AF564389

Introductions to Shakespeare's Tragedies

King Richard II King Richard III Othello King Lear Macbeth

Henry Norman Hudson, Israel Gollancz, C.H. Herford
and other Eminent Shakespearean Authorities

Published by

7/22, Ansari Road, Darya Ganj, New Delhi-110002
Phones : +91-11-40775252, 23273880, 23275880, 23280451
Fax : +91-11-23285873
Web : www.atlanticbooks.com
E-mail : orders@atlanticbooks.com

Branch Office
5, Nallathambi Street, Wallajah Road, Chennai-600002
Phones : +91-44-64611085, 32413319
E-mail : chennai@atlanticbooks.com

First published 1994

Printed in India at Nice Printing Press, A-33/3A, Site-IV, Industrial Area, Sahibabad, Ghaziabad, U.P.

Contents

The Life of William Shakespeare

By James Orchard Halliwell-Phillipps, F.R.S.

In the reign of King Edward the Sixth there lived in Warwickshire a farmer named Richard Shakespeare, who rented a messuage and a considerable quantity of land at Snitterfield, an obscure village in that county. He had two sons, one of whom, named Henry, continued throughout his life to reside in the same parish. John, the other son, left his father's home about the year 1551, and, shortly afterwards, is found residing in the neighboring and comparatively large borough of Stratford-on-Avon, in the locality which has been known from the middle ages to the present day as Henley Street, so called from its being the terminus of the road from Henley-in-Arden, a market-town about eight miles distant.

At this period, and for many generations afterwards, the sanitary condition of the thoroughfares of Stratford-on-Avon was, to our present notions, simply terrible. Under-surface drainage of every kind was then an unknown art in the district. There was a far greater extent of moisture in the land than would now be thought possible, and streamlets of a water-power sufficient for the operations of corn-mills meandered through the town. This general humidity intensified the evils arising from the want of scavengers, or other effective appliances for the preservation of cleanliness. House-slops were recklessly thrown into ill-kept channels that lined the sides of unmetalled roads; pigs and geese too often reveled in the puddles and ruts; while here and there small middens were ever in the course of accumulation, the receptacles of offal and every species of nastiness. A regulation for the removal of these collections to certain specified localities interspersed through the borough, and known as common dunghills, appears to have been the extent of the interference that the authorities ventured or cared to exercise in such matters. Sometimes, when the nuisance was thought to be sufficiently flagrant, they made a raid on those inhabitants who had suffered their refuse to accumulate largely in the highways. On one of these occasions, in April, 1552, John Shakespeare was amerced in the sum of twelve-pence for having amassed what was no doubt a conspicuous *sterquinarium* before his house in Henley Street, and under these unsavory circumstances does the history of the poet's father commence in the records of England. But although there was little excuse for his negligence, one of the public stores of filth being within a stone's throw of his residence, all that can be said to his disparagement is that he was not in advance of his neighbors in such matters, two of whom were coincidently fined for the same offense.

For some years subsequently to this period, John Shakespeare was a humble tradesman at Stratford-on-Avon, holding no conspicuous position in the town; yet still he must have been tolerably successful in business, for in October, 1556, he purchased two small freehold estates, one being the building in Henley Street annexed to that which is now shown as the Birth-Place, and the other situated in Greenhill Street, a road afterwards called More Towns End. In the year 1557, however, his fortunes underwent an important change through an alliance with Mary, the youngest and fondly-loved daughter of Robert Arden, a wealthy farmer of Wilmecote, near Stratford-on-Avon, who had died a few months previously. A wealthy farmer, indeed, for those days, and one who would have been specially so distinguished in the contemporary provincial estimate. He possessed two farm-houses with a hundred acres or more of land at Snitterfield, as well as another one with about fifty acres at Wilmecote, the former being occupied by tenants and the latter by himself. In addition to these he owned a copyhold estate in the last-named parish, the extent of which has not been ascertained. But with all these advantages he was a farmer, and nothing more,—a worthy fellow whose main anxiety, as fully appears from the records, centered in the welfare of his family, and who had no desire to emulate, however remotely, the position of a country gentleman. The appointments of his dwelling were probably, however, superior on the whole to those which were to be found in other residences of the same class, including no fewer than eleven painted-cloths, a species of artistic decoration that was in those days a favorite substitute for the more expensive tapestry. Pictures of the kind that are now familiar to us were then very rarely indeed to be seen, excepting in palaces or in the larger mansions of the nobility. These painted-cloths were generally formed of canvas upon which were depicted the "Seven Ages of Man," the "Story of the Prodigal," and such like; grotesque accompaniments, in one or more of the rooms, to the "bacon in the roof."

The inventory of Robert Arden's goods, which was taken shortly after his death in 1556, enables us to realize the kind of life that was followed by the poet's mother during her girlhood. In the total absence of books or means of intellectual education, her acquirements must have been restricted to an experimental knowledge of matters connected with the farm and its house. There can be no doubt that the maiden with the pretty name, she who has been so often represented as a nymph of the forest, communing with nothing less aesthetic than a nightingale or a waterfall, spent most of her time in the homeliest of rustic employments; and it is not at all improbable that, in common with many other farmers' daughters of the period, she occasionally assisted in the more robust occupations of the field. It is at all events not very likely that a woman, unendowed with an exceptionally healthy and vigorous frame, could have been the parent of a Shakespeare. Of her personal character or social gifts nothing whatever is known, but it would be a grave error to assume that the rude surroundings of her youth were incompatible with the possession of a romantic temperament and the highest form of subjective refinement. Existence, indeed, was passed in her father's house in some respects, we should now say, rather after the manner of pigs than that of human beings. Many of the articles that are considered necessaries in the humblest of modern cottages were not to be seen,—there were no table-knives, no forks, no crockery. The food was manipulated on flat pieces of stout wood, too insignificant in value to be catalogued, and whatever there may have been to supply the places of spoons or cups were no doubt roughly formed of the same material; but some of the larger objects, such as kitchen-pans, may have been of pewter or latten. The means of ablution were lamentably defective, if, indeed, they were not limited to what could have been supplied by an insulated pail of water, for what were called towels were merely used for wiping the hands after a meal, and there was not a single wash-hand basin in the establishment. As for the inmate and other laborers, it was very seldom indeed, if ever, that they either washed their hands or combed their hair, nor is there the least reason for suspecting that those accomplishments were in liberal requisition in the dwellings of their employers. But surely there was nothing in all this to have excluded the unlettered damsel from a fervid taste for oral romance, that which was then chiefly represented by tales of the fairies, the knights, or the giants,—nothing to debar the high probability of her recitals of them having fascinated her illustrious son in the days of his childhood,—nothing to disturb the graceful suggestion that some of his impressions of perfect womanhood had their origin in his recollections of the faultless nature of the matron of Henley Street.

The maiden name of Robert Arden's wife has not been discovered, but it is ascertained that he had contracted a second marriage with Agnes Hill, the widow of a substantial farmer of Bearley, and that, in a settlement which was probably made on that occasion, he had reserved to his daughter Mary the reversion to a portion of a large estate at Snitterfield, her step-mother taking only a life-interest. Some part of this land was in the occupation of Richard Shakespeare, the poet's grandfather, whence may have arisen the acquaintanceship between the two families. In addition to this reversion, Mary Arden received, under the provisions of her father's will, not only a handsome pecuniary legacy, but the fee-simple of a valuable property at Wilmecote, the latter, which was known as Asbies, consisting of a house with nearly sixty acres of land. An estimate of these advantages, viewed relatively to his own position, would no doubt have given John Shakespeare the reputation among his neighbors of having married an opulent heiress, his now comparative affluence investing him with no small degree of local importance. His official career at once commenced by his election in 1557 as one of the ale-tasters, an officer appointed for the supervision of malt liquors and bread. About the same time he was received into the Corporation, taking the lowest rank, as was usual with new comers, that of a burgess; and in the September of the following year, 1558, he was appointed one of the four petty constables by a vote of the jury of the Court Leet. He was re-elected to that quaternion on October 6, 1559, for another year, and on the same day he was chosen one of the affeerors appointed to determine the fines for those offenses which were punishable arbitrarily, and for which no express penalties were prescribed by statute. This latter office he again filled in 1561, when he was elected one of the Chamberlains of the borough, an office that he held for two years, delivering his second account to the Corporation in the first month of 1564.

The ostensible business followed by John Shakespeare was that of a glover, but after his marriage he speculated largely in wool purchased from the neighboring farmers, and occasionally also dealt in corn and other articles. In those days, especially in small provincial towns, the concentration of several trades into the hands of one person was very usual, and, in many cases, no matter how numerous and complicated were the intermediate processes, the producer of the raw material was frequently its manufacturer. Thus a glover might, and sometimes did, rear the sheep that furnished him with meat, skins, wool, and leather. Whether John Shakespeare so conducted his business is unknown, but it is certain that in addition to his trade in gloves, which also, as was usual, included the sale of divers articles made of leather, he entered into a variety of other speculations.

In Henley Street, in what was for those days an unusually large and commodious residence for a provincial tradesman, and upon or almost immediately before April 22, 1564, but most probably on that Saturday, the eldest son of John and Mary Shakespeare, he who was afterwards to be the national poet of England, was born. An apartment on the first floor of that house is shown to this day, through unvarying tradition, as the birth-room of the great dramatist, who was baptized on the following Wednesday, April 26, receiving the Christian name of William. He was then, and continued to be for more than two years, an only child, two girls, daughters of the same parents, who were born previously, having died in their infancy.

The house in which Shakespeare was born must have been erected in the first half of the sixteenth century, but the alterations that it has since undergone have effaced much of its original character. Inhabited at various periods by tradesmen of different occupations, it could not possibly have endured through the long course of upwards of three centuries without having been subjected to numerous repairs and modifications. The general form and arrangement of the tenement that was purchased in 1556 may yet, however, be distinctly traced, and many of the old timbers, as well as pieces of the ancient rough stone-work, still remain. There are also portions of the chimneys, the fire-place surroundings and the stone basement-floor, that have been untouched; but most, if not all, of the lighter wood-work belongs to a more recent period. It may be confidently asserted that there is only one room in the entire building which has not been greatly changed since the days of the poet's boyhood. This is the antique cellar under the sitting-room, from which it is approached by a diminutive flight of steps. It is a very small apartment, measuring only nine by ten feet, but near "that small most greatly liv'd this star of England."

In the July of this year of the poet's birth, 1564, a violent plague, intensified no doubt by sanitary neglect, broke out in the town, but the family in Henley Street providentially escaped its ravages. John Shakespeare contributed on this occasion fairly, at least, if not liberally, both towards the relief of the poor and of those who were attacked by the epidemic.

In March, 1565, John Shakespeare, with the assistance of his former colleague in the same office, made up the accounts of the Chamberlains of the borough for the year ending at the previous Michaelmas. Neither of these worthies could even write their own names, but nearly all tradesmen then reckoned with counters, the results on important occasions being entered by professional scriveners. The poet's father seems to have been an adept in the former kind of work, for in February, 1566, having been elected an alderman in the previous summer, he individually superintended the making up of the accounts of the Chamberlains for the preceding official year, at which time he was paid over three pounds, equivalent to more than thirty of present money, that had been owing to him for some time by the Corporation. In the month of October, 1566, another son, who was christened Gilbert on the thirteenth, was born, the poet being then nearly two and a half years old. This Gilbert, who was educated at the Free School, in after life entered into business in London as a haber-dasher, returning, however, in the early part of the following century, to his native town, where he is found, in 1602, completing an important legal transaction with which he was entrusted by the great dramatist. His Christian name was probably derived from that of one of his father's neighbors, Gilbert Bradley, who was a glover in Henley Street, residing near the Birth-Place and on the same side of the way.

In September, 1567, Robert Perrot, a brewer, John Shakespeare, and Ralph Cawdrey, a butcher, were nominated for the office of the High Bailiff, or, as that dignitary was subsequently called, the Mayor. The last-named candidate was the one who was elected. It is upon this occasion that the poet's father is alluded to for the first time in the local records as "Mr. Shakspeyr." He had been previously therein mentioned either as John Shakespeare, or briefly as Shakespeare, and the addition of the title was in those days no small indication of an advance in social position. There is, indeed, no doubt that, during the early years of Shakespeare's boyhood, his father was one of the leading men in Stratford-on-Avon. On September 4, 1568, John Shakespeare,—"Mr. John Shakysper," as he is called in that day's record,—was chosen High Bailiff, attaining thus the most distinguished official position in the town after an active connection with its affairs during the preceding eleven years. The poet had entered his fifth year in the previous month of April, the family in Henley Street now consisting of his parents, his brother Gilbert, who was very nearly two years old, and himself.

The new religious system was now firmly established at Stratford. Although the churchwardens' accounts are not preserved, and the materials for the local ecclesiastical history are exceedingly scanty, there are entries in the town archives respecting the Guild Chapel which leave no doubt on the subject. The rood-loft is mentioned as having been taken down in the year of the poet's birth, 1564, a number of the images in the building having been previously "defaced," that is to say, at some time between Michaelmas, 1562, and Michaelmas, 1563, John Shakespeare himself having been on the latter occasion one of the chamberlains through whom the expenses of the mutilation were defrayed. Under these circumstances there can be little if any doubt that, at the time of his accession to an office that legally involved the responsibility of taking the oath of supremacy, he had outwardly conformed to the Protestant rule, and there is certainly as little that he was one of the many of those holding a similar position in the Catholic stronghold of Warwickshire who were secretly attached to the old religion. If this had not been the case, it is impossible to believe, no matter how plausible were the explanations that were offered, that his name could, at a subsequent period and after the great penal legislation of 1581, have been included in more than one list of suspected recusants. For this he has been termed an unconscientious hypocrite, but he shared his dissimulation with myriads of his countrymen, and it is altogether unfair to place an enforced in the same category with a spontaneous insincerity. Some anyhow will be found to say a kind word in excuse for a man who, in times of a virulent and crushing persecution, was unwilling to sacrifice the temporal interests of his wife and children as well as his own on the altar of open non-conformity. It should be added that the vestments belonging to the Church of the Holy Trinity, which had been out of use for some years, were sold by the Corporation in 1571; and these were among the last remaining vestiges of a ritual that was not publicly celebrated at Stratford in the life-time of the great dramatist.

It must have been somewhere about this period, 1568, that Shakespeare entered into the mysteries of the horn-book and the A. B. C. Although both his parents were absolutely illiterate, they had the sagacity to appreciate the importance of an education for their son, and the poet, somehow or other, was taught to read and write, the necessary preliminaries to admission into the Free School. There were few persons at that time at Stratford-on-Avon capable of initiating him even into these preparatory accomplishments, but John Shakespeare, in his official position, could hardly have encountered much difficulty in finding a suitable instructor. There was, for instance, Higford, the Steward of the Court of Record, and the person who transcribed some of his accounts when he was the borough Chamberlain; but it is as likely as not that the poet received the first rudiments of education from older boys who were some way advanced in their school career.

A passion for the drama is with some natures an instinct, and it would appear that the poet's father had an express taste in that direction. At all events, dramatic entertainments are first heard of at Stratford-on-Avon during the year of his bailiffship, and were, it may fairly be presumed, introduced in unison with his wishes as they certainly must have been with his sanction. At some period between Michaelmas, 1568, and the same day in 1569, the Queen's and the Earl of Worcester's players visited the town and gave representations before the Council, the former company receiving nine shillings and the latter twelve pence for their first performances, to which the public were admitted without payment. They doubtlessly gave other theatrical entertainments with stated charges for admission, but there would, of course, be no entries of those performances in the municipal accounts; and sometimes there were bodies of actors in the town to whom the official liberality was not extended. No notice whatever of the latter companies would have been registered.

Were it not for the record of a correlative incident, it would have been idle to have hazarded a conjecture on the interesting question,—was the poet, who was then in his fifth or sixth year, a spectator at either of these performances? If, however, it can be shown that, in a neighboring county about the same time, there was an inhabitant of a city who took his little boy, one born in the same year with Shakespeare, 1564, to a free dramatic entertainment exhibited as were those at Stratford-on-Avon before the Corporation under precisely similar conditions, there then arises a reasonable probability that we should be justified in giving an affirmative reply to the enquiry. There is such an evidence in the account left by a person of the name of Willis, of "a stage-play which I saw when I was a child," and included by him in a confidential narrative of his moral and religious life, a sort of autobiography, which, in his old age, he addressed to his wife and children.

The curious narrative given by Willis is in the following terms,—"in the city of Gloucester the manner is, as I think it is in other like corporations, that, when players of enterludes come to towne, they first attend the Mayor to enforme him what noble-mans servants they are, and so to get licence for their publike playing; and if the Mayor like the actors, or would shew respect to their lord and master, he appoints them to play their first play before himselfe and the Aldermen and Common Counsell of the city; and that is called the Mayors play, where every one that will comes in without money, the Mayor giving the players a reward as hee thinks fit to shew respect unto them. At such a play my father tooke me with him, and made mee stand between his leggs as he sate upon one of the benches, where wee saw and heard very well. The play was called the *Cradle of Security*, wherin was personated a king or some great prince, with his courtiers of severall kinds, amongst which three ladies were in speciall grace with him; and they, keeping him in delights and pleasures, drew him from his graver counsellors, hearing of sermons and listning to good counsell and admonitions, that, in the end, they got him to lye downe in a cradle upon the stage, where these three ladies, joyning in a sweet song, rocked him asleepe that he snorted againe; and in the meane time closely conveyed under the cloaths wherewithall he was covered a vizard, like a swine's snout, upon his face, with three wire chaines fastned thereunto, the other end whereof being holden severally by those three ladies who fall to singing againe, and then discovered his face that the spectators might see how they had transformed him, going on with their singing. Whilst all this was acting, there came forth of another doore at the farthest end of the stage two old men, the one in blew with a serjeant-at-armes his mace on his shoulder, the other in red with a drawn sword in his hand and leaning with the other hand upon the others shoulder; and so they two went along in a soft pace round about by the skirt of the stage, till at last they came to the cradle, when all the court was in greatest jollity; and then the foremost old man with his mace stroke a fearfull blow upon the cradle, whereat all the courtiers, with the three ladies and the vizard, all vanished; and the desolate prince starting up bare-faced, and finding himselfe thus sent for to judgement, made a lamentable complaint of his miserable case, and so was carried away by wicked spirits. This prince did personate in the morrall the Wicked of the World; the three ladies, Pride, Covetousnesse and Luxury; the two old men, the End of the World and the Last Judgment. This sight tooke such impression in me that, when I came towards mans estate, it was as fresh in my memory as if I had seen it newly acted," (Willis's *Mount Tabor or Private Exercises of a Penitent Sinner*, published in the yeare of his age 75, anno Dom. 1639, pp. 110-113). Who can be so pitiless to the imagination as not to erase the name of Gloucester in the preceding anecdote, and replace it by that of Stratford-on-Avon?

Homely and rude as such an allegorical drama as the Cradle of Security would now be considered, it was yet an advance in dramatic construction upon the medieval religious plays generally known as mysteries, which were still in favor with the public and were of an exceedingly primitive description. The latter were, however, put on the stage with far more elaborate appliances, there being no reason for believing that the itinerant platform of the later drama was provided with much beyond a few properties. The theater of the mysteries consisted of a movable wooden rectangular structure of two rooms one over the other, the lower closed, the upper one, that in which the performances took place, being open at least on one side to the audience. The vehicle itself, every portion of which that was visible to the audience was grotesquely painted, was furnished in the upper room with tapestries that answered the purposes of scenery, and with mechanical appliances for the disposition of the various objects introduced, such as hell-mouth, a favorite property on the ancient English stage. This consisted of a huge face constructed of painted canvas exhibiting glaring eyes and a red nose of enormous dimensions; the whole so contrived with movable jaws of large, projecting teeth, that, when the mouth opened, flames could be seen within the hideous aperture; the fire being probably represented by the skillful management of links or torches held behind the painted canvas. There was frequently at the back of the stage a raised platform to which there was an ascent by steps from the floor of the pageant and sometimes an important part of the action of the mystery was enacted upon it. Some of the properties however rude, must have been of large dimensions. They were generally made of wood, which was invariably painted, but some appear to have been constructed of basket-work covered over with painted cloths. The larger ones were cities with pinnacles and towers, kings' palaces, temples, castles and such like, some probably not very unlike decorated sentry-boxes. Among the miscellaneous properties may be named "a rybbe colleryd red," which was no doubt used in the mystery of the creation. Clouds were represented by painted cloths so contrived that they could open and show angels in the heavens. Horses and other like animals were generally formed with hoops and laths that were wrapped in canvas, the latter being afterwards painted in imitation of nature. Artificial trees were introduced, and so were beds, tombs, pulpits, ships, ladders, and numerous other articles. One of the quaintest contrivances was that which was intended to convey the idea of an earthquake, which seems to have been attempted by means of some mechanism within a barrel. In the lower room, connected with pulleys in the upper part of the pageant, was a windlass used for the purpose of lowering or raising the larger properties, and for various objects for which movable ropes could be employed. Some of the other machinery was evidently of an ingenious character, but its exact nature has not been ascertained.

The costumes of many of the personages in the mysteries were of a grotesque and fanciful description but in some instances, as in those of Adam and Eve, there was an attempt to make the dresses harmonize with the circumstances of the history. Some writers, interpreting the stage-directions too literally, have asserted that those characters were introduced upon the pageant in a state of nudity. This was certainly not the case. When they were presumed to be destitute of clothing, they appeared in dresses made either of white leather or of flesh-colored cloths, over which at the proper time were thrown the garments of skins. There were no doubt some incidents represented in the old English mysteries which would now be considered indecorous, but it should be borne in mind that every age has, within certain limits, its own conventional and frequently irrational sentiments of toleration and propriety. Adam and Eve attired in white leather and pensonified by men, for actresses were then unknown, scarcely could have realized to the spectator even a generic idea of the nude, but at all events there was nothing in any of the theatrical costumes of the early drama which can be fairly considered to be of an immodest character, although many of them were extravagantly whimsical. Thus Herod was always introduced wearing red gloves, while his clothes and head-gear seem to have been painted or dyed in a variety of colors, so that, as far as costume could assist the deception, he probably appeared, when brandishing his flaming sword, as fierce and hideous a tyrant as could well have been represented. Pontius Pilate was usually enwrapped in a large green cloak, which opened in front to enable him to wield an immense club. The latter was humanely adapted to his strength by the weight being chiefly restricted to that of the outer case, the inside being lightly stuffed with wool. The Devil was another important character, who was also grotesquely arrayed and had a mask or false head which frequently required either mending or painting. Masks were worn by several other personages, though it would appear that in some instances the operation of painting the faces of the actors was substituted. Wigs of false hair, either gilded or of red, yellow, and other colors, were also much in request.

That Shakespeare, in his early youth, witnessed representations of some of these mysteries, cannot admit of a reasonable doubt; for although the ordinary church-plays were by no means extinct, they survived only in particular localities, and do not appear to have been retained in Stratford or its neighborhood. The performances which then took place nearly every year at Coventry attracted hosts of spectators from all parts of the country, while, at occasional intervals, the mystery players of that city made theatrical progresses to various other places.

It is not known whether they favored Stratford-on-Avon with a professional visit, but it is not at all improbable that they did, for they must have passed through the town in their way to Bristol, where it is recorded that they gave a performance in the year 1570. Among the mysteries probably recollected by Shakespeare was one in which the King was introduced as Herod of Jewry, in which the children of Bethlehem were barbarously speared, the soldiers disregarding the frantic shrieks of the bereaved mothers. In the collection known as the *Coventry Mysteries,* a soldier appears before Herod with a child on the end of his spear in evidence of the accomplishment of the King's commands, a scene to be remembered, however rude may have been the property which represented the infant; while the extravagance of rage, which formed one of the then main dramatic characteristics of that sovereign, must have made a deep impression on a youthful spectator. The idea of such a history being susceptible of exaggeration into burlesque never entered a spectator's mind in those days, and the impression made upon him was probably increased by the style of Herod's costume.

Besides the allusions made by the great dramatist to the Herod of the Coventry players, there are indications that other grotesque performers were occasionally in his recollection, those who with blackened faces acted the parts of the Black Souls. There are several references in Shakespeare to condemned souls being of this color, and in one place there is an illusion to them in the language of the mysteries. Falstaff is reported to have said of a flea on Bardolph's red nose that "it was a black soul burning in hell;" and, in the Coventry plays, the Black or Damned Souls appeared with sooty faces and attired in a motley costume of yellow and black. It is certainly just possible that the notions of Herod and the Black Souls may have been derived from other sources, but the more natural probability is that they are absolute recollections of the Coventry plays.

The period of Shakespeare's boyhood was also that of what was practically the last era of the real ancient English mystery. There were, it is true, occasional performances of them up to the reign of James the First, but they became obsolete throughout nearly all the country about the year 1580. Previously to the latter date they had for many generations served as media for religious instruction. In days when education of any kind was a rarity, and spiritual religion an impossibility or at least restricted to very few, appeals to the senses in illustration of theological subjects were wisely encouraged by the Church. The impression made on the rude and uninstructed mind by the representations of incidents in sacred history and religious tradition by living characters, must have been far more profound than any which could have been conveyed by the genius of the sculptor or painter, or by the eloquence of the priest. Notwithstanding, therefore, the opposition that these performances encountered at the hands of a section of churchmen, who apprehended that the introduction of the comic element would ultimately tend to feelings of irreverence, it is found that, in spite of occasional abuses, they long continued to be one of the most effectual means of disseminating a knowledge of Scriptural history and of inculcating belief in the doctrines of the Church. In the Hundred Mery Talys, a collection which was very popular in England throughout the sixteenth century, there is a story of a village priest in Warwickshire who preached a sermon on the Articles of the Creed, telling the congregation at the end of his discourse,—"these artycles ye be bounde to beleve; for they be trew and of auctoryté; and yf you beleve not me, then for a more suerté and suffycyent auctoryté go your way to Conventré, and there ye shall se them all playd in Corpus Cristi playe." Although this is related as a mere anecdote, it well illustrates the value which was then attached to the teachings of the ancient stage. Even as lately as the middle of the seventeenth century there could have been found in England an example of a person whose knowledge of the Scriptures was limited to his recollections of the performance of a mystery. The Rev. John Shaw, who was the temporary chaplain in a village in Lancashire in 1644, narrates the following curious anecdote respecting one of its inhabitants,—"one day an old man about sixty, sensible enough in other things, and living in the parish of Cartmel, coming to me about some business, I told him that he belonged to my care and charge, and I desired to be informed in his knowledge of religion;—I asked him how many Gods there were; he said, he knew not;—I, informing him, asked him again how he thought to be saved; he answered he could not tell, yet thought that was a harder question than the other;—I told him that the way to salvation was by Jesus Christ, God-man, who, as He was man, shed His blood for us on the crosse, etc. Oh, sir, said he, I think I heard of that man you speak of once in a play at Kendall called *Corpus Christi Play*, where there was a man on a tree and blood ran downe, etc., and after he professed that he could not remember that ever he heard of salvation by Jesus Christ but in that play." It is impossible to say to what extent even the Scriptural allusions in the works of Shakespeare himself may not be attributed to recollections of such performances, for in one instance at least the reference by the great dramatist is to the history as represented in those plays, not to that recorded in the New Testament. The English mysteries, indeed, never lost their position as religious instructors, a fact which, viewed in connection with that of a widely-spread affection for the old religion, appears to account for their long continuance in a practically unaltered state while other forms of the drama were being developed by their side. From the fourteenth century until the termination of Shakespeare's youthful days they remained the simple poetic versions in dialogue of religious incidents of various kinds, enlivened by the occasional admission of humorous scenes. In some few instances the theological narrative was made subservient to the comic action, but as a rule the mysteries were designed to bring before the audience merely the personages and events of religious history. Allegorical characters had been occasionally introduced, and about the middle of the fifteenth century there appeared a new kind of English dramatic composition apparently borrowed from France, in which the personages were either wholly or almost exclusively of that description. When the chief object of a performance of this nature, like that of the *Cradle of Security* previously described, was to inculcate a moral lesson, it was sometimes called either a Moral or a Moral-play, terms which continued in use till the seventeenth century, and were licentiously applied by some early writers to any dramas which were of an ethical or educational character. Morals were not only performed in Shakespeare's day, but continued to be a then recognized form of dramatic composition. Some of them were nearly as simple and inartificial as the mysteries, but others were not destitute of originality, or even of the delineation of character and manners. There was, however, no consecutive or systematic development of either the mystery into the moral or the moral into the historical and romantic drama, although there are examples in which the specialities of each are curiously intermingled. Each species of the early English drama appears for the most part to have pursued its own separate and independent career.

In April, 1569, the poet's sister, Joan, was born. She was baptized on the fifteenth of that month, and, by a prevalent fashion which has created so much perplexity in discussions on longevities, was named after an elder child of the same parents who was born in 1558 and had died some time previously to the arrival of her younger sister. Joan was then so common a name that it is hazardous to venture on a conjecture respecting the child's sponsor, but she was very likely so called after her maternal aunt, Mrs. Lambert of Barton-on-the-Heath. John Shakespeare's term of office as High Bailiff expired in the September of the same year, 1569, his successor being one Robert Salisbury, a substantial yeoman then residing in a large house on the eastern side of Church Street.

Although there is no certain information on the subject, it may perhaps be assumed that, at this time, boys usually entered the Free School at the age of seven, according to the custom followed at a later period. If so, the poet commenced his studies there in the spring of the year 1571, and unless its system of instruction differed essentially from that pursued in other establishments of a similar character, his earliest knowledge of Latin was derived from two well-known books of the time, the *Accidence* and the *Sententiæ Pueriles*. From the first of these works the improvised examination of Master Page in the *Merry Wives of Windsor* is so almost verbally remembered, that one might imagine that the William of the scene was a resuscitation of the poet at school. Recollections of the same book are to be traced in other of his plays. The *Sententiæ Pueriles* was, in all probability, the little manual by the aid of which he first learned to construe Latin, for in one place, at least, he all but literally translates a brief passage, and there are in his plays several adaptations of its sentiments. It was then sold for a penny, equivalent to about our present shilling, and contains a large collection of brief sentences collected from a variety of authors, with a distinct selection of moral and religious paragraphs, the latter intended for the use of boys on Saint's Days.

The best authorities unite in telling us that the poet imbibed a certain amount of Latin at school, but that his acquaintance with that language was, throughout his life of a very limited character. It is not probable that scholastic learning was ever congenial to his tastes, and it should be recollected that books in most parts of the country were then of very rare occurrence. Lilly's *Grammar* and a few classical works, chained to the desks of the Free School, were probably the only volumes of the kind to be found at Stratford-on-Avon. Exclusive of Bibles, Church Services, Psalters, and education manuals, there were certainly not more than two or three dozen books, if so many, in the whole town. The copy of the black-letter English history, so often depicted as well thumbed by Shakespeare in his father's parlor, never existed out of the imagination. Fortunately for us, the youthful dramatist had, excepting in the school-room, little opportunity of studying any but a grander volume, the infinite book of nature, the pages of which were ready to be unfolded to him in the lane and field, amongst the copses of Snitterfield, by the side of the river or that of his uncle's hedgerows.

Henry Shakespeare, the poet's uncle, resided on a large farm near Snitterfield church. The house has long disappeared, but two of the old enclosures that he rented, Burmans and Red Hill, are still to be observed on the right of the highway to Luscombe, with the ancient boundaries, and under the same names, by which they were distinguished in the days of Shakespeare's early youth. Nearly every one of the boy's connections, as well as his uncle Henry, was a farmer. There was the brother of Agnes Arden, Alexander Webbe of Snitterfield, who died in 1573, appointing "to be my overseers to see this my last will and testament performed, satisfied and fulfilled, according to my will, John Shackespere of Stret-ford-upon-Aven, John Hill of Bearley, and for theyre paynes taken I geve them xij.*d.* a pece." Henry

Shakespeare was present at the execution of this will, and there is other evidence that the poet's family were on friendly terms with the Hills of Bearley, who were connections by marriage with the Ardens. Then there were the Lamberts of Barton-on-the-Heath, the Stringers of Bearley, the Etkyns of Wilmecote, all of whom were engaged in agricultural business, and Agnes Arden, who was still alive and farming at Wilmecote.

On March 11, 1574, "Richard, sonne to Mr. John Shakspeer," was baptized at Stratford, the Christian name of the infant having probably been adopted in recollection of his grandfather of Snitterfield, who had been removed by the hand of death some years previously. Independently of this new baby, there were now four other children,—Anne, who was in her third, Joan in her fifth, Gilbert in his eighth, and the poet in his tenth year. The father's circumstances were not yet on the wane, so there is every reason for believing that the eldest son, blessed with, as it has been well termed, the precious gift of sisters to a loving boy, returned to a happy fire-side after he had been tormented by the disciplinarian routine that was destined to terminate in the acquisition of "small Latin and less Greek."

The defective classical education of the poet is not, however, to be attributed to the conductors of the local seminary, for enough of Latin was taught to enable the more advanced pupils to display familiar correspondence in that language. It was really owing to his being removed from school long before the usual age, his father requiring his assistance in one of the branches of the Henley Street business. Rowe's words, published in 1709, are these,—"he had bred him, 'tis true, for some time at a free-school, where 'tis probable he acquir'd that little Latin he was master of; but the narrowness of his circumstances, and the want of his assistance at home, forc'd his father to withdraw him from thence, and unhappily prevented his further proficiency in that language." John Shakespeare's circumstances had begun to decline in the year 1577, and, in all probability, he removed the future dramatist from school when the latter was about thirteen, allowing Gilbert, then between ten and eleven, to continue his studies. The selection of the former for home-work may have partially arisen from his having been the elder and the stronger, but it also exhibits the father's presentiment of those talents for business which distinguished the latter part of his son's career.

The conflict of evidences now becomes so exceedingly perplexing, that it is hardly possible to completely reconcile them. All that can prudently be said is that the inclination of the testimonies leans towards the belief that John Shakespeare, following the ordinary usage of the tradesmen of the locality in binding their children to special occupations, eventually apprenticed his eldest son to a butcher. That appellation was sometimes given to persons who, without keeping meat-shops, killed cattle and pigs for others; and as there is no telling how many adjuncts the worthy glover had to his legitimate business, it is very possible that the lad may have served his articles under his own father. With respect to the unpoetical selection of a trade for the great dramatist, it is of course necessary for the biographer to draw attention to the fact that he was no ordinary executioner, but, to use the words of Aubrey, "when he killed a calf, he would do it in a high style and make a speech." It may be doubted if even this palliative will suffice to reconcile the employment with our present ideal of the gentle Shakespeare, but he was not one of the few destined, at all events in early life, to be exempt from the laws which so frequently ordain mortals to be the reluctant victims of circumstances.

The tradition reported by the parish clerk in 1693 is the only known evidence of Shakespeare having been an apprentice, but his assertion that the poet commenced his practical life as a butcher is supported by the earlier testimony of Aubrey. If the clerk's story be rejected, we must then rely on the account furnished by Betterton, who informs us, through Rowe, that John Shakespeare "was a considerable dealer in wool," and that the great dramatist, after leaving school, was brought up to follow the same occupation, continuing in the business until his departure from Warwickshire. Whichever version be thought the more probable, the student will do well, before arriving at a decision, to bear in mind that many butchers of those days were partially farmers, and that those of Stratford-on-Avon largely represented the wealth and commercial intelligence of the town. Among the latter was Ralph Cawdrey, who had then twice served the office of High Bailiff, and had been for many years a colleague of the poet's father. Nor were the accessories of the trade viewed in the repulsive light that some of them are at the present time. The refined and lively Rosalind would have been somewhat astonished if she had been told of the day when her allusion to the washing of a sheep's heart would have been pronounced indecorous and more than unladylike.

Although the information at present accessible does not enable us to determine the exact natures of Shakespeare's occupations from his fourteenth to his eighteenth year, that is to say, from 1577 to 1582, there can be no hesitation in concluding that, during that animated and receptive period of life, he was mercifully released from what, to a spirit like his, must have been the deleterious monotony of a school education. Whether he passed those years as a butcher or a wool-dealer does not greatly matter. In either capacity, or in any other that could then have been found at Stratford, he was unconsciously acquiring a more perfect knowledge of the world and human nature than could have been derived from a study of the classics. During nearly if not all the time to which reference is now being made, he had also the opportunity of witnessing theatrical performances by some of the leading companies of the day. But trouble and sorrow invaded the paternal home. In the autumn of 1578, his father affected the then large mortgage of 40*l.* on the estate of Asbies, and the records of subsequent transactions indicate that he was suffering from pecuniary embarrassments in the two years immediately following. In the midst of these struggles he lost, in 1579, his daughter Anne, who was then in her eighth year. It cannot be doubted that the poet acutely felt the death of his little sister, nor that he followed her to the grave at a funeral which was conducted by the parents with affectionate tributes. In the next year their last child was born. He was christened Edmund on May 3, 1580, no doubt receiving that name from the husband of his maternal aunt, Mrs. Lambert. It was this gentleman who held the mortgage on Asbies, but on John Shakespeare tendering payment to him in the following autumn, the money was refused until other sums due the same creditor were also repaid. This must have been a great disappointment to the worthy glover, who had only in the previous year disposed of his wife's reversionary interests at Snitterfield for the exact amount that he had borrowed from the Lamberts in 1578, a transfer that he had perhaps arranged with a view to the redemption of the matrimonial estate at Wilmecote. It must be borne in mind that it was at that time the practice in mortgages to name a special day for the repayment of a loan, the security falling into the indefeasible ownership of the mortgagee when the terms of the contract were not rigidly observed. There was not then the general equity of redemption which, at a later period, guarded the legitimate interests of the borrower.

The reversion that was parted with in the year 1579 consisted of a share in a considerable landed estate that had belonged to the poet's maternal grandfather, a share to which John and Mary Shakespeare would have become absolutely entitled upon the death of Agnes Arden, who was described as "aged and impotent" in the July of the following year, 1580, and who died a few months afterwards, her burial at Aston Cantlowe having taken place on December 29. In her will, that of a substantial lady farmer of the period, there is no direct mention of the Shakespeares, but it is not unlikely that one or more of their sons may be included in the bequest,—"to everi on of my god-children xij.*d.* a-peece,"—the absence of the testator's own Christian name from their pedigree being a sufficient evidence that her baptismal responsibilities were not extended to their daughters. Taking merely a life-interest in a portion of the family estates, and Mary having received more than an equitable interest in them, she might naturally have felt herself absolved from bestowing larger gifts upon her Henley Street connections.

It was the usual custom at Stratford-on-Avon for apprentices to be bound either for seven or ten years, so that, if Shakespeare were one of them, it was not likely that he was out of his articles at the time of his marriage, an event that took place in 1582, when he was only in his nineteenth year. At that period, before a license for wedlock could be obtained, it was necessary to lodge at the Consistory Court a bond entered into by two responsible sureties, who by that document certified, under a heavy penalty in case of misrepresentation, that there was no impediment of precontract or consanguinity, the former of course alluding to a precontract of either of the affianced parties with a third person.

The bond given in anticipation of the marriage of William Shakespeare with Anne Hathaway, a proof in itself that there was no clandestine intention in the arrangements, is dated November 28, 1582. Their first child, Susanna, was baptized on Sunday, May 26, 1583. With those numerous moralists who do not consider it necessary for rigid enquiry to precede condemnation, these facts taint the husband with dishonor, although, even according to modern notions, that very marriage may have been induced on his part by a sentiment in itself the very essence of honor. If we assume, however, as we reasonably may, that cohabitation had previously taken place, no question of morals would in those days have arisen, or could have been entertained. The precontract, which was usually celebrated two or three months before marriage, *was not only legally recognized, but it invalidated a subsequent union of either of the parties with any one else.* There was a statute, indeed; of 32 Henry VIII, 1540, c. 38, s. 2, by which certain marriages were legalized notwithstanding precontracts, but the clause was repealed by the Act of 2 & 3 Edward VI, 1548, c. 23, s. 2, and the whole statute by 1 & 2 Phil. and Mar., 1554, c. 8, s. 19, while the Act of I Elizabeth, 1558, c. 1, s. 11, expressly confirms the revocation made by Edward VI. The ascertained facts respecting Shakespeare's marriage clearly indicate the high probability of there having been a precontract, a ceremony which substantially had the validity of the more formal one, and the improbability of that marriage having been celebrated under mysterious or unusual circumstances. Whether the early alliance was a prudent one in a worldly point of view may admit of doubt, but that the married pair continued on affectionate terms, until they were separated by the poet's death, may be gathered from the early local tradition that his wife "did earnestly desire to be laid in the same grave with him." The legacy to her of the second-best bed is an evidence which does not in any way negative the later testimony.

The poet's two sureties, Fulk Sandells and John Richardson, were inhabitants of the little hamlet of Shottery, and on the only inscribed seal attached to the bond are the initials R.H., while the consent of friends is in that document limited to those of the bride. No conclusion can be safely drawn from the last-named clause, it being one very usual in such instruments, but it may perhaps be inferred from the other circumstances that the marriage was arranged under the special auspices of the Hathaway family, and that the engagement was not received with favor in Henley Street. The case, however, admits of another explanation. It may be that the nuptials of Shakespeare, like those of so many others of that time, had been privately celebrated some months before under the illegal forms of the Catholic Church, and that the relatives were now anxious for the marriage to be openly acknowledged.

It was extremely common at that time, among the local tradespeople, for the sanction of parents to be given to early marriages in cases where there was no money, and but narrow means of support, on either side. It is not, therefore, likely that the consent of John and Mary Shakespeare to the poet's marriage was withheld on such grounds, nor, with the exception of the indications in the bond, are there other reasons for suspecting that they were averse to the union. But whether they were so or not is a question that does not invalidate the assumption that the lovers followed the all but universal rule of consolidating their engagement by means of a precontract. This ceremony was generally a solemn affair enacted with the immediate concurrence of all the parents, but it was at times informally conducted separately by the betrothing parties, evidence of the fact, communicated by them to independent persons, having been held, at least in Warwickshire, to confer a sufficient legal validity on the transaction. Thus, in 1585, William Holder and Alice Shaw, having privately made a contract, came voluntarily before two witnesses, one of whom was a person named Willis and the other a John Maides of Snitterfield, on purpose to acknowledge that they were irrevocably pledged to wedlock. The lady evidently considered herself already as good as married, saying to Holder,—"I do confesse that I am your wief and have forsaken all my frendes for your sake, and I hope you will use me well;" and thereupon she "gave him her hand." Then, as Maides observes, "the said Holder, *mutatis mutandis*, used the like words unto her in effect, and toke her by the hand, and kissed together in the presence of this deponent and the said Willis." These proceedings are afterwards referred to in the same depositions as constituting a definite "contract of marriage." On another occasion, in 1588, there was a precontract meeting at Alcester, the young lady arriving there unaccompanied by any of her friends. When requested to explain the reason of this omission, "she answered that her leasure wold not lett her and that she thought she cold not obtaine her mother's goodwill, but, quoth she, nevertheless I am the same woman that I was before." The future bridegroom was perfectly satisfied with this assurance, merely asking her "whether she was content to betake herself unto him, and she answered, offring her hand, which he also tooke upon thoffer that she was content by her trothe, and thereto, said she, I geve thee my faith, and before these witnesses, that I am thy wief; and then he likewise answered in theis wordes, vidz., and I geve thee my faith and troth, and become thy husband." These instances, to which several others could be added, prove decisively that Shakespeare could have entered, under any circumstances whatever, into a precontract with Anne Hathaway. It may be worth adding that espousals of this kind were, in the Midland counties, almost invariably terminated by the lady's acceptance of a bent sixpence. One lover, who was betrothed in the same year in which Shakespeare was engaged to Anne Hathaway, gave also a pair of gloves, two oranges, two handkerchiefs and a girdle of broad red silk. A present of gloves on such an occasion was, indeed, nearly as universal as that of a sixpence.

It can never be right for a biographer, when he is unsupported by the least particle of evidence, to assume that the subject of his memoir departed unnecessarily from the ordinary usages of life and society. In Shakespeare's matrimonial case, those who imagine that there was no precontract have to make another extravagant admission. They must ask us also to believe that the lady of his choice was as disreputable as the flax-wench, and gratuitously united with the poet in a moral wrong that could have been converted, by the smallest expenditure of trouble, into a moral right. The whole theory is absolutely incredible,

We may then feel certain that, in the summer of the year 1582, William Shakespeare and Anne Hathaway were betrothed either formally or informally, but, at all events, under conditions that could, if necessary, have been legally ratified.

There are reasons for believing that later in the century cohabitation between the precontract and the marriage began to be generally regarded with much disfavor, but the only means of arriving at an equitable judgment upon the merits of the present case lay in a determination to investigate it strictly in its relation with practices the legitimacy of which was acknowledged in Warwickshire in the days of the poet's youth. If the antecedents of Shakespeare's union with Miss Hathaway were regarded with equanimity by their own neighbors, relatives, and friends, upon what grounds can a modern critic fairly impugn the propriety of their conduct? And that they were so regarded is all but indisputable. Assuming, as we have a right to assume, that the poet's mother must have been a woman of sensitive purity, was she now entertaining the remotest apprehension that her son's honor was imperiled? Assuredly not, for she had passed her youth amid a society who believed that a precontract had all the validity of a marriage, the former being really considered a more significant and important ceremony than the other. When her own father, Robert Arden, settled part of an estate upon his daughter Agnes, on July 17, 1550, he introduces her as *nunc uxor Thome Stringer, ac nuper uxor Johannis Hewyns*, and yet the marriage was not solemnized until three months afterwards. "1550, 15 October, was maryed Thomas Stringer unto Agnes Hwens, wyddow," (Bearley register). Let us hope that, after the production of this decisive testimony, nothing more will be heard of the insinuations that have hitherto thrown an unpleasant shadow over one of the most interesting periods of our author's career.

The marriage, in accordance with the general practice, no doubt took place within two or three days after the execution of the bond on November 28, 1582, the "once asking of the bans" being included in the ceremonial service. The name of the parish in which the nuptials were celebrated has not been ascertained, but it must have been one of those places in the diocese of Worcester the early registers of which have been lost.

Early marriages are not, however, at least with men, invariably preceded by a dispersion of the wild oats; and it appears that Shakespeare had neglected to complete that usually desirable operation, but now a fortunate omission that necessitated his removal to the only locality in which it was probable that his dramatic genius could have arrived at complete maturity. Three or four years after his union with Anne Hathaway, he had, observes Rowe, "by a misfortune common enough to young fellows, fallen into ill company, and, among them, some, that made a frequent practice of deer-stealing, engaged him with them more than once in robbing a park that belonged to Sir Thomas Lucy of Charlecote, near Stratford;—for this he was prosecuted by that gentleman, as he thought, somewhat too severely, and, in order to revenge that ill-usage, he made a ballad upon him; and though this, probably the first essay of his poetry, be lost yet it is said to have been so very bitter that it redoubled the prosecution against him to that degree, that he was obliged to leave his business and family in Warwickshire for some time, and shelter himself in London." If we accept this narrative, which is the most reliable account of the incident that has been preserved, the date of the poet's departure from his native town may be reasonably assigned to the year 1585. He certainly could not have left the neighborhood before the summer of 1584, the baptisms of his youngest children, the twin Hamnet and Judith, having been registered at Stratford-on-Avon on February 2 in the following year; neither could his retreat have been enforced during his oppressor's attendance at the Parliament which sat from November 23, 1584, to March 29, 1585. It is worthy of remark that Sir Thomas had the charge, early in the last-named month, of a bill "for the preservation of grain and game," so it is clear that the knight of Charlecote was a zealous game-preserver, even if the introduction of the proposed measure were not the result of the depredations committed by the poet and his companions.

Another version of the narrative has been recorded by Archdeacon Davies, who was the vicar of Sapperton, a village in the neighboring county of Gloucester, and who died there in the year 1708. According to this authority the future great dramatist was "much given to all unluckiness in stealing venison and rabbits, particularly from Sir Thomas Lucy, who had him oft whipped and sometimes imprisoned, and at last made him fly his native county to his great advancement; but his revenge was so great that he is his Justice Clodpate, and calls him a great man, and that in allusion to his name bore three louses rampant for his arms." It is evident, therefore, from the independent testimonies of Rowe and Davies, that the deer-stealing history was accepted in the poet's native town and in the neighborhood during the latter part of the seventeenth century. That it has a solid basis of fact cannot admit of a reasonable doubt. It was current at a period in the history of Shakespearean appreciation before tales of the kind became liable to intentional falsification, and the impressive story of the penniless fugitive, who afterwards became a leading inhabitant of Stratford and the owner of New Place, was one likely to be handed down with passable fidelity to the grandchildren of his contemporaries. It is, moreover, one which exactly harmonizes with circumstances that materially add to its probability,—with the satirical allusions to the Lucys in their immediate relation to a poaching adventure, and with the certainty that there must have been some very grave reason to induce him to leave his wife and children to seek his unaided fortunes in a distant part of the country, rendering himself at the same time liable to imprisonment (5 Eliz. c. 4. s. 47) for violating the conditions of his apprenticeship. If there had been no such grave reason, how should there have been the provincial belief in 1693 that he had ran "from his master to London, and there received into the play-house as a servitor?" What but a strong and compulsory motive could have driven him so far away from a locality to which, as we gather from subsequent events, he was sensitively attached? The only theory, indeed, that would sanction the unconditional rejection of the traditions is that which assumes that they were designed in explanation of the allusions in the *Merry Wives of Windsor*, but surely, if that had been the case, there would have been a more explicit reference to the accusations of Master Shallow, charges that are in the aggregate of a more formidable description than those which have been transmitted by hearsay. "You have hurt my keeper, kill'd my dogs, stol'n my deer" (ed. 1602). "You have beaten my men, kill'd my deer, and broke open my lodge" (ed. 1623). It is also exceedingly improbable that there should have been any one at Stratford-on-Avon at the time of Betterton's visit who would have cared to elucidate the justice's implications, and it would appear, from the incorrect quotations which are given by Davies, that even the archdeacon was somewhat better acquainted with the history of Sir Thomas Lucy than he was with the comedy.

Neither the best citizens nor the most amiable men are always those whose cautious and dispassionate temperaments have enabled them to pass through the heats of youth without getting into scrapes. Those only, indeed, who consider it their duty to invest the greatest of dramatists with the honors of canonization will be distressed to hear that the poet, in the years of his apprenticeship to a cheerless business, got into trouble by netting rabbits and occasionally joining in the class of adventures that were then known under the title of "unlawful huntings." The general tradition among the rustics of the neighborhood was, and perhaps still is, that he was wild in his younger days, an impression delivered, as I have heard it in years gone by, in no tone or spirit of detraction; and he was wild in the least reprehensible of all irregular directions, not in the slums of Warwick, nor with roisterers in the taverns of Stratford, but in sports of the wood and the field that may have been illegally pursued, but were nevertheless regarded by the multitude as indications of manly spirit and gallantry. Sir Philip Sydney's May-Lady terms deer-stealing a "prettie service," and this was the light in which it was usually viewed so long as the keepers were outwitted. These were days when youthful raids for fruit or animals were not only excusable in the eyes of society, but apt to be considered desirable features of education, and we accordingly find a writer of the next century, Francis Osborn, born about the year 1589, bitterly lamenting that, owing to the mild character of his home-training, he had lost the advantages which others had derived from a participation in such-like kind of exploits; for, to quote his own words, "not undergoing the same discipline, I must needs come short of their experience that are bred up in free-schools, who, by plotting to rob an orchard, &c., run through all the subtleties required in taking of a town; being made by use familiar to secrecy and compliance with opportunity, qualities never after to be attained at cheaper rates than the hazard of all; whereas these see the danger of trusting others and the rocks they fall upon by a too obstinate adhering to their own imprudent resolutions, and all this under no higher penalty than a whipping." Then there was the curious fact that the students of Oxford, the center of the kingdom's learning and intelligence, had been for many generations the most notorious poachers in all England. An Act of the fifteenth century, under which disorderly hunters were to be banished from the university, does not appear to have been very effective, for their serious depredations in the reign of Henry VIII, positively led, as recorded by Leland, to the disparking of Radley, near Abingdon, a park that was about four miles distant from the scholastic city. The same lawless spirit prevailed among the younger collegians for many years. Dr. Forman relates how two students in 1573,—one of them John Thornborough, then aged twenty-one, afterwards Dean of York and Bishop of Worcester,—"never studied nor gave themselves to their books, but to go to schools of defence, to the dancing-schools, to steal deer and conies, and to hunt the hare, and to wooing of wenches." This was pretty well, and yet we are told, on the excellent authority of Anthony Wood, that Thornborough "was a person well-furnish'd with learning wisdom, courage, and other as well episcopal as temporal accomplishments beseeming a gentleman, a dean, and a bishop"; so it is clear that his attachment to the recreation of game-stealing at Shakespeare's poaching-age was not in any way detrimental to his subsequent reputation. He would, indeed, have suffered far more in the estimation of his contemporaries if he had been the Oxford freshman who, as recorded in the old jest-books, joining his fellow-students in one of their favorite clandestine expeditions upon the understanding that he was to maintain a rigid silence, vexatiously frightened away a choice herd of rabbits by exclaiming, "*Ececcuniculi multi*"; thus excusing himself when reproved for his folly,—who in the world, said he, would have thought that conies could have understood Latin?

But although it will be gathered from these evidences that amateur poaching was not always visited in those days with a distinct loss of character, it must not be inferred that its votaries, when detected, did not sometimes get into trouble and a certain amount of attendant disgrace. Much would depend upon the extent and nature of the depredations, and no little of course on the special tastes and pursuits of the owners. The landed gentry had suffered so much inconvenience from the practice that many of them had long been anxious for the establishment of stricter game-laws. Strenuous efforts had been made to render even rabbit-taking a felony, and it is not probable that Sir Thomas Lucy, an enthusiastic sportsman and an advocate for game-preservation, could have regarded the doings of Shakespeare and his companions with equanimity. It was natural that he should do his best to protect his covers from spoliation, and it is easy to believe that there may have been a display of arbitrary and undue severity in the process. There could have been no one among the poachers who would have been likely to have offered a successful resistance, or who would have dared to have appealed to a superior court in respect to a matter in which all of them were incipiently in the wrong; and it must be borne in mind that the future poet was then no more either to Sir Thomas or to the world than Peter Turf or Henry Pimpernell. They might have been indicted under an Act of the thirteenth of Richard II, c. 13, which provided that "no manner of layman which hath not lands or tenements to the value of forty shillings by year shall have or keep any greyhound, hound, nor other dog to hunt; nor shall they use ferrets, hays, nets, hare-pipes, nor cords nor other engines for to take or destroy deer, hares, nor conies, nor other gentlemen's game, upon pain of one year's imprisonment;" but the county records of the time not being extant, it is now impossible to ascertain the course of any proceedings that may have been taken in the matter. And even if the Session Rolls had been preserved, it is not likely that all the particulars of the case would have been revealed, for in all probability Sir Thomas Lucy frequently took it upon himself to exercise a summary jurisdiction in regard to minor offenses. Such a method of settlement may have been on occasion convenient to both parties if, for example, he had sent delinquents to jail on his own responsibility for two or three months when a legal conviction would have secured their imprisonment for twelve. It must be remembered that the rural magistrates of those days assumed very large discretionary powers, their "luxuriant authority," as it was termed by an Elizabethan legislator, having been a frequent subject of complaint. That the magistrates in the vicinity of Stratford-on-Avon were accustomed to exercise a despotic sway over the poorer inhabitants may be gathered from the fact that at a somewhat later period William Combe, the squire of Welcombe, sent a person of the name of Hiccox to Warwick jail, and refused bail, merely because he "did not behave himself with such respect in his presence it seemeth he looked for." What would he not have done if he had first caught his disrespectful visitor marching off with his rabbits and deer, and then, with unprecedented temerity, electrifying the neighborhood by the circulation of a poetical lampoon reflecting upon the intelligence and judgment of His Worship? Now Shakespeare, in his poaching days, the penniless son of an impecunious father, and without friends of appreciable influence, would assuredly have fared no better on such occasions than poor Hiccox, unless he had been, as he obviously was not, high in the favor of Davy, the servingman; and the most rational mode of accounting for and excusing his long-sustained resentment is to recognize a substantial groundwork of facts in the early traditions. They are in unison with possibilities that furnish an intelligible explanation of the known circumstances, and all becomes clear if it be assumed that a persistive, harsh, and injudicial treatment elicited the obnoxious ballad. Its author could have been severely punished under the common law for its exhibition, and there can be little doubt that it was a contemplated movement in reference to the libel, in addition, perhaps, to some other indictment, that occasioned his flight to the metropolis.

The Sir Thomas Lucy who received the honor of knighthood in 1565, and had thus accidentally diverted the course of what might otherwise have been an unnoted life, was the head of one of the most opulent and influential families in the county of Warwick. Owning estates in various parts of the country, including, within a few miles of Stratford-on-Avon, the manors of Sherbourn, Hampton Lucy and Charlecote, they had been settled at the last-named demain for many generations. Sir Thomas was born in 1588, and was therefore about fifty-three years of age at the time of the poet's sprightly adventures. He married in early life Joyce Acton, a rich heiress, through whom he became possessed of Sutton Park, near Tenbury, then and for long afterwards one of the most important deer-enclosures in Worcestershire, where he was high sheriff in 1586. He was elected to the Parliaments of 1571 and 1584, but his absenteeisms from Warwickshire were exceptional, and there he held a social position little inferior to that of the higher nobility. His only son was knighted in 1593, and thus it curiously happened that, from that year until his death in 1600, there were two Sir Thomas Lucys of Charlecote, the one known as the younger and the other as the elder. The ancestral manor house, which the latter rebuilt in the first of Elizabeth, 1558 and 1559, was arranged, out of compliment to that sovereign, in the form of the capital letter E, and it remains to this day the "goodly dwelling and a rich," a visible monument of his wealth and residential dignity. It is situated on the eastern bank of the Avon, upon ground of a slightly undulating character, about four miles from Stratford through the bye-paths that the trespassers would most likely have followed. Although the whole edifice has been seriously modernized, the back especially having been nearly transformed, the front-exterior still retains the general characteristics of the original structure; but by far the most genuine and interesting object is the ancient gatehouse, which stands in advance at a little distance from the mansion, and which, with its turrets and elegant oriel window, is essentially in the state in which it would have been recognized by the now celebrated poachers of 1585.

At the period of Shakespeare's arrival in London, any reputable kind of employment was obtained with considerable difficulty. There is an evidence of this in the history of the early life of John Sadler, a native of Stratford-on-Avon and one of the poet's contemporaries, who tried his fortunes in the metropolis under similar though less discouraging circumstances. This youth, upon quitting Stratford, "join'd himself to the carrier, and came to London, where he had never been before, and sold his horse in Smithfield; and, having no acquaintance in London to recommend him or assist him, he went from street to street, and house to house, asking if they wanted an apprentice, and though he met with many discouraging scorns and a thousand denials, he went on till he light on Mr. Brokesbank, a grocer in Bucklersbury, who, though he long denied him for want of sureties for his fidelity, and because the money he had (but ten pounds) was so disproportionate to what he used to receive with apprentices, yet, upon his discreet account he gave of himself and the motives which put him upon that course, and promise to compensate with diligent and faithfull service whatever else was short of his expectation, he ventured to receive him upon trial, in which he so well approved himself that he accepted him into his service, to which he bound him for eight years." It is to be gathered, from the account given by Rowe, that Shakespeare, a fugitive, leaving his native town unexpectedly, must have reached London more unfavorably circumstanced than Sadler, although the latter experienced so much trouble in finding occupation. At all events, there would have been greater difficulty in the poet's case in accounting satisfactorily to employers for his sudden departure from home. That he was also nearly, if not quite, moneyless, is to be inferred from tradition, the latter supported by the ascertained fact of the adverse circumstances of his father at the time rendering it impossible for him to have received effectual assistance from his parents; nor is there reason for believing that he was likely to have obtained substantial aid from the relatives of his wife. Johnson no doubt accurately reported the tradition of his day, when, in 1765, he stated that Shakespeare "came to London a needy adventurer, and lived for a time by very mean employments." To the same effect is the earlier testimony given by the author of *Ratseis Ghost*, 1605, where the strolling player, in a passage reasonably believed to refer to the great dramatist, observes in reference to actors, "I have heard, indeede, of some that have gone to London *very meanly* and have come in time to be exceedingly wealthy." The author of the last-named tract was evidently well acquainted with the theatrical gossip of his day, so that his nearly contemporary evidence on the subject may be fairly accepted as a truthful record of the current belief.

It has been repeatedly observed that the visits of theatrical companies to the poet's native town suffice to explain the history of his connection with the stage, but it is difficult to understand how this could have been the case. There is no good evidence that a single one of the actors belonged to his neighborhood, and even if he had casually made the acquaintance of some of the itinerants, it is extremely unlikely that any extent of such intimacy would have secured the admission of an inexperienced person into their ranks. The histrionic art is not learned in a day, and it was altogether unusual with the sharers to receive into the company men who had not had the advantage of a very early training in the profession. It might, therefore, have been reasonably inferred, even in the absence of tradition, that at this time Shakespeare could only have obtained employment at the theater in a very subordinate capacity, nor can it be safely assumed that there would have been an opening for him of any kind. The quotations above given seem to indicate that his earlier occupation was something of a still lower character. A traditional anecdote was current about the middle of the last century, according to which it would appear that the great dramatist, if connected in any sort of manner with the theater immediately upon his arrival in London, could only have been engaged in a servile capacity, and that there was, in the career of the great poet, an interval which some may consider one of degradation; to be regarded with either incredulity or sorrow. Others may, with more discernment and without reluctance, receive the story as a testimony to his practical wisdom in accepting any kind of honest occupation in preference to starvation or mendicancy, and cheerfully making the best of the circumstances by which he was surrounded. The tale is related by several writers, but perhaps the best version is the one recorded by Dr. Johnson, in 1765, in the following terms,—"in the time of Elizabeth, coaches being yet uncommon and hired coaches not at all in use, those who were too proud, too tender or too idle to walk, went on horseback to any distant business or diversion;—many came on horseback to the play, and when Shakespeare fled to London from the terror of a criminal prosecution, his first expedient was to wait at the door of the play-house, and hold the horses of those that had no servants that they might be ready again after the performance;—in this office he became so conspicuous for his care and readiness, that in a short time every man as he alighted called for Will

Shakespeare, and scarcely any other waiter was trusted with a horse while Will Shakespeare could be had;—this was the first dawn of better fortune;—Shakespeare, finding more horses put into his hand than he could hold, hired boys to wait under his inspection, who, when Will Shakespeare was summoned, were immediately to present themselves, 'I am Shakespeare's boy, sir;'—in time Shakespeare found higher employment, but as long as the practice of riding to the play-house continued the waiters that held the horses retained the appellation of Shakespeare's Boys." Dr. Johnson received this anecdote from Pope, to whom it had been communicated by Rowe; and it appears to have reached the last-named writer through Betterton and Davenant.

It has been and is the fashion with most biographers to discredit the horse tradition entirely, but that it was originally related by Sir William Davenant, and belongs in some form to the earlier half of the seventeenth century, cannot reasonably be doubted. The circumstance of the anecdote being founded upon the practice of gentleman riding to the theaters, a custom obsolete after the Restoration, is sufficient to establish the antiquity of the story. In a little volume of epigrams by Sir John Davis, printed at Middleborough in or about the year 1599, a man of inferior position is ridiculed for being constantly on horseback, imitating in that respect persons of higher rank, riding even "into the fieldes playes to behold." Most of these horsemen were probably accustomed to a somewhat lavish expenditure, and it may very well be assumed that Shakespeare not unfrequently received more than the ordinary fee of a tester for his services. There is, at all events, no valid reason for enrolling the tradition among the absolute fictions that have been circulated respecting the poet. Several writers have taken that course mainly on the ground that, although it was known to Rowe, he does not allude to it in his Life of Shakespeare, 1709; but there is no improbability in the supposition that the story was not related to him until after the publication of that work, the second edition of which in 1714 is a mere reprint of the first. Other reasons for the omission may be suggested, but even if it be conceded that the anecdote was rejected as suspicious and improbable, that circumstance alone cannot be decisive against the opinion that there may be glimmerings of truth in it. This is, indeed, all that is contended for. Few would be disposed to accept the story literally as related by Johnson, but when it is considered that the tradition must be a very early one, that its genealogy is respectable, and that it harmonizes with the general old belief of the great poet having, when first in London, subsisted by "very mean employments," little doubt can fairly be entertained that it has at least in some way or other a foundation in real occurrences. It should also be remembered that horse-stealing was one of the very commonest offenses of the period, and one which was probably stimulated by the facility with which delinquents of that class obtained pardons. The safe custody of a horse was a matter of serious import, and a person who had satisfactorily fulfilled such a trust would not be lightly estimated.

It is important to observe that all the early traditions, to which any value can be attached, concur in the belief that Shakespeare did not leave his native town with histrionic intention. Even in the absence of those evidences, although it might not necessarily, still it might, and most likely would, be a fallacy to assume that his dramatic tastes impelled him to undertake an arduous and premeditated journey to encounter the risk of an engagement at a metropolitan theater, however powerfully they may have influenced his choice of a profession after he had once arrived in London. For, residing throughout his youth in what may fairly be considered a theatrical neighborhood, with continual facilities for the cultivation of those tastes, if he had yielded in his boyish days to an impulsive fascination for the stage, it is most likely that he would in some way have joined the profession while its doors were readily accessible through one of the numerous itinerant companies, and before, not after, such inclinations must have been in some measure restrained by the local domestic ties that resulted from his marriage. If he had quitted Stratford-on-Avon in his early youth, there would be no difficulty in understanding that he became one of the elder player's boys or apprentices, but it is extremely unlikely that, at the age of twenty-one, he would have voluntarily left a wife and three children in Warwickshire for the sake of obtaining a miserable position on the London boards.

It is not, therefore, requisite to assume that Shakespeare rushed in the first instance to the theater or its neighborhood in search of employment, and a plausible explanation can be given of the circumstances which led him to the occupation mentioned in the Davenant anecdote. It appears that James Burbage, the owner of the theater, rented premises close by Smithfield in which he "usually kept horses at liverye for sundry persons"; his assistant, or rather manager, of the stable being "a northerne man usually called by the name of Robyn," possibly the same individual whose life was afterwards sacrificed by the unfortunate rise in the price of oats. If the course adopted by Sadler on his arrival in London was, as is most likely, the one also taken by the poet, the latter would at once have proceeded to Smithfield to obtain the best price for the horse which carried him to the metropolis, the further retention of the animal being no doubt beyond his means. He might readily upon this occasion have become acquainted with James Burbage at a time when he was desirous of obtaining any kind of situation that presented itself, the tradition leading to the inference that he was engaged by the latter to act in some equestrian capacity. If so, one of his duties would have been the care, during the performances, of the horses of those of Burbage's Smithfield customers who visited the theater. This enterprising manager was also the landlord of a tavern in Shoreditch, where it is possible that his own horses may have been kept. He must, at all events, have been just the kind of person to be ready to take an active and intelligent rustic into his service, without being too inquisitive respecting the history of the young man's antecedents.

The transition from the stable and the fields to the interior of the theater may not have been long deferred, but all the evidences unite in affirming that Shakespeare entered the latter in a very humble capacity. The best authority on this point is one William Castle, who was the parish-clerk of Stratford-on-Avon during nearly all the latter part of the seventeenth century, and used to tell visitors that the poet "was received into the playhouse as a serviture," in other words, an attendant on the performers. A later account is somewhat more explicit. We are informed by Malone, writing in 1780, that there was "a stage tradition that his first office in the theater was that of prompter's attendant, whose employment it is to give the performers notice to be ready to enter as often as the business of the play requires their appearance on the stage"; nor can the future eminence of Shakespeare be considered to be opposed to the reception of the tradition. "I have known men within my remembrance," observes Downes, in 1710, "arrive to the highest dignities of the theater, who made their entrance in the quality of mutes, joint-stools, flower-pots, and tapestry hangings." The office of prompter's attendant was at least as respectable as any of the occupations which are here enumerated.

No one has recorded the name of the first theater with which Shakespeare was connected, but if, as is almost certain, he came to London in or soon after the year 1585, there were at the time of his arrival only two in the metropolis, both of them on the north of the Thames. The earliest legitimate theater on the south was the Rose, the erection of which was contemplated in the year 1587, but it would seem from Henslowe's *Diary* that the building was not opened till early in 1592. The circus at Paris Garden, though perhaps occasionally used for dramatic performances, was not a regular theater. Admitting, however, the possibility that companies of players could have hired the latter establishment, there is good reason for concluding that Southwark was not the locality alluded to in the Davenant tradition. The usual mode of transit, for those Londoners who desired to attend theatrical performances in Southwark, was certainly by water. The boatmen of the Thames were perpetually asserting at a somewhat later period that their living depended on the continuance of the Southwark, and the suppression of the London, theaters. Some few of the courtly members of the audience, perhaps for the mere sake of appearances, might occasionally have arrived at their destination on horseback, having taken what would be to most of them the circuitous route over London Bridge; but the large majority would select the more convenient passage by boat. The Southwark audiences mainly consisted of Londoners, for in the then sparsely inhabited condition of Kent and Surrey very few could have arrived from those counties. The number of riders to the Bankside theaters must, therefore, always have been very limited, too much so for the remunerative employment of horse-holders, whose services would be required merely in regard to the still fewer persons who were unattended by their lackeys. The only theaters upon the other side of the Thames, when the poet arrived in London, were the Theater and the Curtain, for, notwithstanding some apparent testimonies to the contrary, the Blackfriars Theater, as will be afterwards seen, was not then in existence. It was to the Theater or to the Curtain that the satirist alluded when he speaks of the fashionable youth riding "into the fieldes playes to behold." Both these theaters were situated in the parish of Shoreditch, in the fields of the Liberty of Halliwell, in which locality, if the Davenant tradition is in the 'slightest degree to be trusted, Shakespeare must have commenced his metropolitan life. This new career, however, was initiated not absolutely in London, but in a thinly populated outskirt about half a mile from the city walls, a locality possessing outwardly the appearance of a country village, but inwardly sustaining much of the bustle and all the vices of the town. These latter inconveniences could easily be avoided, for there were in the neighboring meadows ample opportunities for quiet meditation or scientific enquiry. Here it was that Gerard, the celebrated botanist, stumbled a few years afterwards upon a new kind of crow-foot which he describes as being similar to the ordinary plant, "saving that his leaves are fatter, thicker, and greener, and his small twiggie stalkes stand upright, otherwise it is like; of which kinde it chanced that, walking in the fielde next unto the Theater by London, in company of a worshipfull marchant named master Nicholas Lete, I founde one of this kinde there with double flowers, which before that time I had not seene," (The Herball, 1597, p. 804). Thus Shakespeare's observation of the wild flowers was not necessarily limited, as has been supposed, to his provincial experiences, two of the principal theaters with which he was connected having been situated in a rural suburb, and green fields being throughout his life within an easy walk from any part of London.

Nothing has been discovered respecting the history of Shakespeare's early theatrical life, but there is an interesting evidence that no estrangement between his parents and himself had followed the circumstances that led him to the metropolis, a fact which is established by his concurrence with them in an endeavor that they were making in 1587 to obtain favorable terms for a proposed relinquishment of Asbies. Nine years previously they had borrowed the sum of £40, on the security of that estate, from their connection, Edmund Lambert of Barton-on-the-Heath. The loan remaining unpaid, and the mortgagee dying in April, 1587, his son and heir, John, threatened shortly after that event with the institution of a law-suit for the recovery of the property, was naturally desirous of having the matter settled, and it was arranged in the following September that Lambert should, on canceling the mortgage and paying also the sum of £20, receive from the Shakespeares an absolute title to the estate, or, to speak more accurately, the best title which it was in their power to grant. Having obtained the assent of William, who was his mother's heir-apparent, they were enabled to offer all but a perfect security; but it appears, from the records of a subsequent litigation, that the intended compromise was abandoned.

It clearly appears, from the account given by Rowe, that Shakespeare returned to his native town after the dangers from the Lucy prosecution had subsided. The same writer informs us that the visit occurred subsequently to his junction with one of the theatrical companies. The exact dates of these events are unknown, but it is not likely that he would have ventured into Sir Thomas's neighborhood for a considerable time after his escapade. Country justices wielded in those days tremendous power in adjudication on minor offenses. There were no newspapers to carry the intelligence of provincial tyranny to the ears of a sensitive public opinion, and there is no doubt that a youth in Shakespeare's position, who had dared to lampoon the most influential magistrate of the locality, would have been for some time in a critical position. However greatly he may have desired to rejoin his family, it is, therefore, not probable that the poet would be found again at Stratford-on-Avon before the year 1587, and then we have, in the Lambert episode, a substantial reason for believing that he had at that time a conference with his parents on the subject of the Asbies mortgage. The sum of £20, equivalent to at least £240 now-a-days, to be paid in cash by Lambert, would have been an element of serious importance to them all in their then financial circumstances. It must have been a subject for anxious deliberation, one that could hardly have been arranged without a personal interview, and, in the presence of Rowe's testimony, it may fairly be assumed that the meeting took place at Stratford, not in London.

In the same year, 1587, an unusual number of companies of actors visited Stratford-on-Avon, including the Queen's Players and those of Lords Essex, Leicester, and Stafford. This circumstance has given rise to a variety of speculations respecting the company to which the poet may then have belonged; but the fact is that we are destitute of any information, and have no relative means of forming an opinion on the subject. Even if it be conceded that Burbage's theater was the first with which Shakespeare was connected, no progress is made in the enquiry. That personage, who had retired from the stage, was in the habit of letting the building to any public entertainers who would remunerate him either in cash or by a share of profits. There was no establishment at that time devoted for a long continuous period to the use of a single company.

It is, however, all but certain that the favorite theory of Shakespeare having been one of the Queen's servants at this period is incorrect, for his name is not found in the official list belonging to the following year; so that, if he was connected in any way with them, he could at the latter date have been merely one of the underlings who were not in a position of sufficient importance to be included in the register. With the single exception of the absence of his name from that list, no evidence whatever has been discovered to warrant a conjecture on the subject. But although there is no reason for believing that he was ever one of the royal actors, we may be sure that he must have witnessed, either at Stratford or London, some of the inimitable performances of the company's star, the celebrated Richard Tarlton. This individual, the "pleasant Willy" of Spenser, who died in September, 1588, was the most popular comedian of the day, one of those instinctive humorists who have merely to show their faces to be greeted with roars of merriment. It may have been, when the part of Derick, the clown, was in his hands, that

Shakespeare became acquainted with the *Famous Victories of Henry the Fifth*, a lively play, some of the incidents of which he unquestionably recollected when composing his histories of that sovereign and his predecessor. There was another drama that was played in London about the same time, one in which Tarlton's personation of a dissolute youth was singularly popular and long remembered. In this latter was a death-bed scene, a notice of which may be worth giving as an example of the dramatic incidents that were relished in the poet's early days;—A wealthy father, in the last extremity of illness, communicates his testamentary intentions to his three sons. His landed estates are alloted to the eldest, who, overcome with emotion, expresses a fervent wish that the invalid may yet survive to enjoy them himself. To the next, who is a scholar, are left a handsome annuity and a very large sum of money for the purchase of books. Affected equally with his brother, he declares that he has no wish for such gifts, and only hopes that the testator may live to enjoy them himself. The third son, represented by Tarlton, was now summoned to the bed-side, and a grotesque figure he must have appeared in a costume which is described by an eye-witness as including a torn and dirty shirt, a one-sleeved coat, stockings out at heels, and a head-dress of feathers and straw. "As for you, sirrah," quoths the indignant parent, "you know how often I have fetched you out of Newgate and Bridewell;—you have been an ungracious villain;—I have nothing to bequeath to you but the gallows and a rope." Following the example of the others, Tarlton bursts into a flood of tears, and then, falling on his knees, sobbingly exclaims,—"O, father, I do not desire them;—I trust to Heaven you shall live to enjoy them yourself."

It may be gathered, from the poet's subsequent history, that his return to Stratford-on-Avon was merely of a temporary character. The actors of those days were, as a rule, individual wanderers, spending a large portion of their time at a distance from their families; and there is every reason for believing that this was the case with Shakespeare from the period of his arrival in London until nearly the end of his life. All the old theatrical companies were more or less of an itinerant character, and it is all but impossible that he should not have already commenced his provincial tours. But what were their directions, or who were his associates, have not been discovered. There is not, indeed, a single particle of evidence respecting his career during the next five years, that is to say, from the time of the Lambert negotiation, in 1587, until he is discovered as a rising actor and dramatist in 1592.

This interval must have been the chief period of Shakespeare's literary education. Removed prematurely from school; residing with illiterate relatives in a bookless neighborhood; thrown into the midst of occupations adverse to scholastic progress—it is difficult to believe that, when he first left Stratford, he was not all but destitute of polished accomplishments. He could not, at all events, under the circumstances in which he had then so long been placed, have had the opportunity of acquiring a refined style of composition. After he had once, however, gained a footing in London, he would have been placed under different conditions. Books of many kinds would have been accessible to him, and he would have been almost daily within hearing of the best dramatic poetry of the age. There would also no doubt have been occasional facilities for picking up a little smattering of the continental languages, and it is almost beyond a doubt that he added somewhat to his classical knowledge during his residence in the metropolis. It is, for instance, hardly possible that the *Amoves* of Ovid, whence he derived his earliest motto, could have been one of his school-books.

Although Shakespeare had exhibited a taste for poetic composition before his first departure from Stratford-on-Avon, all traditions agree in the statement that he was a recognized actor before he joined the ranks of the dramatists. This latter event appears to have occurred on March 3, 1592, when a new drama, entitled *Henry*, or *Harry, the Sixth*, was brought out by Lord Strange's Servants, then acting either at Newington or Southwark under an arrangement with Henslowe, a wealthy stage manager, to whom no doubt the author had sold the play. In this year, as we learn on unquestionable authority, Shakespeare was first rising into prominent notice, so that the history then produced, now known as the *First Part of Henry the Sixth*, was, in all probability, his earliest complete dramatic work. Its extraordinary success must have secured for the author a substantial position in the theatrical world of the day. The play had, for those times, an unusually long run, so that Nash, writing in or before the following month of July, states that the performances of it had, in that short interval, been witnessed by "ten thousand spectators at least," and, although this estimate may be overstrained, there can be no hesitation in receiving it as a valid testimony to the singular popularity of the new drama. The *Second Part of Henry the Sixth* must have appeared soon afterward, but no record of its production on the stage has been preserved. The former drama was published for the first time in the collective edition of 1623. A garbled and spurious version of the second play, the unskillful work of some one who had not access to a perfect copy of the original, appeared in the year 1594 under the title of the *First Part of the Contention betwixt the Houses of York and Lancaster*. It was published by Millington, the same bookseller who afterwards issued the surreptitious edition of *Henry the Fifth*.

Robert Greene, a popular writer and dramatist, who had commenced his literary career nine years previously, died on September 3, 1592. In a work entitled the *Groatsworth of Wit*, written shortly before his death, he had travestied, in an interesting sarcastic episode respecting some of his contemporaries, a line from one of Shakespeare's then recent compositions,—O, *tiger's heart, wrapp'd in a woman's hide!* This line is of extreme interest as including the earliest record of words composed by the great dramatist. It forms part of a vigorous speech which is as Shakespearean in its natural characterial fidelity, as it is Marlowean in its diction. That speech of the unfortunate Duke of York's is one of the most striking in the play, and the above line was probably selected for quotation by Greene on account of its popularity through effective delivery. The quotation shows that the *Third Part of Henry the Sixth* was written previously to September, 1592, and hence it may be concluded that all Shakespeare's plays on the subject of that reign, although perhaps subsequently revised in a few places by the author, were originally produced in that year. A surreptitious and tinkered version of the third part, made up by an inferior hand chiefly out of imperfect materials, appeared in 1595 under the title of the *Tragedy of Richard Duke of York*, and therein stated to have been "sundry times acted by the Earl of Pembroke's servants."

There is no reason for wonder in the style of a young author being influenced by that of a popular and accomplished contemporary, and judgment on the authorship of much of the above-named plays should not be ruled by a criticism which can only fairly be applied to the rapidly approaching period when the great dramatist had outlived the possibility of appearing in the character of an imitative writer. That Shakespeare commenced his literary vocation as, to some extent, a follower of Marlowe can hardly be denied, even were the line quoted by Greene the only remnant of his early plays; and that the three parts of *Henry the Sixth* had been some years on the stage, when *Henry the Fifth* was produced in 1599, may be gathered from that interesting relic of literary autobiography, the final chorus to the latter play. No theory respecting the history of the former dramas is wholly free from embarrassing perplexities, but that which best agrees with the positive evidences is that which concedes the authorship of the three plays to Shakespeare, their production to the year 1592, and the quarto editions of the second and third parts as vamped, imperfect, and blundering versions of the poet's own original dramas.

The *Groatsworth of Wit* was published very soon after the unfortunate writer's decease, that is to say, it appeared towards the end of September, 1592; and it is clear that one portion of it had been composed under the influence of a profound jealousy of Shakespeare. Greene is addressing his fellow-dramatists, and speaking of the actors of their plays, thus introduces his satirical observations on the author of the *Third Part of Henry the Sixth*, with a travesty of the line above mentioned,—"trust them not, for there is an upstart crow, beautified with our feathers, that, with his *Tygers heart wrapt in a Players hide*, supposes he is as well able to bumbast out a blanke verse as the best of you; and being an absolute *Johannes factotum*, is, in his owne conceit, the onely Shake-scene in a countrie." It was natural that these impertinent remarks should have annoyed the object of them, and that they were so far effective may be gathered from an interesting statement made by the editor, Henry Chettle, in a work of his own, entitled *Kind-Heart's Dream*, that he published a few weeks afterward, in which he specially regrets that the attack had proved offensive to Shakespeare, whom, he observes,—"at that time I did not so much spare as since I wish I had, for that, as I have moderated the heate of living writers, and might have usde my owne discretion, especially in such a case, the author beeing dead, that I did not I am as sory as if the originall fault had beene my fault, because myselfe have seene his demeanor no lesse civill than he exelent in the qualitie he professes; besides, divers of worship have reported his uprightnes of dealing, which argues his honesty, and his facetious grace in writting, that aprooves his art." Apologies of this kind are so apt to be overstrained that we can hardly gather more from the present one than the respectable position Shakespeare held as a writer and actor, and that Chettle, having made his acquaintance, was desirous of keeping friends with one who was beginning to be appreciated by the higher classes of society. The annoyance, however, occasioned by Greene's posthumous criticism was soon forgotten by the poet amid the triumphs of his subsequent career.

Removing now the scene of our fragmentary history from the metropolis to the country, we find, at the time of Greene's lampoonry, the poet's father busily engaged with his counters in appraising the goods of one Henry Field, a tanner of Stratford-on-Avon, whose inventory, attached to his will, was taken in August, 1592. This tradesman's son, Richard, who was apprenticed to a printer in London in the year 1579, took up his freedom in 1587, and soon afterwards commenced business on his own account, an elegant copy of Ovid's *Metamorphoses*, 1589, being among the numerous works that issued from his press. It is most likely, indeed all but certain, that Shakespeare participated in his father's acquaintance with the printer's relatives, and at all events there was the provincial tie, so specially dear to Englishmen when at a distance from the town of their birth, between the poet and Richard Field. When, therefore, the latter is discovered, early in the year 1593, engaged in the production of *Venus and Adonis*, it is only reasonable to infer that the author had a control over the typographical arrangements. The purity of the text and the nature of the dedication may be thought to strengthen this opinion, and although poems were not then generally introduced to the public in the same glowing terms usually accorded to dramatic pieces, the singularly brief and anonymous title-page does not bear the appearance of a publisher's handywork. Field, however, registered the copyright to himself on April 18, and the work was offered for sale, at the White Greyhound in St. Paul's Churchyard, by his friend, John Harrison, the publisher of the first three editions, and who next year became the owner both of the *Venus* and *Lucrece*. It may be well to record that the publication had what was probably the vicarious sanction of no less an individual than the Archbishop of Canterbury, who, although no Puritan, would scarcely have considered its exquisite versification sufficient to atone for its voluptuous character.

The poem of *Venus and Adonis*, which was favorably received and long continued to be the most popular book of the kind, is termed by the author "the first heir of my invention." If these words are to be literally interpreted, it must have been written in or before the year 1592; but Shakespeare may be referring only to works of a strictly poetical character, which were then held in far higher estimation than dramatic compositions. However that may be, the oft-repeated belief that *Venus and Adonis* was a production of his younger days at Stratford-on-Avon can hardly be sustained. It is extremely improbable that an epic, so highly finished and so completely devoid of patois, could have been produced under the circumstances of his then domestic surroundings, while, moreover, the notion is opposed to the best and earliest traditional opinions. It is also to be observed that there is nothing in the dedication in favor of such a conjecture, although the fact, had it been one, would have formed a ready and natural defense against the writer's obvious timidity. The work was inscribed, apparently without permission, to Lord Southampton, a young nobleman then only in his twentieth year, who about this time had commenced to exhibit a special disposition to encourage the rising authors of the metropolis.

Literature, in Shakespeare's time, was nearly the only passport of the lower and middle class to the countenance and friendship of the great. It was no wonder that the poet, in days when interest was all but omnipotent, should have wished to secure the advantages that could hardly fail to be derived from a special association with an individual in the favored position, and with the exceptionally generous character, of Lord Southampton. Wealthy, accomplished and romantic,—with a temperament that could listen to a metrical narrative of the follies of Venus without yielding to hysterics,—the young nobleman was presumably the most eligible dedicatee that Shakespeare could have desired for the introduction of his first poem to the literary world. It is evident, however, that, when he was penning the inscription to *Venus and Adonis*, whatever presentiment he may have entertained on the subject, he was by no means sure that his lordship would give a friendly, reception to, much less so that he would be gratified by, the intended compliment. But all doubts upon these points were speedily removed, and little more than a twelve month elapsed before the poet is found warmly attached to Lord Southampton, and eagerly taking the opportunity, in his second address, of tendering his gratitude for favors conferred in the interval.

In the winter season of 1593–94, Shakespeare's earliest tragedy, which was, unfortunately, based on a repulsive tale, was brought out by the Earl of Sussex's actors, who were then performing, after a tour in the provinces, at one of the Surrey theaters. They were either hired by, or playing under some financial arrangement with, Henslowe, who, after the representation of a number of revivals, ventured upon the production of a drama on the story of *Titus Andronicus*, the only new play introduced during the season. This tragedy, having been successfully produced before a large audience on January 23, 1594, was shortly afterward entered on the books of the Stationers' Company and published by Danter. It was also performed, almost if not quite simultaneously, by the servants of the Earls of Derby and Pembroke. Thus it appears that Shakespeare, up to this period, had written all his dramas for Henslowe, and that they were acted, under the sanction of that manager, by the various companies performing from 1592 to 1594 at the Rose Theater and Newington Butts. The acting copies of *Titus Andronicus* and the three parts of *Henry the Sixth* must of course have been afterwards transferred by Henslowe to the Lord Chamberlain's company.

Hideous and repulsive as the story of Tamora and the Andronici is now considered, it was anything but repugnant to the taste of the general public in Henslowe's day. Neither was it regarded as out of the pale of the legitimate drama by the most cultivated, otherwise so able a scholar and critic as Meres would hardly, several years after the appearance of *Titus Andronicus*, have inserted its title among those of the noteworthy tragedies of Shakespeare. The audiences of Elizabeth's time reveled in the very crudity of the horrible, so much so that nearly every kind of bodily torture and mutilation, or even more revolting incidents, formed part of the stock business of the theater. Murders were in special request in all kinds of serious dramas. Wilson, one of Lord Leicester's servants, was thought in 1581 to be just the person to write a play then urgently desired, which was not only to "be original and amusing," but was also to include "plenty of mystery," and "be full of all sorts of murders, immorality, and robberies." Nor was the taste for the predominance of the worst kind of sensational incidents restricted to the public stage, as any one may see who will care to peruse the *Misfortunes of Arthur*, produced with great flourish by the students of Gray's Inn in 1588. This deplorable fancy was nearly in its zenith at the time of the appearance of Titus Andronicus. In the same year, 1594, there was published the *Tragicall Raigne of Selimus, Emperour of the Turkes*, a composition offering similar attractions, but the writer was so afraid of his massacres being considered too insipid, he thus reveals his misgivings to the audience,—

> If this First Part, gentles, do like you well,
> The Second Part shall greater murders tell.

The character of the theatrical speculations of Henslowe was obviously influenced, in common with that of nearly all managers, by the current tastes of the public, and, in an age like the one now spoken of, is it wonderful that he should have considered the story of Titus Andronicus a fit theme for the dramatist? Is it also marvelous that Shakespeare, a young author then struggling into position, should not have felt it his duty, on æsthetic grounds, to reject an offer the acceptance of which invited no hostile criticism, while it opened out a prospect of material advantages? Henslowe's judgment, regulated by thoughts of the money-box, not by those of attempted reforms of the drama, were no doubt in his own opinion amply justified by the result. A certain deference to the expectations of a popular audience is, indeed, nearly always essential to the continuous support of a theater, and it is not unlikely that the very incidents now so offensive were those which mainly contributed to the success of the tragedy. As for the poet's share in the transaction, we are too apt to consider it indefensible under any measure of temptation, without reflecting to what extent a familiarity with representative horrors might produce an unconscious indifference to their ghastliness even in the tenderest of natures. Such horrors belong to the taste of the age, not to that of the individual. We must try to reconcile ourselves, as best we may, to the obvious fact that Shakespeare did not always consider it necessary to deviate from the course of his foundation-tales for the sake of avoiding the barbarities of the ancient stage. Had it been otherwise, the story of *Titus Andronicus* might have been purified, and we also mercifully spared from a contemplation of the appalling eye-scene in the tragedy of *Lear*.

No discussion on either of the last-named plays, or on many of the others, can be satisfactorily conducted so long as the influences of the older drama, and the theatric usages of the time, are not ever carefully borne in mind. It is a fallacy to admit, with many, the necessity of true criticism being grounded upon a reverential belief that the whole of Shakespeare's plays, in the forms in which they have descended to us, are examples of the unvarying perfection of the writer's judgment and dramatic art. That he was endowed with an exquisite judgment there is ample evidence, but that it was not always utilized is equally indisputable. It is obvious that, in several instances, when vivifying some of the most popular old English dramas, he was contented to transfer irrational plots and defective constructions that had been firmly established in public favor. The latter were sometimes adopted without an effort to bring them into harmony with the conduct of the action; and there appears to have been generally a disinclination on his part to originate either plots or incidents. So numerous were the popular and other tales that were suited for contemporary dramatic purposes, there was, as a rule, no theatrical necessity for his inventing either; while the creation of a new story, never an easy and generally a hazardous task for a dramatist, might have been more trouble to him than the composition of a play. Shakespeare was leading a busy life, and there are no indications that he would have delayed the completion of any one of his works for the sake of art. It should be remembered that his dramas were not written for posterity, but as a matter of business, never for his own speculation but always for that of the managers of the theater, the choice of subject being occasionally dictated by them or by patrons of the stage; his task having been to construct out of certain given or elected materials successful dramas for the audiences of the day. It is not pretended that he did not invariably take an earnest interest in his work, his intense sympathy with each character forbidding such an assumption; but simply that his other tastes were subordinated when necessary to his duty to his employers. If the managers considered that the popular feeling was likely to encourage, or if an influential patron or the Court desired, the production of a drama on some special theme, it was composed to order on that subject, no matter how repulsive the character of the plot or how intrinsically it was unfitted for dramatic purposes. Working thus under the domination of a commercial spirit, it is impossible to say to what extent his work was affected by unfavorable influences; such, for example, as the necessity of finishing a drama with undue haste, the whole, as it may have been, especially in his early days, written under disturbing circumstances in the room of a noisy tavern or in an inconvenient lodging that served him for "parlor, kitchen, and hall." And, again, besides the incongruities derived from the older plays or novels, his control over his art was occasionally liable to be governed by the customs and exigencies of the ancient stage, so much so that, in a few instances, the action of a scene was diverted for the express purpose of complying with those necessities. From some of these causes may have arisen simultaneous inequalities in taste and art which otherwise appear to be inexplicable, and which would doubtlessly have been removed had Shakespeare lived to have given the public a revised edition of his works during his retirement at Stratford-on-Avon, and had also wished to display that uniformity of excellence which he alone, of all prolific writers, might have achieved.

The Burbages, however, had no conception of his intellectual supremacy, and, if they had, it is certain that they would not have deviated on that account from the course they were in the habit of pursuing. In their estimation, however, he was merely, to use their own words, a "deserving man," an effective actor and a popular writer, one who would not have been considered so valuable a member of their staff had he not also worked as a practical man of business, knowing that the success of the theater was identified with his own, and that, within certain limits, it was necessary that his art should be regulated by expediency. There is, indeed, no evidence that Shakespeare wrote, at any period of his life, without a constant reference to the immediate effect of his dramas upon the theatrical public of his own day; and it may reasonably be suspected that there is not one of them which is the result of an express or cherished literary design. He was sometimes, moreover, in such a hurry of composition that a reference to the original foundation-story is necessary for the complete elucidation of his meaning, another circumstance which is incompatible with a resolute desire for the construction of perfect artistic work. This is one of the several indications which lead to the high probability that his theatrical success was neither the result of a devotion to art, nor of a solicitude for the eulogy of readers, but of his unrivaled power of characterization, of his intimate knowledge of stage business, and of a fidelity to mental nature that touched the hearts of all. These qualities, although less prominently developed in *Titus Andronicus* than in many other of his plays, are yet to be observed in that inferior work. Even amid its display of barbarous and abandoned personages, neither sternness nor profligacy is permitted to altogether extinguish the natural emotions, while, at the same time, the unities of character are well sustained. It is by tests such as these, not by counting its syllables or analyzing its peculiarities of style, that the authenticity of Shakespeare's earliest tragedy should be determined.

Although it is dangerous nowadays to enter upon the history of Shakespeare's art with the language of common-sense, the risk must be encountered if we are not contented to lose interesting examples of the poet's youthful genius. If, indeed, all is to be discarded that offends the extra-judicial taste of modern purists, the object of our idolatry will be converted into a king of dramatic shreds and patches. The evil arises from the practice of discussing the intricacies of that art without reference to the conditions under which it was evolved. Those which have been above-mentioned will go far to explain many difficulties, and especially the singular variations of power that are occasionally to be traced in one and the same drama. A few words on the general question may now be added. In one sense, that of being the delineator of the passions and character, Shakespeare was the greatest artist that ever lived, as he was also in melody, in humor, and in all kinds of dramatic expression. But in another and very usual meaning of that personal term, in that of being an elaborator intent on rendering his component work artistically faultless in the eye of criticism, he can hardly be thought to have even a slight claim to the title. When Ben Jonson told Drummond of Hawthornden, in 1619, that "Shakespeare wanted art," he referred no doubt to his general negligence in the latter respect, and perhaps especially to his occasional defects in construction. One of Shakespeare's most wonderful gifts was his unlimited power of a characterial invention to suit any kind of plot, no matter how ill-advised, and, at the same time harmonize with theatrical expediencies, however incongruous, which might have been considered by the managers or actors to have been essential to the maintenance of popularity. "His wit," observes the same Rare Ben, dissatisfied with what he no doubt thought a reckless mode of composition, "was in his own power;—would *the rule* of it had been so too!" It was natural that Jonson, with his reverence for classical models, should regard his great contemporary's indifference to them with dismay. But Shakespeare, endowed with an universal genius, created his personages by unfettered instinct, and, most happily, the times and circumstances were alike favorable to the development of the dramatic power by which alone the perfect results of that genius could have been exhibited. Commencing his public life as an actor, he had the inestimable advantage of gaining a preliminary knowledge of all that was most likely to be effective on the stage, the then conventionalities of which, moreover, by their very simplicity, and notwithstanding one or two drawbacks, were eminently calculated for the fullest exercise of an author's poetic and imaginative faculties. Then there was a language which, having for some time past been emancipated from the influence of literal terminations, had attained a form that gave matchless facilities for the display of nervous expression, and this in the brightest period of earnest and vigorous English thought. That language found in Shakespeare its felicitous and unrivaled exponent, and although on occasion his words either imperfectly represent the thought or are philologically erroneous, becoming thus to mere readers inextricably obscure, it may be confidently averred that there is not one speech, the essential meanings of which, if it were properly delivered, would not have been directly intelligible to the auditory. He had also ready prepared to his hands the matured outward form of a drama, its personages and their histories, all waiting for the hand that was to endow them with grace and life. It was then his unconscious mission through the most effective agency, that of the stage, to interpret human nature to the people. That interpretation was fortunately neither cramped nor distorted by the necessity of adherence to literary rule, while the popular tastes sanctioned its uncontrolled application to every variety of character, through all kinds of probable or improbable situation,—before fairy-land had been exiled, and the thunder of fie-foh-fum had lost its solemnity. Writing first for a living, and then for affluence, his sole aim was to please an audience, most of whom, be it remembered, were not only illiterate, but unable to either read or write. But this very ignorance of the large majority of his public, so far from being a disadvantage, enabled him to disregard restrictive canons and the tastes of scholars,—to make that appeal to the heart and intellect which can only be universal when it reaches the intuitive perceptions of the lowliest,—and by exhibiting his marvelous conceptions in the pristine form in which they had instinctively emanated, become the poet of nature instead of the poet of art. That Shakespeare wrote without effort, by inspiration not by design, was, so far as it has been recorded, the unanimous belief of his contemporaries and immediate successors. It was surely to this comprehensive truth, and not exclusively to the natural music of his verse, that Milton referred when, in two of the most exquisite lines respecting him that were ever penned, he speaks of Fancy's child warbling "his native wood-notes wild." If those notes had been cabined by philosophy and methodically cultivated, they might have been as intrinsically powerful, but they would assuredly have lost much of their present charm.

It cannot be absolutely observed of Shakespeare, as it has been of another great poet, that he woke up one morning to discover that he was famous, but there is reason for believing that the publication of his *Lucrece*, in the May of this year, 1594, almost immediately secured for its author a higher reputation than would then have been established by the most brilliant efforts of dramatic art. This magnificent poem, which was originally proposed to be entitled the *Ravishment of Lucrece*, must have been written after the dedication to *Venus and Adonis*, and before the entry of the former work at Stationers' Hall, that is to say, at some time between April, 1593, and May, 1594. There can be no doubt of the estimation in which it was held in the year of publication, the author of an elegy on Lady Helen Branch, 1594, including among our *greater poetes*,—"you that have writ of chaste Lucretia, = whose death was witnesse of her spotlesse life;" and Drayton, in his *Matilda*, of the same date, speaking of *Lucrece*, "lately reviv'd to live another age." Shakespeare's new poem is also mentioned in Willobie's *Avisa*, published in September, 1594, the earliest contemporary work in which he is introduced by name; and in the following year, "Lucrecia—sweet Shakespeare," is a marginal note to Polimanteia, 1595, one which implies that it was then considered his best work. Later references testify its continued appreciation, and it was received as the perfect exposition of woman's chastity, a sequel, or rather perhaps a companion, to the earlier one of her profligacy. The contemporaries of Shakespeare allude more than once to the two poems as being his most important works, and as these on which his literary distinction chiefly rested.

The prefixes to the *Venus* and *Lucrece* are, in the presence of so few biographical memorials, inestimable records of their author. The two dedications to Lord Southampton and the argument to the second work are the only non-dramatic prose compositions of Shakespeare that have descended to modern times, while the former are, alas, the sole remaining samples of his epistolary writings. The latter are of course by far the more interesting, and, making allowances for the inordinate deference to rank which then prevailed, they are perfect examples of the judicious fusion of independence with courtesy in a suggestive application for a favor, and in expressions of gratitude for its concession.

In the June of this same year, 1594, *Titus Andronicus* was performed at Newington Butts by the Lord Chamberlain's, then acting in conjunction with the Lord Admiral's, Servants, the poet most likely taking a part in the representation. The earliest definite notice, however, of his appearance on the stage, is one in which he is recorded as having been a player in two comedies that were acted before Queen Elizabeth in the following December, at Greenwich Palace. He was then described as one of the Lord Chamberlain's Servants, and was associated in the performances with Kemp and Burbage, the former of whom was the most favorite comedian of the day. It is not known to what company or companies Shakespeare belonged previously to his adhesion to the one last named; but the probabilities are these.— It is well ascertained that Henslowe was an exceeding grasping manager, and it is therefore, most unlikely that he would have speculated in new plays that were not intended for immediate use. We may then fairly assume that every drama composed for him would be, in the first instance, produced by the actors that occupied his theater when the manuscript was purchased. Now, as Shakespeare was an actor as well as a dramatist, there is an inclination towards the belief that he would have been engaged at Henslowe's theater when employed to write for that personage, and, if we accept the theory of early production, would have belonged to those companies by whom the first representations of his dramas were given. If this view be taken, it would appear not altogether unlikely that the poet was one of Lord Strange's actors in March, 1592; one of Lord Pembroke's a few months later; and that he had joined the company of the Earl of Sussex in or before January, 1594.

There were rare doings at Gray's Inn in the Christmas holidays of the year last mentioned. The students of that house had usually excelled in their festive arrangements, and now they were making preparations for revels on a scale of exceptional magnificence, sports that were to include burlesque performances, masques, plays and dances, as well as processions through London and on the Thames. A mock Court was held at the Inn under the presidency of one Henry Helmes, a Norfolk gentleman, who was elected Prince of Purpoole, the ancient name of the manor, other students being elected to serve under him in all the various offices then appertaining to royalty and government. The grand entertainment of all was arranged for the evening of Innocent's Day, December 28, on which occasion high scaffolds had been erected in the hall for the accommodation of the revelers and the principal guests, a larger number of the latter having received invitations. Among the guests, the students of the Inner Temple, joining in the humor of their professional neighbors, and appearing as an embassy credited by their Emporer, arrived about nine o'clock "very gallantly appointed." The ambassador, we are told, was "brought in very solemnly, with sound of trumpets, the King-at-Arms and Lords of Purpoole making to his company, which marched before him in order;—he was received very kindly by the Prince, and placed in a chair beside his Highness, to the end that he might be partaker of the sports intended." Complimentary addresses were then exchanged between the Prince and the Ambassador, but, owing to defective arrangements for a limitation of the number of those entitled to admission on the stage, there followed a scene of confusion which ended in the Templarians retiring in dudgeon. "After their departure," as we are told in the original narrative, "the throngs and tumults did somewhat cease, although so much of them continued as was able to disorder and confound any good inventions whatsoever; in regard whereof, as also for that the sports intended were especially for the gracing of the Templarians, it was thought good not to offer anything of account saving dancing and reveling with gentlewomen; and, after such sports, a *Comedy of Errors*, like to Plautus his *Menechmus*, was played by the players; so that night was begun and continued to the end in nothing but confusion and errors, whereupon it was afterwards called the Night of Errors." This is the earliest notice of the comedy which has yet been discovered, but that it was written before the year 1594 may be inferred from an allusion in it to the civil war for and against Henry IV, the Protestant heir to the French throne, a contest which terminated in 1593.

The spacious and elegant open-roofed hall of Gray's Inn, the erection of which was completed in the year 1560, is one of the only two buildings now remaining in London in which, so far as we know, any of the plays of Shakespeare were performed in his own time. In accordance with the then usual custom of the Inns of Court, professional actors were engaged for the representation of the *Comedy of Errors*, and although their names are not mentioned, it may be safely inferred that the play was acted by the Lord Chamberlain's Company, that to which Shakespeare was then attached, and the owners of the copyright. The performance must have taken place very late on the night following the day in which the poet appeared before Queen Elizabeth at Greenwich. On the next evening there was a Commission of Oyer and Terminer at Gray's Inn to enquire into the circumstances of the misfortunes of the previous night, the cause of the tumult being assigned to the intervention of a sorcerer; but it is hardly pleasant to be told, even in burlesque, that this personage was accused of having "foisted a company of base and common fellows to make up our disorders with a play of errors and confusions." The *Comedy of Errors*, the perfection of dramatic farce, long continued an acting play, it having been performed before James I on December 28, 1604.

When Greene thought to be sarcastic in terming Shakespeare "an absolute Johannes Factotum," he furnished an independent and valuable testimony to the poet's conspicuous activity. It is but reasonable to assume that part of this energy in theatrical matters was devoted, in accordance with the ordinary practice of the time, to the revision and enlargement of the plays of others, work then assigned by managers to any convenient hands, without reference to sentimental views of authorial integrity. No record, however, has been discovered of the name of even one drama so treated by Shakespeare in the early period of his career, so that, if any such composition is preserved, the identification necessarily depends upon, the tests of internal evidence. These are valueless in the chief direction, for there is surely not a known possible example in which is to be traced the incontestible supremacy of dramatic power that would on that account sanction the positive attribution of even one of its scenes to the pen of the great dramatist. Other tests, such as those of phraseology and mannerism, are nearly always illusory, but in an anonymous and popular drama entitled the *Reign of King Edward III*, produced in or before the year 1595, there are occasional passages which, by most judgments, will be accepted as having been written either by Shakespeare, or by an exceedingly dexterous and successful imitator of one of his then favorite styles of composition. For who but one or the other could have endowed a kind and gentle lady with the ability of replying to the impertinent addresses of a foolish sovereign in words such as these,—

> As easy may my intellectual soul
> Be lent away, and yet my body live,
> As lend my body, palace to my soul,
> Away from her, and yet retain my soul.
> My body is her bower, her court, her abbey,
> And she an angel,—pure, divine, unspotted!
> If I should lend her house, my lord, to thee,
> I kill my poor soul, and my poor soul me.

or have enabled the king, when instinctively acknowledging the dread effect of her beauty, to thus express a wish that "ugly treason" might lie,—

> No farther off than her conspiring eye,
> Which shoots infected poison in my heart,
> Beyond repulse of wit or cure of art.
> Now in the sun alone it doth not lie,
> With light to take light from a mortal eye;
> For here two day-stars, that mine eyes would see,
> More than the sun steal mine own light from me.
> Contemplative desire!—desire to be
> In contemplation that may master thee.

or have made the royal secretary convey his impression of the lady's conquest in the following lines,—

I might perceive his eye in her eye lost,
His ear to drink her sweet tongue's utterance;
And changing passion, like inconstant clouds,
That rackt upon the carriage of the winds,
Increase and die in his disturbed cheeks.
Lo! when she blush'd even then did he look pale,
As if her cheeks, by some enchanted power,
Attracted had the cherry blood from his.
Anon, with reverent fear, when she grew pale,
His cheeks put on their scarlet ornaments,
But no more like her oriental red
Than brick to coral, or live things to dead.

but, as it is possible that *Edward III* was composed some time before the year 1595, it may, of course, be assumed that Shakespeare himself was the imitator, in his own acknowledged works, of the style of the writer of this anonymous play, or that of some other author, the predecessor of both. Not one in fifty of the dramas of this period having descended to modern times, much of the reasoning upon this and similar questions must be received with grave suspicion of its validity, and the exact history of the composition of the play above quoted will most likely remain for ever a mystery. If, however, it is thought probable that Shakespeare's career of imitation expired with his treading in some of the footsteps of Marlowe, and that he had not, at the latest time when *Edward III* could have appeared, achieved a popularity sufficient to attract imitators of his own style, then there will be at least an excusable surmise that his work is to be traced in parts of that historical drama. Every now and then one meets in it with passages, especially in the scenes referring to the King's infatuation for the Countess of Salisbury, which are so infinitely superior in composition to the rest of the play, and so exactly in Shakespeare's manner, this presumption, under the above named premises, can scarcely be avoided. Whether this view be accepted or not, *Edward III* will, under any circumstances, be indissolubly connected with the literary history of the great dramatist, for one of its lines is also found in his ninety-fourth sonnet. As the last-named poem, even if it had been written as early as 1595, was not printed for many years afterwards, it is unlikely that the line in question could have been transplanted from the sonnet into the play by any one but Shakespeare himself, who, however, might have reversed the operation, whether he were or were not the original author of the words. This is the passage in the drama in which the line of the sonnet is introduced,—

> A spacious field of reasons could I urge
> Between his gloomy daughter and thy shame,—
> That poison shows worst in a golden cup;
> Dark night seems darker by the lightning flash;
> *Lilies that fester smell far worse than weeds*;
> And every glory that inclines to sin,
> The shame is treble by the opposite.

In the summer of the year 1596, upon the death of the Lord Chamberlain on July 22, the company of actors to which the poet belonged became the servants of that nobleman's eldest son, Lord Hunsdon, and one of the first dramas selected by them, while in their new position, was Shakespeare's tragedy of *Romeo and Juliet,* which was produced at the Curtain Theater and met with great success. *Romeo and Juliet* may be said, indeed, to have taken the metropolies by storm and to have become *the* play of the season. Its popularity led to the compilation of an imperfect and unauthorized edition which issued from Danter's press in the following year, one got up in such haste that two fonts of type were engaged in its composition. In 1599, Cuthbert Burby, a bookseller, whose shop was near the Royal exchange, published the tragedy with the overstrained announcement that it had been "newly corrected, augmented and amended." This is the version of the drama which is now accepted, and it appears to be an authentic copy of the tragedy produced in 1596, after a few passages in the letter had been revised by the author. The long-continued popularity of *Romeo and Juliet* may be inferred from several early allusions, as well as from the express testimony of Leonard Digges, but it is rather singular that the author's name is not mentioned in any of the old editions until some time after the year 1609. An interesting tradition respecting one of the characters in this tragedy is recorded in 1672 by Dryden, who observes that the great dramatist "showed the best of his skill in his Mercutio, and he said himself that he was forced to kill him in the third act, to prevent being killed by him." The eminent narrator of this little anecdote ingenuously adds,—"but, for my part, I cannot find he was so dangerous a person;—I see nothing in him but what was so exceeding harmless that he might have lived to the end of the play, and died in his bed, without offense to any man."

A severe domestic affliction marred the pleasure that the author might otherwise have derived from his last-mentioned triumph. His only son Hamnet, then in his twelfth year, died early in August, 1596, and was buried at Stratford-on-Avon on the eleventh of that month. At the close of the year the poet also lost his uncle Henry, the farmer of Snitterfield, during the same Christmas holidays in which his company had the honor of performing on two occasions before Queen Elizabeth at Whitehall Palace.

No positive information on the subject has been recorded, but the few evidences there are lead to the belief that the Shakespeare family continued, throughout his life, to reside in the poet's native town. They had not accompanied him in his first visit to the metropolis, and, from the circumstance of the burial of Hamnet at Stratford-on-Avon, it may be confidently inferred that they were living there at the time of the poor youth's decease. It is in the highest degree unlikely that they could have taken up an abode anywhere else but in London, and no hint is given of the latter having been the case. Let it also be borne in mind that Shakespeare's occupations debarred him from the possibility of his sustaining even an approach to a continuous domestic life, so that, when his known attachment to Stratford is taken into consideration, it seems all but certain that his wife and children were but waiting there under economical circumstances, perhaps with his parents in Henley Street, until he could provide them with a comfortable residence of their own. Every particular that is known indicates that he admitted no disgrace in the irresponsible persecution which occasioned his retreat to London, and that he persistently entertained the wish to make Stratford his and his family's only permanent home. This desire was too confirmed to be materially affected even by the death of his only son, for, shortly after that event, he is discovered taking a fancy to one of the largest houses in the town, and becoming its purchaser in the following year. At this time, 1596, he appears to have been residing, when in town, in lodgings near the Bear Garden in Southwark.

There is preserved at the College of Arms the draft of a grant of coat-armor to John Shakespeare, dated in October, 1596, the result of an application made no doubt some little time previously. It may be safely inferred, from the unprosperous circumstances of the grantee, that this attempt to confer gentility on the family was made at the poet's expense. This is the first evidence that we have of his rising pecuniary fortunes, and of his determination to advance in social position.

Early in the year 1597,—on New Year's Day, Twelfth Night, Shrove Sunday, and Shrove Tuesday,—Shakespeare's company again performed before the Queen at Whitehall. In the summer they made a tour through Sussex and Kent, visiting Faversham and Rye in August, and acting at Dover on September 3. In their progress to the latter town, he who was hereafter to be the author of *Lear* might, have witnessed, and been impressed with, the samphire gatherers on the celebrated rock that was afterwards to be regarded the type of Edgar's imaginary precipice. By the end of the month they had quitted the southern counties, and traveled westward as far as Bristol; acting about the same time at Marlborough and Bath.

In the spring of this year the great dramatist made his first investment in realty by the purchase of New Place, consisting of a mansion and nearly an acre of land in the center of the town of Stratford-on-Avon. The estate was sold to him for £60, a moderate sum for so considerable a property, but in a paper of the time of Edward VI the residence is described as having then been for some time "in great ruyne and decay and unrepayred," so that it was probably in a dilapidated condition when it was transferred to Shakespeare. There are reasons for believing that it was renovated by the new owner; but whatever may have been its state of repair at the time of its acquisition, it was unquestionably one of the largest domiciles in the town, there having been no other, with the single exception of the College, that was conspicuously more important. Sir Hugh Clopton, for whom it was erected, speaks of it in 1496 as his "great house," a title under which, as it will be observed anon, it was popularly known at Stratford for upwards of two centuries. Neither its history nor its magnitude sufficed, however, to attract the serious consideration of our early topographers, and thus it is that scarcely any details of a precise character have been discovered respecting the nature of the house, one which, if now in existence, would have been the most interesting edifice on the surface of the globe. We know indeed, that it was mainly constructed of brick raised on stone foundations, that it was gabled, and that there was a bay-window on the eastern or garden side, but little beyond this. Two eye-witnesses only, out of the numbers who had seen the building previously to its destruction, have left memorials, and those but faint notices, of its appearance. Leland, who wrote about the year 1540, simply describes it as "a praty house of bricke and tymbre," words which may imply either that the upper part was formed entirely of wood or that there were large portions of bricknogging in the outer walls. Our other informant was a native of Stratford-on-Avon, one Richard Grimmitt, who was very familiar with New Place in the years immediately preceding its demolition, and whose old-age dim memory of the locality in 1767 is thus recorded by the Rev. Joseph Greene, an intelligent Warwickshire antiquary of the last century,—"this Richard said he in his youth had been a playfellow with Edward Clopton, senior, eldest son of Sir John Clopton, knight, and had been often with him in the Great House near the Chapel in Stratford call'd New Place; that, to the best of his remembrance, there was a brick wall next the street, with a kind of porch at that end of it next the Chapel, when they cross'd a small kind of green court before they enter'd the house, which was bearing to the left and fronted with brick, with plain windows, consisting of common panes of glass set in lead, as at this time." It appears from this statement that the main entrance was then in Chapel-lane, and this was so doubt the case at a much earlier period, arrangements of that kind being very rarely changed. We may rest assured, therefore, that, when Ben Jonson or Drayton visited the provincial home of the author of *Twelfth Night*, he would arrive there from the lane through a porched gateway, entering in front of the lawn, a barn on his right hand and the house on the left. All this is in consonance with what is known respecting the surroundings of a large number of other contemporary mansions. "The architecture of an old English gentleman's house," observes Aubrey, alluding to the Shakespearean era, "was a good high strong wall, a gate-house, a great hall and parlor, and within the little green court where you come in stood on one side the barne;—they then thought not the noise of the threshold ill musique." In the poet's time there were two barns on the Chapel-lane side of New Place between the open area mentioned by Grimmitt and the eastern termination of the grounds, but this is all that we know respecting the outbuildings, unless, indeed, there can be included under the latter term an ancient well, the stone-work of which yet remains in a nearly perfect condition. The chief fact of interest, however, in the personal annals of this year, 1597, is the remarkable circumstance that Shakespeare, after leaving his native town in indigence only twelve years previously, should now have been enabled to become, so far as material advantages were concerned, one of its leading inhabitants.

However limited may have been the character of the poet's visits to his native town, there is no doubt that New Place was henceforward to be accepted as his established residence. Early in the following year, on February 4, 1598, corn being then at an unprecedented and almost famine price at Stratford-on-Avon, he is returned as the holder of ten quarters in the Chapel Street Ward, that in which the newly acquired property was situated, and in none of the indentures is he described as a Londoner, but always as "William Shakespeare of Stratford-on-Avon, in the county of Warwick, gentleman." There is an evidence in the same direction in the interest that he took in the maintenance of his grounds, a fact elicited from two circumstances that are worthy of record. It appears from a comparison of descriptions of parcels, 1597 and 1602, that in the earlier years of his occupancy, he arranged a fruit-orchard in that portion of his garden which adjoined the neighboring premises in Chapel Street. Then there is the well-authenticated tradition that, in another locality near the back of the house, he planted with his own hands the first mulberry-tree that had ever been brought to Stratford-on-Avon.

The date of the latter occurrence has not been recorded, but it may be assigned, with a high degree of probability, to the spring of 1609, in which year a Frenchman named Verton distributed an immense number of young mulberry plants through the midland counties of England. This novel arrangement was carried out by the order of James I, who vigorously encouraged the cultivation of that tree, vainly hoping that silk might thence become one of the staple productions of England.

The establishment of the fruit-orchard and the tradition respecting the mulberry-tree are the only evidences which have reached us of any sort of interest taken by the great dramatist in horticulture. It has, indeed, been attempted to prove his attachment to such pursuits by various allusions in his works, but no inferences as to his personal tastes can be safely drawn from any number of cognate references. There was, no doubt, treasured in the storehouse of his perfect memory, and ready for immediate use, every technical expression, and every morsel of contemporary popular belief, that had once come within his hearing. So marvelous also was Shakespeare's all but intuitive perception of nearly every variety of human thought and knowledge, the result of an unrivaled power of rapid observation and deduction, if once the hazardous course of attempting to realize the personal characteristics or habits of the author through his writings be indulged in, there is scarcely an occupation that he might not be suspected of having adopted at one period or other of his life. That he was familiar with and fondly appreciated the beauty of the wild flowers; that he was acquainted with many of the cultivated plants and trees; that he had witnessed and understood a few of the processes of gardening;—these facts may be admitted, but they do not prove that he was ever a botanist or a gardener. Neither are his numerous allusions to wild flowers and plants, not one of which appears to be peculiar to Warwickshire, evidences, as has been suggested, of the frequency of his visits to Stratford-on-Avon. It would be about as reasonable to surmise that he must have taken a journey to Elsinore before or when he was engaged on the tragedy of *Hamlet*, as to adopt the oft-repeated suggestion that the nosegay of Perdita could only have been conceived when he was wandering on the banks of the Avon. To judge in that manner from allusions in the plays it might be inferred that *The Winter's Tale* must have been written in London, for there is little probability that a specimen of one of the flowers therein mentioned, the crown-imperial, could have been then seen in the provinces, whereas there is Gerard's excellent authority that it had "been brought from Constantinople among other bulbus rootes, and made denizons in our London gardens" (Herball, ed. 1597, p. 154). All inductions of this kind must be received with the utmost caution. Surely the poet's memory was not so feeble that it is necessary to assume that the selection of his imagery depended upon the objects to be met with in the locality in which he was writing. Even were this extravagant supposition to be maintained, no conclusion can be derived from it, for it is not probable that London would have had the exclusive possession of any cultivated flower, while it is certain that Stratford had not the monopoly of every wild one. It should be recollected that the line of demarcation between country and town life was not strongly marked in Shakespeare's day. The great dramatist may be practically considered never to have relinquished a country life during any part of his career, for even when in the metropolis he must always have been within a walk of green fields, woods and plant-bordered streams, and within a few steps of some of the gardens which were then to be found in all parts of London, not even excepting the limited area of the city. Wild plants, as has been previously observed, were to be seen in the immediate vicinity of the Shoreditch theaters, and there is perhaps no specimen mentioned by Shakespeare which was not to be met with in or near the metropolis; but even were this not the case, surely the fact of his having resided in Warwickshire during at least the first eighteen years of his life is sufficient to account for his knowledge of them. Then again at a later period he must, in those days of slow and leisurely travel, have been well acquainted with the rural life and natural objects of many other parts of the country which were traversed by him when the members of his company made their professional tours, and with the district between London and Stratford-on-Avon he must of course have been specially familiar.

The metropolis in those days was the main abode of English letters and refined culture, but in other respects there could have been very few experiences that were absolutely restricted to its limits. If this is carefully borne in mind, it will save us from falling into numerous delusions, and, among others, into the common one of fancying that Shakespeare must have drawn his tavern-life from an acquaintance with its character as it was exhibited on the banks of the Thames. There was no more necessity for him to have traveled from London in search of flowers than there was to have gone there for the,—"anon, anon, sir; score a pint of bastard in the Half Moon." We have, indeed, the direct testimony of Harrison, in 1586, to the effect that the metropolitan were then inferior to many of the provincial hotels. There was certainly at least one inn at Stratford-on-Avon which could bear comparison in essential respects with any to be found elsewhere in England. The Bear near the foot of the bridge possessed its large hall, its nominated rooms such as the Lion and Talbot chambers, an enormous quantity of house linen, a whole pipe of claret, two butts of sack, plenty of beer, upwards of forty tankards of different sizes, and, among its plate, "one goblet of silver, parcel-gilt." The last-named vessel need not be converted into the prototype of the one used by Mrs. Quickly in the Dolphin, nor, as a rule, in the absence of palpable evidence to the contrary, are there grounds for believing that the great dramatist was thinking of special localities when he was penning his various allusions or characterizations.

When the amazing number of different characters in the plays of Shakespeare is borne in mind, it is curious that he should have left so few traces in them of what is exclusively provincial. There are yet fewer, if any, of language or customs that can be thought to be absolutely peculiar to Stratford-upon-Avon, but examples of both are frequently to be met with that may fairly be supposed to have been primarily derived from the poet's local experiences. Among these is the expression,—*aroint thee, witch!*—one that is so rare in our literature, either in print or manuscript, that the combined labors of philologists have failed to produce a single early instance of its use in the works of other authors. That it was, however, a familiar phrase in Shakespeare's time with the lower classes of his native place, is apparent from one of the town records. It is there narrated how one Goodie Bromlie, in an altercation with a woman named Holder, was so exceedingly free-spoken that she had the audacity to wind up a torrent of abuse with the unseemly execration,—*arent the, witch!* There is no doubt that Stratford yielded many another unusual expression,—many a quaint observation,—to the recollection of the great dramatist, and it is just possible that an occasional specimen may yet be met with in the locality. One of the inhabitants, so recently as the year 1843, was put into stocks for intoxication, and a passer-by, asking the captive how he liked the discipline, was met with the reply,—"I beant the first mon as ever were in the stocks, so I don't care a farden about it." If it were not an impossible view of the case, it might be fancied that the jovial delinquent had been travestying one of the reflections that Richard II is made to utter in the dungeon of Pomfret Castle.

Those who would desire to realize the general appearance of the Stratford-on-Avon of the poet's days must deplore the absence, not merely of a genuine sketch of New Place, but of any kind of view or engraving of the town as it appeared in the sixteenth or seventeenth centuries. Its aspect must then have been essentially different from that exhibited at a subsequent period. Relatively to ourselves, Shakespeare may practically be considered to have existed in a different land, not more than glimpses of the real nature of which are now to be obtained by the most careful study of existing documents and material remains. Many enthusiasts of these times who visit Stratford-on-Avon are under the delusion that they behold a locality which recalls the days of the great dramatist, but, with the exception of a few diffused buildings, scarcely one of which is precisely in its original condition, there is no resemblance between the present town and the Shakespearean borough,—the latter with its medieval and Elizabethan buildings, its crosses, its numerous barns and thatched hovels, its water-mills, its street bridges and rivulets, its mud walls, its dunghills and fetid ditches, its unpaved walks and its wooden-spired church, with the common fields reaching nearly to the gardens of the Birth-Place. Neither can there be a much greater resemblance between the ancient and modern general views of the town from any of the neighboring elevations. The tower and lower part of the church, the top of the Guild Chapel, a few old tall chimneys, the course of the river, the mill-dam, and the outlines of the surrounding hills, would be nearly all that would be common to both prospects. There were, however, until the last few years, the old mill-bridge, which, excepting that rails had been added, preserved its Elizabethan form, the Cross-on-the-Hill, and the Wier Brake, the two latter fully retaining their original character. Now, alas, a hideous railway has obliterated all trace of the picturesque from what was one of the most interesting and charming spots in Warwickshire.

A former inhabitant of Stratford-on-Avon, writing in the year 1759, asserts that "the unanimous tradition of this neighborhood is that, by the uncommon bounty of the Earl of Southampton, he was enabled to purchase houses and land at Stratford." According to Rowe,—"there is one instance so singular in the magnificence of this patron of Shakespeare's that, if I had not been assured that the story was handed down by Sir William D'Avenant, who was probably very well acquainted with his affairs, I should not have ventured to have inserted; that my Lord Southampton at one time gave him a thousand pounds to enable him to go through with a purchase which he heard he had a mind to." A comparison of these versions would indicate that, if the anecdote is based on truth, the gift was made on the occasion of the purchase of New Place in 1597; and it is probable that it was larger than the sum required for that object, although the amount named by Rowe must be an exaggeration. Unless the general truth of the story be accepted, it is difficult to believe that Shakespeare could have obtained, so early in his career, the ample means he certainly possessed in that and the following year. The largest emoluments that could have been derived from his professional avocations would hardly have sufficed to have accomplished such a result, and the necessity of forwarding continual remittances to Stratford-on-Avon must not be overlooked.

It was not until the year 1597 that Shakespeare's public reputation as a dramatist was sufficiently established for the booksellers to be anxious to secure the copyright of his plays.

The first of his dramas so honored was the successful and popular one of King Richard II, which was entered as a tragedy on the books of the Stationers' Company by Andrew Wise, a publisher in St. Paul's Churchyard, on August 29, 1597. In the impression heralded by this entry the deposition scene was omitted for political reasons, objections having been made to its introduction on the public stage, and it was not inserted by the publishers of the history until some years after the accession of James. Considering the small space that it occupies and its inoffensive character, the omission may appear rather singular, but during the few years that closed the eventful reign of Elizabeth, the subject of the deposition of Richard II bore so close an analogy, in the important respects of the wishes of those who desired a repetition of a similar occurrence, it was an exceedingly dangerous theme for the pen of contemporary writers.

One of the most popular subjects for the historical drama at this period was the story of Richard III. A piece on the events of this reign had been acted by the Queen's Company in or before the month of June, 1594, but there is no evidence that this production was known to the great dramatist. The earliest notice of Shakespeare's play hitherto discovered is in an entry of it as a tragedy on the books of the Stationers' Company in October, 1597, and it was published by Wise in the same year. The historical portions are to a certain extent taken from More and Holinshed, but with an utter defiance of chronology, the imprisonment of Clarence, for instance, preceding the funeral of Henry VI. There are, also, slight traces of an older play to be observed, passages which may belong to an inferior hand, and incidents, such as that of the rising of the ghosts, suggested probably by similar ones in a more ancient composition. That the play of *King Richard III*, as we now have it, is essentially Shakespeare's, cannot admit of a doubt; but as little can it be questioned that to the circumstance of an anterior work on the subject having been used do we owe some of its weakness and excessively turbulent character. No copy of this older play is known to exist, but one brief speech and the two following lines have been accidentally preserved—"My liege, the Duke of Buckingham is ta'en, = And Banister is come for his reward"—

from which it is clear that the new dramatist did not hesitate to adopt an occasional line from his predecessor, although he entirely omitted the character of Banister. Both plays must have been successful, for, notwithstanding the great popularity of Shakespeare's, the more ancient one sustained its ground on the English stage until the reign of Charles I.

Dick Burbage, the celebrated actor, undertook the character of Richard III, a part in which he was particularly celebrated. There was especially one telling speech in this most fiery of tragedies,—"a horse! a horse! my kingdom for a horse!"—which was enunciated by him with so much vigor and effect that the line became an object for the imitation, and occasionally for the ridicule, of contemporary writers. The speech made such an impression on Marston that it appears in his works not merely in its authentic form, but satirized and travestied into such lines as,—"a man! a man! a kingdom for a man" (*Scourge of Villanie*, ed. 1598)—"a boate, a boate, a boate, a full hundred markes for a boate" (*Eastward Hoe*, 1605)—"a foole, a foole, a foole, my coxcombe for a foole" (*Parasitaster*, 1606). Burbage continued to enact the part of Richard until his death in 1619, and his supremacy in the character lingered for many years in the recollection of the public; so that Bishop Corbet, writing in the reign of Charles I, and giving a description of the battle of Bosworth as narrated to him on the field by a provincial tavern-keeper, tells us that, when the perspicuous guide—"would have said, King Richard died, = And called, a horse! a horse! he Burbage cried."

In the autumn of 1597, in the midst of the incipient popularity of this animated drama, John and Mary Shakespeare filed a bill in Chancery against Lambert for the recovery of Asbies, a design that the poet must have been very desirous of furthering to the utmost of his ability. It is most likely that he furnished the means for the prosecution of the suit, a course to which he would have been impelled not merely from a knowledge of the slender resources of his aged parents, but also from his having, as his mother's heir, so large a prospective interest in the success of the litigation. The acquisition of the farm had now become a matter of special importance. There were not merely the associations twining around the possession of a family estate to stimulate a desire for its restoration, but there was nearly at hand a very large increase in its annual value through the termination of a lease under which all but the dwelling was held from 1580 to 1601 at the inadequate rental of half a quarter of wheat and half a quarter of barley. Our knowledge of the course taken by the plaintiffs in furtherance of their object is imperfect, Lambert, in his answer to the above-mentioned bill, declaring that another one of like import had been afterwards exhibited against him by John Shakespeare in his individual capacity, and of this independent action no explanatory records have been discovered. The mere facts, however, of the last-named suit having been instituted, and of John Shakespeare having taken out two commissions under it for the examination of witnesses, show that there was a tolerably well-furnished purse at his disposal, a circumstance which, unless the expense were borne by the poet, is difficult to reconcile with the plaintive appeal of his wife and himself when they asked the Court to bear in mind that "the sayde John Lamberte ys of greate wealthe and abilitie, and well frended and alied amongest gentlemen and freeholders of the countrey in the saide countie of Warwicke, where he dwelleth, and your saide oratours are of small wealthe, and verey fewe frends and alyance in the saide countie." The terms of this sample of legal policy must be attributed to the Counsel, but the facts, so far at least as they affect the parents of the great dramatist, were no doubt correctly stated. It appears that the suit was carried on for very nearly two years, publication having been granted in October, 1599, but, as no decree is recorded, it is all but certain that either the plaintiffs retired from the contest or that there was a compromise in favor of the possession of the land by the defendants. Had it been otherwise, something must have been afterwards heard of the Shakespearean ownership of the estate.

Queen Elizabeth held her court at Whitehall in the Christmas holidays of 1597, and among the plays then performed was, on December 26, the comedy of *Love's Labor's Lost,* printed early in the following year, 1598, under the title of,—*A Pleasant Conceited Comedie called, Loues labors lost.* No record bas been discovered of the time at which this drama was first produced, but on the present occasion it had been, "newly corrected and augmented," that is to say, it had received some additions and improvements from the hands of the author, but the play itself had not been re-written. A few scraps of the original version of the comedy have been accidentally preserved, and are of extreme interest as distinctly exhibiting Shakespeare's method of working in the revision of a play. Thus, for example, the following three lines of the earlier drama,—

From women's eyes this doctrine I derive;
They are the ground, the books, the academes
From whence doth spring the true Promethean fire.

are thus gracefully expanded in the corrected version which has so fortunately descended to us,—

From women's eyes this doctrine I derive;
They sparkle still the right Promethean fire;
They are the books, the arts, the academes,
That show, contain, and nourish all the world;
Else none at all in ought proves excellent.

Love's Labor's Lost is mentioned by Tofte and Meres in 1598, and was no doubt successful on the stage, or otherwise it would scarcely have been revised and published. Burbage, at all events, had a high opinion of the comedy, for when the company to which the author belonged selected it for a contemplated representation before Queen Anne of Denmark at Southampton House early in the year 1605, he observed that it was one "which for wit and mirth will please her exceedingly." That the great actor correctly estimated its attractions may he gathered from its being performed about the same time before the Court.

The *First Part of Henry IV*, the appearance of which on the stage may be confidently assigned to the spring of the year 1597, was followed immediately, or a few months afterwards, by the composition of the second part. It is recorded that both these plays were very favorably received by Elizabeth, the Queen especially relishing the character of Falstaff, and they were most probably among the dramas represented before that sovereign in the Christmas holidays of 1597-1598. At this time, or then very recently, the renowned hero of the Boar's Head Tavern had been introduced as Sir John Oldcastle, but the Queen ordered Shakespeare to alter the name of the character. This step was taken in consequence of the representations of some member or members of the Cobham family, who had taken offense at their illustrious ancestor, Sir John Oldcastle, Lord Cobham, the Protestant martyr, being disparagingly introduced on the stage; and, accordingly, in or before the February of the following year, Falstaff took the place of Oldcastle, the former being probably one of the few names invented by Shakespeare.

The great dramatist himself, having nominally adopted Oldcastle from a character who is one of Prince Henry's profligate companions in a previous drama, a composition which had been several years before the public, and had not encountered effective remonstrance, could have had no idea that his appropriation of the name would have given so much displeasure. The subject, however, was viewed by the Cobhams in a very serious light. This is clearly shown, not merely by the action taken by the Queen, but by the anxiety exhibited by Shakespeare, in the epilogue to the second part, to place the matter beyond all doubt by the explicit declaration that there was in Falstaff no kind of association, satirical or otherwise, with the martyred Oldcastle. The whole incident is a testimony to the popularity of, and the importance attached to, these dramas of Shakespeare's at their first appearance, and it may be fairly questioned if any comedy on the early English stage was more immediately or enthusiastically appreciated than was the *First Part of Henry IV.* Two editions of the latter play appeared in 1598, and, the same year, there were quoted from it passages that had evidently already become familiar household words in the mouths of the public. Strangely enough, however, the earliest edition that bore the author's name on the title-page was not published till the following year.

The inimitable humor of Falstaff was appreciated at the Court as heartily as by the public. The Queen was so taken with the delineation of that marvelous character in the two parts of *Henry IV,* that she commanded Shakespeare to write a third part in which the fat knight should be exhibited as a victim to the power of love. Sovereigns in the olden time, especially one of Elizabeth's temperament, would never have dreamed of consulting the author as to the risk of the selected additional passion not harmonizing with the original conception. Shakespeare's business was to obey, not to indulge in what would have been considered an insolent and unintelligible remonstrance. His intention of continuing the history of the same Falstaff in a play on the subject of *Henry V* was, therefore, abandoned, and thus we have, in the *Merry Wives of Windsor,* a comedy in which some of the names are adopted from the previous dramas, but the natures of the characters to which those names are attached are either modified or altogether transformed. The transient allusions which bring the latter play into the historical series are so trivial that they would appear to have been introduced merely out of deference to the Queen's expressed wishes for a continuation. The comedy diverges in every other respect from the two parts of *Henry IV,* and remains, with the induction to the *Taming of the Shrew*, the only examples in the works of Shakespeare of absolute and continuous representations of English life and manners of the author's own time.

There is an old tradition which avers that the *Merry Wives of Windsor* was written, at the desire of the Queen, in the brief space of a fortnight, and that it gave immense satisfaction at the Court. Nor in those days of rapid dramatic composition, when brevity of time in the execution of such work was frequently part of an ordinary theatrical agreement, could such a feat have been impossible to Shakespeare. It could have been no trouble to him to write, and the exceptional celerity of his pen is recorded by several of his friends. Hence, probably, are to be traced most of the numerous little discrepancies which, by a careful analysis, may be detected throughout the works of the great dramatist, and which are seen perhaps more conspicuously in this play than in most of the others. Shakespeare had evidently, as a writer, neither a topographical nor a chronometrical mind, and took small care to avoid inconsistencies arising from errors in his dispositions of localities and periods of time; provided always of course that such oversights were not sufficiently palpable in the action to disturb the complete reception of the latter by the audience. We may rest assured that the poet, when engaged in dramatic writing, neither placed before his eyes an elaborate map of the scenes of the plot; nor reckoned the exact number of hours to be taken by a character in moving from one spot to another; nor, in the composition of each line of verse, repeated the syllables to ascertain if they developed the style of meter it was his duty to posterity to be using at that special period of his life. Such precautions may best be indefinitely reserved for the use of that visionary personage—a scientific and arithmetical Shakespeare.

The earliest notice of the *Merry Wives of Windsor*, hitherto discovered, is in an entry on the registers of the Stationers' Company bearing date in January, 1602, in which year a catch-penny publisher surreptitiously issued a very defective copy, one made up by some poetaster, with the aid of short-hand notes, into the form of a play. That it was composed, however, before the death of Sir Thomas Lucy in July, 1600, may be safely taken for granted, for it is contrary to all records of Shakespeare's nature to believe that the more than playful allusions it contains to that individual would have been written after the decease of Shallow's prototype; and most probably also before the production of *King Henry V* in the summer of 1559, the royal command being the most feasible explanation that can be given of the author's change of purpose in the elimination of Falstaff from the action of the latter drama.

The *Second Part of Henry IV* and the *Merry Wives of Windsor* are, so far as we know, the only dramas of Shakespeare that are in any way connected with his personal history. They include scenes that could not have been written exactly in their present form if the great dramatist had not entertained an acute grudge against Sir Thomas Lucy. The knight of Charlecote was to be lampooned on the stage, then by far the most effective medium for public derision, and hence arose the necessity of making Falstaff take his circuitous journeys to the "old pike's" house in Gloucestershire, to a locality within reach of Stratford-on-Avon and Henley-in-Arden, towns that are faintly veiled under the names of Stamford and Hinckley. Hence also the direct and practically undisguised banter of the Lucys in the *Merry Wives*, for no one in Warwickshire could possibly have mistaken the allusion to the luces, the fishes otherwise termed pikes, that held so conspicuous a position in the family shield; and hence the rapidity with which the quarrel with Falstaff is dismissed after the object of its introduction had been satisfied. And although it may be consistent with dramatic possibilities that Shallow, when he arrives at Windsor on a mission of complaint to the King, should be welcomed there by an intimate friend, an inhabitant of that town, and at the same time a fellow-sportsman on the Cotswold,—one may be pardoned for suspecting that the Gloucestershire magistrate would not have been transferred to the royal borough if his presence had not been required for the effective illustration of the Charlecote escapade. Be this as it may, there is sufficient outside the region of conjecture to enable us to infer that the poet designed, in his satirical notices of the justice, an individual as well as a general application, and where could the listeners be found that would be likely to appreciate the former? Certainly neither in London nor at the Court, even on the very unlikely supposition that intelligence of the deer-stealing affair had reached so far, for Sir Thomas's public life, at the earliest date at which either of the comedies could have been produced, had for many years been restricted to the midland counties. It may, therefore, be assumed that the great dramatist had in view representations of his pieces that he knew would be organized at or near Stratford after the termination of their first runs in the metropolis. But although a long-sustained resentment, under conditions of special insult or oppression, is not incompatible with the possession of an essentially gentle nature, it is not at all necessary to fancy that Shakespeare was here acting in the mere irrational spirit of retaliation. The owner of New Place had a social position to consolidate in his native town, and he took the best means of neutralizing a vexatious piece of scandal by holding up to local ridicule the individual whose line of treatment had attached to him whatever there was in the matter of personal degradation. And he would have been encouraged by the sympathy of the many who detested Sir Thomas's fanatical policy, even if the quarrel with him had not been in itself a passport to their favor. The news of the performance would somehow or other reach the ears of that potentate, who would naturally have been highly incensed at the unpardonable liberty that had been taken; the more so if, as it would appear, he was peculiarly sensitive to the opinion of his neighbors. The flight to London is an incontestable evidence that Shakespeare had no dread at that time of a metropolitan prosecution, and it was probably now, if ever, that Sir Thomas threatened to make his conduct, even at that late day, the subject of an appeal to the Star Chamber. Then would have followed the more pointed attack in the opening scene at Windsor, that in which his judicial dignities and his coat-armor, as well as the poaching adventure itself, are so mercilessly caricatured. It is not probable, however, that the entire significance of that dialogue will ever be ascertained. Much that is now obscure was no doubt immensely relished by the contemporary Stratfordians. It is easy to imagine, for example, the roars of laughter that might have greeted the poet's declaration made through Falstaff, that he had never kissed the keeper's daughter, if so be that the lady in question had chanced to have been one of nature's scarecrows; and who will venture to be confident that there is no quaint hidden meanings in the references to the salt fish and the old coat? And again, as the assiduous knight never appears to have declined an invitation to take a glass of wine, it is very likely that the bacchanalian tournament with Silence is no overdrawn picture, one, moreover, that would have been thoroughly enjoyed in a neighborhood in which the jovial host had taken an active part in a commission for the reformation of tipplers.

Exaggeration is one of the legitimate resources of satirical art, and that it has largely affected the dramatic portraiture of Sir Thomas Lucy cannot admit of a reasonable doubt. A tolerable degree of business and even of administrative capacity is, indeed, sometimes to be observed in men of no great wisdom, but there are substantial reasons for believing that Sir Thomas could not have been the precise intellectual counterpart of Justice Shallow. This may be gathered from a perusal of his correspondence, from the notices of his parliamentary doings, and, so far as marble can be a faithful guide in such matters, from the expression of his features in the Charlecote effigy, the only authentic likeness of him known to exist. Neither would it be inferred from that memorial that he could have been correctly represented as a starveling, but here allowance must be made for Falstaff's imagery having been in a great measure dependent upon his relative estimate of the standard of personal expanse. That there was much, however, of existing personation in the dramatic character and surroundings of the Gloucestershire justice that would have been readily interpreted by the Stratford audience is unquestionable. Although our supplies of information on this point are very defective, there are still contemporary records which tell us of the special interest taken by Sir Thomas in the details of archery, of the hospitality that was the order of his mansion, of his familiarity with recruits and the muster-roll, of the antiquity of his family, and, above all, of that appreciation of "friends at court" through whose influence he contrived to bask in the divergent sunshines of Mary and Elizabeth. Nor is there the least reason for suspecting that his violent Protestantism, so convenient in the latter reign, was in any way connected with an asceticism that would have decried the stage or excluded a festive evening with a brother magistrate. We know, on the contrary, that he was the patron of a company of itinerant actors, and that he had an intelligent estimate of the virtues of sack. Much, indeed, has been said of his dislike to the Shakespeares on religious grounds, but there is really nothing to warrant such an assumption beyond the bare and inadequate fact that he served on a commission under which the poet's father was named in a list of suspected recusants.

Two plays, the titles of which have not been recorded, were acted by Shakespeare's company in the early part of the year 1598, the poet being then in London. It is certain, however, that his thoughts were not at this time absorbed by literature or the stage. So far from this being the case there are good reasons for concluding that they were largely occupied with matters relating to pecuniary affairs, and to the progress of his influence at Stratford-on-Avon. He was then considering the advisability of purchasing an "odd yard land or other" in the neighborhood, and this circumstance, indicating the possession of redundant means, becoming known, his friend, Richard Quiney, who was in the metropolis, was strongly urged both in English and Latin to suggest to him the policy of trying to obtain one of the valuable tithe-leases, and to name, among other inducements,—"by the friends he can make therefore, we think it a fair mark for him to shoot at;—it obtained would advance him in deed and would do us much good," letter of Abraham Sturley dated from Stratford-on-Avon, January 24, 1598. These expressions indicate that Shakespeare's desire to establish a good position for himself in his native town was well known to his provincial friends.

When Shakespeare was meditating the purchase of the "odd yard," that is to say, most likely rather more than forty acres of land or thereabouts, he appears to have had a predilection in favor of Shottery, a hamlet in the immediate neighborhood of Stratford. It was in this village that he is generally believed, but on somewhat inconclusive grounds, to have met with his future wife, and hence has arisen the inevitable surmise that the inclination in favor of the particular investment emanated from recollections of the days of courtship. Some of those days may, indeed, have been passed in that locality, but whether this be the case or no, it is obvious, from the terms in which the contemplated acquisition is introduced that he was desirous of becoming one of the proprietors of its open fields. These latter, which were very extensive, comprising altogether about sixteen hundred acres, have long been enclosed, while there is nothing on their site, and little in their vicinity, to recall the Shottery that was now in the poet's thoughts. Most of its numerous ancient footpaths have been suppressed; its mud-walls have disappeared; very few of its dwellings exhibit outward traces of genuine Elizabethan work, and a hideous culvert is the modern substitute for what was once a stepping-stone passage across a gurgling brook. It may be confidently stated that there is only one of its buildings that can be thought to have retained an approach to a complete preservation of its original external features, a farm-house that belonged to a family of the name of Hathaway, and one that is usually considered to be the birth-place of Shakespeare's own Anne. But although it cannot be said that "the report of her is extended more than can be thought to begin from such a cottage," the truthful biographer is compelled to admit, in my case more than reluctantly, that the balance of evidence is hardly in favor of the attribution.

It was natural that the poet, having not only himself bitterly felt the want of resources not so many years previously, but seen so much inconvenience arising from a similar deficiency in his father's household, should now be determining to avoid the chance of a recurrence of the infliction. That he did not love money for its own sake, or for more than its relative advantages, may be gathered from his liberal expenditure in after life; but that he had the wisdom to make other tastes subservient to its acquisition, so long as that course was suggested by prudence, is a fact that cannot fairly be questioned. However repugnant it may be to the flowery sentiments of the æsthetic critics, no doubt can arise, in the minds of those who will listen to evidence, that when Pope asserted that—

> Shakespeare, whom you and ev'ry playhouse bill
> Style the divine, the matchless, what you will,
> For gain, not glory, wing'd his roving flight,
> And grew immortal in his own despight.

he not only expressed the traditional belief of his own day, but one which later researches have unerringly verified. With all Shakespeare's gentleness of disposition and amiable qualities, it is evident from the records that there was very little of the merely sentimental in his nature; that is to say, of such matters as a desire for posthumous fame, or the excitable sympathy which is so often recklessly appeased without thought of results. In the year now under consideration, 1598, he appears not only as an advancer of money, but also one who negotiated loans through other capitalists.

The comedy of *The Merchant of Venice*, the plot of which was either grounded on that of an older drama, or formed out of tales long familiar to the public, was represented with success in London in or before the month of July, 1598. It then had another title, being "otherwise called *The Jew of Venice*," and a bookseller named Roberts was anxious to secure the copyright, but the registrars of Stationers' Hall withheld their consent until he had obtained the sanction of the Lord Chamberlain, in other words, that of the author and his colleagues; and upwards of two years elapsed before the earliest editions of the comedy appeared. It continued for a long time to be one of the acting plays of

Shakespeare's company, and, as lately as 1605, it attracted the favorable notice of James I, who was so much pleased with one performance that he ordered a repetition of it two days afterward.

One of the most interesting of the recorded events of Shakespeare's life occurred in the present year. In September, 1598, Ben Jonson's famous comedy of *Every Man in his Humor* was produced by the Lord Chamberlain's company, and there is every probability that both writer and manager were indebted for its acceptance to the sagacity of the great dramatist, who was one of the leading actors on the occasion. "His acquaintance with Ben Jonson," observes Rowe, "began with a remarkable piece of humanity and good nature; Mr. Jonson, who was at that time altogether unknown to the world, had offered one of his plays to the players in order to have it acted, and the persons into whose hands it was put, after having turned it carelessly and superciliously over, were just upon returning it to him with an ill-natured answer that it would be of no service to their company, when Shakespeare luckily cast his eye upon it, and found something so well in it as to engage him first to read it through, and afterwards to recommend Mr. Jonson and his writings to the public." The statement that Rare Ben was then absolutely new to literature is certainly erroneous, however ignorant the Burbages or their colleagues may have been of his primitive efforts; but he was in a state of indigence, rendering the judgment on his manuscript of vital consequence, and the services of a friendly advocate of inestimable value. He had been engaged in dramatic work for Henslowe some months before the appearance of the new comedy, but about that time there seems to have been a misunderstanding between them, the latter alluding to Jonson simply as a bricklayer, not as one of his company, in his record of the unfortunate duel with Gabriel. There had been, in all probability, a theatrical disturbance resulting in the last-named event, and in Ben's temporary secession from the Rose. Then there are the words of Jonson himself, who, unbiased by the recollection that he had been defeated in, at all events, one literary skirmish with the great dramatist, speaks of him in language that would appear hyperbolical had it not been sanctioned by a feeling of gratitude for a definite and important service,—"I loved the man and do honor his memory, on this side idolatry, as much as any." This was a personal idolatry, not one solely in reference to his works, moderately adverse criticisms upon which immediately follow the generous panegyric. It may, then, fairly be said that the evidences at our disposal favor, on the whole, the general credibility of the anecdote narrated by Rowe.

In the same month in which Shakespeare was acting in Ben Jonson's comedy,—September, 1598,—there appeared in London the *Palladis Tamia*, a work that contains more elaborate notices of the great dramatist than are elsewhere to be found in all contemporary literature. Its author was one Francis Meres, a native of Lincolnshire, who had been educated at Cambridge, but for some time past resident in the metropolis. Although his studies were mostly of a theological character, he was interested in all branches of literature, and had formed intimacies with some of its chief representatives. He had been favored with access to the unpublished writings of Drayton and Shakespeare, and had either seen a manuscript, or witnessed a representation, of Rare Ben's earliest tragedy. In the important enumeration of Shakespeare's plays given by Meres, four of them,—*The Two Gentlemen of Verona*, *Love Labors Won*, *The Midsummer Night's Dream*, and *King John*,—are mentioned for the first time. There can be no doubt that the first of these dramas had been written some years previously, and *Love Labors Won*, a production which is nowhere else alluded to, is one of the numerous works of that time which have long since perished, unless its graceful appellation be the original or a secondary title of some other comedy. Neither *King John* nor *The Two Gentlemen of Verona* was printed during the author's lifetime, but two editions of *The Midsummer Night's Dream* appeared in the year 1600. This last-mentioned circumstance indicates the then popularity of that exquisite but singular drama, the comic scenes of which appear to have been those specially relished by the public. One little fragment of the contemporary stage humor, displayed in the representation of this play, has been recorded. When Thisbe killed herself, she fell on the scabbard; not on the trusty sword, the interlude doubtlessly having been acted in that spirit of extreme farce which was naturally evolved from the stupidity and nervousness of the clowns.

It is in the *Palladis Tamia*, 1598, that we first hear of those remarkable productions, the *Sonnets*. "As the soul of Euphorbus," observes Meres in that quaint collection of similitudes, "was thought to live in Pythagoras, so the sweet witty soul of Ovid lives in mellifluous and honey-tongued Shakespeare; witness his *Venus and Adonis*, his *Lucrece*, his sugared Sonnets among his private friends," etc. These last-mentioned dainty poems were clearly not then intended for general circulation, and even transcripts of a few were obtainable with difficulty. A publisher named Jaggard who, in the following year, 1599, attempted to form a collection of new Shakespearean poems, did not manage to obtain more than two of the *Sonnets*. The words of Meres, and the insignificant result of Jaggard's efforts, when viewed in connection with the nature of these strange poems, lead to the inference that some of them were written in clusters, and others as separate exercises, either being contributions made by their writer to the albums of his friends, probably no two of the latter being favored with identical compositions. There was no tradition adverse to a belief in their fragmentary character in the generation immediately following the author's death, as may be gathered from the arrangement found in Benson's edition of 1640; and this concludes the little real evidence on the subject that has descended to us. It was reserved for the students of the last century, who have ascertained so much respecting Shakespeare that was unsuspected by his own friends and contemporaries, to discover that his innermost earnest thoughts, his mental conflicts, and so on, are revealed in what would then be the most powerful lyrics yet given to the world. But the victim of spiritual emotions that involve criminatory reflections does not usually protrude them voluntarily on the consideration of society: and, if the personal theory be accepted, we must concede the possibility of our national dramatist gratuitously confessing his sins and revealing those of others, proclaiming his disgrace and avowing his repentance, in poetical circulars distributed by the delinquent himself among his most intimate friends.

There are no external testimonies of any description in favor of a personal application of the *Sonnets*, while there are abundant difficulties arising from the reception of such a theory. Among the latter is one deserving of special notice, for its investigation will tend to remove the displeasing interpretation all but universally given of two of the poems, those in which reference is supposed to be made to a bitter feeling of personal degradation allowed by Shakespeare to result from his connection with the stage. Is it conceivable that a man who encouraged a sentiment of this nature, one which must have been accompanied with a distaste and contempt for his profession, would have remained an actor years and years after any real necessity for such a course had expired? By the spring of 1602 at the latest, if not previously, he had acquired a secure and definite competence independently of his emoluments as a dramatist, and yet, eight years afterwards, in 1610, he is discovered playing in company with Burbage and Hemmings at the Blackfriars Theater. When, in addition to this voluntary long continuance on the boards, we bear in mind the vivid interest in the stage, and in the purity of the acted drama, which is exhibited in the well-known dialogue in *Hamlet*, and that the poet's last wishes included affectionate recollections of three of his fellow-players, it is difficult to believe that he could have nourished a real antipathy to his lower vocation. It is, on the contrary, to be inferred that, however greatly he may have deplored the unfortunate estimation in which the stage was held by the immense majority of his countrymen, he himself entertained a love for it that was too sincere to be repressed by contemporary disdain. If there is, among the defective records of the poet's life, one feature demanding special respect, it is the unflinching courage with which, notwithstanding his desire for social position, he braved public opinion in favor of a continued adherence to that which he felt was in itself a noble profession, and this at a time when it was not merely despised, but surrounded by an aggressive fanaticism that prohibited its exercise even in his own native town.

These considerations may suffice to eliminate a personal application from the two sonnets above mentioned, and as to the remainder, if the only safe method, that of discarding all mere assumptions, be strictly followed, the clearer the ideality of most of them, and the futility of arguments resting on any other basis, will be perceived. It will be observed that all the hypotheses, which aim at a complete biographical exposition of the *Sonnets*, necessitate the acceptance of interpretations that are too subtle for dispassionate reasoners. Even in the few instances where there is a reasonable possibility that Shakespeare was thinking of living individuals, as when he refers to an unknown poetical rival or quibbles on his own Christian name, scarcely any, if any, light is thrown on his personal feelings or character. In the latter case, it is a mere assumption that the second Will is the youth of the opening series, or, at least, that position cannot be sustained without tortuous interpretations of much which is found in the interval. With respect to other suggested personal revelations, such as those which are thought to be chronicled in Shakespeare's addresses to the dark-eyed beauty of more than questionable reputation,—unless, with a criminal indifference to the risk of the scandal traveling to the ears of his family, he had desired to proclaim to his acquaintances his own infidelity and folly,—he might, perhaps, have repeated the words of the author of *Licia*, who published his own sonnets in the year 1593, and thus writes of their probable effects,—"for the matter of love, it may bee I am so devoted to some one, into whose hands these may light by chance, that she may say, which thou nowe saiest, that surelie he is in love, which if she doe, then have I the full recompence of my labour, and the poems have dealt sufficientlie for the discharge of their owne duetie." The disguise of the ideal under the personal was then, indeed, an ordinary expedient.

In the Christmas holidays of 1598-1599, three plays, one of them in all probability having been the *Merry Wives of Windsor*, were acted by Shakespeare's company before the Queen at Whitehall, after which they do not appear to have performed at Court until the following December, an the 26th of which month they were at Richmond Palace. The poet's distinguished friend, Lord Southampton, was in London in the autumn of this year, and no doubt favored more than one theater with his attendance. In a letter dated October 11, 1599, his lordship is alluded to as spending his time "merrily in going to plays every day."

In March, 1599, the Earl of Essex departed on his ill-starred expedition to Ireland, leaving the metropolis amid the enthusiastic cheers of the inhabitants. He was then the most popular man in all England, hosts of the middle and lower classes regarding him as their chief hope for the redress of their grievances. At some time in May or June, while the suppression of the Irish was considered in his able hands a mere work of time, Shakespeare completed his play of *King Henry the Fifth,* taking the opportunity of introducing in it a graceful compliment to the Earl, in terms which indicate that the poet himself sympathized with the thousands of Londoners who fondly expected hereafter to welcome his victorious return to England. Independently, however, of his appreciation of Essex, it was natural that the great dramatist should have taken a special interest in the course of affairs in Ireland, his great patron and friend, Lord Southampton, holding the distinguished position of General of the Horse in the Earl's army. There is no record of this drama in the year of its composition, but there is little or rather no doubt that it was produced on the diminutive boards of the Curtain Theater in the summer of 1599. It was favorably received and the character of Pistol appears to have been specially relished by the audiences. In or before the August of the following year, 1600, an unsuccessful attempt was made to obtain a license for its publication, but the only copy of it, printed in the author's lifetime, was a miserably imperfect and garbled one which was surreptitiously published about that time by Millington and Busby, and transferred by them very soon afterwards to Thomas Pavier, the latter reprinting this spurious edition in 1602 and 1608. It is curious that Pavier, who was so unscrupulous in other instances in the use of Shakespeare's name, should have refrained from placing it on the title-pages of any of those impressions. There are unequivocal indications that the edition of 1600 was fraudulently printed from a copy made up from notes taken at the theater.

Toward the close of this year, 1599, a renewed attempt was made by the poet to obtain a grant of coat-armor to his father. It was now proposed to impale the arms of Shakespeare with those of Arden, and on each occasion ridiculous statements were made respecting the claims of the two families. Both were really descended from obscure English country yeomen, but the heralds made out that the predecessors of John Shakespeare were rewarded by the Crown for distinguished services, and that his wife's ancestors were entitled to armorial bearings. Although the poet's relatives at a later date assumed his right to the coat suggested for his father in 1596, it does not appear that either of the proposed grants was ratified by the college, and certainly nothing more is heard of the Arden impalement.

The *Sonnets*, first mentioned in the previous year, are now again brought into notice. They had evidently obtained a recognition in literary circles, but restrictive suggestions had possibly been made to the recipients, for, as previously observed, when Jaggard, in 1599, issued a tiny volume under the fanciful title of *The Passionate Pilgrim*, he was apparently not enabled to secure more, than two of them. These are in the first part of the book, the second being entitled *Sonnets to Sundry Notes of Music*, but Shakespeare's name is not attached to the latter division. The publisher seems to have had few materials of any description that he could venture to insert under either title, for, in order to make something like a book with them, he adopted the very unusual course of having nearly the whole of the tract printed upon one side only of each leaf. Not keeping a shop, he entrusted the sale to Leake, who was then the owner of the copyright of *Venus and Adonis*, and who published an edition of that poem in the same year, the two little volumes no doubt being displayed together on the stall of the latter at the Greyhound in St. Paul's Churchyard. With the exception of the two sonnets above alluded to, and a few verses taken from the already published comedy of *Love's Labor's Lost*, Jaggard's collection does not include a single line that can be positively ascribed to the pen of the great dramatist, but much that has been ascertained to have been the composition of others. The entire publication bears evident marks of an attempted fraud, and it may well be doubted if any of its untraced contents, with perhaps three exceptions, justify the announcement of the title-page. The three pieces alluded to are those on the subject of *Venus and Adonis*, and these, with the beautiful little poem called *The Lover's Complaint*, may be included in the significant *et cetera* by which Meres clearly implies that Shakespeare was the author of other poetical essays besides those which he enumerates.

It is extremely improbable that Shakespeare, in that age of small London and few publishers, could have been ignorant of the use made of his name in the first edition of the *Passionate Pilgrim*, Although he may, however, have been displeased at Jaggard's unwarrantable conduct in the matter, it appears that he took no strenuous measures to induce him to disavow or suppress the ascription in the title-page of that work. There was, it is true, no legal remedy, but there is reason for believing that, in this case, at least, a personal remonstrance would have been effective. Owing, perhaps, to the apathy exhibited by Shakespeare on this occasion, a far more remarkable operation in the same kind of knavery was perpetrated in the latter part of the following year by the publisher of the *First Part of the Life of Sir John Oldcastle,* 1600, a play mainly concerned with the romantic adventures of Lord Cobham. Although this drama is known not only to have been composed by other dramatists, but also to have belonged to a theatrical company with whom Shakespeare had then no manner of connection, it was unblushingly announced as his work by the publisher, Thomas Pavier, a shifty bookseller, residing at the grotesque sign of the Cat and Parrots near the Royal Exchange. Two editions were issued in the same year by Pavier, the one most largely distributed being that which was assigned to the pen of the great dramatist, and another to which no writer's name is attached. As there are no means of ascertaining which of these editions is the first in order of publication, it is impossible to say with certainty whether the introduction of Shakespeare's name was an afterthought, or if it were withdrawn for a special reason, perhaps either at his instigation or at that of the real authors. It is most likely, however, that the anonymous impression was the first that was published, that the ascribed edition was the second, and that there was no cancel of the poet's name in either.

The most celebrated theater the world has ever seen was now to receive a local habitation and a name. The wooden structure belonging to the Burbages in Shoreditch had fallen into desuetude in 1598, and, very early in 1599, they had pulled it down and removed the materials to Southwark, using them in the erection of a new building which was completed towards the end of the year and opened early in 1600 under the title of the Globe. Ben

Jonson's comedy of *Every Man Out of his Humour* was one of the first plays there exhibited, the author, in an epilogue written probably for the occasion, distinctly appealing to the judgment of "the happier spirits in this faire-fild Globe" (ed. 1600). Among the Shakespearean dramas acted at the old Globe before its destruction by fire in 1613 may be mentioned, *Romeo and Juliet*, *Richard the Second*, *King Lear*, *Troilus and Cressida*, *Pericles*, *Othello*, *Macbeth*, and *The Winter's Tale*.

Shakespeare's company acted before Queen Elizabeth at Richmond Palace on Twelfth Night and Shrove Sunday, 1600, and at Whitehall on December 26. On March 6 they were at Somerset House, and there performed, before Lord Hunsdon and some foreign ambassadors, another drama on the subject of Oldcastle. A few weeks after the last occurrence, the poet, who was then in London, brought an action against one John Clayton to recover the sum of £7, and duly succeeded in obtaining a verdict in his favor. This is one of the several evidences that distinctly prove the great dramatist to have been a man of business, thoroughly realizing the necessity of careful attention to his pecuniary affairs. Here we have the highest example of all to tell us that the financial discretion is not incompatible with the possession of literary genius.

One of the most exquisite of Shakespeare's comedies, *As You Like It*, was most likely produced in the summer of this year, and was, as might be expected, favorably received. The celebrated speech of Jacques on the seven ages of man would have had an appropriate significance when uttered below the Latin motto under the sign of the Globe Theater, but the coincidence was no doubt accidental. An attempt to publish this drama was frustrated by an appeal to the Stationers' Company, a fact which testifies to its popularity; and one of its ditties was set to music by Thomas Morley, an eminent composer of the day, who published it, with some others of a cognate description, in his *First Booke of Ayres, or Little Short Songs*, a small thin folio volume printed at London in the same year, 1600.

According to a tradition mentioned by several writers of the last century, there was a character in *As You Like It* that was performed by the author of the comedy. "One of Shakespeare's younger brothers," says Oldys, "who lived to a good old age, even some years, as I compute, after the restoration of King Charles II, would in his younger days come to London to visit his brother Will, as he called him, and be a spectator of him as an actor in some of his own plays. This custom, as his brother's fame enlarged, and his dramatic entertainments grew the greatest support of our principal, if not of all our theaters, he continued, it seems, so long after his brother's death, as even to the latter end of his own life. The curiosity at this time of the most noted actors to learn something from him of his brother, etc., they justly held him in the highest veneration; and it may be well believed, as there was besides a kinsman and descendant of the family, who was then a celebrated actor among them, this opportunity made them greedily inquisitive into every little circumstance, more especially in his dramatic character, which his brother could relate of him. But he, it seems, was so stricken in years, and possibly his memory so weakened with infirmities, which might make him the easier pass for a man of weak intellects, that he could give them but little light into their inquiries; and all that could be recollected from him of his brother Will in that station was the faint, general, and almost lost ideas he had of having once seen him act a part in one of his own comedies, wherein, being to personate a decrepit old man, he wore a long beard, and appeared so weak and drooping and unable to walk, that he was forced to be supported and carried by another person to a table, at which he was seated among some company who were eating, and one of them sung a song." This account contains several discrepancies, but there is reason for believing that it includes a glimmering of truth which is founded on an earlier tradition.

The earliest notice of the comedy of *Much Ado About Nothing* occurs in the entry in which we also first hear of *As You Like It*. Its attempted publication was stopped by an application made by the Stationers' Company on or before August 4, 1600, but, on the 23rd of the same month, Wise and Aspley succeeded in obtaining a license. It is not known if the prohibition was directed against the latter publication and afterwards removed, or whether it refers to a fraudulent attempt by some other bookseller to issue a surreptitious copy. Although *Much Ado*

About Nothing was not reprinted in the author's lifetime, there is no doubt of its continued popularity.

The scene of this comedy is laid in Messina, but the satire on the constables obviously refers to those of the England of the author's own time. Aubrey, whose statements are always to be cautiously received, asserts that Shakespeare "happened to take" the "humor" of one of them "at Grendon in Bucks, which is in the road from London to Stratford, and there was living that constable about 1642." The eccentric biographer no doubt refers to Dogberry or Verges, but if the poet really had a special individual in his mind when portraying either of those characters, it is not likely that the Grendon constable could have been the person so honored, for unless he had attained an incredible age in the year 1642, he would have been too young for the prototype. It is far more likely that the satire was generally applicable to the English constables of the author's period, to such as were those in the neighborhood of London at the time of his arrival there, and who are so graphically thus described in a letter from Lord Burghley to Sir Francis Walsingham, written in 1586,—"as I came from London homeward in my coach, I saw at every town's end the number of ten or twelve standing with long staves, and, until I came to Enfield, I thought no other of them but that they had stayed for avoiding of the rain, or to drink at some alehouses, for so they did stand under pentices at alehouses; but at Enfield, finding a dozen in a plump when there was no rain, I bethought myself that they were appointed as watchmen for the apprehending of such as are missing; and thereupon I called some of them to me apart, and asked them wherefore they stood there, and one of them answered, to take three young men; and, demanding how they should know the persons,—Marry, said they, one of the parties hath a hooked nose; and have you, quoth I, no other mark? No, said they. Surely, sir, these watchmen stand so openly in plumps as no suspected person will come near them, and if they be no better instructed but to find three persons by one of them having a hooked nose, they may miss thereof."

It was toward the close of the present year, 1600, or at some time in the following one, that Shakespeare, for the first and only time, came forward in the avowed character of a philosophical writer. One Robert Chester was the author of a long and tedious poem, which was issued in 1601, under the title of,—*Love's Martyr or Rosalins Complaint, allegorically shadowing the truth of Love in the constant fate of the Phœnix and Turtle,* and *to these are added some new compositions of severall moderne writers, whose names are subscribed to their severall workes, upon the first subject; viz., the Phœnix and Turtle.* The latter were stated, in a separate title-page, to have been "done by the best and chiefest of our moderne writers, with their names subscribed to their particular workes; never before extant; and now first consecrated by them all generally to the love and merite of the true-noble knight, Sir John Salisburie",—the names of Shakespeare, Marston, Chapman, and Jonson being attached to the recognized pieces of this latter series. The contribution of the great dramatist is a remarkable poem in which he makes a notice of the obsequies of the phœnix and turtle-dove subservient, to the delineation of spiritual union. It is generally thought that, in his own works, Chester meditated a personal allegory, but, if that be the case, there is nothing to indicate that Shakespeare participated in the design, nor even that he had endured the punishment of reading *Love's Martyr.*

The commencement of this year, 1601, is memorable for the development and suppression of the Essex conspiracy, one of the most singular events of the Queen's reign, and one in which Shakespeare's company was transiently implicated. The general history of this remarkable movement is too familiar to us all to sanction its repetition, but it is not so generally known that the Earl's friends, in their anxiety to seize every opportunity of influencing public opinion in favor of their schemes, negotiated with the Lord Chamberlain's Servants for the representation at the Globe Theater of a drama that evinced a political significance in its treatment of the deposition of Richard II. The conspirators had selected as the one most suitable for their design a play that had been already exhibited on the stage, but, in a discussion on the subject with a few of the actors, it was strongly urged by the latter that the composition in question had so out-grown its popularity that a serious loss on its revival would inevitably accrue; and, under these circumstances, it was arranged that forty shillings should be paid to the company in augmentation of their receipts on the occasion. The interview at which this compromise was effected took place on Friday, February 6, a "play of the deposing and killing of King Richard," one which also dealt, it would appear, with a portion of the reign of his successor, being represented at the Globe on the afternoon of the following day; but none of the persons engaged in these transactions had then the remotest idea that the latter were to be immediately followed by the premature outbreak of the insurrection.

The rapidity, indeed, with which events now moved have most likely hidden from us forever the contemporary light in which the proceedings at the Globe were viewed; but that the public exhibition at this juncture of the history of the deposition of Richard was an unwonted bold step on the part of the company cannot admit of a question. Some of its members, at all events, and most probably all, must have been aware of the Queen's preternatural sensitiveness in everything that related to that history; so that it is difficult to avoid the impression that the leaders of the theater shared in the all but universal desire of the community for the restoration of Essex to power. It is true that Shakespeare's friend and colleague, Augustine Phillipps, in an affidavit sworn before three of the judges eleven days afterwards, assigns the initiative of the pecuniary offer to the conspirators, but that offer of forty shillings, if viewed on either side as a bribe, was certainly too moderate an amount to have overcome the scruples of unwilling agents in so considerable a risk, and too much reliance should not be placed upon the terms of a document that may have been signed under conditions that admitted of serious peril to the witness and his friends. Now that the game was irretrievably lost, and the power of a despotic government again supreme, it is most likely that Phillipps dexterously said as little about the affair as he dared, and yet just enough to save himself and the other actors at the Globe from being, to use an expressive phrase of the time, "wrecked on the Essex coast." That they altogether escaped this calamity may be gathered from the fact that they performed before the Queen at Richmond Palace on Shrove Tuesday, February 24, the very evening before the lamented death of Essex; but it should be borne in mind that the selection of that movable feast-day for the performance was merely owing to the following of a long-established custom, not the result of a special order; and Elizabeth, now that the dangers to which she had been exposed were over, had too much wisdom, whatever she may have known or thought respecting their doings on the seventh, to make an impolitic display of superfluous animosities. Least of all is it probable that she would have been inclined, excepting in a case of dire emergency, to have visited her displeasure upon the humble ministers of one of her favorite amusements, persons, moreover, who were then regarded in about the same light with jugglers and buffoons. As to her appearance at a theatrical representation the night before the execution, that was not more unseemly than her amusing herself by playing on the virginals the following morning, all this outward heartlessness emanating from a determination to assume before the court a demeanor of indifference to the cruel destiny of her quondam favorite.

That the poet was intimately acquainted, so far at least as the extreme social distinctions of the age permitted, with some of the leading members of the conspiracy, may be fairly assumed. It is all but impossible that he should not have been well-known to the readily-accessible Essex,—the object of the graceful compliment in the last act of *King Henry the Fifth*,—one who was not only distinguished by his widely extended impartial and generous patronage of literature and its votaries, but the bosom friend of Shakespeare's own Mæcenas. Then there were the Earl of Rutland, the frequent companion of the latter at the public theaters, and Sir Charles Percy, who, only a few weeks before the performance at the Globe, had shown how deeply he had been impressed by the humor of the *Second Part of Henry the Fourth*. But there is no evidence that tends to associate the great dramatist with any kind of participation in the furtherance of the objects of the conspirators beyond, of course, the natural inference that he shared with his colleagues the responsibility of their theatrical proceedings on February 7.

Apart from all this, even if it were thought possible that Shakespeare could have been altogether ignorant of the treasonable designs of Essex and Southampton, there can be no doubt that his obligations to and relations with the latter, irrespective of other considerations, made him regard the memorable events of the following day,—in whatever way they may have come to his knowledge, either partially as an eye-witness or otherwise,—with feelings of the deepest anxiety and personal interest. The history of that Sunday thus becomes in a manner a portion of his own biography.

The poet's father,—Mr. Johannes Shakespeare, as he is called in the register,—was buried at Stratford-on-Avon on September 8, 1601; having no doubt expired a few days previously at his residence in Henley Street, which is noticed so recently as 1597 as being then in his occupation. He is mentioned as having been concerned with others in the former year in the discussion of matters respecting an action brought by Sir Edward Greville against the town, so there are no reasons for believing that his latest years were accompanied by decrepitude. In all probability the old man died intestate, and the great dramatist appears to have succeeded, as his eldest son and heir-at-law, to the ownership of the freehold tenements in Henley Street. It is not likely that the widow acquired more than her right to dower in that property but there can be no hesitation in assuming that such a claim would have been merged in a liberal allowance from her son.

Twelfth Night, the perfection of English comedy and the most fascinating drama in the language, was produced in the season of 1601-2, most probably on January 5. There is preserved a curious notice of its performance in the following month before the benchers of the Middle Temple in their beautiful hall, nearly the only building now remaining in London in which it is known that any of Shakespeare's dramas were represented during the author's lifetime. The record of this interesting occurrence is embedded in the minutely written contemporary diary of one John Manningham, a student at that inn of court, who appears to have been specially impressed with the character of Malvolio. "A good practice in it," he observes, "to make the steward believe his lady widow was in love with him, by counterfeiting a letter as from his lady in general terms, telling him what she liked best in him, and prescribing his gesture in smiling, his apparel, etc., and then, when he came to practice, making him believe they took him to be mad." This representation of *Twelfth Night* took place at the Feast of the Purification, February 2, one of the two grand festival days of the lawyers, on which occasion professional actors were annually engaged at the Middle Temple, the then liberal sum of ten pounds being given to them for a single performance. There is no doubt that the comedy was performed by the Lord Chamberlain's servants, and very little that Shakespeare himself was one of the actors who were engaged. *Twelfth Night* was appreciated at an early period as one of the author's most popular creations. There is not only the testimony of Manningham in its favor, but Leonard Digges, in the verses describing this most attractive of Shakespeare's acting dramas, expressly alludes to the estimation in which the part of Malvolio was held by the frequenters of the theater.

The Queen kept her Court at Whitehall in the Christmas of 1601-1602, and, during the holidays, four plays, one of them most probably *Twelfth Night*, were exhibited before her by Shakespeare's company. In the following May, the great dramatist purchased from the Combes, for the sum of £320, one hundred and seven acres of land near Stratford-on-Avon, but, owing to his absence from that town, the conveyance was delivered for his use to his brother Gilbert. It is not likely, indeed, that he visited the locality within any brief period after this transaction, for otherwise the counterpart of the indenture, which was duly engrossed in complete readiness for the purchaser's attestation, would hardly have been permitted to remain without his signature. But this was not the only legal business of the year in which the poet was interested. It appears that a flaw had been discovered in the validity of his title to New Place, the vendor's relative, Hercules Underhill, possessing some unknown kind of interest that had not been effectually barred by the terms of the conveyance. In order to meet this difficulty it was necessary for a fine to be levied through which the absolute ownership of the purchaser should be recognized by Hercules, and of so much importance was this considered that, upon the deforciant representing in June, 1602, that the state of his health prevented his undertaking a journey to London, a special commission was arranged for obtaining his acknowledgment. This important ratification was procured in Northamptonshire in the following October, Shakespeare no doubt being responsible for the considerable expenditure that must have been incurred by these transactions, which, there is reason to believe, were conducted exclusively by his own professional advisers.

The pecuniary resources of Shakespeare must now have been very considerable, for, notwithstanding the serious expenditure incurred by this last acquisition, a few months afterwards he is recorded as the purchaser of a small copyhold estate near his country residence. On September 28, 1602, at a Court Baron of the Manor of Rowington, one Walter Getley transferred to the poet a cottage and garden which were situated in Chapel Lane opposite the lower grounds of New Place. They covered the space of a quarter of an acre, with a frontage in the lane of forty feet, and were held practically in fee simple at the annual rental of two shillings and sixpence. It appears from the roll that Shakespeare did not attend the manorial court then held at Rowington, there being a stipulation that the estate should remain in the hands of the lady of the manor until he appeared in person to complete the transaction with the usual formalities. At a later period he was admitted to the copyhold, and then he surrendered it to the use of himself for life, with a remainder to his two daughters in fee. The cottage was replaced about the year 1690 by a brick and tiled building, and no representation of the original tenement is known to be in existence. The latter, in all probability, had, like most other cottages at Stratford-on-Avon in the poet's time, a thatched roof supported by mud walls. The adjoining boundary wall that enclosed the vicarage garden on the lane side continued to be one of mud until the latter part of the eighteenth century.

In the spring of this year, 1602, the tragedy, known originally under the title of *The Revenge of Hamlet, Prince of Denmark*, was in course of representation by the Lord Chamberlain's players at the Globe Theater, and had then, in all probability, been recently composed. Its popularity led to an unsuccessful attempt by Roberts, a London publisher, to include it among his dramatic issues, but it was not printed until the summer of the following year, 1603, when two booksellers, named Ling and Trundell, employed an inferior and clumsy writer to work up, in his own fashion, what scraps of the play had been furtively obtained from shorthand notes or other memoranda into the semblance of a perfect drama, which they had the audacity to publish as Shakespeare's own work. It is possible, however, that the appearance of this surreptitious edition, which contains several abnormous variations from the complete work, may have led the sharers of the theater to be less averse to the publication of their own copy. At all events, Ling in some way obtained an authentic transcript of the play in the following year, and it was "newly imprinted" by Roberts for that publisher, "enlarged to almost as much againe as it was, according to the true and perfect coppie," 1604. The appearance of subsequent editions and various early notices evince the favor in which the tragedy was held by the public in the time of its author. The hero was admirably portrayed by Burbage, and has ever since, as then, been accepted as the leading character of the greatest actor of the passing day. It is worth notice that the incident of Hamlet leaping into Ophelia's grave, now sometimes omitted, was considered in Burbage's time to be one of the most striking features of the acted tragedy; and there is a high probability that a singular little by-play drollery, enacted by the First Grave-digger, was also introduced at the Globe performances. The once popular stage-trick of that personage taking off a number of waistcoats one after the other, previously to the serious commencement of his work, is an artifice which has only been laid aside in comparatively recent years.

In February, 1603, Roberts, one of the Shakespearean printers, attempted to obtain a license for an impression of the play of *Troilus and Cressida*, then in the course of representation by the Lord Chamberlain's servants. The subject had been dramatized by Decker and Chettle for the Lord Admiral's servants in 1599, but although the two companies may have been then, as in former years, on friendly terms, there is no probability that their copyrights were exchangeable, so that the application made by Roberts is not likely to refer to the jointly-written drama. When that printer applied for a license for the publication of the new tragedy, he had not obtained, nor is there any reason for believing that he ever succeeded in procuring, the company's sanction to his projected speculation. At all events, Shakespeare's *Troilus and Cressida* was not printed until early in the year 1609, when two other publishers, Bonian and Walley, having surreptitiously procured a copy, ventured on its publication, and, in the hope of attracting purchasers, they had the audacity to state, in an unusual preface, that it had never been represented on the stage. They even appeared to exult in having treacherously obtained a manuscript of the tragedy, but the triumph of their artifices was of brief duration. The deceptive temptation they offered of novelty must have been immediately exposed, and a pressure was no doubt exerted upon them by the company, who probably withdrew their opposition on payment of compensation, for, by January 28, the printers had received a license from the Lord Chamberlain for the publication. The preface was then entirely canceled, and the falsity of the assertion that *Troilus and Cressida* had never been acted was conspicuously admitted by the reissue professing to appear "as it *was* acted by the King's Majesty's Servants at the Globe,"—when is not stated. The suppressed preface could hardly have been written had the drama been one of the acting plays of the season of 1608-1609, and, indeed, the whole tenor of that preamble is against the validity of such an assumption. There can be little doubt that *Troilus and Cressida* was originally produced at the Globe in the winter season of 1602-1603.

The career of the illustrious sovereign, who had so highly appreciated the dramas of our national poet, was now drawing to an end. Shakespeare's company, who had acted before her at Whitehall on December 26, 1602, were summoned to Richmond for another performance on the following Candlemas Day, February 2, 1603. The Queen was then in a very precarious state of health, and this was the last occasion on which the poet could have had the opportunity of appearing before her. Elizabeth died on March 24, but, among the numerous poetical tributes to her memory that were elicited by her decease, there was not one from the pen of Shakespeare.

The poetical apathy exhibited by the great dramatist on this occasion, although specially lamented by a contemporary writer, can easily be accounted for in more than one way; if, indeed, an explanation is needed beyond a reference to the then agitated and bewildered state of the public mind. The company to which he belonged might have been absent, as several others were at the time, on a provincial tour. Again, they were no doubt intent on obtaining the patronage of the new sovereign, and may have fancied that too enthusiastic a display of grief for Elizabeth would have been considered inseparable from a regret for the change of dynasty. However that may be, James I arrived in London on May 7, 1603, and ten days afterwards he granted, by bill of Privy Signet, a license to Shakespeare and the other members of his company to perform in London at the Globe Theater, and, in the provinces, at town-halls or other suitable buildings. They itinerated a good deal during the next few months, records of their performances being found at Bath, Coventry, Shrewsbury, and Ipswich. It was either in this year, or early in the following one, and under this license, that the company, including the poet himself, acted at the Globe in Ben Jonson's new comedy of *Sejanus*.

The King was staying in December, 1603, at Wilton, the seat of one of Shakespeare's patron's, William Herbert, third Earl of Pembroke, and on the second of that month the company had the honor of performing before the distinguished party then assembled in that noble mansion. In the following Christmas holidays, 1603-1604, they were acting on several occasions at Hampton Court, the play selected for representation on the first evening of the new year being mentioned by one of the audience under the name of *Robin Goodfellow*, possibly a familiar title of *The Midsummer Night's Dream*. Their services were again invoked by royalty at Candlemas and on Shrove Sunday, on the former occasion at Hampton Court before the Florentine ambassador, and on the latter at Whitehall. At this time they were prohibited from acting in or near London, in fear that public gatherings might imperil the diminution of the pestilence, the King making the company on that account the then very handsome present of thirty pounds.

Owing in some degree to the severe plague of 1603, and more perhaps to royal disinclination, the public entry of the King into the metropolis did not take place until nearly a year after the death of Elizabeth. It was on March 15, 1604, that James undertook his formal march from the Tower to Westminister, amid emphatic demonstrations of welcome, and passing every now and then under the most elaborate triumphal arches London had ever seen. In the royal train were the nine actors to whom the special license had been granted the previous year, including of course Shakespeare and his three friends, Burbage, Hemmings, and Condell. Each of them was presented with four yards and a half of scarlet cloth, the usual dress allowance to players belonging to the household. The poet and his colleagues were termed the King's Servants, and took rank at Court among the Grooms of the Chamber.

Shortly after this event the poet made a visit to Stratford-on-Avon. It appears, from a declaration filed in the local court, that he had sold in that town to one Philip Rogers several bushels of malt at various times between March 27 and the end of May, 1604, and that the latter did not, or could not, pay the debt thus incurred, amounting to £1. 15s. 10d. Shakespeare had sold him malt to the value of £1. 19s. 10d., and, on June 25, Rogers borrowed two shillings of the poet at Stratford, making in all £2. 1s. 10d. Six shillings of this were afterwards paid, and the action was brought to recover the balance.

In the following August the great dramatist was in London, there having been a special order, issued in that month by desire of the King, for every member of the company to be in attendance at Somerset House. This was on the occasion of the visit of the Spanish ambassador to England, but it may be perhaps that their professional services were not required, for no notice of them has been discovered.

The tragedy of *Othello*, originally known under the title of *The Moor of Venice*, is first heard of in 1604, it having been performed by the King's players, who then included Shakespeare himself, before the Court, in the Banqueting House at Whitehall, on the evening of Hallowmas day, November 1. This drama was very popular, Leonard Digges speaking of the audiences preferring it to the labored compositions of Ben Jonson. In 1609, a stage-loving parent, one William Bishop, of Shoreditch, who had perhaps been taken with the representation of the tragedy, gave the name of Othello's perfect wife to one of his twin daughters. A performance at the Globe in the April of the following year, 1610, was honored with the presence of the German ambassador and his suite, and it was again represented at Court before Prince Charles, the Princess Elizabeth, and the Elector Palatine, in May, 1613. These scattered notices, accidentally preserved, doubtlessly out of many others that might have been recorded, are indicative of its continuance as an acting play; a result that may, without disparagement to the author, be attributed in some measure to the leading character having been assigned to the most accomplished tragic actor of the day,—Richard Burbage. The name of the first performer of Iago is not known, but there is a curious tradition, which can be traced as far back as the close of the seventeenth century, to the effect that the part was originally undertaken by a popular comedian, and that Shakespeare adapted some of the speeches of that character to the peculiar talents of the actor.

The company are found playing at Oxford in the early part of the summer of 1604. In the Christmas holidays of the same year, on the evening of December 26, the comedy of *Measure for Measure* was performed before the Court at Whitehall, and if it were written for that special occasion, it seems probable that the lines, those in which Angelo deprecates the thronging of the multitude to royalty, were introduced out of special consideration to James I, who, as is well known, had a great dislike to encountering crowds of people. The lines in the mouth of Angelo appear to be somewhat forced, while their metrical disposition is consistent with the idea that they might have been the result of an afterthought.

Shakespeare's company performed a number of dramas before the Court early in the following year, 1605, including several of his own. About the same time a curious old play, termed *The London Prodigal*, which had been previously acted by them, was impudently submitted by Nathaniel Butter to the reading public as one of the compositions of the great dramatist. On May 4, a few days before his death, the poet's colleague, Augustine Phillips, made his will, leaving "to my fellowe, William Shakespeare, a thirty shillinges peece in, goold." And in the following July, Shakespeare made the largest, and, in a monetary sense very likely the most judicious, purchase he ever completed, giving the sum of £440 for the unexpired term of the moiety of a valuable lease of the tithes of Stratford, Old Stratford, Bishopton and Welcombe.

On October 9 in the same year, 1605, Shakespeare's company, having previously traveled as far as Barnstaple, gave another performance before the Mayor and Corporation of Oxford. If the poet, as was most likely the case, was one of the actors on the occasion, he would have been lodging at the Crown Inn, a wine-tavern kept by one John Davenant, who had taken out his license in the previous year, 1604. The landlord was a highly respectable man, filling in succession the chief municipal offices, but, although of a peculiarly grave and saturnine disposition, he was, as recorded by Wood in 1692, "an admirer and lover of the plays and play-makers, especially Shakespeare, who frequented his house in his journies between Warwickshire and London." His wife is described by the same writer as "a very beautiful woman, of a good wit and conversation." Early in the following year the latter presented her husband with a son, who was christened at St. Martin's Church on March 3, 1606, receiving there the name of William. They had several other children, and their married life was one of such exceptional harmony that it elicited the unusual honor of metrical tributes. A more devoted pair the city of Oxford had never seen, and John Davenant, in his will, 1622, expressly desires that he should be "buryed in the parish of St. Martin's in Oxford as nere my wife as the place will give leave where shee lyeth."

It was the general belief in Oxford, in the latter part of the seventeenth century, that Shakespeare was William Davenant's godfather, and there is no reason for questioning the accuracy of the tradition. Anthony Wood alludes to the special regard in which the poet was held by the worthy innkeeper, while the Christian name that was selected was a new one in the family of the latter. There was also current in the same town a favorite anecdote, in which a person was warned not to speak of his godfather lest he should incur the risk of breaking the Third

Commandment. This was a kind of representative story, one which could be told of any individual at the pleasure of the narrator, and it is found in the generic form in a collection of tavern pleasantries made by Taylor, the Water-Poet, in 1629. This last fact alone is sufficient to invest a personal application with the gravest doubt, and to lead to the inference that the subsequent version related of Shakespeare was altogether unauthorized. If so, there can be little doubt that with the spurious tale originated its necessary foundation,—the oft-repeated intimation that Sir William Davenant was the natural son of the great dramatist. The latter surmise is first heard of in one of the manuscripts of Aubrey, written in or before the year 1680, in which he says, after mentioning the Crown tavern,—"Mr. William Shakespeare was wont to goe into Warwickshire once a yeare, and did commonly in his journey lye at this house in Oxen, where he was exceedingly respected." He then proceeds to tell us that Sir William, considering himself equal in genius to Shakespeare, was not averse to being taken for his son, and would occasionally make these confessions in his drinking bouts with Sam Butler and other friends. The writer's language is obscure, and might have been thought to mean simply that Davenant wished to appear in the light of a son in the poetical acceptation of the term, but the reckless gossip must needs add that Sir William's mother not only "had a very light report," but was looked upon in her own day as a perfect Thais. Sufficient is known of the family history of the Davenants, and of their social position and respectability, to enable us to be certain that this onslaught upon the lady's reputation is a scandalous mis-statement. Anthony Wood also, the conscientious Oxonian biographer, who had the free use of Aubrey's papers, eliminates every kind of insinuation against the character of either Shakespeare or Mrs. Davenant. He may have known from reliable sources that there could have been no truth in the alleged illegitimacy, and anyhow he no doubt had the independent sagacity to observe that the reception of the libel involved extravagant admissions. It would require us to believe that the guilty parties, with incredible callousness, united at the font to perpetuate their own recollection of the crime; and this in the presence of the injured husband, who must be presumed to have been then, and throughout his life, unconscious of a secret which was so insecurely kept that it furnished ample materials for future slander. Even Aubrey himself tacitly concedes that the scandal had not transpired in the poet's time, for he mentions the great respect in which the latter was held at Oxford. Then, as if to make assurance to posterity doubly sure, there is preserved at Alnwick Castle a very elaborate manuscript poem on the Oxford gossip of the time of James I, including especially everything that could be raked up against its innkeepers and taverns, and in that manuscript there is no mention either of the Crown Inn or of the Davenants.

It is, indeed, easy to perceive that we should never have heard any scandal respecting Mrs. Davenant, if she had not been noted in her own time, and for long afterwards, for her exceptional personal attractions. Her history ought to be a consolation to ugly girls, that is to say, if the existence of such rarities as the latter be not altogether mythical. Listen to the antique words of Flecknoe, 1654, referring to Lord Exeter's observation that the world spoke kindly of none but people of the ordinary types. "There is no great danger," he writes, even of the latter escaping censure, "calumny being so universal a trade now, as every one is of it; nor is there any action so good they cannot find a bad name for, nor entail upon 't an ill intention; insomuch as one was so injurious to his mistress's beauty not long since to say,—she has more beauty than becomes the chaste."

A considerable portion of this year, 1606, was spent by the King's company in provincial travel. They were at Oxford in July, at Leicester in August, at Dover in September, and, at some unrecorded periods, at Maidstone, Saffron Walden, and Marlborough. Before the winter had set in they had returned to London, and in the Christmas holidays, on the evening of December 26, the tragedy of *King Lear*, some of the incidents of which were adopted from one or more older dramas on the same legend, was represented before King James at Whitehall, having no doubt been produced at the Globe in the summer of that year. No record of the character of its reception by the Court has been preserved, but it must have been successful at the theater for the booksellers, late in the November of the following year, made an arrangement with the company to enable them to obtain the sanction of the Master at the Revels for the publication of the tragedy, two editions of which shortly afterwards appeared, both dated in 1608. In these issues the author's name is curiously given in one line of large type at the very commencement of each title-page, a singular and even unique testimony to the popularity of a dramatic author of the period.

The poet's eldest daughter, Susanna, then in her twenty-fifth year, was married at Stratford-on-Avon on June 5, 1607, to John Hall, M.A., a physician who afterwards rose to great provincial eminence. He was born in the year 1575, and was most probably connected with the Halls of Acton, co. Middlesex, but he was not a native of that village. In his early days, as was usual with the more highly educated youths of the time, he had traveled on the continent, and attained a proficiency in the French language. The period of his arrival at Stratford-on-Avon is unknown, but, from the absence of all notice of him in the local records previously to his marriage, it may be presumed that his settlement there had not then been of long duration. It might even have been the result of his engagement with the poet's daughter. He appears to have, taken up his first Stratford abode in a road termed the Old Town, a street leading from the churchyard to the main portion of the borough. With the further exceptions that, in 1611, his name is found in a list of supporters to a highway bill, and that, in 1612, he commenced leasing from the Corporation a small piece of wooded land on the outskirts of the town, nothing whatever is known of his career during the lifetime of Shakespeare.

Shakespeare's company were playing at Oxford on September 7, 1607, and towards the close of the same year he lost his brother Edmund, who, on Thursday, December 31, was buried at Southwark, in the church of St. Saviour's, "with a forenoone knell of the great bell." It may fairly be assumed that the burial in the church, a mark of respect which was seldom paid to an actor, and which added very considerably to the expenses of the funeral, resulted from the poet's own affectionate directions; while the selection of the morning for the ceremony, then unusual at St. Saviour's, may have arisen from a wish to give some of the members of the Globe company the opportunity of attendance.

Edmund Shakespeare was in the twenty-eighth year of his age at the time of his death, and is described in the register as a player. There can be little doubt that he was introduced to the stage by the great dramatist, but, from the absence of professional notice of him, it may be concluded that he did not attain to much theatrical eminence.

Elizabeth, the only child of the Halls, was born in February, 1608, an event which conferred on Shakespeare the dignity of grandfather. The poet lived to see her attain the engaging age of eight, and the fact of his entertaining a great affection for her does not require the support of probability derived from his traditionally recorded love of children. If he had not been extremely fond of the little girl, it is not likely that he would have specifically bequeathed so mere a child nearly the whole of his plate in addition to a valuable contingent interest in his pecuniary estate. It appears, from the records of some chancery proceedings, that she inherited in after life the shrewd business qualities of her grandfather, but, with this exception, nothing is known of her disposition or character.

In the spring of the year 1608, the apparently inartificial drama of *Pericles* was represented at the Globe Theater. It seems to have been well received, and Edward Blount, a London bookseller, lost no time in obtaining the personal sanction of Sir George Buck, the Master of the Revels, for its publication, but the emoluments derived from the stage performances were probably too large for the company to incur the risk of their being diminished by the circulation of the printed drama. Blount was perhaps either too friendly or too conscientious to persist in his designs against the wishes of the actors, and it was reserved for a less respectable publisher to issue the first edition of *Pericles* early in the following year, 1609, an impression followed by another surreptitious one in 1611. As Blount, the legitimate owner of the copyright, was one of the proprietors of the first folio it may safely be inferred that the editors of that work did not consider that the poet's share in the composition of *Pericles* was sufficiently large to entitle it to a place in their collection. This curious drama has, in fact, the appearance of being an earlier production, one to which, in its present form,

Shakespeare was merely responsible for a number of re-castings and other improvements.

About the time that *Pericles* was so well received at the Globe, the tragedy of *Antony and Cleopatra* was in course of performance at the same theater, but, although successful, it did not equal the former in popularity. It was, however, sufficiently attractive for Blount to secure the consent of the Master of the Revels to its publication, and also for the company to frustrate his immediate design.

Almost simultaneously with the contemplated publication of the admirable tragedy last mentioned, an insignificant piece, of some little merit but no dramatic power, entitled *The Yorkshire Tragedy*, was dishonestly introduced to the public as having been "written by W. Shakespeare." It was "printed by R.B. for Thomas Pavier" in 1608, the latter being a well-known unscrupulous publisher of the day, but it is of considerable interest as one of the few domestic tragedies of the kind and period that have descended to us, as well as from the circumstance of its having been performed by Shakespeare's company at the Globe Theater. When originally produced, it appears to have had the title of *All's One*, belonging to a series of four diminutive plays that were consecutively acted by the company as a single performance in lieu of a regular five-act-drama. This was a curious practice of the early stage of which there are several other examples. *The Yorkshire Tragedy*, the only one of this Globe series now preserved, was founded on a real occurrence which happened in the spring of the year 1605,—one of those exceptionally terrible murders that every now and then electrify and sadden the public. A Yorkshire squire of good family, maddened by losses resulting from a career of dissipation, having killed two of his sons, unsuccessfully attempted the destruction of his wife and her then sole remaining child. The event created a great sensation in London at the time, and it is most likely that this drama on the subject was produced at the theater shortly after the occurrence, or, at least, before the public excitement respecting it had subsided. This is probable, not merely from the haste with which it was apparently written, but from its somewhat abrupt termination indicating that it was completed before the execution of the murderer at York in August, 1605. It appears to have been the criminal's professed object to blot out the family in sight of their impending ruin, intending perhaps to consummate the work by suicide, but he exhibited at the last some kind of desire to atone for his unnatural cruelty. In order to save the remnant of the family estates for the benefit of his wife and surviving child, he refused to plead to the indictment, thus practically electing to suffer the then inevitable and fearful alternative of being pressed to death.

It is not unlikely that the publisher of *The Yorkshire Tragedy* took advantage of the departure of Shakespeare from London to perpetrate his nominated fraud, for the poet's company were traveling on the southern coast about the time of its appearance. A few months later the great dramatist was destined to lose his mother, the Mary Arden of former days, who was buried at Stratford-on-Avon on September 9, 1608. He would naturally have desired, if possible, to attend the funeral, and it is nearly certain that he was at his native town in the following month. On October 16 he was the principal godfather at the baptism of the William Walker to whom, in 1616, he bequeathed "twenty shillings in gold." This child was the son of Henry Walker, a mercer and one of the aldermen of the town. It should be added that the King's Servants were playing at Coventry on the twenty-ninth of the last-named month, and that they acted in the same year upon some unknown occasion at Marlborough.

The records of Stratford exhibit the poet, in 1608 and 1609, engaged in a suit with a townsman for the recovery of a debt. In the August of the former year he commenced an action against one John Addenbroke, but it then seems to have been in abeyance for a time, the first precept for a jury in the cause being dated December 21, 1608; after which there was another delay, possibly in the hope of the matter being amicably arranged, a peremptory summons to the same jury having been issued on February 15, in the following year. A verdict was then given in favor of the poet for £6 and £1. 4s. costs, and execution went forth against the defendant; but the sergeant-at-mace returning that he was not to be found within the liberty of the borough, Shakespeare proceeded against a person of the name of Horneby, who had become bail for Addenbroke. This last process is dated on June 7, 1609, so that nearly a year elapsed during the prosecution of the suit. It must not be assumed that the great dramatist attended personally to these matters, although of course the proceedings were carried on under his instructions. The precepts, as appears from memoranda in the originals, were issued by the poet's cousin, Thomas Greene, who was then residing, under some unknown conditions, at New Place.

The spring of the year 1609 is remarkable in literary history for the appearance of one of the most singular volumes that ever issued from the press. It was entered at Stationers' Hall on May 20, and published by one Thomas Thorpe under the title of—*Shake-speares Sonnets, neuer before imprinted*,—the first two words being given in large capitals, so that they might attract their full share of public notice. This little book, a very small quarto of forty leaves, was sold at what would now be considered the trifling price of five-pence. The exact manner in which these sonnets were acquired for publication remains a mystery, but it is most probable that they were obtained from one of the poet's intimate friends who alone would be likely to have copies, not only of so many of those pieces but also one of *The Lover's Complaint*. However that may be, Thorpe,—the well-wishing *adventurer*,—was so elated with the opportunity of entering into the speculation that he dedicated the work to the factor in the acquisition, one Mr. W.H., in language of hyperbolical gratitude, wishing him every happiness and an eternity, the latter in terms which are altogether inexplicable. The surname of the addressee, which has not been recorded, has been the subject of numerous futile conjectures; but the use of initials in the place of names, especially if they referred to private individuals, was then so extremely common that it is not necessary to assume that there was an intentional reservation.

At the time that the *Sonnets* issued from the press the author's company were itinerating in Kent, playing at Hythe on May 16 and at New Romney on the following day. They were also at Shrewsbury at some unrecorded period in the same year, a memorable one in the theatrical biography of the great dramatist, for in the following December, the eyry of children quitted the

Blackfriars Theater to be replaced by Shakespeare's company. The latter then included Hemmings, Condell, Burbage, and the poet himself.

The exact period is unknown, but it was in the same year, 1609, or not very long afterwards, that Shakespeare and two other individuals either commenced or devised a law-suit bearing upon a question in which he was interested as a partial owner of the Stratford tithes. Our only information on the subject is derived from the draft of a bill of complaint, one that was penned under the following circumstances.—Nearly all the valuable possessions of the local college, including the tithes of Stratford-on-Avon, Old Stratford, Welcombe and Bishopton were granted by Edward VI, a few days before his death in 1553, to the Corporation, but the gift was subject to the unexpired term of a lease for ninety-two years which had been executed in 1544 by the then proprietors in favor of one William Barker. The next owner of the lease, John Barker, assigned it in 1580 to Sir John Huband, but he reserved to himself a rent charge of £27. 13s. 4d., with the usual power of reëntry in case of non-payment. The above-mentioned tithes were of course involved in this liability, but, when Shakespeare purchased a moiety of them in 1605, it was arranged that his share of that charge should be commuted by an annual payment of £5. An observance of this condition should have absolved the poet from further trouble in the matter, but this unfortunately was not the case. When the bill of complaint was drafted there were about forty persons who had interests under Barker's lease, and commutations of the shares of the rent-charge had only been made in two cases, that is to say, in those of the owners of the tithe-moieties. A number of the other tenants had expressed their willingness to join in an equitable arrangement, provided that it was legally carried out; but there were some who declined altogether to contribute, and hence arose the necessity of taking measures to compel them to do so, a few, including Shakespeare, having had to pay more than their due proportions to avoid the forfeitures of their several estates. The result of the legal proceedings, if any were instituted, is not known, but there are reasons for believing that the movement terminated in some way in favor of the complainants.

The annual income which Shakespeare derived from his moiety is estimated in the bill of complaint at £60, but this was not only subject to the payment of the above-named £5, but also to that of one-half of another rent-charge, one of £34, that belonged to the Corporation of Stratford. His net income from the tithes would thus be reduced to £38, but it was necessarily of a fluctuating character, the probability, however, being that there was a tendency towards increase, especially in the latter part of his career. It is most likely that he entered into an agreement each year with a collector, whose province it would have been to relieve him of all trouble in the matter, and pay over a stipulated amount. It is not probable that he himself visited the harvest field to mark, as was then the local practice, every tenth sheaf with a dock, or that he personally attended to the destination of each of his tithe-pigs.

The next year, 1610, is nearly barren of recorded incidents, but in the early part of it Shakespeare purchased twenty acres of pasture land from the Combes, adding them to the valuable freeholds that he had obtained from those parties in 1602. After this transaction he owned no fewer than a hundred and twenty-seven acres in the common fields of Stratford and its neighborhood. His first purchase consisted entirely of arable land, but although he had the usual privilege of common of pasture that was attached to it, the new acquisition was no doubt a desirable one. The concord of the fine that was prepared on the latter occasion is dated April 13, 1610, and, as it was acknowledged before Commissioners, it may be inferred that Shakespeare was not in London at the time. His company were at Dover in July, at Oxford in August, and at Shrewsbury at some period of the year which has not been recorded.

There are an unusual number of evidences of Shakespeare's dramatic popularity in the fallowing year. We now first hear of his plays of *Macbeth, The Winter's Tale, Cymbeline,* and *The Tempest.* New impressions of *Titus Andronicus, Hamlet,* and *Pericles* also appeared in 1611, and, in the same year, a publisher named Helme issued an edition of the old play of *King John,* that which Shakespeare so marvelously re-dramatized, with the deceptive imputation of the authorship to one W. Sh., a clear proof, if any were needed, of the early commercial value of his name.

The tragedy of *Macbeth* was acted at the Globe Theater, in April, 1611, and Forman, the celebrated astrologer, has recorded a graphic account of its performance on that occasion, the only contemporary notice of it that has been discovered. The eccentric Doctor appears to have given some of the details inaccurately, but he could hardly have been mistaken in the statement that Macbeth and Banquo made their first appearance on horseback, a curious testimony to the rude endeavors of the stage-managers of the day to invest their representations with something of reality. The weird sisters were personated by men whose heads were disguised by grotesque periwigs. Forman's narrative decides a question, which has frequently been raised, as to whether the Ghost of Banquo should appear, or only be imagined, by Macbeth. There is no doubt that the Ghost was personally introduced on the early stage as well as long afterwards, when the tragedy was revived by Davenant; but the audiences of the seventeenth century were indoctrinated with the common belief that spirits were generally visible only to those connected with their object or mission, so in this play, as in some others of the period, an artificial stimulus to credulity in that direction was unnecessary. It is a singular circumstance that, in Davenant's time, Banquo and his Ghost were performed by different actors, a practice not impossibly derived from that of former times.

A performance of the comedy of *The Winter's Tale*, the name of which is probably owing to its having been originally produced in the winter season, was witnessed by Dr. Forman at the Globe Theater on May 15, 1611. It was also the play chosen for representation before the Court on November 15 in the same year. Although it is extremely unlikely that Camillo's speech respecting "anointed Kings" influenced the selection of the comedy, there can hardly be a doubt that a sentiment so appropriate to the anniversary celebrated on that day was favorably received by a Whitehall audience. *The Winter's Tale* was also performed in the year 1613 before Prince Charles, the Lady Elizabeth and the Elector Palatine, some time before the close of the month of April, at which period the two last of the above-named personages left England for the Continent.

Among the performances of other dramas witnessed by Dr. Forman was one of the tragedy of *Cymbeline*, and although he does not record either the date or the locality, there can be little hesitation in referring the incident to the spring of the year 1611; at all events, to a period not later than the following September, when that marvelously eccentric astrologer died suddenly in a boat while passing over the Thames from Southwark to Puddle Dock. It may be suspected that the poet was in London at the time of that occurrence, for in a subscription list originated at Stratford-on-Avon on the eleventh of that month, his name is the only one found on the margin, as if it were a later insertion in a folio page of donors "towardes the charge of prosecutyng the bill in Parliament for the better repayre of the highe waies." The moneys were raised in anticipation of a Parliament which was then expected to be summoned, but which did not meet until long afterwards. The list includes the names of all the leading inhabitants of the town, so that it is impossible to say whether the poet took a special interest in the proposed design, or if he allowed his name to appear merely out of consideration for its promoters.

The comedy of *The Tempest*, having most likely been produced at one of the Shakespearean theaters in 1611, was represented before King James and the Court at Whitehall on the evening of November 1 in that year, the incidental music having been composed by Robert Johnson, one of the Royal "musicians for the lutes." The record of the performance includes the earliest notice of that drama which has yet been discovered. It was also acted with success at the Blackfriars Theater, and it was one of the plays selected early in the year 1613 for the entertainment of Prince Charles, the Lady Elizabeth and the Elector Palatine.

The four years and a half that intervened between the performance of *The Tempest* in 1611 and the author's death, could not have been one of his periods of great literary activity. So many of his plays are known to have been in existence at the former date, it follows that there are only six which could by any possibility have been written after that time, and it is not likely that the whole of those belong to so late an era. These facts lead irresistibly to the conclusion that the poet abandoned literary occupation a considerable period before his decease, and, in all probability, when he disposed of his theatrical property. So long as he continued to be a shareholder in the Globe Theater, it was incumbent upon him to supply the company with two plays annually. It may therefore, be reasonably inferred that he parted with his shares within two or three years after the performance above alluded to, the drama of *King Henry the Eighth* being, most likely, his concluding work.

Among the six plays above-mentioned is the amusing comedy of *The Taming of the Shrew*. Most of the incidents of that drama, as well as those of its exquisite induction, are taken from an old farce which was written at some time before May, 1594, and published in that year under the nearly identical title of *The Taming of a Shrew*. This latter work had then been acted by the Earl of Pembroke's servants, and was probably well known to Shakespeare when he was connected with that company, or shortly afterwards, for it was one of the plays represented at the Newington Butts Theater by the Lord Admiral's and the Lord Chamberlain's men in the June of the same year. The period at which he wrote the new comedy is at present a matter solely of conjecture; but its local allusions might induce an opinion that it was composed with a view to a contemplated representation before a provincial audience. That delicious episode, the induction, presents us with a fragment of the rural life with which Shakespeare himself must have been familiar in his native county. With such animated power is it written that we almost appear to personally witness the affray between Marian Hacket, the fat ale-wife of Wincot, and Christopher Sly, to see the nobleman on his return from the chase discovering the insensible drunkard, and to hear the strolling actors make the offer of professional services that was requited by the cordial welcome to the buttery. Wincot is a secluded hamlet near Stratford-on-Avon, and there is an old tradition that the ale-house frequented by Sly was often resorted to by Shakespeare for the sake of diverting himself with a fool who belonged to a neighboring mill. Stephen Sly, one of the tinker's friends or relatives, was a known character at

Stratford-on-Avon, and is several times mentioned in the records of that town. This fact, taken in conjunction with the references to Wilmecote and Barton-on-the-Heath, definitely proves that the scene of the induction was intended to be in the neighborhood of Stratford-on-Avon, the water-mill tradition leading to the belief that Little Wilmecote, the part of the hamlet nearest to the poet's native town, is the Wincot alluded to in the comedy. If—but the virtuous character of that interesting particle must not be overlooked—the local imagery extends to the nobleman, the play itself must be supposed to be represented at Clopton House, the only large private residence near the scene of Sly's intemperance; but if so, not until 1605, in the May of which year Sir George became Baron Carew of Clopton.

It was the general opinion in the convivial days of Shakespeare "that a quart of ale is a dish for a king." So impressed were nearly all classes of society by its attractions, it was imbibed wherever it was to be found, and there was no possible idea of degradation attached to the poet's occasional visits to the house of entertainment at Wincot. If, indeed, he had been observed in that village and to pass Mrs. Hacket's door without taking a sip of ale with the vigorous landlady, he might perhaps no longer have been enrolled among the members of good-fellowship. Such a notion, at all events, is at variance with the proclivities recorded in the famous crab-tree anecdote, one which is of sufficient antiquity to deserve a notice among the more trivial records of Shakespearean biography. It would appear from this tradition that the poet, one summer's morning, set out from his native town for a walk over Bardon Hill to the village of Bidford, six miles distant, a place said to have been then noted for its revelry. When he had nearly reached his destination, he happened to meet with a shepherd, and jocosely enquired of him if the Bidford Drinkers were at home. The rustic, perfectly equal to the occasion, replied that the Drinkers were absent, but that he would easily find the Sippers, and that the latter might perhaps be sufficiently jolly to meet his expectations. The anticipations of the shepherd were fully realized, and Shakespeare, in bending his way homeward late in the evening, found an acceptable interval of rest under the branches of a crab-tree which was situated about a mile from Bidford. There is no great wonder and no special offense to record, when it is added that he was overtaken by drowsiness, and that he did not renew the course of his journey until early in the following morning. The whole story, indeed, when viewed strictly with reference to the habits and opinions of those days, presents no features that suggest disgrace to the principal actor, or imposition on the part of the narrator. With our ancestors the ludicrous aspect of intoxication completely neutralized, or rather, to speak more correctly, excluded the thought of attendant discredit. The affair would have been merely regarded in the light of an unusually good joke, and that there is, at least, some foundation for the tale may be gathered from the fact that, as early as the year 1762, the tree, then known as Shakespeare's Canopy, was regarded at Stratford-on-Avon as an object of great interest.

In the year 1612 the third edition of *The Passionate Pilgrim* made its appearance, the publisher seeking to attract a special class of buyers by describing it as consisting of "Certain Amorous Sonnets between Venus and Adonis." These were announced as the work of Shakespeare, but it is also stated that to them were "newly added two love-epistles, the first from Paris to Helen, and Helen's answer back again to Paris;" the name of the author of the last two poems not being mentioned. The wording of the title might imply that the latter were also the compositions of the great dramatist, but they were in fact written by Thomas Heywood, and had been impudently taken from his Troia Britanica, a large poetical work that had appeared three years previously, 1609. "Here, likewise," observes that writer, speaking in 1612 of the last-named production, "I must necessarily insert a manifest injury done me in that worke by taking the two Epistles of Paris to Helen, and Helen to Paris, and printing them in a lesse volume under the name of another, which may put the world in opinion I might steale them from him; and hee, to doe himselfe right, hath since published them in his owne name; but as I must acknowledge my lines not worthy his patronage under whom he hath publisht them, so the author I know much offended with M. Jaggard that (altogether unknowne to him) presumed to make so bold with his name."

Although Heywood thus ingeniously endeavors to make it appear that his chief objection to the piracy arose from a desire to shield himself against a charge of plagiarism, it is apparent that he was highly incensed at the liberty that had been taken; and a new title-page to *The Passionate Pilgrim* of 1612, from which Shakepeare's name was withdrawn, was afterwards issued. There can be little doubt that this step was taken mainly in consequence of the remonstrances of Heywood addressed to Shakespeare, who may certainly have been displeased at Jaggard's proceedings, but as clearly required pressure to induce him to act in the matter. If the publisher would now so readily listen to Shakespeare's wishes, it is difficult to believe that he would not have been equally compliant had he been expostulated with either at the first appearance of the work in 1599, or at any period during the following twelve years of its circulation. It is pleasing to notice that Heywood, in observing that the poet was ignorant of Jaggard's intentions, entirely acquits the former of any blame in the matter.

In the course of this year the King's Servants are found playing at Folkestone, New Romney, and Shrewsbury; and early in the following one, 1613, the great dramatist lost his younger, most probably now his only surviving, brother, Richard, who was buried at Stratford-on-Avon on Thursday, February 4. He was in the thirty-ninth year of his age. Beyond the records of his baptism and funeral no biographical particulars respecting him have been discovered; but it may be suspected that all the poet's brothers were at times more or less dependent on his purse or influence. When the parish-clerk told Dowdall, in 1693, that Shakespeare "was the best of his family," he used a provincial expression which implied not only that its other members of the same sex were less amiable than himself, but that they were not held in very favorable estimation.

There is no record of the exact period at which the great dramatist retired from the stage in favor of a retreat at New Place, but it is not likely that he made the latter a permanent residence until 1613 at the earliest. Had this step been taken previously, it is improbable that he would, in the March of that year, have been anxious to secure possession of an estate in London, a property consisting of a house and a yard, the lower part of the former having been then and for long previously a haberdasher's shop. The premises referred to, situated within one or two hundred yards to the east of the Blackfriars Theater, were bought by the poet for the sum of £140, and for some reason or other, he was so intent on its acquisition that he permitted a considerable amount, £60, of the purchase-money to remain on mortgage. That reason can hardly be found in the notion that the property was merely a desirable investment, for it would appear to have been purchased at a somewhat extravagant rate, the vendor, one Henry Walker, a London musician, having paid but £100 for it in the year 1604. If intended for conversion into Shakespeare's own residence, that design was afterwards abandoned, for, at some time previously to his death, he had granted a lease of it to John Robinson, who was, oddly enough, one of the persons who had violently opposed the establishment of the neighboring theater. It does not appear that Shakespeare lived to redeem the mortgage, for the legal estate remained in the trustees until the year 1618. Among the latter was one described as John Hemyng of London, gentleman, who signs himself Heminges, but it is not likely that he was the poet's friend and colleague of the same name.

The conveyance-deeds of this house bear the date of March 10, 1613, but in all probability they were not executed until the following day, and at the same time that the mortgage was effected. The latter transaction was completed in Shakespeare's presence on the eleventh, and that the occurrence took place in London or in the immediate neighborhood is apparent from the fact that the vendor deposited the original conveyance on the same day for enrollment in the Court of Chancery. The independent witnesses present on the occasion consisted of Atkinson, who was the Clerk of the Brewers' Company, and a person of the name of Overy. To these were joined the then usual official attestors, the scrivener who drew up the deeds and his assistant, the latter, one Henry Lawrence, having the honor of lending his seal to the great dramatist, who thus, to the disappointment of posterity, impressed the wax of both his labels with the initials H.L. instead of those of his own name.

This Blackfriars estate was the only London property that Shakespeare is known for certain to have ever owned. It consisted of a dwelling-house, the first story of which was erected partially over a gateway, and either at the side or back, included in the premises, was a diminutive enclosed plot of land. The house was situated on the west side of St. Andrew's Hill, formerly otherwise termed Puddle Hill or Puddle Dock Hill, and it was either partially on or very near the locality now and for more than two centuries known as Ireland Yard. At the bottom of the hill was Puddle Dock, a narrow creek of the Thames which may yet be traced, with its repulsive very gradually inclined surface of mud at low water, and, at high, an admirable representative of its name. Stow, in his *Survay of London*, ed. 1603, p. 41, mentions "a water gate at Puddle Wharfe, of one Puddle that kept a wharfe on the west side thereof, and now of puddle water, by meanes of many horses watred there." It is scarcely necessary to observe that every vestige of the Shakepearean house was obliterated in the great fire of 1666. So complete was the destruction of all this quarter of London that, perhaps, the only fragment of its ancient buildings that remained to the present century is a doorway of the old church or priory of the Blackfriars, a relic which was afterwards built into the outer wall of a parish lumber-house adjoining St. Anne's burying ground.

The Globe Theater was destroyed by fire on Tuesday, June 29, 1613. The great dramatist was probably at Stratford-on-Avon at the time of this lamentable occurrence. At all events, his name is not mentioned in any of the notices of the calamity, nor is there a probability that he was the author of the new drama on the history of Henry VIII, which was then produced, the first one on the public stage in which the efforts of the dramatist were subordinated to theatrical display. It is true that some of the historical incidents in the piece that was in course of representation when the accident occurred are also introduced into Shakespeare's play, but it is not likely that there was any other resemblance between the two works. Among the actors engaged at the theater on this fatal day were Burbage, Hemmings, Condell, and one who enacted the part of the Fool, the two last being so dilatory in quitting the building that fears were entertained for their safety. Up to this period, therefore, it may reasonably be inferred that the stage-fool had been introduced into every play on the subject of Henry VIII, so that when Shakespeare's pageant-drama appeared some time afterwards, the prologue is careful to inform the audience that there was to be a novel treatment of the history divested of some of the former accompaniments. This theory of a late date is in consonance with the internal evidence. The temperate introduction of lines with the hypermetrical syllable has often a pleasing effect, but during the last few years of the poet's career, their immoderate use was affected by other dramatists, and although, for the most part, Shakespeare's meter was a free offspring of the ear, owing little but its generic form to his predecessors and contemporaries, it appears certain that, in the present instance, he suffered himself to be overruled by this disagreeable innovation.

When Shakespeare's *King Henry VIII* was produced, the character of the King was undertaken by Lowin, a very accomplished actor. This fact, which was stated on the authority of an old manuscript note in a copy of the second folio preserved at Windsor Castle, is confirmed by Downes, in 1708, and by Roberts, the actor, in a tract published in 1729, the latter observing,—"I am apt to think, he (Lowin) did not rise to his perfection and most exalted state in the theater till after Burbage, tho' he play'd what we call second and third characters in his time and particularly *Henry VIII* originally; from an observation of whose acting it in his later days Sir William Davenant convey'd his instructions to Mr. Betterton." According to Downes, Betterton was instructed in the acting of the part by Davenant, "who had it from old Mr. Lowin, that had his instructions from Mr. Shakespeare himself." There is a stage-tradition that, in Shakespeare's drama, as was also probably the case in all the old plays on the subject, the King's exclamation of *ha* was peculiarly emphasized. A story told by Fuller of a boy-actor in the part whose feeble utterance of this particle occasioned a colleague to warn him that, if he did not pronounce it more vigorously, his Parliament would never give him "a penny of money."

Shortly before the destruction of the Globe Theater in 1613, and in the same month of June, there was a malicious bit of gossip in circulation at Stratford-on-Avon respecting Mrs. Hall, Shakespeare's eldest daughter, and one Ralph Smith. The rumor was traced to an individual of the name of Lane, who was accordingly summoned to the Ecclesiastical Court to atone for the offense. The case was opened at Worcester on July 15, 1613, the poet's friend, Robert Whatcot, being the chief witness on behalf of the plaintiff. Nothing beyond the formal proceedings in the suit has been recorded, but there can be little doubt that Lane was one of those mean social basilisks who attack the personal honor of any one whom they may happen to be offended with. Slanderers, however, are notorious cowards. Neither the defendant nor his proctor ventured to appear before the court, and, in the end, the lady's character was vindicated by the excommunication of the former on July 27.

When itinerant preachers visited Stratford-on-Avon it was the fashion in those days for the Corporation to make them complimentary offerings. In the spring of the following year, 1614, one of these gentlemen arrived in town, and being either quartered at New Place, or spending a few hours in that house, was there presented by the municipal authorities with one quart of sack and another of claret. There is no evidence that Shakespeare participated in the clerical festivity, the earliest notice of him in this year being in July, when John Combe, one of the leading inhabitants, died bequeathing him the then handsome legacy of £5. It is clear therefore, that, at the time the will was made, there was no unfriendliness between the two parties, and that the lines commencing, "Ten-in-the-hundred," if genuine, must have been composed at a later period. The first two lines of that mock elegy are, however, undoubtedly spurious, and are omitted in the earliest discovered version of it, dated 1630, preserved at Thirlestane House. There is, moreover, no reason for believing that Combe was an usurious money-lender, ten per cent being then the legal and ordinary rate of interest. That rate was not lowered until after the death of Shakespeare.

The Globe Theater which had been rebuilt at a very large cost, had then been recently opened; and Chamberlain, writing from London on June 30, 1614, to a lady at Venice, says, "I heare much speach of this new playhouse, which is saide to be the fayrest that ever was in England."

In the autumn of the same year, 1614, there was great excitement at Stratford-on-Avon respecting an attempted enclosure of a large portion of the neighboring common-fields,—not commons, as so many biographers have inadvertently stated. The design was resisted by the Corporation, under the natural impression that, if it were realized, both the number of agricultural employees and the value of the tithes would be seriously diminished. There is no doubt that this would have been the case, and, as might have been expected, William Combe, the squire of Welcombe, who originated the movement, encountered a determined and, in the end, a successful opposition. He spared, however, no exertions to accomplish the object, and, in many instances, if we may believe contemporary allegations, tormented the poor and coaxed the rich into an acquiescence with his views. It appears most probable that Shakespeare was one of the latter who were so influenced, and that, among perhaps other inducements, he was allured to the unpopular side by Combe's agent, one Replingham, guaranteeing him from prospective loss. However that may be, it is certain that the poet was in favor of the enclosures, for, on December 23, the Corporation addressed a letter of remonstrance to him on the subject, and another on the same day to a Mr. Manwaring. The latter, who had been practically bribed by some land arrangements at Welcombe, undertook to protect the interests of Shakespeare, so there can be no doubt that the three parties were acting in unison.

It appears that Shakespeare was in the metropolis when the Corporation decided upon the expostulary letter of December 23, 1614, and that he had arrived there on Wednesday, November 16, almost certainly, in those days of arduous travel, spending the entire interval in London. We are indebted for the knowledge of the former circumstances to the diary of Thomas Greene, the town-clerk of Stratford-on-Avon, who has recorded in that manuscript the following too brief, but still extremely curious, notices of the great dramatist in connection with the subject of the enclosures:

> (a) Jovis, 17 Nov., my cosen Shakspeare comyng yesterday to towne, I went to see him how he did. He told me that they assured him they ment to inclose noe

a contingent reversionary interest, his wearing apparel, twenty pounds in money, and a life-interest in the Henley Street property, the last being subject to the manorial rent of twelve-pence. This limitation of real estate to Mrs. Hart, the anxiety displayed to secure the integrity of the little Rowington copyhold, and the subsequent devises to his eldest daughter, exhibit very clearly his determination to place under legal settlement every foot of land that he possessed. With this object in view, he settles his estates in tail male, with the usual remainders over, all of which, however, so far as the predominant intention was concerned, turned out to be merely exponents of the vanity of human wishes. Before half a century had elapsed, all possibility of the continuance of the family entail had been dispelled.

The most celebrated interlineation is that in which Shakespeare leaves his widow his "second-best bed with the furniture," the first-best being that generally reserved for visitors, and one which may possibly have descended as a family heir-loom, becoming in that way the undevisable property of his eldest daughter. Bedsteads were sometimes of elaborate workmanship, and gifts of them are often to be met with in ancient wills. The notion of indifference to his wife, so frequently deduced from the above-mentioned entry, cannot be sustained on that account. So far from being considered of trifling import, beds were even sometimes selected as portions of compensation for dower; and bequests of personal articles of the most insignificant description were never formerly held in any light but that of marks of affection. Among the smaller legacies of former days may be enumerated kettles, chairs, gowns, hats, pewter cups, feather bolsters, and cullenders. In the year 1642 one John Shakespeare of Budbrook, near Warwick, considered it a sufficient mark of respect to his father-in-law to leave him "his best boots."

The expression "second-best" has, however, been so repeatedly and so seriously canvassed to the testator's prejudice, it is important to produce evidence of its strictly inoffensive character. Such evidence is to be found in instances of its testamentary use in cases where an approach to a disparaging significance could not have been entertained. Thus the younger Sir Thomas Lucy of Charlecote, in a will made in the year

1600, bequeathed to his son Richard "my second-best horse and furnyture"; and among the legacies given by Bartholomew Hathaway to his son Edmund, in 1621, is "my second brass pott." But there is another example that is conclusive in itself, without other testimony, of the position which is here advocated. It is in the will, dated in April, 1610, of one John Harris, a well-to-do notary of Lincoln, who, while leaving his wife a freehold estate and other property, also bequeaths to her "the standing bedstead in the litle chaumber, *with the second-best featherbed I have, with a whole furniture therto belonging*, and allso a trundle-bedsted with a featherbed, and the furniture therto belonging, and six payer of sheetes, three payer of the better sorte and three payer of the meaner sorte." This extremely interesting parallel disposes of the most plausible reason that has ever been given for the notion that there was at one time some kind of estrangement between Shakespeare and his Anne. Let us be permitted to add that the opportunity which has thus presented itself of refuting such aspersion is more than satisfactory,—it is a consolation; for there are few surer tests of the want either of a man's real amiability or of his moral conduct than his incompetence, excepting in very special cases, to remain on affectionate terms with the partner of his choice. And it is altogether impossible that there could have been an exculpatory special case in the present instance.

The conjugal history of Shakespeare would not have been so tarnished had more regard been given to contemporary practices. It has generally been considered that the terms of the marriage-bond favor a suspicion of haste and irregularity, but it will be seen on examination that they are merely copies of the ordinary forms in use at Worcester. We should not inspect these matters through the glasses of modern life. For the gift of a bed let us substitute that of one of its present correlatives, a valuable diamond-ring for example, and we should then instinctively feel not only that the gift was one of affection, but that its isolation was most probably due to the circumstance of a special provision of livelihood for her being unnecessary. This was undoubtedly the case in the present instance. The interests of the survivor were nearly always duly considered in the voluntary settlements formerly so often made between husband and wife, but even if

further then to Gospell Bushe, and soe upp straight (leavyng out part of the Dyngles to the Field) to the Gate in Clopton hedge, and take in Salisburyes peece; and that they mean in Aprill to survey the land, and then to gyve satisfaccion, and not before; and he and Mr. Hall say they think ther will be nothyng done at all.

(b) 23 Dec. A hall. Lettres wryten, on to Mr. Maneryng, another to Mr. Shakspeare, with almost all the companies handes to eyther. I alsoe wrytte of myself to my cosen Shakspear the coppyes of all our actes, and then also a not of the inconvenyences wold happen by the inclosure.

(c) 9 Jan. 1614. Mr. Replyngham, 28 Octobris, article with Mr. Shakspear, and then I was putt in by T. Lucas.

(d) 11 Januarii, 1614. Mr. Manyryng and his agreement for me with my cosen Shakspeare.

(e) Sept. Mr. Shakspeare tellyng J. Greene that I was not able to beare the encloseing of Welcombe.

Greene was in London at the date of the first entry, and at Stratford at that of the second. The exact day on which the fifth memorandum was written is not given, but it was certainly penned before September 5. Why the last observation should have been chronicled at all is a mystery, but the note has a mournful interest as the register of the latest recorded spoken words of the great dramatist. They were uttered in the autumn of the year 1615, when the end was very near at hand.

Had it not been for its untimely termination, the concluding period of Shakespeare's life would have been regarded with unmixed pleasure. It "was spent," observes Rowe, "as all men of good sense will wish theirs may be, in ease, retirement, and conversation of his friends." The latter were not restricted to his provincial associates, for he retained his literary intimacies until the end; while it is clear, from what is above recorded, that his retirement to Stratford did not exclude an occasional visit to the metropolis. He had, moreover, the practical wisdom to be contented with the fortune his incessant labors had secured. He had gathered, writes his first real biographer, "an estate equal to his occasion, and, in that, *to his wish*," language which suggests a traditional belief that the days of accumulation had passed. In other words, he was one of the few who knew when to commence the enjoyment of acquired wealth, avoiding the too common error of desiring more when in full possession of whatever there is in the ability of money to contribute to happiness.

It is not likely that the poet, with his systematic forethought, had hitherto neglected to provide for the ultimate devolution of his estates, but, as usual, it is only the latest will that has been preserved. This important record was prepared in January, 1616, either by or under the directions of Francis Collins, a solicitor then residing at Warwick, and it appears, from the date given to the superscription and from some of the erasures in the manuscript itself, that it was a corrected draft ready for an engrossment that was to have been signed by the testator on Thursday, the twenty-fifth of that month. For some unknown reason, but most probably owing to circumstances relating to Judith's matrimonial engagement, the appointment for that day was postponed, at Shakespeare's request, in anticipation of further instructions, and before Collins had ordered a fair copy to be made. The draft, therefore, remained in his custody, his client being then "in perfect health," and taking no doubt a lively interest in all that concerned his daughter's marriage. Under such conditions a few weeks easily pass away unheeded, so that, when he was unexpectedly seized with a dangerous fever in March, it is not very surprising that the business of the will should be found to have been neglected. Hence it was that his lawyer was hurriedly summoned from Warwick, that it was not considered advisable to wait for the preparation of a regular transcript, and that the papers were signed after a few more alterations had been hastily effected. An unusual number of witnesses were called in to secure the validity of the informally written document, its draftsman, according to the almost invariable custom at that time, being the first to sign.

The corrected draft of the will was so hastily revised at Shakespeare's bedside, that even the alteration of the day of the month was overlooked. It is probable that the melancholy gathering at New Place happened somewhat later than March 25, the fourth week after a serious attack of fever being generally the most fatal period. We may at all events safely assume that, if death resulted from such a cause on April 23, the seizure could not have occurred much before the end of the preceding month. It is satisfactory to know that the invalid's mind was as yet unclouded, several of the interlineations that were added on the occasion having obviously emanated from himself. And it is not necessary to follow the general opinion that the signatures betray the tremulous hand of illness, although portions of them may indicate that they were written from an inconvenient position. It may be observed that the words, *by me*, which, the autographs excepted, are the only ones in the poet's handwriting known to exist, appear to have been penned with ordinary firmness.

The first interlineation, that which refers to Judith, was apparently the result of her marriage, an event considered as a probability on January 25, and shortly afterwards, that is to say in less than three weeks, definitely arranged. That the poet, as is so often assumed, was ignorant, in January, of an attachment which resulted in a marriage in February, is altogether incredible. It is especially so when it is recollected that the Quiney and Shakespear families were at least on visiting terms, and all residing in a small country town, where the rudiment of every love-affair must have been immediately enrolled among the desirable ingredients of the gossips' caldron. But there is evidence in the will itself that Shakespeare not only contemplated Judith's marriage, but was extremely anxious for her husband to settle on her an estate in land equivalent in value to the bequest of £150. He makes the failure of that settlement an absolute bar to the husband's life or other personal interest in the money, rigidly securing the integrity of the capital against the possibility of the condition being evaded so long as Judith or any of her issue were living. The singular limitation of the three years from the date of the will, not from that of the testator's decease, may perhaps be explained by the possibility of Thomas Quiney having a landed reversion accruing to him at the end of that period, such as a bequest contingent on his reaching the age of thirty. However that may be, it seems certain that the interlineated words, *in discharge of her marriage porcion*, must have reference to an engagement on the part of Shakespeare, one entered into after the will was first drawn up and before that paragraph was inserted, to give Judith the sum of £100 on the occasion of her marriage with Thomas Quiney. That event took place in their native town on Saturday, February 10, 1616. There was some reason for accelerating the nuptials, for they were married without a license, an irregularity for which, a few weeks afterwards, they were fined and threatened with excommunication by the ecclesiastical court at Worcester. No evidence, however, has been discovered to warrant the frequent suggestion that the poet disapproved of the alliance. So far as is known, there was nothing in the bridegroom's position or then character to authorize a parent's opposition, nor have good reasons been adduced for the suspicion that there was ever any unpleasantness between the married Quineys and their Shakespeare connections. Their first-born son was christened after the great dramatist, and they remained on good terms with the Halls. Judith, the first and one of the most prominent legatees named in the will, was a tenant-for-life in remainder under the provisions of that document, so there is not the least reason for suspecting that the partiality therein exhibited to the testator's eldest daughter was otherwise than one elicited by aristocratic tendencies. It is not likely that it was viewed in any other light by the younger sister, who received what were for those days exceedingly liberal pecuniary legacies, while the special gift to her of "my broad silver gilt bole" is an unmistakable testimony of affection. Shakespeare, in devising his real estates to one child, followed the example of his maternal grandfather and the general custom of landed proprietors. He evidently desired that their undivided ownership should continue in the family, but that he had no other motive may be inferred from the absence of conditions for the perpetuation of his own name.

Following the bequests to the Quineys are those to the poet's sister Joan, then in her forty-seventh year, and five pounds a-piece to his nephews, her three children, lads of the respective ages of sixteen, eleven, and eight. To this lady, who became a widow very shortly before his own decease, he leaves, besides there had been no such arrangements in this case, the latter would have been well provided for by free-bench in the Rowington copyhold, and by dower on the rest of the property.

It is curious that the only real ground for a belief in any kind of estrangement between them should not hitherto have been noticed, but something to favor that impression may be fancied to be visible in Shakespeare's neglect to give his widow a life-interest either in their own residence at New Place or in its furniture. However liberally she may have been provided for, that circumstance would hardly reconcile us to the somewhat ungracious divorce of a wife from the control of her own household. It is clear that there must have been some valid reason for this arrangement, for the grant of such an interest would not have affected the testator's evident desire to perpetuate a family estate, and there appears to be no other obvious design with which a limited gift of the mansion could have interfered. Perhaps the only theory that would be consistent with the terms of the will, and with the deep affection which she is traditionally recorded to have entertained for him to the end of her life, is the possibility of her having been afflicted with some chronic infirmity of a nature that precluded all hope of recovery. In such a case, to relieve her from household anxieties and select a comfortable apartment at New Place, where she would be under the care of an affectionate daughter and an experienced physician, would have been the wisest and kindest measure that could have been adopted.

It has been observed that a man's character is more fully revealed in a will than in any other less solemn document, and the experiences of most people will tend to favor the impression that nothing is so likely to be a really faithful record of natural impulses. Dismissing, as unworthy of consideration, the possibility of there having been an intentional neglect of his wife, it is pleasing to notice in Shakespeare's indications of the designer having been a conscientious and kind-hearted man, and one who was devoid of any sort of affectation. Independently of the bequests that amply provided for his children and sister, there are found in it a very unusual number of legacies to personal friends, and if some of its omissions, such as those of reference to the Hathaways, appear to be mysterious, it must be recollected that we are entirely unacquainted with family arrangements, the knowledge of some of which might explain them all. It has, moreover, been objected that "the will contains less of sentiment than might be wished," that is to say, it may be presumed, by those who fancy that the great dramatist must have been, by virtue of his art, of an æsthetic and sentimental temperament. When Mr. West of Alscot was the first, in 1747, to exhibit a biographical interest in this relic, the Rev. Joseph Greene, master of the grammar-school of Stratford-on-Avon, who made a transcript for him, was also disappointed with its contents, and could not help observing that it was "absolutely void of the least particle of that spirit which animated our great poet." It might be thought from this impeachment that the worthy preceptor expected to find it written in blank-verse.

The preponderance of Shakespeare's domestic over his literary sympathies is strikingly exhibited in this final record. Not only is there no mention of Drayton, Ben Jonson, or any of his other literary friends, but an entire absence of reference to his own compositions. When these facts are considered adjunctively with his want of vigilance in not having previously secured authorized publications of any one of his dramas, and with other episodes of his life, it is difficult to resist the conviction that he was indifferent to the posthumous fate of his own writings. The editors of the first folio speak, indeed, in a tone of regret at his death having rendered a personal edition an impossibility; but they merely allude to this as a matter of fact or destiny, and as a reason for the devolution of the task upon themselves. They nowhere say, as they might naturally have done had it been the case, that the poet himself had meditated such an undertaking, or even that the slightest preparations for it had been made during the years of his retirement. They distinctly assure us, however, that Shakespeare was in the habit of furnishing them with the autograph manuscripts of his plays, so that, if he had retained transcripts of them for his own ultimate use, or had afterwards collected them, it is reasonable to assume that they would have used his materials and not been so careful to mention that they themselves were the only gatherers. It may, indeed, be safely averred that the leading facts in the case, especially the apathy exhibited by the poet in his days of leisure, all tend to the persuasion that the composition of his immortal dramas was mainly stimulated by pecuniary results that were desired for the realization of social and domestic advantages. It has been frequently observed that, if this view be accepted, it is at the expense of investing him with a mean and sordid disposition. Such a conclusion may well be questioned. Literary ambition confers no moral grace, while its possession, as it might in Shakespeare's case, too often jeopardizes the attainment of independence as well as the paramount claims of family and kindred. That a solicitude in these latter directions should have predominated over vanity is a fact that should enhance our appreciation of his personal character, however it may affect the direct gratitude of posterity for the infinite pleasure and instruction derived from his writings.

One more section of the poet's will has yet to be considered, that solemn one which has been so frequently held to express the limits of his faith; but the terms in which the soul was devised were almost invariably those that were thought to reflect the doctrine of the prevailing religion, so that the opening clause is no more a declaration that he was a Protestant than is the bequest by his maternal grandfather, Robert Arden, of "my soul to Almighty God, and to our blessed Lady, Saint Mary, and to all the holy company of Heaven," a proof in itself that the last-named testator was a Catholic. Neither can it be determined that Shakespeare was one or the other from what is fancied to be the internal evidence on the subject afforded by his writings, for this has been the theme of innumerable essays with the result that the advocates for his Protestantism and those for his Catholicism are as nearly as may be on a level in respect to the validity of their inferences. Those who endeavor to ascertain a dramatist's own religious sentiments from the utterances of his characters,—each of whom should be to himself religiously true at the due moments of religious expression,—or from the variations in his mode of treating materials that had been dramatically fashioned by his predecessors, can only be successful amid the works of less impartial artists. With respect to allusions to facts that are dependent upon knowledge and become in that way a species of evidence, there is only one, the reference to evening-mass, which is of practical value in the enquiry; but this, assuming it to be as hopelessly incorrect as is generally represented, is either a casual oversight or due to the very little opportunity that the author could have had for becoming familiar with Catholic practice. And if the merciless rigor with which the Catholic ministrations were suppressed is fairly borne in mind, no heed will be given to arguments based on the resort of the Shakespeares to those of the governmental Church. The poet, moreover, was educated under the Protestant direction, or he would not have been educated at all. But there is no doubt that John Shakespeare nourished all the while a latent attachment to the old religion, and although, like most unconverted conformists of ordinary discretion who were exposed to the inquisitorial tactics of the authorities, he may have attempted to conceal his views even from the members of his own household; yet still, however determinately he may have refrained from giving them expression, it generally happens in such cases that a wave from the religious spirit of a parent will imperceptibly reach the hearts of his children and exercise more or less influence on their perceptions. And this last presumption is an important consideration in assessing the degree of credit to be given to the earliest notice that has come down to us respecting the character of Shakespeare's own belief,—the assertion of Davies that "he died a Papist." That this was the local tradition in the latter part of the seventeenth century does not admit of rational question. If the statement had emanated from a man like Prynne, addressing fanatics whose hatred of a stage player would if possible have been intensified by the knowledge that he was a Romanist, then indeed a legitimate suspicion might have been entertained of the narrator's integrity; but here we have the testimony of a sober clergyman, who could have had no conceivable motive for deception, in what is obviously the casual note of a provincial hearsay. An element of fact in this testimony must be accepted in a biography in which the best, in this instance the only, direct evidence takes precedence over theories that are based on mere credibilities. At the same time it is anything but necessary to conclude that the great dramatist had very strong or pronounced views on theological matters. If that were the case, it is almost certain that there would have been some other early allusion to them, and perhaps in himself less of that spirit of toleration for every kind of opinion which rendered him at home with all sorts and conditions of men,—as well as less of that freedom from inflexible preconceptions that might have affected the fidelity of his dramatic work. Many will hold that there was sufficient of those qualities to betray a general indifference to creeds and rituals, and, at all events, whatever there was of Catholicism in his faith did not exclude the maintenance of affectionate relations with his ultra-protestant son-in-law. There is nothing in the will, in the list of witnesses, in the monumental inscription, in selection of friends, in the history of his professional career, in the little that tells of his personal character,—there is nothing, in short, in a single one of the contemporary evidences to indicate that he ever entered any of the circles of religious partisanship. Assuming, as we fairly may, that he had a leaning to the faith of his ancestors, we may yet be sure that the inclination was not of a nature that materially disturbed the easygoing acquiescence in the conditions of his surrounding world that added so much to the happiness of his later days. With perhaps one exception. It is surely within the bounds of possibility that he gave utterance to that inclination in the course of his last illness, and that he then declined, almost in the same breath in which he directed the kindly remembrances to his fellow-actors, the offices of a vicar who preached the abolition of the stage, and regarded the writers of plays as so many Anti-Christs. This hypothesis would fully explain the currency of the tradition recorded by Davies, and at the same time meet the other conditions of the problem.

There was a funeral as well as a marriage in the family during the last days of Shakespeare. William Hart, who was carrying on the business of a hatter at the premises now known as the Birth-place, and who was the husband of the poet's sister Joan, was buried at Stratford-on-Avon on April 17, 1616. Before another week had elapsed, the spirit of the great dramatist himself had fled.

Among the numerous popular errors of our ancestors was the belief that fevers often resulted from convivial indulgences. This was the current notion in England until a comparatively recent period, and its prevalence affected the traditional history of the poet's last illness. The facts were these. Late in the March of this calamitous year, or, accepting our computation, early in April, Shakespeare and his two friends, Drayton and Ben Jonson, were regaling themselves at an entertainment in one of the taverns at Stratford-on-Avon. It is recorded that the party was a jovial one, and according to a late but apparently genuine tradition, when the great dramatist was returning to New Place in the evening, he had taken more wine than was conducive to pedestrian accuracy. Shortly or immediately afterwards he was seized by the lamentable fever which terminated fatally on Tuesday, April 23, 1616, a day, which, according to our present mode of computation, would be May 3. The cause of the malady, then attributed to undue festivity, would now be readily discernible in the wretched sanitary conditions surrounding his residence. If truth, and not romance, is to be invoked, were there the woodbine and sweet honeysuckle within reach of the poet's death-bed, their fragrance would have been neutralized by their vicinity to middens, fetid watercourses, mud-walls and piggeries.

The funeral was solemnized on the following Thursday, April 25, when all that was mortal of the great dramatist was consigned to his final resting-place in the beautiful parish-church of his native town. His remains were deposited in the chancel, the selection of the locality for the interment being due to the circumstance of its then being the legal and customary burial-place of the owners of the tithes.

The grave is situated near the northern wall of the chancel, within a few paces of the ancient charnel-house, the arch of the doorway that opened to the latter, with its antique corbels, still remaining. The sepulcher was covered with a slab that bore the fallowing inscription,—

> Good frend, for Iesvs sake forbeare
> To Digg The Dvst Encloased Heare;
> Bleste Be The Man That Spares Thes Stones,
> And cvrst be he that moves my bones.

—lines which, according to an early tradition, were selected by the poet himself for his epitaph. There is another early but less probable statement that they were the poet's own composition; but, at all events, it may be safely gathered that they originated in some way from an aversion on his part to the idea of a disturbance of his remains. It should be remembered that the transfer of bones from graves to the charnel-house was then an ordinary practice at Stratford-on-Avon. There has long been a tradition that Shakespeare's feelings on this subject arose from a reflection on the ghastly appearance of that receptacle, which the elder Ireland, writing in the year 1795, describes as then containing "the largest assemblage of human bones" he had ever beheld. But whether this be the truth, or if it were merely the natural wish of a sensitive and thoughtful mind, it is a source of congratulation that the simple verses should have protected his ashes from sacrilege. The nearest approach to an excavation into the grave of Shakespeare was made in the summer of the year 1796, in digging a vault in the immediate locality, when an opening appeared which was presumed to indicate the commencement of the site of the bard's remains. The most scrupulous care, however, was taken not to disturb the neighboring earth in the slightest degree, the clerk having been placed there, until the brickwork of the adjoining vault was completed, to prevent anyone making an examination. No relics whatever were visible through the small opening that thus presented itself, and as the poet was buried in the ground, not in a vault, the chancel earth, moreover, formerly absorbing a large degree of moisture, the great probability is that dust alone remains. This consideration may tend to discourage an irreverent opinion expressed by some, that it is due to the interests of science to unfold to the world the material abode which once held so great an intellect. It is not many years since a phalanx of trouble-tombs, lanterns and spades in hand, assembled in the chancel at dead of night, intent on disobeying the solemn injunction that the bones of Shakespeare were not to be disturbed. But the supplicatory lines prevailed. There were some among the number who, at the last moment, refused to incur the warning condemnation, and so the design was happily abandoned.

King Richard II

Preface

By Israel Gollancz, M.A.

THE EARLY EDITIONS

Richard II was first published, in quarto, in 1597, in which year it was entered on the Register of the Stationers' Company. The title-page of the First Quarto was as follows:

> The Tragedie of King Richard the Second, As it hath been publikely acted by the Right Honourable the Lord Chamberlaine his Servants, London. Printed by Valentine Simmes for Andrew Wise, and are to be sold at his shop in Paules Church Yard at the Signe of the Angel. 1597.[1]

A Second Quarto, with Shakespeare's name on the title-page, was published in 1597.

In the year 1608 a third Quarto appeared, "with new additions of the Parliament Sceane, and the deposing of King Richard, as it hath been lately acted by the Kinges Majesties servantes, at the Globe." The Fourth Quarto, a mere reprint of this, appeared in 1615.

The text of the play in the 1623 Folio was evidently derived from the Fourth Quarto, "corrected with some care, and prepared for stage representation.... In the 'new additions of the Parliament Sceane,' it would appear that the defective text of the Quarto had been corrected from the author's MS. For this part, therefore,

1. *Cp*. Facsimile editions of this and other Quartos by Messrs. Griggs and Prætorius.

the First Folio is our highest authority; for all the rest of the play the First Quarto affords the best text" (Cambridge Editors).

A Fifth Quarto was published in 1634, based for the most part on the text of the Second Folio (1633); its readings "in a few cases are entirely independent of previous editions."

THE NEW ADDITIONS

The subject of "the deposition of Richard II" was regarded with considerable suspicion towards the end of Queen Elizabeth's reign,[1] and the suppression of lines 154–318 in the first scene of the fourth act in the two editions of the play published during the Queen's lifetime must be taken in connection with certain well-known incidents:—(i) in 1599 Sir John Hayward was imprisoned for publishing his *History of the Life and Raigne of Henry the Fourth*, i.e. the story of the deposition of Richard II; (ii) in 1601, on the afternoon before the rebellion of Essex, Merrick, one of his adherents, "with a great company of others that afterwards were all in the action, had procured to be played before them the *Play of Deposing of King Richard the Second*. Neither was it casual, but a play bespoken by Merrick";[2] (iii) it is recorded how the Queen on one occasion, probably soon after the revolt of Essex, when Lambarde, the Keeper of the Records in the Tower, was showing her his rolls, suddenly exclaimed, on coming to the reign of Richard II:—"I am Richard II; know ye not that," and she told Lambarde how "this tragedy was played forty times in open streets and houses."[3]

PLAYS ON THE SUBJECT OF RICHARD II

(i) Merrick's play was in all probability not Shakespeare's, though it is singular that the actor who provided the play was a member of the Globe Theater, Augustine Philipps; the piece in question is described as "an obsolete tragedy" (*exoletam*

1. In 1596 a Papal Bull was issued against the Queen, inciting her subjects to rebellion.
2. Bacon's "*Declaration of the practices and treasons attempted and committed by Robert, late Earl of Essex, and his complices against her Majesty and her kingdom.*" *Cp.* also *State Trials*, p. 1445 (ed. 1809).
3. Nichol's *Progresses of Queen Elizabeth*.

tragoediam de tragica abdicatione regis Ric. II, according to Camden), and the players complained that "they should have loss in playing it, because few would come to it."[1] (ii) Dr. Simon Forman saw a play of Richard II, at the Globe, on April 30, 1611; it dealt with the tumult of Jack Straw and the death of the Duke of Gloucester, i.e., with earlier events of the reign; (i) and (ii) were possibly the first and second parts of a chronicle history of the whole reign of Richard II. (iii) In 1870 Mr. T. Halliwell printed, for the first time, from the Egerton MSS. (in the British Museum), "*The Tragedy of Richard II, concluding with the murder of the Duke of Gloster at Calais*"; Mr. Halliwell claimed that the play was composed before Shakespeare's; but this view has been rightly contested (*cp. New Shakespeare Society's Transactions*, April 10, 1885), and in all probability the production belongs to the end of the first quarter of the seventeenth century.

THE DATE OF COMPOSITION

The publication of the First Quarto in 1597 gives us one hint for the date of composition, which may be safely assigned to about the year 1593. A noticeable piece of external evidence is perhaps to be found in the second edition of Daniel's *Civil Wars*, published in 1595, which contains certain striking parallels with Shakespeare's play not found in the earlier version. The likeness may possibly be purely accidental; on the other hand, we know that Daniel was addicted to the vice of plagiarism.[2]

The relation of *Richard II* to Marlowe's *Edward II* (not earlier than 1590) throws valuable light on the date of composition. As regards versification, it is to be noted that Shakespeare broke

---

1. Prof. Hales considers it unlikely that there were two plays answering the same description "in the field" of the Globe—two plays dealing with the dosing years of Richard II (*Notes and Essays on Shakespeare*, p. 208).
2. *Cp.* "*Only let him more sparingly make use*
   Of others' wit, and use his own the more,
   That well may scorn base imitation."—
   Return from Parnassus.

   In the second play of the trilogy the author makes it quite clear that Daniel showed at times too palpably the influence exercised upon him by Shakespeare.

away from Marlowe's example, and in place of a rigid use of blank verse, made free use of rhyme: no less than one-fifth of *Richard II* is in rhymed verse. The proportion of rhyme cannot be taken as an absolute test in placing the piece: it may perhaps be due to an intentional experiment on Shakespeare's part to produce that "unity of lyrical effect" which is the play's most striking characteristic. In the avoidance of prose, however, the Marlowan precedent is still followed, as in the case of *Richard III* and *King John.* A general consideration of the metrical tests places *Richard II* between *Richard III* and *Henry IV, Romeo and Juliet* and *King John* belonging to nearly the same date. But in dramatic method, no less than in versification, Shakespeare's play shows resistance of Marlowe's influence, though the subject of *Richard II* may, as is very probable, have been suggested by the similar theme of *Edward II.*[1] "The reluctant pangs of abdicating royalty in *Edward II*" may have, in Charles Lamb's famous words, "furnished hints which Shakespeare scarcely improved in his *Richard II.*" Outwardly the two plays have much in common; in tragic pathos, arising from the collision of incident and character, as opposed to tragic horror, Shakespeare had left his predecessor far behind.

THE SOURCE OF THE PLAY

Shakespeare's main source for the historical facts of *Richard II* was Holinshed's *Chronicle of Englande, Scotland, and Ireland*; probably the second edition of the work published in 1586, which alone contains the withering of the bay-trees (II. iv. 8). Stowe's *Annals* (1580) seems to have supplied the story of Mowbray's career in Palestine (IV. i. 97). Other sources were used by Shakespeare, but they are unknown; neither Hall nor Holinshed stat—that the Bishop of Carlisle was committed to the custody of the Abbot of Westminster. On the whole, Holinshed has been carefully followed by Shakespeare; among the chief divergences are—(i) the re-creation of characters of the Queen,

1. It is perhaps worth while pointing out that the parallel of Edward and Richard is brought out by Hayward in his *History of Henry the Fourth*, where Richard's last words refer to his great-grandfather, King Edward the Second, "being in this manner deposed, imprisoned, and murdered," &c.

and Gaunt; (ii) the death-bed scene of Gaunt, and the deposition scene of Richard; (iii) the introduction of the gardener, the servant, and the groom; (iv) changes in historic time and place, etc. (*cp.* Riechelman's *Abhandlung zu Richard II und Holinshed*).

DURATION OF ACTION

The time of *Richard II.* covers fourteen days, with intervals; the historic period is from April 29, 1398, to the beginning of March, 1400, "at which time the body of Richard, or what was declared to be such, was brought to London" (*cp.* Daniel's Time-Analysis, *Trans. New Shakespeare Society*, 1877-79, p. 269).

Introduction

By Henry Norman Hudson, A.M.

The earliest notice that has been discovered of *The Life and Death of King Richard the Second* is an entry by Andrew Wise in the Stationers' Register, dated August 29, 1597. The same year was published a quarto pamphlet of thirty-seven leaves, with a title-page reading as follows: "The Tragedy of King Richard the Second: As it hath been publicly acted by the Right Honourable the Lord Chamberlain his Servants. London: Printed by Valentine Simmes for Andrew Wise, and are to be sold at his shop in Paul's Church-yard at the sign of the Angel. 1597." It will be observed that in this edition the author's name was not given. In 1598 another edition was put forth having the same title-page, save the announcement "By William Shakespeare." There was a third issue in 1608, the title-page varying thus: "With new additions of the Parliament Scene, and the deposing of King Richard. As it hath been lately acted by the King's Majesty's Servants, at the Globe. Printed by W.W. for Matthew Law, and are to be sold at his shop in Paul's Church-yard, at the sign of the Fox." In 1615 appeared a fourth edition with a title-page precisely the same as that of 1608, save that it lacks the printer's initials.

At the accession of James I in the spring of 1603, "The Lord Chamberlain's Servants" became "His Majesty's Servants;" so that the play was still in the hands of the same company. The "new additions" of 1608 are in Act iv. sc. 1, being a hundred and sixty-four lines, or about half the Act. In the folio of 1623 this play makes the second in the list of histories, has the acts and scenes regularly marked, wherein it differs from all the quartos, and appears in other respects to have been printed from the issue of 1615, with an occasional reference to some other authority. In the folio, however, several passages, comprising in all just fifty lines, are unaccountably omitted. Of these five editions, Mr. Collier, who has carefully collated them, pronounces the first, that of 1597, "beyond all dispute the most valuable for its readings and general accuracy;" and we concur with him therein.—The only other certain contemporary notice of this play is in Meres' *Palladis Tamia*, 1598, where he mentions it in witness of Shakespeare's excellence in Tragedy.

As to the date of the composition we have nothing firm to build upon other than what has been stated above. Malone assigned the writing to 1593, and Chalmers to 1596; though their reasons for doing so are either not given, or such that they had better been withheld. To our judgment, the internal evidence, the abundance of rhymes, the frequent passages of elaborate verbal trifling, the general smooth-flowing current of the verse, and the comparative uncompactness of logical texture, make strongly in favor of the earlier date. In all these respects a comparison of *Richard II* with the *First Part of Henry IV*, which latter, even as it now stands, could not have been written later than 1597, will, we think, satisfy almost any one that the former must have preceded by several years. And an argument of considerable force to that effect might be made out from another sort of evidence. The first four books of Daniel's *History of the Civil Wars*, three of which are wholly taken up with the closing passages of Richard's government and life, were originally published in 1595. Daniel was himself a star, not indeed of the first magnitude, nor, perhaps, of the second, but yet a star in that matchless constellation of wits contemporary with Elizabeth and James I, which has since made England the brightness of the whole earth. Shakespeare and Daniel are known to have been personally acquainted, and the latter was a man of too high and pure a taste not to have relished the offspring of his friend's unapproachable genius. Being, moreover, himself a writer of plays, and an aspirant for dramatic honors, it is scarce to be supposed that he would be away from the theater when "the applause, delight, the wonder of our stage" was making the place glorious with his "Delphic lines."

The poem and the play in question have several passages so similar in thought and language as to argue that one of the authors must have drawn from the other; though this of itself will by no means conclude which way the obligation ran. But there is another sort of resemblance more pertinent to the matter in hand. Shakespeare, in strict keeping with the scope and purpose of his work, makes the queen in mind, character, and deportment a full-grown woman, whereas in fact she was at the time only twelve years old, having been married when she was but eight;—a liberty of art every way justifiable in an historical drama, and such as he never scruples to take when the proper ends of dramatic representation can be furthered thereby. With Daniel, however, the plan of his work, no less than the bent of his mind, caused him to write for the most part with the historical accuracy of a chronicle, insomuch that the fine deep vein of poetry that was in him had not fair play, being overmuch hampered and clogged by the stiffness and rigidity of literal truth. Yet he makes a similar departure from fact in case of the queen, representing her very much as she is in the play;—a thing for which the only hint of authority has been discovered is a sentence in Froissart's description of the marriage: "As I have been informed, it was a goodly sight to see her behavior; for all that she was but young, right pleasantly she bare the port of a queen." The point, then, is, that such a departure from historical truth, however justifiable in either case, seems more likely to have been original in the play than in the poem: in the one it grew naturally from the purpose of the work and the usual method of the workman; in the other its cause appears to be rather in the force of example: in short, Shakespeare was more apt to do it, because, artistically speaking, it ought so to be; Daniel, because it had been so done with success. And it is considerable that Daniel pushes this divergence even further than Shakespeare; in which excess we may easily detect the influence of a model: for what proceeds by the reason and laws of art naturally stops with them; but in proceeding by the measure of examples and effects such is not the case; and hence it is that mere imitation is so apt to "overstep the modesty of nature." To all which if we add, what may be safely added, that both this and the other resemblances are such withal as would naturally result from the impressions of the stage, the whole seems to make at least something of probability for the point in question.

There was certainly one and perhaps two other plays in Shakespeare's time on the subject of Richard II. This we learn unmistakably from the *Diary* of Dr. Simon Forman. Under the date of April 30, 1611, he gives a particular account of a play called *Richard II*, which he had just seen at the Globe Theater. The leading events of the play as there stated are as follows: "How Jack Straw was suddenly stabbed at Smithfield Bars by Walworth, the mayor of London, and he and his whole army overthrown: How the duke of Gloucester and others, crossing the king in his humors about the duke of Ireland and Busby, were glad to fly, and raise a host of men; and when Ireland came by night with three hundred men to surprise them, they, being warned thereof, kept the gates fast, and would not suffer him to enter the castle; so he went back with a fly in his ear, and was afterwards slain in battle by the earl of Arundel: That when Gloucester and Arundel came to London with their army the king went forth to meet them, and gave them fair words, promising them pardon, and that all should be well, if they would discharge their army; and after they had done so, having bid them all to a banquet, he betrayed them, and cut off their heads, because they had not the pardon under his hand and seal: How the duke of Lancaster privily contrived to set them all by the ears, and to make the nobility envy the king, and mislike his government; whereby he made his own son king, which was Henry Bolingbroke: And how Lancaster asked a wise man whether himself should ever be king; and being told that he should not, but his son should, he hanged the man for his labor, lest he should speak thereof to others."

From this account it is clear the play could not have been Shakespeare's, though performed at the theater for which he had so long been used to write. It should be observed that Forman says nothing distinctly about the deposing of the king; which event he would hardly have failed to make special mention of, had it been represented in the play. This brings us to a strange matter of state that took place in the year 1601. In Lord Bacon's papers concerning "the treason of Robert, earl of Essex," we meet with the following statement, being a part of what was charged against Sir Gilly Merrick: "That the afternoon before the rebellion, Merrick, with a great company of others that afterwards were all in the action, had procured to be played before them *The Play of Deposing King Richard the Second.* Neither was it casual, but a play bespoken by Merrick. And not so only, but when it was told him by one of the players that the *play was old*, and they should have loss in playing it, because few would come to it, there were forty shillings extraordinary given to play it, and so thereupon played it was. So earnest he was to satisfy his eyes with the sight of that tragedy, which he thought soon after his lordship should bring from the stage to the state."

That this may have been the same play witnessed by Forman ten years later is indeed possible, but appears, to say the least, rather improbable. Whether, granting it not to have been that, it was Shakespeare's *Richard II*, or a third play on the same subject, that has not elsewhere been heard of, is a question not very likely to be solved. Malone conjectured that the "new additions" of 1608 formed a part of the play as originally written, but were left out of the first two quartos from fear of offending the queen, to whose ears the deposing of monarchs was a very ungrateful theme, especially after the part she had in deposing from both crown and life her enchanting and ill-starred kinswoman, the witty and beautiful Mary of Scotland. Her sensitive jealousy on this score appears in that Hayward all but incurred a prosecution in 1599 for his *First Part of the Life and Reign of King Henry IV*, wherein the deposing of Richard II was set forth. So that, allowing the deposition-scene to have been originally a part of Shakespeare's play, we have here sufficient reason for its being omitted in the printed copy of 1597. Nor do the new additions themselves yield any argument or indication of having been written at a later period than the rest of the play. All which being considered, it does not well appear but that Shakespeare's *Richard II* may have been the play referred to in the state paper quoted above. To this the chief, if not the only objection is, that the one there spoken of is called an "old play"; whereby, however, we need understand no more than that the play had lost the charm of novelty; a thing which, considering the marvelous fertility of the time in dramatic productions, might well enough come about in the course of four or five years. And it is worth remarking withal, that the players could afford to call the play an old one, since this gave them the chance of an extra forty shillings. So that, upon the whole, the objection in hand cannot pass for much. Our own judgment therefore is, though we claim nothing better than fragile probabilities for its basis, that Shakespeare's *Richard II* was written before 1595; that it was the play referred to in the trial of Essex and his accomplices; and that for reasons of state the deposition-scene was withheld from the press till some time after the accession of James I, when all apprehensions on that score were done away.

The leading events, the manners, and all the persons of this drama, except the queen, its whole substance, movement, and interest, are purely historical, with only such heightening of effect, such vividness of coloring, and such vital invigoration as poetry can add without anywise marring or displacing the truth of history; the Poet having entirely forborne that noble freedom of art in representative character, which elsewhere issued in such everlasting delectations as Faulconbridge and Falstaff. For the materials of *Richard II* Shakespeare need not have gone beyond the pages of Holinshed, and it is clear that he drew directly from this source. In the current of that writer's narrative, the quarrel of Bolingbroke and Mowbray strikes in so abruptly and unexpectedly, is so inexplicable in its origin and so teeming with great results, as to form naturally and of itself the beginning of the manifold national tragedy which ends only with the catastrophe of Richard III. The cause of that quarrel is hardly less obscure in the history than in the drama: it stands out almost as something uncaused, so that there was no need of going behind it; while at the same time it proves the germ of such a vast and varied procession of historical events and heroic passages, as to give it the highest importance. The following abstract of Holinshed's narrative will explain both the nature of the Poet's studies, and the use he made of them.

For some years the violence and weakness of Richard's government had been filling the state more and more with strifes and factions. Of late these contests had mostly resulted in the king's setting himself above the law, his ear being engrossed by upstarts and parasites, who still encouraged him in all sorts of outrages on the rights and liberties of the nation. At length his misgovernment grew to the point that all parties seemed likely to unite against him. In 1398, being the twenty-first year of his reign, the king held a Parliament at Shrewsbury, where sundry of the nobles showed their griefs to those by whom the king was misled, hoping that either they might thereby be induced to counsel him better, or else that he, knowing what evil report went of him, would mend his ways. But this likelihood of amendment was thwarted by a new quarrel that broke out between the dukes of Hereford and Norfolk, who had generally acted together in the preceding troubles. The issue proved that their confidence in each other had been but the seed-time of a most deadly enmity. During the Parliament at Shrewsbury Hereford accused Norfolk of certain disloyal words uttered in a talk lately had by them as they were riding together between London and Brainford; and, in further proof thereof, he challenged him to the field as a traitor to the king and the realm. The king, having heard the challenge and the reply, had both parties arrested in his name; whereupon the dukes of Lancaster, York, and Surrey undertook as pledges for Hereford; but Norfolk was not suffered to put in pledges, but order was given to have him safely kept at Windsor castle till such time as should be fixed upon for the trial.

The Parliament being dissolved, about six weeks after, on the day appointed, the king came to Windsor with the nobles and prelates, to hear find determine the cause between the two dukes. The appellant and defendant being sent for to come before him, he required them to grow to some agreement, assuring them of his readiness to pardon all that had been said or done amiss on either side; but they answered that it was not possible to have any peace or agreement betwixt them. The king then asked Hereford what it was that he demanded of Norfolk, and why they could not make peace together and become friends. Thereupon a knight stood forth and answered thus in Hereford's name: "Right dear and sovereign lord, here is Henry of Lancaster, duke of Hereford and earl of Derby, who saith, and I say for him, that Thomas Mowbray, duke of Norfolk, is a traitor to your royal majesty and your whole realm : likewise, that he hath received eight thousand nobles to pay the soldiers that keep your town of Calais, which he hath not done: furthermore, that he hath been the cause of all the treason contrived in your realm for the space of these eighteen years, and by his false suggestions and malicious counsels hath caused your uncle, the duke of Gloucester, to be murdered: moreover, that he will prove this with his body against the body of Norfolk within the lists." The king then waxing angry, and asking Hereford if these were his words, he replied,—"Right dear lord, they are my words, and hereof I require right, and the battle against him." Then stood forth another knight, and made answer for the defendant thus: "Right dear and sovereign lord, here is Thomas Mowbray, duke of Norfolk, who saith, and I say for him, that all which Henry of Lancaster hath said is a lie, and that he both has been and is a traitor against you, your crown, majesty, and realm. This will I prove, as becometh a loyal knight, with my body against his." The king then asked Norfolk if these were his words, and whether he had any more to say; and he answered for himself: "Right dear sir, true it is, that I received so much gold to pay your people of Calais, which I have done; and I avouch that the town is as well kept now as it ever was before, and that no complaint of me has ever been brought to you by any of that town. For the voyage that I made to France about your marriage, I never received any money of you, nor for the voyage that the duke of Aumerle and I made to Almaine, where we spent great treasure. Marry, true it is, that I once laid an ambush to slay the duke of Lancaster, who sitteth there; but he hath pardoned me for that, and there was good peace made betwixt us, for which I yield him hearty thanks. This is my answer; and I am ready to defend myself against my adversary: I beseech you therefore to have the battle against him in upright judgment." Then the king, after taking the advice of his council, caused the parties to be asked again if they would agree and make peace together, but they both flatly refused, Hereford throwing down his gage, and Norfolk taking it up; whereupon the king swore by St. John the

Baptist that he would never seek to make peace betwixt them again. The battle was ordered to take place at Coventry, upon St. Lambert's day, being the seventeenth of September, as some say, though writers differ much as to the time.

At the time appointed all the parties, in fine array and numerously attended, were at Coventry, where a sumptuous scaffold and royal lists were erected for the trial. The day before they should fight, Hereford came to the king to take leave of him; and early the next morning Norfolk did likewise. Hereford then armed himself in his tent, which was set up near the lists; but Norfolk put on his armor in a house between the gate and the barrier of the town. About the hour of prime Hereford made his appearance, mounted on a white courser, his trappings of green and blue velvet, richly embroidered with swans and antelopes of goldsmith's work. The constable and marshal demanding of him who he was, he answered, "I am Henry of Lancaster, duke of Hereford, and have come to do my endeavor against Thomas Mowbray, duke of Norfolk, as a traitor to God, the king, his realm, and me." Then, having sworn upon the Evangelists that his quarrel was just, he put up his sword, drew down his visor, made a cross on his horse, and with spear in hand entered the lists, dismounted, and sat down in a chair of green velvet, to wait the coming of his adversary. Soon after, the king entered the field in great triumph, accompanied by all the peers of the realm, and having above ten thousand armed men on the ground, lest some fray or tumult should arise among the nobles. When the king was seated, he had proclamation made, forbidding any one to approach or touch the lists upon pain of death, except such as were appointed to order the field. Then another herald cried,—"Behold here the duke of Hereford appellant, who has entered the lists to do his endeavor against the duke of Norfolk defendant, on pain to be found false and recreant." Meanwhile, Norfolk was hovering on horseback at the entrance of the lists, his caparisons being of crimson velvet, embroidered richly with lions of silver and mulberry trees. Having made oath that his quarrel was just, he entered the lists manfully, saying aloud, "God aid him that hath the right:" then, dismounting, he sat down in his chair, which was of crimson velvet, curtained with white and red damask. The marshal, having viewed their spears to see that they were of equal length, handed one to Hereford, and sent the other to Norfolk by a knight; and thereupon a herald commanded them in the king's behalf to mount, and address themselves to the battle. A trumpet being sounded, Hereford set forward bravely towards his enemy six or seven paces; but Norfolk had not fully started when the king threw down his warder to stop the combat. Their spears were then taken away from them, and they were remanded to their chairs, where they sat two hours, while the king and his counsel deliberated what order was best to be taken concerning them. The order finally hit upon was, that Hereford should within fifteen days go into exile, not to return upon pain of death till the end of ten years, unless he were repealed home by the king; and that Norfolk should likewise avoid the realm, and never return to England, nor approach the borders thereof on pain of death. This sentence being announced, the king called both parties before him, and made them swear they would never willingly meet nor keep company together in any foreign region; which oath they gave, and forthwith went into banishment.

These proceedings were soon followed by a further invasion of the rights and liberties of the people; the king growing more and more reckless in his misgovernment, and in giving effect to the counsels of his creatures and favorites. Meanwhile the duke of Lancaster having died, Richard forthwith seized into his own hands all his estates and revenues, which should have devolved to Hereford; and at the same time revoked the letters-patent before granted, whereby his attorneys might sue for the delivery of whatever possessions might fall to him, thus showing plainly that he meant no less than his utter undoing. Against this hard dealing all ranks of men cried out, and grew to a thorough hatred of the king. Hitherto the duke of York had borne things as patiently as he could, though some of them touched him very near, especially the death of his brother Gloucester, and the banishment of his nephew: but now, seeing that neither law nor equity could stand where the king's will was bent on any wrong purpose, he considered that the glory of his country must needs decay through the king's lack of wisdom, and his want of such as would faithfully admonish him of his duty. Divers other tyrannical outrages followed in quick succession, such as the forcing of some to lend large sums of money, with no securities but what were revocable at the king's pleasure; the compelling of others to put their hands and seals to blanks, wherein the king's officers might write whatsoever they listed: finally, many old, infirm, and sickly persons were apprehended and put in prison, and might not be discharged, unless they would justify themselves in single combat with their accusers, who for the most part were lusty, young, and valiant.

While such was the state of things in England, the king was certified that a flaming rebellion had broken out in Ireland. Having drawn together with all convenient haste a great power of armed men and archers, in the spring of 1399 he set sail from Milford for that country with two hundred ships, leaving his uncle the duke of York to act as regent in his absence. The duke of Aumerle was to have followed him forthwith with another fleet of an hundred sail; but he did not arrive till about two months after: whether this delay were through his own fault or not, he was greatly suspected of some evil purpose in being so much behind his time. However, what with the valor and the policy of Richard and his men, the wild Irish were soon tamed and reduced to obedience. Meantime divers of the nobility and local magistrates in England, seeing how the realm drew to utter ruin, and was not likely to recover while Richard reigned, devised with great care to send letters to Hereford, promising him all their aid and power, if he would expel Richard, as a man unfit for the office he bore, and take upon himself the government of his native land; all which he was not slow in consenting to. As soon as York was apprised of these designs, he called a council to advise what were best to be done; and their advice was to gather an army at St. Alban's, to resist the duke in his landing; but how vain was this their counsel appeared in that the most of those who came boldly protested that they would not fight against the duke, whom they knew to be evilly dealt withal. Thereupon the earl of Wiltshire, who was lord treasurer, Bushy, Bagot, and Green, perceiving that the commons would take part with Hereford, slipped away, leaving the regent and the chancellor to make what shift they could: Bagot fled to Chester, and thence into Ireland; the others to Bristol, hoping to be safe there. After hovering some time near the coast, and finding how the people were affected towards him, the duke landed about the first of July in Yorkshire, at a place called Ravenspurg, and with him not more than threescore persons; but he was so well received by the lords, knights, and gentlemen of those parts, that a great number of people were quickly assembled to further his cause. At Doncaster he met the earl of Northumberland and his son Henry Percy, to whom he swore that he would but claim the lands inherited from his father, and in right of his wife; promising, withal, that he would bring the king to good government, and remove from him the creatures who sustained him in his evil courses. Leaving Doncaster with a great army he came with all speed by Evesham to Berkley; and within three days all the royal castles in those parts were surrendered to him. At Berkley he found the duke of York, who, all his plans of defense having failed, had gone thither to meet the king at his coming from Ireland. The next day he passed onward, still gathering power at every step, towards Bristol, where Wiltshire, Green, and Bushy prepared to make resistance; but in this they were soon defeated, taken prisoners, found guilty of treason, and forthwith beheaded.

All this while the king was detained in Ireland, the seas being so tempestuous and the winds so contrary that he could not even hear any news of what was doing in England; and when, after the lapse of six weeks, he understood how Hereford was carrying all before him, instead of setting forth at once, he still lingered till all his ships should be ready for the passage; but sent over the earl of Salisbury to gather a power in Wales and Cheshire with all possible speed, that they might be ready against his arrival. The earl, landing at Conway, sent forth letters to the king's friends, to levy their people, and come quickly to assist the king; which they did most willingly, insomuch that within four days an army of forty thousand men were ready to march with the king, if himself had been there in person. But, he not appearing, a report began to prevail that he was dead; which so wrought with the Welchmen and others that Salisbury could barely induce them to wait fourteen days, to see if he would come; and at the end of that time, he not coming, they dispersed and went home. A few days after, the king, with the bishop of Carlisle, the dukes of Aumerle, Surrey, Exeter, and others, landed near Bark-loughly castle in Wales; and, learning how matters stood in England, he hastened on towards Conway, where Salisbury had been waiting for him. At first he went forward with good courage; but when he heard how all the castles were already in Hereford's hands, how the nobles and commons on all sides were fully bent to side with the duke against him, and how his trusty friends had lost their heads at Bristol, he became very sorrowful, and, utterly despairing of his own safety, he called his army together, and gave every man leave to go home. The soldiers besought him to be of good cheer, swearing to stand by him unto death; but this did not encourage him at all; and the following night he stole from the army with Carlisle, Surrey, Exeter, Sir Stephen Scroop, and a few others and went to Conway castle, where he found Salisbury, who was resolved to hold himself there, till he should see better times.

When the duke of Lancaster heard of the king's return, he hastened into Wales, and sent Northumberland to the king with four hundred lances and a thousand archers. The earl, having placed his men in ambush, pushed on with a small company to Conway, and by fair promises drew forth the king with a few attendants, and, before he suspected any danger, they were at the place where the ambush was laid; so that Richard was now entirely in his power, and there was no way but for him to go with them to Flint castle, which was already at Lancaster's disposal. The duke, being constantly informed of the earl's doings, came thither the next day, and mustered his army in sight of the king, who viewed them from the walls of the castle. Here again the earl was employed to manage affairs with the king. Finally the duke himself came to the castle, all armed, but stayed at the first gate, and sent for the king to come to an interview with him there; whereupon he came forth, with a few attendants, into the lower court of the castle, and sat down in a place prepared for him. As soon as the duke saw him, he showed a reverent duty, bowing his knee, and coming forward, till the king took him by the hand, and lifted him up, saying,—"Dear cousin, ye are welcome;" and he, humbly thanking him, said,—"My sovereign lord and king, the cause of my coming is to have restitution of my person, lands, and heritage, through your favorite license." To which the king answered,—"Dear cousin, I am ready to accomplish your will, so that you may enjoy all that is yours." Then, having drunk wine together, they mounted on horseback, and set out for London; whither they came after riding several days, the king not being even allowed all this while to change his apparel.

Shortly after, the duke sent out writs in the king's name for a Parliament which met September 13, 1399, at Westminster; whereupon many heinous acts of injustice and misgovernment, drawn up and digested into thirty-three articles, were charged upon the king. Then a committee of nobles, prelates, knights, and lawyers, being sent to Richard, got his hand to an instrument acknowledging his unfitness for the kingly office, resigning the crown and all belonging to it, and releasing all his subjects from their allegiance. The signature being given, Lancaster was then brought in presence, and the king, in token of what he had done, took the signet ring from his finger and put it on the duke's, and requested the bishops standing by to inform the Parliament of his voluntary resignation, and of the good will he bare towards his cousin of Lancaster, to have him for his successor to the throne. The instrument of resignation was afterwards accepted and ratified by both houses of Parliament; and finally a sentence was passed whereby Richard was solemnly deposed, and all men forbidden to pay him any kind of obedience. All which being done, the duke of Lancaster stood forth, and, after making the sign of the cross on his forehead and also on his breast, laid claim to the crown "in the name of the Father, and of the Son, and of the Holy Ghost."

Afterwards a conspiracy against King Henry's life was devised mainly by the abbot of Westminster, he being moved thereto, as was reported, chiefly because he had heard the king say many years before, that princes had too little, and priests too much. The abbot, having felt the minds of divers lords, and found them apt for his purpose, among whom were Exeter, Surrey, Aumerle, Salisbury, and the bishop of Carlisle, had them to a feast at his house, where they arranged to hold a tournament at Oxford, to engage the king to be present, and then to slay him suddenly while he was busy with the pastime. An indenture to that effect was signed and sealed by them, whereby they stood bound to each other, and they swore upon the Evangelists to be true and secret even to the point of death. When all things were ready, Exeter went to the king, earnestly desiring him to grace the occasion with his presence; which he readily promised to do, as Exeter was his brother-in-law. Their purpose was to restore the crown to Richard, who was yet alive; but their plot was disclosed to King Henry through the folly or the treachery of Aumerle; and most of the conspirators soon lost their heads for their pains. The knowledge how great danger he had thus escaped doubtless rendered the king more anxious than ever to have Richard put out of the way. He was relieved from this anxiety soon after.

This dry skeleton will show that the Poet followed the chronicler very closely in the events of the drama. Holinshed had not the art, (as indeed what modern historian has?) nor did it fall within his purpose, to give a special lifelike portraiture of the persons: yet in respect of these Shakespeare is, to say the least, equally true to history as in the events; still informing the bald diagrams of humanity with vital spirit and efficacy, and thus enabling us not so much to hear or read *about* the men of a former age, as to see them passing before us. Hints to that purpose there are indeed in the narrative; but these for the most part are so slight, and withal so overlaid with other matter, that perhaps no eye but Shakespeare's could have detected them and drawn forth their secret meaning. So that, looking through his eyes, we can now see things in the chronicler that we could by no means have discerned with our own. Thus, by a sort of poetical comparative anatomy, from a few fragments, such as would have escaped any perception less apprehensive and quick than his, he could reconstruct the whole order and complexion of characteristic traits and lineaments. And, which is very remarkable, the laws of fact appear to sit as easy upon him as those of imagination: with the prescribed scope of an unchangeable past he has all the freedom of reason: within the hard stiff lines of historical truth his creative faculties are as unstraitened and uncramped, they move with as much grace, facility, and spirit, as when owning no restraints but such as are self-imposed. Than which perhaps nothing could more forcibly approve the strength and rectitude of his genius. But then, in fact, his freedom here is much the same as in the world of pure fiction, because in either case it is the truth that makes him free.

It is probably on some such ground as this that Coleridge, speaking of *Richard II*, says he "feels no hesitation in placing it as the first and most admirable of Shakespeare's historical plays." For in all the qualities of a work of art, as an exhibition of intense dramatic power working on predetermined materials, it is inferior to several others, and is nowise comparable to the two parts of *Henry IV*. So that it excels the others only in that the Poet's creative powers are here strictly confined to the work of reproduction; whereas in the others, and especially in *Henry IV*, a part of their task lies in the producing of characters purely imaginary, though at the same time making them the vehicle of a larger moral history than would otherwise consist with the laws of dramatic reason and truth. And, indeed, it is in this sense that Coleridge himself assigns the first place to *Richard II*. And he rightly suggests that a drama is rendered historical, not merely by being made up of historical matter, but by the peculiar relation which that matter bears to the plot. For *Macbeth* has much of historical matter, yet is in no proper sense an historical drama, because the history neither forms nor directs, but only *subserves* the plot. Nor, on the other hand, does the having of much besides historical matter any-wise hinder a drama from being properly historical: ideal events and characters do not at all change the nature of the work, provided they be made to serve the truth of history, instead of overruling it. Which brings us to the distinction between *Richard II* and *Henry IV*. Both are in the strictest sense historical plays, the difference between them being that in the former the history makes the plot, but in the latter rather guides and controls it: in the one, history furnishes the whole matter and order of the work; in the other, it furnishes a part, and at the same time molds and governs whatsoever is added by the creative imagination.

Of course, Bolingbroke is the moving and controlling spirit of this play, the center and spring-head of the entire action. Every thing waits upon his firm-set, but noiseless potency of will, and is made alive with his most silent, all-pervading, inly-working efficacy of thought and purpose. For, though Richard be much the more prominent character, this is nowise as the mover of things, but only as the receiver of movements caused by another; the effects lighting upon him, while the worker of them is comparatively unseen and unheard. For the main peculiarity of Bolingbroke is that he looks solely to results, and, like a true artist and a skillful, as he is, the better to secure these, he keeps his designs and processes most carefully hidden: a thorough-paced politician, his policy, however, is emphatically an art, and he is far too deep and subtle therein to make use of any artifice; his agency thus being so stealthy and invisible, his power flowing forth so secretly, that in whatsoever he does, the thing seems to have done itself to his hand, and himself to have had no part in bringing it to pass. How intense his enthusiasm, yet how perfect, and how imperturbable his coolness and composure! so that we might almost ask,—"Was ever breast contained so much, and made so little noise?" And then how pregnant and forcible, always, yet how calm and gentle, and at times how terrible his speech! how easily and unconcernedly the words drop from him, and, therewithal, how pat and home they are to the persons for whom and the circumstances wherein they are spoken! as if his eyes burned itself a passage right straight to the heart of whomsoever he looked upon, and at the same time gave out the light whereby to read whatsoever was written there. To all which add a flaming thirst of power, a most aspiring and mounting ambition, and the result explains much of his character and fortune as developed in the subsequent plays wherein he figures. For the Poet keeps him the same man throughout. So that in this play we have, done to the life, though somewhat in miniature, what is afterwards drawn out and unfolded at full length,—the quick, keen sagacity, the firm, steady, but easy self-control, molding his whole action, and making every thing about him bend and converge to a set purpose;—a character hard and cold indeed to the feelings, but written all over with success; which has no impulsive gushes or starts, but all is study, forecast, design, and calm suiting of means to pre-appointed ends, every cord and muscle being subdued to the quality of his aim, and pliant to the working of his thought. And this perfect self-command is in great part the true secret of his strange power over others, making them almost as docile and pliant to his purpose as are the cords and muscles of his own body: so that, as the event proves, he grows great by their feeding, till he can compass food enough without their help, and, if they go to hinder him, can eat them up. The main points of his character are admirably put by Hazlitt, thus: "Patient for occasion, and then steadily availing himself of it; seeing his advantage afar off, but only seizing on it when he has it within his reach; humble, crafty, bold, and aspiring; encroaching by regular but slow degrees, building power on opinion, and cementing opinion by power."

With such an antagonist to ply him, it is no wonder that Richard's ricketty, unknit, jaunty nature soon goes to pieces. He is a man of large powers and good dispositions, but there is no concert, or composition, or reciprocity among them; for which cause he acts in each of them by turns, but never in all of them together: will, understanding, imagination, and conscience are all strong and vigorous in him, yet somehow they never grow to cohesion and unity, to be all in each and each in all; so that, though he often talks shrewdly and acts stoutly, yet he is never truly wise and strong in either. Hence, when he is stripped of power, and can no longer enact the tyrant, he forthwith turns philosopher, poet, and moralist, as if in revenge of his miscarriages as a prince, and to atone for his faults as a man. However, as soon as, in default of other resources, he betakes himself to these latter, whatever is excellent and amiable in his mind and character begins to come out, and henceforth he brings up wonderfully in our good opinion, insomuch that before the close we are fain to forget what he has done and been, and cannot choose but pity the misfortunes that have ennobled and endeared him; though we still have a strong undercurrent of suspicion that he is but flirting with the Muses and the Graces, to beguile the sense and memory of his follies and crimes; as men often fall to a special cherishing of virtuous thoughts and sentiments in order to delude themselves into a persuasion of their being the reverse of what their acts have proved them to be. At all events, his course yields shrewd argument that a sentimentalist is but a profligate without means, as faction is said to be tyranny out of office. Nevertheless, his redundancy of thought and fancy, though sometimes running into puerility and platitude, sheds a sort of perfusive and unifying eloquence over the whole play.

Coleridge seems to have dwelt with peculiar intentness on the character of Richard, and his statement thereof is proportionably apt and rich. "It is clear," says he, "that Shakespeare never meant to represent Richard as a vulgar debauchee, but a man with a wantonness of spirit in external show, a feminine *friendism*, an intensity of womanlike love of those immediately about him, and a mistaking of the delight of being loved by him for a love of him. The amiable part of his character is brought full upon us by the queen's few words, 'so sweet a guest as my sweet Richard;' and Shakespeare has carefully shown in him an intense love of his country, well knowing how that feeling would, in a pure historic drama, redeem him in the hearts of his audience. Yet even in this love there is something feminine and personal. With this is combined a constant overflow of emotions from a total incapability of controlling them, and thence a waste of that energy, which should have been reserved for actions, in the passion and effort of mere resolves and menaces. The consequence is moral exhaustion, and rapid alternations of unmanly despair and ungrounded hope, every feeling being abandoned for its direct opposite upon the pressure of external accident. And yet when his inward weakness appears to seek refuge in despair, and his exhaustion counterfeits repose, the old habit of kingliness, the effect of flatterers from his infancy, is ever and anon producing in him a sort of wordy courage which only serves to betray more clearly his internal impotence."

Comments

By Shakespearean Scholars

SHAKESPEARE'S KINGS

No! Shakespeare's Kings are not, nor are meant to be, great men: rather, little or quite ordinary humanity, thrust upon greatness, with those pathetic results, the natural self-pity of the weak heightened in them into irresistible appeal to others as the net result of their royal prerogative. One after another, they seem to lie composed in Shakespeare's embalming pages, with just that touch of nature about them, making the whole world akin, which has infused into their tombs at Westminster a rare poetic grace. It is that irony of Kingship, the sense that it is in its happiness child's play, in its sorrows, after all, but children's grief, which gives its finer accent to all the changeful feeling of these wonderful speeches:—the great meekness of the graceful, wild creature, tamed at last,—

Give Richard leave to live till Richard die!...

And as sometimes happens with children, he attains contentment finally in the merely passive recognition of superior strength, in the naturalness of the result of the great battle as a matter of course, and experiences something of the royal prerogative of poetry to obscure, or at least to attune and soften men's griefs.—Pater.

EXILE

The right assumed by sovereign power to trifle at its will with the happiness of others as a matter of course, or to remit its exercise as a matter of favor, is strikingly shown in the sentence of banishment so unjustly pronounced on Bolingbroke and Mowbray, and in what Bolingbroke says when four years of his banishment are taken off, with as little reason.

> How long a time lies in one little word!
> Four lagging winters and four wanton springs
> End in a word: such is the breath of kings.

A more affecting image of the loneliness of a state of exile can hardly be given than by what Bolingbroke afterwards observes of his having "sighed his English breath in foreign clouds"; or than that conveyed in Mowbray's complaint at being banished for life.

> The language I have learned these forty years,
> My native English, now I must forego;
> And now my tongue's use is to me no more
> Than an unstringed viol or a harp,
> Or like a cunning instrument cas'd up,
> Or being open, put into his hands
> That knows no touch to tune the harmony.
> I am too old to fawn upon a nurse,
> Too far in years to be a pupil now.—

How very beautiful is all this, and at the same time how very *English* too!—Hazlitt, *Characters of Shakespeare's Plays.*

RICHARD II

His effeminate outward beauty, which wins for him the title of "sweet lovely rose," is matched by a puerile grace of fancy that tinges the facts of life with an unreal, pseudo-poetic glow. Instead of grappling with its stern necessities, he takes an æsthetic delight in the situations which it provides. His whole attitude is that of an onlooker, a dilettante whose will has never been braced to mold and fashion circumstances; he is, as Dowden has summed it up, "an amateur in living, not an artist." Thus, on an occasion which requires the resolute exercise of authority, he is satisfied with making a grandiloquent comparison, while he suffers his command to be defied, and is forced to fix a day for the ordeal of battle between the rival lords. But in the lists at Coventry he gives more signal proof of impulsive weakness.

Before the combatants can close, he flings down his warder, stops the tourney, and banishes Bolingbroke for six years and Mowbray for life. This act, as Mowbray's son asserts at a later period in *Henry IV*, Part II, was the beginning of all the evils that befall him later:

> O when the king did throw his warder down,
> His own life hung upon the staff he threw,
> Then threw he himself down.

For Richard, alarmed at the popular manifestations in Bolingbroke's favor, sends to perpetual exile the man whom he loves, and who would have proved faithful to him, while he inflicts a lighter and yet exasperating penalty upon the aspiring lord whom he secretly fears.—Boas, *Shakspere and his Predecessors.*

THE QUEEN

The queen, even in the time of prosperity, was oppressed by a "nameless woe," and looked towards the future with a foreboding dread, i.e. with a conviction that Richard's unholy actions could lead only to misery; yet she has neither the energy nor the will to prevent that which was in her power. She is the partner of her husband's un-kingly extravagance, and, at the death-bed of old Gaunt, listens tacitly to his fruitless warnings, to Richard's insulting speeches, and to his command to seize the revenues and property of the duchy of Lancaster, therefore, she justly shares her consort's fate. Misfortune, however, raises both above their fate, and shows us the sparks of light which slumbered in Richard's originally noble nature. For he is not merely a weakly, shallow, and dissolute voluptuary, he is intelligent, rich in imagination, of strong but too excitable feelings, and of acute judgment (as is proved by his remarks upon young Bolingbroke, who had been banished); but his lively imagination blinds his judgment, the exuberance of his feelings overpowers his will.... He is devotedly fond of his wife, his friends and favorites, but his wife is like a weak and pliant reed, incapable of affording him support, and his friends are common, selfish flatterers, who only encourage him in his weaknesses and take advantage of his favor in the meanest and most selfish manner.—Ulrici, *Shakspeare's Dramatic Art.*

JOHN OF GAUNT AND THE DUKE OF YORK

The Duke of York is a good sketch, but in his senile bluster of words, and his weak reversal of them when any action is required, and in his soft yielding to fate, he is only a faded representation of what Richard, without his touch of genius, might have been as an old man. Even in his furious demand for his son's death as a pledge of his loyalty to Bolingbroke—a scene which is quite unworthy of Shakespeare—he is another image of the excess into which weakness of will is so often betrayed. His haste, his fury, his exaggerated defiance of natural feeling—how could a father ask the King to slay his son?—are nothing more than weakness desperately trying to convince itself that it is strong, a condition of soul into which Richard falls again and again. His loyalty, which is his religion, is first broken down by the iniquity of the King, yet in principle is retained. Then circumstance steals his principle away, and he joins Bolingbroke. Then he recovers his principle by transferring his loyalty to Bolingbroke. In a word, he is a very old man, and his words and acts are carefully studied from weak old age. The sketch may well be contrasted with that of Gaunt, who is as old a man, but who has not lost his will, his power, or his courage. He stays but a short time, only in two scenes, but we see him as if he were alive before us; one of the old school of Edward III; chivalrous, honorable, fit for the works and the trials of war, as fit as Richard was unfit for them; of deep experience in life, yet tender; rigid in justice even to blaming the King; honoring his own caste, yet loving the people; knowing his duties to them and pressing those duties on the King; loving his son, yet loving England more. Old and with trembling angers of age, as well as its sorrows; old and dying, but never truer, more valiant, more patriotic, and more sorrowful than in death. As we stand by his deathbed, we see the trouble of the land and presage the doom of Richard.—Brooke, *On Ten Plays of Shakespeare*.

The characters of old John of Gaunt and of his brother York, uncles to the King, the one stern and foreboding, the other honest, good-natured, doing all for the best, and therefore doing nothing, are well kept up. The speech of the former, in praise of England, is one of the most eloquent that ever was penned.—Hazlitt, *Characters of Shakespeare's Plays*.

THE DEATH OF JOHN OF GAUNT

The death scene of John of Gaunt is a dramatic invention, but Shakspeare has made an admirable historical use of it, by putting into the mouth of Lancaster, not only a dying man's prophecy of the ruin that is to follow Richard's riotous misrule, but also one of those magnificent poetic eulogies on England, by which the poet has fostered the national feeling of his countrymen. The misgovernment in Richard's reign grieves the spirit of the dying Lancaster; because remembering the splendor and the strength of his father's reign, he thinks of that small island England, as—

This royal throne of kings, this scepter'd isle,
This earth of majesty, this seat of Mars,
This other Eden, demi-paradise,
This fortress built by Nature for herself
Against infection and the hand of war,
This happy breed of men, this little world,
This precious stone set in the silver sea,
Which serves it in the office of a wall
Or as a moat defensive to a house
Against the envy of less happier lands,
This blessed plot, this earth, this realm, this England.

The remonstrance and the warnings of his dying uncle are of no avail to stop the headlong course of the king; they serve but to exasperate his royal pride.—Reed, *Lectures on English History as illustrated by Shakspeare.*

BOLINGBROKE

Of a totally reverse character to Richard's was that of Bolingbroke: cold, crafty, determined, persevering, designing, and treacherous; politically plausible, and insolently unjust; an oppressor with a heart of ice,—and there is no tyrant like that;—a demagogue, a traitor, and a violator of his oath. He swore by the tomb of his grandfather, Edward III (an impressive and solemn oath in that age), that he had no design upon the crown; yet, as it were, in the same breath, he assumed the prerogative of royalty, condemning to death the favorites of Richard; and in a few weeks after he deposed and imprisoned his relation and sovereign.—Clarke, *Shakespeare-Characters.*

The character of Bolingbroke is less elaborately wrought out, emphasizing by its very severity of outline and color the unsubstantial pageantry of Richard's mind. Every trait tends to heighten the contrast between the two,—a contrast hardly surpassed for subtlety and suggestiveness in the whole range of the Histories. Bolingbroke's astute compliance with the laws is pointedly opposed to Richard's reckless and insane defiance of law. He pursues his ends by constitutional forms, knows how to bide his time, uses violence only to vindicate justice, and controls while appearing to obey. The historical Bolingbroke was not averse from ruder methods. Shakespeare tells us nothing of the plot laid by him in June, 1397, in concert with Mowbray and Gloucester, to seize and imprison Richard, and his uncles York and Lancaster, and to put the rest of the council to death. His first step towards bringing Gloucester's murder home to the king is the cautious "indirection" of accusing his accomplice Mowbray. His return from banishment has an excuse as well as a pretext in Richard's flagrant confiscation of his inheritance. Once landed, he finds himself at the head of a national uprising which bears him by its own momentum to the throne; and he is already a king in power before he has put off the obeisances of the subject.—Herford, *The Eversley Shakespeare*.

INTERPRETATION OF THE PLAY

The best commentator on the character of Richard would be a great actor; and the same remark applies to other characters in this play. It is scarcely possible, in reading the play to oneself, to appreciate the exact feeling which dictates words that in literal acceptation are at variance with the feeling of the speaker. Henry speaks words of truth and repentance when he purposes to wash off his guilt in the Holy Land, and yet his speech is dictated by politic hypocrisy; precisely as at the commencement of the ensuing play he smoothly opens the council with happy words on the end of civil conflict, while he all the while has letters in his pocket and the messenger waiting his summons, to announce the contumacy of the Percies. The reader, or the spectator, must form his own judgment how far a character is to be understood as willfully deceiving others, or unconsciously deceiving himself; and the poet appears to desire to reduce the positive indications of insincerity to the lowest degree, and leave as much as possible to the sagacity of his audience, recognizing motive in the flow and rhythm of lines which in purport are at entire variance with these motives. Thus the hollow loyalty of the challenger, Bolingbroke, in the first act, is expressed, but not in words; by what he does not say it appears, rather than by what he does; or by what he says as betraying by tone and occasion, that it must be interpreted by reverse. I am inclined to think that this refinement is sometimes overwrought, even for the spectator, now the actors are gone who enjoyed the author's own instructions, or could dispense with them; but of course we cannot impeach Shakespeare, who wrote for the stage, for not considering a reader. The interpretation of many scenes can only be correctly obtained by the same study that an actor must give of his entire part, and that only an accomplished actor is capable of giving. His rendering and intonation of one scene is governed by those which he knows must follow, but that the reader for the first time is of course ignorant of, and gaining no aid from previous scenes, is unprepared for when they arrive. So refined is the finesse that I believe that, in some instances, the clue to the spirit of the speaker is only obtainable from the impression of the flow and rhythm of his words in actual recitation.

Simply on this account the purport of much of the first act of Richard II is obscure to the reader, and the difficulty is enhanced by the assumption of his familiarity with circumstances that perished for him with the earlier play; and if Richard II is ever to be successfully revived on the stage, I think that a chorus-prologue should recite these—but who shall write it?—Lloyd, *Critical Essays*.

THE GAGE

The glove then thrown down was popularly called "a gage" from the French, signifying a pledge, and in *Richard II*, Act IV, Sc. 1, it is so termed by Aumerle:

> There is my gage, the manual seal of death,
> That marks thee out for hell.

In the same play it is also called "honor's pawn." Thus Bolingbroke, Act I, Sc. 1, says to Mowbray:

Pale trembling coward, there I throw my gage,
Disclaiming here the kindred of the king;
And lay aside my high blood's royalty,
Which fear, not reverence, makes thee to except.
If guilty dread have left thee so much strength
As to take up mine honor's pawn, then stoop.

And further on, Act IV, Sc. 1, one of the lords employs the same phrase:

There is my honor's pawn;
Engage to the trial, if thou darest.

It is difficult to discover why the glove was recognized as the sign of defiance. Brand suggests that the custom of dropping or sending the glove, "as the signal of a challenge, may have been derived from the circumstance of its being the cover of the hand, and therefore put for the hand itself. The giving of the hand is well known to intimate that the person who does so will not deceive, but stand to his agreement. To shake hands upon it would not be very delicate in an agreement to fight, and, therefore, gloves may possibly have been deputed as substitutes."—Dyer, *Folklore of Shakespeare.*

King Richard III

Preface

By Israel Gollancz, M.A.

THE EDITIONS

The Tragedy of King Richard the Third was first printed in 1597, with the following title page—"The Tragedy of | King Richard the Third. | Containing, | His treacherous Plots against his brother Clarence: | the pittiefull murther of his innocent nephewes: | his tyranni-call vsurpation: with the whole course | of his detested life, and most deserved death. | As it hath been lately Acted by the | Right honourable the Lord Chamber- | laine his servants. | at London | Printed by Valentine Sims, for Andrew Wise, | dwelling in Paules Church-yard, at the | Sign of the Angell. | 1597. |"

This Edition, known as Q. 1, was reprinted more or less correctly in subsequent Quartos issued in the years 1598 (Q. 2), 1602 (Q. 3), 1605 (Q. 4), 1612 (Q. 5), 1622 (Q. 6), 1629 (Q. 7), 1634 (Q. 8); each of these issues followed its immediate predecessor, except in the case of the 1612-edition, which was printed from the Quarto of 1602: in the second and subsequent Quartos the name of the author (*By* William Shakespeare) was added.

The First and Second Folios give the title of the play as follows:

> The Tragedy of Richard the Third: with the Landing of Earle Richmond, and the Battell at Bosworth Field.

THE TEXT

The textual problems connected with *Richard the Third* are of a complicated nature, owing to the many differences between the Quarto version and that of the Folio. The main differences may be grouped under the following heads—(1) The Folio contains nearly 200 lines which are not found in the Quarto,[1] while the Quarto contains at least one notable passage not found in the Folio (IV, ii. 103-120); (2) it gives alterations of the Quarto, which could not have been intended by Shakespeare;[2] (3) in a great many cases it removes (a) gross and obvious metrical defects,[3] (b) imaginary metrical irregularities of the Quarto;[4] (4) it introduces a number of alterations to avoid repeating the same word;[5] (5) it often modifies "certain terms of phrase and use of words," which had evidently become obsolete, *e.g. which* is changed to *that; betwixt* to *between; thou wert* to *thou wast; yea* to *I* (*aye*)*; moe* to *more*, or *other; you* to *thou;* (6) there are besides certain minute verbal changes in the Folio, the reason for which is not so clear as in the previous cases, but probably in

---

1. *Viz.*:—I. ii. 16, 25, 155-167; iii. 116, 167-169; iv. 36, 37, 69-72, 115-116, 222, 266-269, 273, 275; II. i. 67; ii. 89-100, 123-140; III. i. 172-174; iii. 7, 8, 15; iv. 104-107; v. 7, 103-105; vii. 5, 6, 37, 98, 99, 120, 127, 144-153, 202, 245; IV. i. 2-6, 37, 98-104; iv. 20, 21, 28, 32, 53, 103, 159, 172, 179, 221-234, 276-277, 288-342, 400; V. iii. 27-28, 43.
2. *E.g.* "*Unmannered dog, standst thou when I command*" (I. ii. 39).
   "*Or let me die, to look on earth no more*" (II. iv. 65).
3. *E.g.* "*And when my uncle told me so he wept,*
   And pitied me, and kindly kissed my cheek;
   Bade me rely on him as on my father" (II. ii. 23-25).

   Cp. the Quarto version—
   "*And when he told me so, he wept*
   And hugg'd me in his arm, and kindly kissed my cheek
   And bade me rely on him as on my father."
4. *E.g.* "*I do remember me, Henry the Sixth,*" instead of "*As I remember, Henry the Sixth*" (IV. ii. 98); (i.e. *Henery the Sixth*).
5. *E.g.* "*Methought that Gloucester stumbled; and in stumbling* (Ff., *falling*)
   Struck me, that thought to stay him, overboard" (I. iv. 18).
   "*By heaven my heart* (Ff., *soul*) *is purged from grudging hate*
   And with my hand I seal my true heart's love" (II. i. 9).

most instances they are due to euphony;[1] (7) the stage-directions in the Folio are fuller and more accurate than those in the Quarto.

WHICH IS THE BEST AUTHORITY?

Critics are divided on this point, some championing the cause of the Quartos, others of the Folios; the chief representatives of the former party are the Cambridge Editors; of the latter James Spedding, Delius, Daniel, etc.

(i) According to the Cambridge Editors some such scheme as the following will best account for the phenomena of the text—

Where A_1 is the Author's original MS.; B_1 a transcript by another hand with some accidental omissions and, of course, slips of the pen. From this transcript was printed the Quarto of 1597, while A_2 is the Author's original MS. revised by himself, with corrections and additions, interlinear, marginal, and on inserted leaves; B_2 a copy of this revised MS., made by another hand, probably after the death of the Author, and perhaps a very short time before 1623. From B_2 the Folio text was printed; the writer of B_2 had perhaps occasionally recourse to the Quarto of 1602 to supplement passages which, by its being frayed or stained, had become illegible in A_2 (*v.* page x., Camb. ed.).

"Assuming the truth of this hypothesis," the Cambridge Editors conclude, "the object of an Editor must be to give in the text as near an approximation as possible to A_2, rejecting from F_1 all that is due to the unknown writer of B_2 and supplying its place from Q_1, which, errors of pen and press apart, certainly came from the hand of Shakespeare. In the construction of our text we have steadily borne this principle in mind, only deviating from it in a few instances where we have retained the expanded version of the Folio in preference to the briefer version of the

1. *E.g.*"*To bring* (Ff., *bear*) *this tidings to the bloody King,*" IV. iii, 22. "*The imperial metal circling now thy brow*" (Ff., *head*); IV. iv. 382.

Quarto, even when we incline to think that the earlier form is more terse, and therefore not likely to have been altered by its author.... Cæteris paribus, we have adopted the reading of the Quarto."

(ii) James Spedding, in an exhaustive essay on the subject,[1] contested this view, maintaining "that the text of the Folio (errors being corrected or allowed for) represents the result of Shakespeare's own latest version, and approaches nearest to the form in which he wished it to stand," that the First Quarto was printed without preparation for the press or superintendence by himself, and that he began to prepare a corrected and amended copy, but had not leisure to complete this new version.[2]

Delius anticipated Spedding in his inquiry[3] and came to an even more determined conclusion as regards the superiority of the Folio; according to him a nameless corrector had tampered with the original MS. before it went to the printer in 1597, while the true text appears in the Folio version.

Mr. Daniel (*Facsimile Reprint of Q. 1*) is also in favor of the Folio "as the basis of the text"; after a careful analysis of the early Quartos he comes to the conclusion that the Folio version was printed from a copy of Q. 6, altered "in accordance with the theatrical MS. which the transcriber had before him."

(iii) Surveying all the evidence, the present writer thinks it possible to take a somewhat neutral position; the partisanship of the two schools seems too determined in its devotion to the one text or the other. Whatever may be the history of the First Quarto it certainly goes back to the author's MS., probably abridged for acting purposes; but on the whole it is a careless piece of printing; whatever may be the history of the First Folio version, one can certainly trace in it the touch of a hand other than Shakespeare's;[4] the editor did his work with insufficient

1. *On the corrected edition of Richard III*, pp. 1-75, *New Shakspere Society's Transactions*, 1875-76.
2. *Ibid. v.* p. 190, where Spedding summed up his views, after considering Mr. Pickersgill's objections (pp. 77-124).
3. *v.* German Shakespeare Society's Year Book, Vol. VII.
4. *E.g.* "*My Lady Grey, his wife, Clarence 'tis she*
   That tempts him to this harsh extremity" (I. i. 64).

caution, though comparatively few changes for the worse are intentionally his; he probably had a Third or Sixth Quarto collated with an unabridged MS., ordering an untrustworthy assistant to correct the printed copy, and to add the omitted passages; subsequently he probably read through the whole, amending here and there, and not troubling to consult the MS. too often. Hence the genuineness of most of the added passages, and the doubtful character of so many of the smaller changes.

THE DATE OF COMPOSITION

Authorities are agreed in assigning *Richard III* to 1594 or thereabouts, relying mainly on the internal evidence of style, especially the manifest influence of Marlowe; in considering this influence it must be borne in mind that the play belongs naturally to the group of history plays dealing with the House of York, and links itself intimately to 2 *Henry VI*, and 3 *Henry VI*. Noteworthy Marlowan characteristics are the following—(a) Richard, like Tamberlaine, or Faustus, or Barabas, monopolizes the whole action of the Drama; (b) the characters of this play of passion seem intended, for the most part, merely to set off the hero's "ideal villainy"; (c) the absence of evolution of character in the hero; (d) the hero's consciousness and avowal of his villainy; (e) the tone of the play is often lyrical or epical rather than dramatic (*e.g.* the lamentation of the women, II. ii.; IV. i.); (f) blank verse is used throughout, while prose and the lyrical forms found in the earlier plays are conspicuously absent. The play of Richard III was evidently Shakespeare's experiment—his only experiment—in the Marlowan method of tragedy, but in one respect, at least, Shakespeare shows himself no blind follower of Marlowe; he weaves Nemesis into the play and shows its consummation in Richard's fall, hence the significance of Margaret's fateful presence, haunting the scenes like some prophetic Chorus of ancient Drama.

Q. 1. "*That tempers him to this extremity.*"
Q. 2. "*That tempts him to this extremity.*"
Q. 3. "*That temps him to this extremity.*"

Spedding held there is nothing to choose between the two lines, but there seems all the difference in the world between the Folio and Quarto reading.

In John Weever's *Epigrammes*, printed in 1599, but written in 1595, the 22nd Epigram, addressed *Ad Gulielmum Shakespeare*, mention is made of *Romeo* and *Richard* as well-known characters, and the reference is evidently to *Richard III*, and not to *Richard II*.[1] Possibly, too, the wooing of Estrild in the old play of *Locrine* is imitated, as Mr. Fleay (*Shakespeare Manual*) has suggested, from *Richard III*, I, ii.; *Locrine* was first printed in 1595.

THE SOURCE OF THE PLOT

Sir Thomas More's *Life of Richard the Third*, incorporated by Hall & Holinshed in their histories, is the ultimate source of the play. Shakespeare evidently used the second edition of Holinshed, copying a mistake which occurs only in that edition. The wooing of Queen Anne, as well as Queen Margaret's part, are, however, purely imaginary (*cp*. Courtenay's *Commentaries on the Historical Plays*, II. 60-117).

Possibly Shakespeare borrowed a few hints from an earlier play written before 1588, and published in 1594,—*The True Tragedie of Richard the Third*,[2] etc. To Dr. Legge's Latin play (acted at Cambridge before 1583) he certainly owed nothing.

There were several other plays on this subject, probably one, wholly or in part, by Ben Jonson (*vide* Henslowe's *Diary*, June 22, 1602), called *Richard Crookback*, and another, now lost, perhaps more intimately connected with Shakespeare's.

DURATION OF ACTION

The time of *Richard III*, as analyzed by Mr. Daniel (*New Shakespeare Society Trans*. 1877-79), covers eleven days represented on the stage; with intervals. The total *dramatic* time is probably within one month.

---

1. "*Romeo, Richard; more, whose names I know not.*"
2. Reprinted by *Shakespeare Society*, 1844, from the only perfect copy extant.—*N.B.*—In the old play we find "*A horse, a horse, a fresh horse*," also, Richard's reference to the ghosts of his victims "crying for revenge." The same Society printed *Richard's Vision*, a seventeenth century poem founded on Shakespeare's play, containing an interesting reference thereto.

Day 1. Act I. Sc. i., ii. *Interval.*

Day 2. Act I. Sc. iii., iv.; Act. II. Sc. i., ii.

Day 3. Act II. Sc. iii. *Interval*; for the journey to Ludlow.

Day 4. Act II. Sc. iv.

Day 5. Act III. Sc. i.

Day 6. Act III. Sc. ii.-vii.

Day 7. Act IV. Sc. i.

Day 8. Act IV. Sc. ii.-v. *Interval*; Richard's march to Salisbury.

Day 9. Act V. Sc. i. *Interval*; Richard's march from Salisbury to Leicester.

Day 10. Act V. Sc. ii., and first half of Sc. iii.

Day 11. Act V., second half of Sc. iii.

Day 12. Act V., second half of Sc. iii., and Sc. iv., v.

The *historic* time is from about the date of Henry VI's obsequies, May 1471 to the Battle of Bosworth Field, 22nd August 1485.

Introduction

By Henry Norman Hudson, A.M.

The earliest notice we have of this play is an entry in the Stationers' Register by Andrew Wise, dated October 20, 1597, and running thus: *The Tragedy of King Richard the Third, with the death of the Duke of Clarence*. The same year was published a quarto pamphlet of forty-seven leaves, the title-page reading as follows: "*The Tragedy of King Richard the Third; containing his treacherous plots against his brother Clarence, the pitiful murder of his innocent nephews, his tyrannical usurpation, with the whole course of his detested life, and most deserved death*: As it hath been lately acted by the Right Honourable the Lord Chamberlain his servants. At London: Printed by Valentine Simms for Andrew Wise, dwelling in Paul's Church-yard, at the sign of the Angel. 1597." In this edition the author's name was not given. The play was issued again in 1598, the title-page being the same, except the addition,—"By William Shakespeare," and the substitution of Thomas Creede for Valentine Simms. There was a third issue by the same publisher in 1602; which, though merely a reprint of the former, claimed in the title-page to be "newly augmented." By another entry at the Stationers', bearing date June 27, 1603, it appears that Wise transferred his right in the play to Matthew Law, who published a fourth edition in 1605, and a fifth in 1613. Three other issues of the same text are also known to have been made in quarto, the several dates being 1624, 1629, and 1634; and there is some reason to think that an edition was put forth in 1622, though no copy of that date is known to be extant.

Of these eight editions, all except the first two purport to be "newly augmented;" which, as the text was the same in them all, would seem to infer that the publishers understood the play to have received certain additions, and wanted to have it thought that their copies included them. Accordingly, in the folio of 1623 we have the text not only augmented, but in a multitude of cases slightly altered, thus showing that the play had been carefully revised by the author. The additions, amounting in all to more than a hundred and eighty lines, and in one place to fifty-five, will be pointed out in our notes, as they occur.—In the folio the heading of the play is,—*The Tragedy of Richard the Third, with the Landing of Earl Richmond, and the Battle at Bosworth Field*; and its running title is,—*The Life and Death of Richard the Third*. And the text is there set forth with reasonable care and accuracy, the divisions of acts and scenes being duly marked.

The evidences of revisal presented in the folio will doubtless be held a sufficient reason for adhering mainly to the text as there printed: in doing which we shall in many cases depart, as Knight, Collier, and Verplanck have done, from the text commonly received; this having been made up from the two copies, apparently on no steadier or better principle than editorial caprice. Malone, indeed, assigns, as the reason of his proceeding herein, that "the alterations were made, not by Shakespeare, but by the players;" but as he still keeps flying off every little while from the line to which this reason would bind him, we are apt to doubt whether he fully believed it himself. Steevens, on the other hand, thought the folio gave the better text; wherein he was certainly right, though his motive probably was, as usual, to contradict Malone. To point out all the variations of the folio from the quartos, would encumber our pages overmuch with notes. In a few instances single lines, omitted apparently by accident in the folio, are retained, as being needful, or at least helpful, to the sense. And in Act iv. sc. 2, a most spirited and characteristic piece of dialogue is wanting in the folio: why it should have been omitted is inconceivable; and the matter is such that no modern editor would think of leaving it out. As going to prove that the changes of the folio were made by Shakespeare himself, besides that the additions bear the stamp of no mind but his, it may be observed that those changes often consist but in the substitution of an epithet, of purpose, manifestly, to avoid a too frequent recurrence of the same word; which is just what one would naturally do in a cool review of what he had struck out in the full glow of inspiration. So that there need be no question about taking the folio as the standard text, and using the quartos to ascertain and rectify this, instead of using this as an occasional resort, to clear up what is dark, or fill out what is wanting in those.

The great popularity of *King Richard III* is amply shown in the number of editions called for, wherein it surpasses any other of the Poet's dramas. And the three later issues in quarto prove it to have been in good demand in a separate form some time after the folio collection had appeared. It was also honored above any of its fellows by the notice of contemporary writers: it is mentioned by Meres in his *Palladis Tamia*; Fuller, in his *Church History*, and Milton, in one of his political eruptions, refer to it as being already well known: and in Bishop Corbet's *Iter Boreale*, 1617, we have a quaint description of the author's host at Bosworth, which is exceedingly curious as witnessing both what an impression the play had made in the popular mind, and how thoroughly the character of Richard had become identified with Burbage, the great original performer of it:

Mine host was full of ale and history;
And in the morning, when he brought us nigh
Where the two Roses join'd, you would suppo
Chaucer ne'er made the Romaunt of the Rose.
Hear him: 'See you yon wood? there Richard lay
With his whole army. Look the other way,
And, lo! where Richmond in a bed of gorse
Encamp'd himself all night, and all his force:
Upon this, hill they met.'—Why, he could tell
The inch where Richmond stood, where Richard fell.
Besides what of his knowledge he could say,
He had authentic notice from the play;
Which I might guess by marking up the ghosts,
And policies not incident to hosts;
But chiefly by that one perspicuous thing,

Where he mistook a player for a king:
For when he would have said, 'King Richard died,'
And call'd, 'A horse! a horse!' he Burbage cried.

As to when the play was written, we have no certain external notice of an earlier date than the first entry in the Stationers' Register. Touching this point, however, an inference of some probability has been gathered from a passage in Weever's *Epigrams*, which, it would seem, must have been written in 1595, though not published till 1599. The writer is professedly enumerating the "issue" of "honey-tongued Shakespeare":

Rose-cheek'd Adonis, with his amber tresses,
Fair fire-hot Venus charming him to love her;
Chaste Lucretia, virgin-like her dresses,
Proud lust-stung Tarquin seeking still to prove her;
Romeo, *Richard*, more whose names I know not;
Their sugar'd tongues and power-attractive beauty
Say they are saints, although that saints they show not.

In this stupid euphuism we cannot be certain whether the author is referring to the *Richard III* or the *Richard II* of Shakespeare; for, though the epithet sugar'd would seem to point out the latter, nothing can be argued thence here, the writer is so little used to keep any sort of terms between the phrase and the matter. To the best of our judgment, the internal evidence of the play makes strongly for as early a date as 1593 or 1594: the general style, though rising somewhat above that of the *Second and Third Parts of Henry VI*, is strictly continuous with it; while the history and the characterization show it to have been written with the scenes of those dramas fresh in the author's mind. In Clarence's account of his dream, and in Tyrrel's description of the murder of the young princes, Shakespeare is out in his plenitude of poetical wealth; and the character of the hero is indeed a marvel of sustained vigor and concentrated activity: nevertheless, as a whole, the play evinces considerably less maturity of power, than *King Richard II*: in several cases there is great insubordination of the details to the general plan; as, for instance, in Richard's wooing of lady Anne and of Queen Elizabeth, which have an excess of dialogical epigram, showing indeed a prodigious fertility of resource, but betraying withal a sort of mental incontinence;

and where we quite miss that watchful judgment which, in the Poet's later dramas, tempers all the parts and elements into artistic symmetry and proportion.

It is certain that the history of Richard III had been made the subject of stage performance several years before it fell into Shakespeare's hands. A Latin drama, written by one Dr. Legge, was acted at St. John's College, Cambridge, some time before 1583. Sir John Harrington, in his *Apology for Poetry*, 1591, refers to this play, as one which would "have moved Phalaris the tyrant, and terrified all tyrannous-minded men." Besides, there was an English play on the same subject, entered at the Stationers', June 19, 1594, and published the same year, with a title-page running thus: *The True Tragedy of Richard the Third; wherein is shown the death of Edward the Fourth, with the smothering of the two young Princes in the Tower: With a lamentable end of Shore's wife, an example to all wicked women; and, lastly, the conjunction and joining of the two noble Houses, Lancaster and York*. Mr. Collier says "it was evidently written several years before it came from the press." As it is unlike any other relic of the kind, some account of it probably will not be deemed out of place. The following is an abridgment of the one given by Mr. Collier:

The opening consists of a singular dialogue between Truth and Poetry; after which, the ghost of Clarence having passed over the stage, and made a short speech in its passage, Truth proceeds to deliver the argument of the play. Thus much by way of introduction; whereupon the drama itself begins with a scene representing the death of Edward IV. Thenceforth the story is most clumsily conducted, with characters ill-sustained, and with a total disregard of dates, facts, and places, Shore's wife playing a conspicuous part, and the representation being drawn out long after the battle of Bosworth Field. Richard having been killed, Report enters, and holds a dialogue with a Page, to give information of divers things not exhibited. Then follows a long scene between Richmond, his mother, and the Princess Elizabeth; after which two Messengers come in, and reel off what is to be done and who is to reign, all the way from Richard to Queen Elizabeth, the whole winding up with an elaborate panegyric on the latter. As to the composition of this unique performance, it is written partly in prose and partly in heavy blank-verse, duly interspersed with ten-syllable rhyming couplets and stanzas, and with specimens of the long fourteen-syllable meter.

There are but two instances wherein Shakespeare has with any likelihood been traced to the *True Tragedy*; and in those the resemblance is not such as to infer any more knowledge of the old play than might well enough have been caught in the hearing. Other resemblances there are indeed, but only such as would naturally result from using a common authority; as where Richard opens his breast so freely to the Page concerning the fittest person to be employed about the murdering of the princes. In all other points, whether of conception or of execution, the two plays will bear no comparison; and, save in the way of historical account, one almost had need to ask pardon for naming them together.

The closeness of connection between this play and *The Third Part of Henry VI* is so evident as to leave no occasion for tracing it out. At the very opening of the one we have Richard flouting and snarling in soliloquy at the "stately triumphs" and "mirthful comic shows," with which, at the close of the other, King Edward had proposed to celebrate the final and full establishment of his cause. And it was fitting, no doubt, that on Richard's first appearance as a dramatic hero, we should overhear him at his old practice of ruminating aloud, and thus familiarizing his thoughts in solitude with the villainy which he has in purpose to act. Of course everybody knows that Colley Cibber, being seized with a fit of progress, took upon him to reform Shakespeare's *King Richard III* into fitness for the uses of the stage; and that, as the play in its original shape was too long for representation, his mode of retrenching it within the proper compass was, in part, by transporting into it a scene or two from the foregoing play. From which we may conclude that Cibber saw there was such a continuity of matter and style in the two plays as might well enough admit of their being drawn into one; though, as would seem, he did not perceive the absurdity of setting the catastrophe of one play at the beginning of another. How his mind should have been so taken up with that continuity as to overlook this absurdity, is a question for those to meet, who maintain, with

Malone, that the two plays were not originally by the same hand. For the scene where Richard murders Henry in the Tower is among those parts of the preceding play, which, as was shown near the close of the sixth volume, were least altered from their original state.

Historically considered, the play in hand embraces a period of more than fourteen years, from the death of Henry, May, 1471, till the fall of Richard, August, 1585. Half of this period, however, is despatched in the first act; the funeral of Henry, the marriage of Richard with lady Anne, and the death of Clarence being represented as occurring all about the same time, whereas in fact they were separated by considerable intervals, and the latter did not take place till February, 1478. And there is a similar abridgment, or rather overleaping of time between the first act and the second, as the latter opens with the sickness of Edward, his seeming reconciliation of the peers, and his death, all which took place in April, 1483, thus leaving but two years and four months for the rest of the play. This drawing together of the scattered events seems eminently judicious: for the plan of the drama required no use to be made of them but as subsidiary to the hero's character; and it does not appear how the Poet could have ordered them better, so as to develop in the most forcible manner his idea of that extraordinary man. So that the selection and grouping of the secondary incidents are strictly regulated by the paramount law of the work; and, certainly, they are made to tell with masterly effect in furtherance of the author's purpose.

After the death of Edward IV the events of the drama are disposed for the most part in the order of their actual occurrence. Thenceforward the representation in all its main points is founded directly on the narrative of Sir Thomas More, as it had been given at full length in the *Chronicles* of Hall and Holinshed; the drama being perhaps as true to the history as were practicable or desirable in a work so different in its nature and use. Perhaps it should be observed, however, that More's narrative only comes down to the revolt of Buckingham; after which the account given by Hall, and copied by Holinshed, was made up from other sources. So that More's *History* furnished the basis of the most characteristic passages of the play. What esteem his narrative was held in at that time is testified by Sir John Harrington, in his *Metamorphosis of Ajax*, 1596, thus: "The best part of our *Chronicles*, in all men's opinion, is that of Richard the Third, written, as I have heard, by Morton, but as most suppose, by Sir Thomas More."

Since Shakespeare's time, much has been written to explode the current history of Richard, and to lessen, if not remove, the abhorrence in which his memory had come to be held. The Poet has not been left without his share of criticism and censure for the alleged blackening of his dramatic hero. This attempt at reforming public opinion was led off by Sir George Buck, whose *History of Richard III* was published in 1646. The general drift of his book is thus indicated by Fuller in his *Church History*, who is himself high authority on the matters in question: "He eveneth Richard's shoulders, smootheth his back, planeth his teeth, maketh him in all points a comely and beautiful person. Nor stoppeth he here, but, proceeding from his naturals to his morals, maketh him as virtuous as handsome; concealing most, denying some, defending others of his foulest acts, wherewith in all ages since he standeth charged on record. For mine own part, I confess it no heresy to maintain a paradox in history; nor am I such an enemy to wit as not to allow it leave harmlessly to disport itself for its own content, and the delight of others. But when men do it cordially, in sober sadness, to pervert people's judgments, and therein go against all received records, I say that singularity is the least fault that can be laid to such men's charges. Besides, there are some birds, sea-pies by name, who cannot rise except it be by flying against the wind; as some hope to achieve their advancement by being contrary and paradoxical to all before them."

Something more than a century later, the same work was resumed and carried on with great acuteness and ingenuity by Horace Walpole in his *Historic Doubts*, which, however, in the opinion of Campbell, "are themselves subject to doubts." Also, Carte, Laing, and, in our own day, Caroline A. Halsted have put their hands to the same work. Still the old judgment seems likely to stand, the main substance thereof not having been much shaken yet. Dr. Lingard has carried to the subject his usual candor and research, and, after despatching the strong points urged on the other side, winds up his account of Richard thus: "Writers have indeed in modern times attempted to prove his innocence; but their arguments are rather ingenious than conclusive, and dwindle into groundless conjectures when confronted with the evidence which may be arrayed against them." Of course the killing of the two princes formed the backbone of the guilt laid at his door. That they did actually disappear, is tolerably certain; that upon him fell whatsoever advantage could grow from their death, is equally so; and it is for those who deny the cause uniformly assigned at the time and long after for their disappearance, to tell us how and by whom they were put out of the way. And Sharon Turner, who is perhaps the severest of all sifters of historical fictions and fables, is constrained to admit the murder of his nephews, however he may seem to succeed in washing off his other blood-stains; and so long as this remains, the scouring of others, if it diminish his crimes, will hardly lighten his criminality.

But even if Shakespeare's representation were proved to be essentially untrue to Richard as he was in himself and in his life, still this would nowise touch the standing of the work as a dramatic reproduction of historical matter. For the Poet's vindication on this score, it sufficeth that his Richard, so far at least as regards the moral complexion of the man, is substantially the Richard of the chroniclers, and of all the historical authorities that were received and studied in his time. Besides, to satisfy the nice scruples and queries of historic doubters and dialecticians, is no part of the poet's business: his concern is not with truth in her abstract essence, but with truth in her operative form; and to pursue the former were to anatomize history, not to represent it. For instance, in the case in hand, whether Richard were in fact guilty of such and such crimes, matters little or none; it being enough that he was generally believed to be so, and that this belief was the mother-principle of those national events whereon the drama turns. That Richard was a prince of abundant head; that his government was in the main wise and just; that he was sober in counsel, brave in the field, and farsighted in both; all this only renders it the harder to account for that general desertion which left him almost naked to his foes, but by such a wide-spread impression of his criminality as no puttings-forth of intellect could surmount. Thus his fall, so sudden and so complete, was mainly in virtue of what he was thought to be. And forasmuch as the character generally set upon him at the time, if not the essential truth regarding him, was the stuff out of which were spun his overthrow, and the consequent opening of a new social and political era, thus being the truth that was operative; such, therefore, was the only character that would cohere or consist with the circumstances, and hence the only one that was capable of dramatic development.

Touching the moral complexion of Shakespeare's *Richard*, as thus explained, enough, we trust, will be found in our notes to bear out the delineation. The incidents whereby his character in this respect transpires are nearly all taken from the historians, with only such quickening and heightening as it is the prerogative of poetry to lend, even when most tied to the conditions of actual events. Intellectually, however, his proportions, as they had need to be, are drawn much beyond the conferrings of history, or perhaps of nature. For to have set forth such a moral physiognomy in dramatic form, with only his actual endowment of mind, would scarce consist with so much of pleasure in his skill, as was required to countervail the horror of his crimes. Such a measure of depravity, stripped of the disguise which it necessarily keeps up in real life, might indeed be valuable as truth, but would not do at all as poetry. And this may aptly suggest the different laws of history and art, which we know not how to state better than that the method of the one is to please because it instructs, of the other to instruct because it pleases. The forms of poetry, it scarce need be said, are properly relished, not as being fitted to facts, which is the case with science, but as they fit the mind. Nor does this infer any defect of real instructiveness in art; for whatsoever pleasure springs in virtue of such fitness and congeniality with our better nature must needs carry refreshment and invigoration in its touch.

Practically no man ever understood this matter better than Shakespeare; nor, perhaps, has his understanding thereof been better shown anywhere than in the case of Richard. The lines of his guilt, as traced in history, are considerably deepened in the play, and its features charged with boisterous life, making, all together, a fearful picture, and such as, without counterpoising attractions, would be apt to shock and revolt the beholder. But his intellectuality is idealized so far and in such sort from the Poet's own stock, as to season the impression of his moral deformity with the largest and most various mental entertainment. If he be all villain, he is an all-accomplished one; and any painful sense of his villainy is spirited away by his thronging diversions of thought, his unflagging gayety of spirits, his prompt, piercing, versatile wit. Nay, his very crimes do but beget occasion for these enchantments, while every demand seems in effect to replenish his stock; and thus in his character the hateful is so compensated by the admirable, that we are more than reconciled to his company.

The point in review is well illustrated in Richard's wooing and winning of lady Anne, where the rays of his character are all gathered, as it were, into a focus. Now, whatever may have been the real facts in the case, it is certain that Richard was at the time generally believed by the Lancastrians to have had a hand in killing both Henry VI and Edward his son. It is also certain that within two years after their death Richard was married to Edward's widow, who must in all reason be supposed to have shared in the common belief of her party. How they felt on the subject may well appear in that the late king was revered by them as a martyr, and his tomb hallowed as the abode of miraculous efficacies; for which cause Richard afterwards had his bones removed to a more secluded place. On Richard's part the chief motive to the marriage was, no doubt, to come at a share in the immense estates of the lady's father. For as Clarence, having married the elder daughter, grasped at the whole; and as Richard proposed by taking the younger to succeed to a part; hence arose that fierce strife between them, whence grew the general persuasion that Richard was somehow the cause of his brother's death. Perhaps, as indicating the manner and spirit of their contest, it should be mentioned that Clarence, to thwart the aim of Richard, at first had the lady concealed from his pursuit several months in the disguise of a cook-maid; and that, when at last the former saw he could not prevent the marriage, he swore that the latter "should not part the livelihood with him."

So that the Poet is nowise answerable for this difficulty: it was in the history; and the best he could do was to furnish such a solution of it as would stand with the conditions of dramatic effect; to produce which effect it must perforce be brought within the terms of historical reason and probability. Before solving the difficulty, however, Shakespeare greatly augments it by the suppression of time; heightening the exigency, as if on purpose that he may proportionably heighten the intellectuality that is to meet it. Richard begins and finishes his courtship of the lady over the very coffin of the royal saint whose death she is mourning, and whom he is supposed to have murdered. Yet his triumph, such is the Poet's management, seems owing not to any special vice or defect in her, but simply to his persuasive art and fascinations of wit, so put in play as to disconcert all her powers, and steal from her the very will and spirit, of resistance. His towering audacity, which, springing from entire confidence that his genius will back him up and bear him out, succeeds in part by the very effrontery of its attempts; his flexibility and suppleness of thought, turning himself indifferently to all occasions, forms, and modes of address; his perfect self-possession and presence of mind, never at loss for a shift, nor betrayed into a misstep, nor surprised into a pause; his wily dissimulation, and more wily frankness, silencing her charges by pleading guilty to them, parrying her blows by inviting them, and disarming her hatred by owning its justice;—such are the parts of the sly, subtle, unfearing, remorseless Richard, that are wrought out in his courtship of lady Anne.

This scene indeed is far from being the best, or even among the best, in the play, and is thus pitched upon, as combining a remarkable variety of characteristic points, and as happily exemplifying the Poet's method of diverting off the offensiveness of Richard's acts by the entertainment of his gifts. In these respects wc have a repetition of the scene afterwards, when he in like manner triumphs over the fears and scruples of Elizabeth; where the same difficulty recurring draws on a similar procedure, history being again responsible for the one, and Shakespeare for the other. And surely the Poet was not without a purpose in so ordering the drama, that in our first impression of the full-grown Richard his thought-swarming head should have the start of his bloody hand: which order, by the way, is quite reversed in Cibber's patch-work preparation of the play, where, the murder of the sainted Henry coming first, admiration of Richard's intellect is of course forestalled by abhorrence of his cruelty. By the opening soliloquy, so startling in its abruptness, and so crammed to the utmost with poetry and thought, our minds are duly preëngaged to the man's active, fertile, scheming brain: our first impression is of one, unrelenting indeed, and incapable of fear, but who looks long and well before he strikes, and never does the latter, till he is sure of working his will thereby. And the organic law of the drama plainly requires that this or some such initiative be given to the penetrating and imperturbable sagacity which presides over all other elements in the hero's character, and every where pioneers to his purpose, and in the strength of which he still gains his real ends by feigning others, and conquers by seeming to yield. And thus, in the original arrangement of the play, our feelings are from the first properly toned and set to the scope and measure of the terrible as distinguished from the horrible; the reverse of which takes place in the Cibberian improvement.

One of the authors of that singularly thoughtful and suggestive book, *Guesses at Truth*, has a piece of criticism on *Richard*, which, whether altogether just or not, the reader will doubtless thank us for producing here, "Slow and reluctant as I am," says he, "to think that any thing can be erroneous in Shakespeare, whom Nature had wedded, so to say, for better, for worse, and whom she admitted into all the hidden recesses of her heart, still I cannot help thinking that even he, notwithstanding the firm grasp with which he is wont to hold the reins of his solar chariot, as it circles the world, beholding and bringing out every form of life in it, has somewhat exaggerated the diabolical element in the soliloquies of *Richard the Third*." Then, after quoting parts of the two soliloquies near the close of the foregoing play and at the opening of this, he adds,—"If we compare the way in which Iago's plot is first sown, and springs up and gradually grows and ripens in his brain, with Richard's downright enunciation of his projected series of crimes from the first, we may discern the contrast between the youth and the mature manhood of the mightiest intellect that ever lived upon earth,—a contrast almost equally observable in the difference between the diction and meter of the two plays. There are several things in Richard's position, which justify a great difference in the representation of his inward being. His rank and station pampered a more audacious will. The civil wars had familiarized him with crimes of lawless violence, and the wildest revolutions of fortune. Above all, his deformity,—which Shakespeare received from a tradition he did not think of questioning, and which he purposely brings forward so prominently in both the speeches quoted,—seemed to separate and cut him off from sympathy and communion with his kind, and to be a plea for thinking that, as he was a monster in body, he might also be a monster in heart and conduct. In fact, it is a common result of a natural malformation to awaken and irritate a morbid self-consciousness, by making a person continually and painfully sensible of his inferiority to his fellows. Still I cannot but think that Shakespeare would have made a somewhat different use even of this motive, if he had rewritten the play in the maturity of his intellect. Would not Richard then, like Edmund and Iago, have palliated and excused his crimes to himself, and sophisticated and played tricks with his conscience? Would he not have denied and avowed his wickedness, almost in the same breath, and made the ever-waxing darkness of his purposes, like that of night, at once conceal and betray their hideous enformity?"

These queries certainly go right to the spot, and the most we should venture in answer to them, is to start a few cross-queries; premising that when, in reference to the same point, this acute and ingenious writer says,—"It is as contrary to nature for a man to anatomize his heart and soul thus, as it would be to make him dissect his own body,"—his speech surely is stronger than the subject may well bear. May it not, then, be a natural result of Richard's inordinate, dare-devil intellectuality, that he should inspect and scrutinize himself with the same cold, passionless impartiality as he would another person, or as another would him? And might he not, in the strength of his God-defying pride of intellect, grow and harden into a habit of facing his blackest purposes as unflinchingly as he does his unsightly person, and even take pleasure in exaggerating and overpainting their wickedness to himself, as serving to set off and magnify in his own view the art and spirit which, he feels assured, will carry him safe and victorious through them? And does not his most distinctive and individual feature, as compared with Edmund and Iago stand mainly in this, that intellectual pride is in a more exclusive and operative manner the constituent of his character, and the principle of his action? It should be observed that the question here is not, whether the portrait as a whole be not one of superhuman audacity, and running to a height of guilt where no man could sustain himself in being; but whether the speeches under consideration be not in perfect keeping with the idea of his character as transpiring in his action throughout the play. For in whatsoever he does, no less than in what he there says, it is manifest that his hypocrisy is without the least shade of self-delusion. The most constant, the most versatile, the most perfect of actors, he is never a whit deceived or taken in by his own acting: he has, in consummation, the art to conceal his art from others; and because this is the very thing he chiefly glories in, therefore he takes care that it may never become in any degree a secret unto himself. Moral obliquity so played as to pass for moral rectitude is to him the test and measure of intellectual strength and dexterity; for the which cause he delights to practice it, and, what is more, to contemplate himself while practicing it, and even while designing it. And herein Richard is distinguished from and far above all real-life actors, where it is scarce possible but that hypocrisy and self-deceit should slide into each other; whence it is that hypocrites still end by turning fanatics, and *vice versa*, as every day's observation amply testifies.

But this is making Richard out an improbable character? Perhaps it is so; and our purpose was not so much to vindicate the soliloquies, as to suggest whether the charge so pertinently started touching them will not hold equally against the whole delineation. If we be right in thinking that the speeches in question strictly cohere with his general action, it follows that both are in fault, or neither: so that if the Poet be here in error, he is at the least consistently so; though in this case consistency be no jewel. Instead, therefore, of rejoicing the fine criticism quoted above, we should rather incline to extend it in some sort over the substance and body of the play; in the very conception of which we seem to have somewhat of the mistake, so incident to youthful genius, of seeking for excellence rather by transcending nature, or forcing her into a better path, than by falling heartily in, and going smoothly along, with her.—That we have not spoken altogether without book, may be seen by the choice observations of Coleridge. "Pride of intellect," says he, "is the characteristic of Richard, carried to the extent of even boasting to his own mind of his villainy, whilst others are present to feed his pride of superiority. Shakespeare here develops, in a tone of sublime morality, the dreadful consequences of placing the moral in subordination to the mere intellectual being. In Richard there is a predominance of irony, accompanied with apparently blunt manners to those immediately about him, but formalized into a more set hypocrisy towards the people as represented by their magistrates."

It is plain that such a man as Richard must either cease to be himself, or else must be "himself alone." Isolation, virtual or actual, is his vital air, the breath, the necessary condition, of his life. One of his character without his position would have to find solitude; Richard, by his position, has the alternative of creating it: the former must needs be where none others are; the latter, where all others are, in effect, as though they were not. For society is in its nature a complection of mutualities and reciprocal influences, and every rule pertaining to it works both ways: it is a partnership of individualities, some of them subordinate, indeed, and some superior, yet not in such sort but as to presuppose a net-work of ties running and recurring from each to each, so that no one can urge a right without inferring a duty, or claim a bond without owning himself bound. But Richard's individuality can abide no partner, either as equal, or as second, or in any other degree. For partnership is of members the same in kind, differing only in degree; but whoever would move where Richard moves, must do so as of another kind. There is no sharing any thing with him, in however unequal portions; no acting with him, as original and self-moving agents, but only from him, as the objects and passive recipients of his activity: such is the form and scope of his individuality, that other men's cannot stand in mere subordination to it, but must either crush it, or fly from it, or be absorbed into it; and the moment any one goes to act otherwise than as a limb of his person or organ of his will, there is a virtual declaration of war between them, and the issue must hang on a trial of strength or of statagem.

Hence comes it that there is, properly speaking, no interaction between Richard and the other persons of the drama. He is the all-in-all of the play, the soul of every thing that is done, the theme of every thing that is said: there is scarce a thought, or feeling, or purpose expressed, but what is either from him, or in some way concerning him, he being the author, the subject, or the occasion of it. And herein is this play chiefly distinguished from all the others, and, certainly, as a work of art, not distinguished for the better, that the entire action, in all its parts and stages, so far at least as it has any human origin or purpose, both springs from the hero as its source, and determines in him as its end. So that the drama is not properly a composition of coöperative characters, mutually developing and developed; but the prolonged yet hurried outcome of a single character, to which all the other persons serve but as exponents and conductors; as if he were a volume of electrical activity, disclosing himself by means of others, and quenching their active powers at the very moment of doing so. Observe, we say the other persons, not characters; for however much their forms meet the eye, their inward being is for the most part held in abeyance and kept from transpiring by the virtual ubiquity of the hero.

All which may go far to account for the great and lasting popularity of this play on the stage. There being no one to share with the hero the action and interest of the piece, this of course renders it all the better for theatrical starring; for which reason most of the great actors have naturally been fond of appearing in it, and play-goers of seeing them in it. Besides, the hero is himself essentially an actor, though an actor of many parts, sometimes one after another, and sometimes all of them together; and the fact that his character is much of it assumed, and carried through as a matter of art, probably makes it somewhat easier for another to assume it. At all events, the difficulty, one would suppose, must be much less in proportion to the stage-effect, than in reproducing the deep tragic passions of Lear and Othello, as they burst from the original founts of nature.

This want of dramatic balance and equipoise resulted naturally, no doubt, from the subject, and, however detracting from the play as a work of art, may be considered one of its excellences as a representation of history. For by reason of this unartistic disproportion, the play sets forth with the more awful emphasis the malignant working of that tyranny, where a single person arrogates to himself the life of a whole people, and makes all their thoughts, feelings, aims, interests, rights, and affections, serve but as the sporting-ground of his overmastering and remorseless will;—a state of things which is sure to produce, if indeed it do not rather presuppose, a thorough disorganization of society.

Richard's all-controlling energy of purpose, his thorough mastery of himself and every thing about him, has its strongest exhibition in the catastrophe. He cannot indeed prolong his life, but he makes his death serve in the highest degree the end for which he has lived; dying in a perfect transport and ecstasy of heroism, insomuch that we may truly say, "nothing in his life became him like the leaving it." Nay, he may even be said to compel his own death, when a higher Power than man's has cut off all other means of honor and triumph. Herein, too, the Poet followed history; but in the prerogatives of his art he found a way, which history knew not of, to satisfy the moral feelings, representing him as in Hands that can afford to let him defy all the powers of human avengement. Inaccessible to earthly strokes, or accessible to them only in a way that adds to his earthly honor, yet this dreadful impunity is recompensed in the agonies of an embosomed hell; and our moral nature reaps a stern satisfaction in the retributions which are rendered vocal and articulate by the ghosts that are made to haunt his sleeping moments. For even so God sometimes apparently chooses to vindicate His law by taking the punishment directly and exclusively into His own hands. And, surely, His vengeance is never so terrible, as when subordinate ministries are thus dispensed with.

The only considerable exception to what we have been saying is Queen Margaret, whose individuality shoulders itself in face to face with Richard's, her passionate impulse wrestling evenly with his deliberate purpose, and her ferocious temper being provoked into larger and hotter eruptions by all attempts at restraint or intimidation. This, to be sure, is partly because she can do nothing; while at the same time her tongue is all the more able and eager to blast, forasmuch as she has no hand to strike. Long suffering has deepened her fierceness into sublimity: at once vindictive and broken-hearted, her part runs into a most impressive blending of the terrible and the pathetic. Walpole, in his *Historic Doubts*, remarks, that in this play the Poet "seems to deduce the woes of the house of York from the curses which Queen Margaret had vented against them." Might it not as well be said that her woes are deduced from the curse formerly laid upon her by the duke of York? We can perceive no deduction in either case: each seems but to have a foresight of future woe to the other as the proper consequence of past or present crimes. The truth is, Margaret's curses do but proclaim those moral retributions of which God is the author, and nature His minister; and perhaps the only way her former character could be carried on into these scenes was by making her seek indemnity for her woes in ringing changes upon theirs.

Comments

By Shakespearean Scholars

RICHARD III

In no other play of Shakespeare's, we may surely say, is the leading character so absolutely predominant as here. He absorbs almost the whole of the interest, and it is a triumph of Shakespeare's art that he makes us, in spite of everything, follow him with sympathy. This is partly because several of his victims are so worthless that their fate seems well deserved. Anne's weakness deprives her of our sympathy, and Richard's crime loses something of its horror when we see how lightly it is forgiven by the one who ought to take it most to heart. In spite of all his iniquities, he has wit and courage on his side—a wit which sometimes rises to Mephistophelean humor, a courage which does not fail him even in the moment of disaster, but sheds a glory over his fall which is lacking to the triumph of his coldly correct opponent. However false and hypocritical he may be towards others, he is no hypocrite to himself. He is chemically free from self-delusion, even applying to himself the most derogatory terms; and this candor in the depths of his nature appeals to us. It must be said for him, too, that threats and curses recoil from him innocuous, that neither hatred nor violence nor superior force can dash his courage. Strength of character is such a rare quality that it arouses sympathy even in a criminal. If Richard's reign had lasted longer, he would perhaps have figured in history as a ruler of the type of Louis XI: crafty, always wearing his religion on his sleeve, but far-seeing and resolute. As a matter of fact, in history as in the drama, his whole time was occupied in defending himself in the position to which he had fought his way, like a bloodthirsty beast of prey. His figure stands before us as his contemporaries have drawn it: small and wiry, the right shoulder higher than the left, wearing his rich brown hair long in order to conceal this malformation, biting his under-lip, always restless, always with his hand on his dagger-hilt, sliding it up and down in its sheath, without entirely drawing it. Shakespeare has suceeded in throwing a halo of poetry around this tiger in human shape.—Brandes, *William Shakespeare.*

Pride of intellect is the characteristic of Richard, carried to the extent of even boasting to his own mind of his villany, whilst others are present to feed his pride of superiority; as in his first speech, Act II. Sc. 1. Shakspere here, as in all his great parts, developes in a tone of sublime morality the dreadful consequences of placing the moral in subordination to the mere intellectual being. In Richard there is a predominance of irony, accompanied with apparently blunt manners to those immediately about him, but formalized into a more set hypocrisy towards the people as represented by their magistrates.—Coleridge, *Lectures on Shakspere.*

The deformity of Richard is a circumstance as essential to the rancor of his passion as the blackness of Othello—it wounds his pride and irritates his spite, and stirs his rankling revenge. He hankers for the crown with a diseased imagination that dwells upon the very metallic symbol of royalty itself as personal ornament compensating for natural personal defects. Hence he dwells on the very name of it, and the indications are absolute that after his success his costume is to be completed by constantly wearing it—and the trait is akin to the affection for rich attire ascribed to him by history, and not unusual with the deformed. So again his opening soliloquy refers with bitterness to the disadvantage he stands at with the gay and the fair, while his pretended indifference is belied by persevering reparation to his vanity in the influence he exerts upon them.—Lloyd, *Critical Essays.*

The Richard of Shakespear is towering and lofty; equally impetuous and commanding; haughty, violent, and subtle;

bold and treacherous; confident in his strength as well as in his cunning; raised high by his birth, and higher by his talents and his crimes; a royal usurper, a princely hypocrite, a tyrant, and a murderer of the house of Plan-tagenet.

> But I was born so high:
> Our aery buildeth in the cedar's top,
> And dallies with the wind, and scorns the sun.

The idea conveyed in these lines (which are indeed omitted in the miserable medley acted for Richard III) is never lost sight of by Shakespear, and should not be out of the actor's mind for a moment. The restless and sanguinary Richard is not a man striving to be great, but to be greater than he is; conscious of his strength of will, his power of intellect, his daring courage, his elevated station; and making use of these advantages to commit unheard-of crimes, and to shield himself from remorse and infamy.—Hazlitt, *Characters of Shakespear's Plays.*

The entire play may be said to be the exhibition of the one central character of Richard; all subordinate persons are created that he may wreak his will upon them. This is quite in the manner of Marlowe. Like Marlowe also is the fierce energy of the central character, untempered by moral restraints, the heaping up of violent deeds, the absence of all reserve or mystery in the characterization, the broad and bold touches, the demoniac force, and the intensity of the whole. There is something sublime and terrible in so great and fierce a human energy as that of Richard, concentrated within one withered and distorted body. This is the evil offspring and flower of the long and cruel civil wars—this distorted creature, a hater and scorner of man, an absolute cynic, loveless and alone, disregarding all human bonds and human affections, yet full of intellect, of fire, of power. The figure of Queen Margaret, prophesying destruction to her adversaries, and bitterly rejoicing in the fulfilment of her prophecies, is introduced without historical warrant, but in a manner most impressive. The accumulated crimes of civil war are at last atoned for, and the evil which culminates in Richard falls with Richard from its bad eminence. The loveless solitude, haunted by terrible visions of his victims, on the night before his last battle, almost overmasters his resolution; but the stir and movement of the morning reanimates him, and he dies in a paroxysm of the rage of battle.—Dowden, *Shakspere in the Literature Primers.*

ANNE

Anne, whom he [Richard] woos at the beginning of the play, excites less contempt than pity in her frail womanliness, which is without all moral support. She hates and marries; she curses her who shall be the wife of the man who killed her first husband, and she subjects herself to this curse; afterwards as a wife she is leagued with his enemies against him. Thus, says the poet of the "Ghost of Richard,"

> Women's griefs, nor loves, are dyed in grain,
> For either's color time or men can stain.

Not often has a task been ventured upon like that of the poet in this instance. He produces a scene full of improbability, the principal part in which is played by this Anne, whose character is prepared or delineated in no other scene, in the most unnatural situation. Vanity, self-complacency, and weakness have all to be displayed at once; it is the part of the matron of Ephesus in the tragedy, though it is neither incredible nor forced. We must at the same time bear in view that the murder of her relatives admits of excuse as among the unavoidable evils of war and defense. We must take into account the extraordinary degree of dissimulation, which deceives even experienced men; and for this reason the artist who is to play Richard must woo rather as an actor than as a lover, but must yet go to the very limits of deception even as regards the initiated spectator. We have further to consider how the part of repentance and atonement becomes a valiant soldier, and how pardonable is the womanly weakness which delights in the idea of endeavoring to support and save such a penitent. We must remember that the unwonted mildness of the tyrant is far more effective than the gentleness of the weak; and in the historical examples of our own day we have seen how tender feminine characters have been united to the most brutal, in the consciousness of at any rate restraining the human barbarity at home.—Gervinus, *Shakspeare Commentaries.*

RICHMOND

The race of Henry IV is ultimately quite rooted out; of the house of York, with the exception of the childless Richard,[1] there survives but one daughter of Edward IV, to connect the old with the new era. This had to be. The deliverer and founder of the new era had necessarily to be of a different blood; yet his title had, at the same time, in some measure to mediate between the past and the future. Such was the case with Henry, duke of Richmond, afterwards Henry VII, and the husband of Elizabeth, the above-named daughter of Edward IV—of the House of Lancaster (Gaunt), it is true, but not a descendant of Henry IV. He appears a gentle, pious youth, not a distinguished or eminent person. For the age is so demoralized that it not only cannot offer any resistance to the tyrant Richard, but is also unable to provide a deliverer from within itself. Very justly, therefore, Henry considers himself "God's captain," and does not center his hope in himself, in the prevailing circumstances or in the strength of his army; it is simply his consciousness that it is the will of God that gives him the energy he exhibits in the great enterprise. He is the man whom God sent, whom the age required, and who alone was entitled to act; the invisible hand, which ever guides the course of history, maintains and protects him. How beautifully the poet has contrived to express this is shown in that scene of the fifth act, so frequently censured, in which appear the ghosts of those members of the royal family whom Richard had murdered.—Ulrici, *Shakespeare's Dramatic Art.*

MARGARET OF ANJOU

The second idea of the drama comes in (Act I. Sc. iii) with the presence of Margaret, the incarnate Fury of the Civil Wars, who has been their incessant urger, and is now the Pythoness of their punishment. "Small joy have I," cries Elizabeth, "in being England's queen." And Margaret, her first entrance into the action, mutters from the background—

And lessen'd be that small, God, I beseech him.

1. His son, whom Shakespeare does not mention, died one year before him.

She is a terrible figure, the Fate and Fury together of the play. She does nothing for its movement; she is outside of that. But she broods above its action, with hands outstretched in cursing. Worn, like "a wrinkled witch," her tongue edged with bitter fire, with all the venom of the Civil Wars bubbling in her heart; grey-haired, tall, with the habit of command, she has not been, like Richard, without love or exiled from human nature. But all she loved are dead. She has outlived humanity, and passed into an elemental Power, hopeless, pitiless, joyless save for the joy of vengeance. It is not till she finds the Duchess of York and Edward's queen sunk in their hopeless pain that she feels herself at one, even for a moment, with any human creature. She sits down and curses with them, but soon leaves them, as one removed; towering over them as she flings back on them her parting curse, incensed that she has been even for that moment at one with their feeble wrath. Her eloquence is that of primeval sorrow and hate. Her curses have the intensity of an immortal's passion.

"O, well skilled in curses," cries the Queen Elizabeth, "teach me how to curse." "Life is her shame," Margaret says, but she will not die till she has vengeance. 'Tis the only thing which brings a smile to her withered lips. And her vengeance is felt, like an actual presence in the air, by all who die. Shakespeare takes pains to mark that out. She is not only Margaret and hate to them, but the spirit through whom divine justice works its wrath upon them. And when she sees the end, she passes away, still alive, like one who cannot die; departs in an awful joy—

These English woes will make me smile in France.

—Brooke, *On Ten Plays of Shakespeare.*

Margaret, in bold defiance of history, but with fine dramatic effect, is introduced again in the gorgeous and polluted court of Edward the Fourth. There she stalks around the seat of her former greatness, like a terrible phantom of departed majesty, uncrowned, unsceptred, desolate, powerless—or like a vampire thirsting for blood—or like a grim prophetess of evil, imprecating that ruin on the head of her enemies, which she lived to see realized. The scene following the murder of the princes in the Tower, in which Queen Elizabeth and the Duchess of York sit down on the ground bewailing their desolation, and Margaret suddenly appears from behind them, like the very personification of woe, and seats herself beside them revelling in their despair, is, in the general conception and effect, grand and appalling.—Mrs. Jameson, *Shakespeare's Heroines*.

THE PRINCES

The figures of the two boy princes, Edward's sons, stand in the strongest contrast to Richard. The eldest child already shows greatness of soul, a kingly spirit, with a deep feeling for the import of historic achievement. The fact that Julius Cæsar built the Tower, he says, even were it not registered, ought to live from age to age. He is full of the thought that while Cæsar's "valor did enrich his wit," yet it was his wit "that made his valor live," and he exclaims with enthusiasm, "Death makes no conquest of this conqueror." The younger brother is childishly witty, imaginative, full of boyish mockery for his uncle's grimness, and eager to play with his dagger and sword. In a very few touches Shakespeare has endowed these young brothers with the most exquisite grace. The murderers "weep like to children in their death's sad story":

> Their lips were four red roses on a stalk,
> Which in their summer beauty kiss'd each other.

—Brandes, *William Shakespeare*.

ELIZABETH, QUEEN TO EDWARD IV

Elizabeth, queen of Edward, mother of the princes of the Tower, is admirable. She may have been a light woman and indiscreet. She may have forwarded too busily the fortunes of her family, but this is a trait of human, not especially of woman, nature, and has its noble side. We must maintain that she overreached Richard in the end, by the keen unscrupulousness of a loving woman when those she loves are in peril. For her deception and ruse of acquiescence, we may have great charity.—Warner, *English History in Shakespeare's Plays*.

THE MURDERERS

The two murderers employed by Gloster to despatch Clarence are drawn with a terribly bold and masterly hand. They are not only designed with a marked difference from any others of Shakespeare's murderers, but these have such perfect individuality as to be unlike and quite distinct from each other. Throughout the scene you recognize the one ruffian from his companion though no otherwise designated than as "1st Murderer and 2nd Murderer," being third or fourth class characters in the play. From the preliminary short interview with Gloster, where the 1st Murderer alone speaks, and assures the duke,—

> Fear not, my lord, we will not stand to prate;
> Talkers are no good doers: be assured
> We come to use our hands and not our tongues;

down to the scene where they perpetrate the deed, the first man displays the bold, ruthless, callous villain, dashed with a spice of ferocious humor; and the other is a vacillating creature, whom circumstances, and not predisposition, have made what he is.—Clarke, *Shakespeare-Characters*.

THE LAW OF NEMESIS

While the figure of the hunchback king throws all other characters into a subordinate place, the full intent of the drama is missed, unless Richard's fate is seen as the climax of a series of Nemeses upon the guilty House of York. Clarence, King Edward, the Queen's kindred, Hastings, Buckingham, follow one another to their doom, and in each case, as will be evident on careful study of the play, there is a turn of the wheel with the result that "those who triumph in one Nemesis become the victims of the next." But each incident, in addition, goes to form a chain of triumph for Richard, while the catastrophe of his fate, as the gathering of the ghosts testifies, is the retribution for them all. Yet further, alike he and his victims suffer in common expiation of the sins of York against Lancaster, so that a complicated law of Nemesis controls the issues of the play. So uniform indeed is its working that it runs a risk of appearing automatic, and thus losing something of its moral significance. In view of this danger Shakspere varies the action by a number of devices, of which the most striking is the introduction upon the scene, in weirdly impressive contrast, of the two women, the Duchess of York and the Lancastrian Queen Margaret, who epitomize, as it were, the whole story of the crime and its retribution. They are less human personages than monumental figures, embodiments of suffering and of doom. The aged Duchess, widow of the great Duke of York, mother of Edward, Clarence and Richard, grandmother of the boy princes, gathers up into her own breast all the spear-points of penal destiny; as she herself exclaims:

> Alas! I am the mother of these moans:
> Their woes are parcelled, mine are general,

and Queen Margaret, like some Fury of old, chants over her the wild paean of sated, or all-but sated, revenge:

> Thy Edward he is dead, that killed my Edward;
> Thy other Edward dead, to quit my Edward;
> Young York he is but boot, because both they
> Match not the high perfection of my loss:
> Thy Clarence he is dead that stabbed my Edward;
> And the beholders of this frantic play,
> The adulterate Hastings, Rivers, Vaughan, Grey,
> Untimely smothered in their dusky graves.

One last victim is still due, "hell's black intelligencer," Richard, but that culminating debt is at length paid, and the account between the Houses made even. Then, and not till then, may the White Rose mingle with the Red, and "fair prosperous days" once more dawn over a re-united land. If, as is probable, *Richard III* was Shakespeare's first serious play, it gave convincing proof that the new dramatist, however tolerant in some ways, held rigidly to the doctrine that evil-doing, whether in the individual or in the State, is dogged by a Nemesis that wrings its penalty, even to the uttermost farthing.—Boas, *Shakspere and his Predecessors.*

EDWARD IV

The play must not be dismissed without one word spoken of King Edward IV. He did not interest the imagination of Shakspere. Edward is the self-indulgent, luxurious king. The one thing which Shakspere cared to say about him was, that his pleasant delusion of peace-making shortly before his death, was a poor and insufficient compensation for a life spent in ease and luxury rather than in laying the hard and strong bases of a substantial peace. A few soft words, and placing of hands in hands will not repair the ravage of fierce years, and the decay of sound human bonds during soft, effeminate years. Just as the peacemaking is perfect, Richard is present on the scene:

> There wanteth now our brother Gloster here
> To make the blessed period of our peace.

And Gloster stands before the dying king to announce that Clarence lies murdered in the Tower. This is Shakspere's comment upon and condemnation of the self-indulgent King.—Dowden, *Shakspere—His Mind and Art.*

SHAKESPEARE'S FAMILIARITY WITH HIS SUBJECT

Matured, especially in its wonderful exhibition of character, as the Richard III is, we cannot doubt that the subject was very early familiar to the young poet's mind. The Battle of Bosworth Field was the great event of his own locality, which for a century had fixed the government of England. The course of the Reformation, and especially the dissolution of the Monasteries, had produced great social changes, which were in operation at the time in which William Shakspere was born; whose effects, for good and for evil, he must have seen working around him, as he grew from year to year in knowledge and experience. But those events were too recent, and indeed of too delicate a nature, to assume the poetical aspect in his mind. They abided still in the region of prejudice and controversy. It was dangerous to speak of the great religious divisions of the kingdom with a tolerant impartiality. History could scarcely deal with these opinions in a spirit of justice. Poetry, thus, which has regard to what is permanent and universal, has passed by these matters, important as they are. But the great event which placed the Tudor family on the throne, and gave England a stable government, however occasionally distracted by civil and religious division, was an event which would seize fast upon such a mind as that of William Shakspere. His ancestor, there can be little doubt, had been an adherent of the Earl of Richmond. For his faithful services to the conqueror at Bosworth he was rewarded, as we are assured, by lands in Warwickshire. That field at Bosworth would therefore have to him a family as well as a local interest.

Burton, the historian of Leicestershire, who was born about ten years after William Shakspere, tells us "that his great-great-grandfather, John Hardwick, of Lindley, near Bosworth, a man of very short stature, but active and courageous, tendered his service to Henry, with some troops of horse, the night he lay at Atherston, became his guide to the field, advised him in the attack, and how to profit by the sun and by the wind." Burton further says, writing in 1622, that the inhabitants living around the plain called Bosworth Field, more properly the plain of Sutton, "have many occurrences and passages yet fresh in memory, by reason that some persons thereabout, which saw the battle fought, were living within less than forty years, of which persons myself have seen some, and have heard of their disclosures, though related by the second hand." This "living within less than forty years" would take us back to about the period which we are now viewing in relation to the life of Shakspere. But certainly there is something over-marvellous in Burton's story, to enable us to think that William Shakspere, even as a very young boy, could have conversed with "some persons thereabout" who had seen a battle fought in 1485. That, as Burton more reasonably of himself says, he might have "heard their discourses at second-hand" is probable enough. Bosworth Field is about thirty miles from Stratford. Burton says that the plain derives its name from Bosworth, "not that this battle was fought at this place (it being fought in a large, flat plain, and spacious ground, three miles distant from this town, between the towns of Shenton, Sutton, Dadlington, and Stoke); but for that this town was the most worthy town of note near adjacent, and was therefore called Bosworth Field. That this battle was fought in this plain appeareth by many remarkable places: By a little mount cast up, where the common report is, that at the first beginning of the battle Henry Earl of Richmond made his parænetical oration to his army; by divers pieces of armor, weapons, and other warlike accouterments, and by many arrowheads here found, whereof, about twenty years since, at the enclosure of the lordship of Stoke, great store were digged up, of which some I have now (1622) in my custody, being of a long, large and big proportion, far greater than any now in use; as also by relation of the inhabitants, who have many occurrences and passages yet fresh in memory." Burton goes on to tell two stories connected with the eventful battle. The one was the vision of King Richard, of "divers fearful ghosts running about him, not suffering him to take any rest, still crying 'Revenge.'" Hall relates the tradition thus:—"The fame went that he had the same night a dreadful and a terrible dream, for it seemed to him, being asleep, that he saw divers images like terrible devils, not suffering him to take any quiet or rest." Burton says, previous to his description of the dream, "The vision is reported to be in this manner." And certainly his account of the fearful ghosts "still crying Revenge" is essentially different from that of the chronicler. Shakspere has followed the more poetical account of the old local historian; which, however, could not have been known to him:

> Methought the souls of all that I have murther'd
> Came to my tent: and every one did threat
> To-morrow's vengeance on the head of Richard.

Did Shakspere obtain his notion from the same source as Burton—from "relation of the inhabitants who have many occurrences and passages yet fresh in memory?" The topographer has another story, not quite so poetical, which the dramatist does not touch: "It was foretold, that if ever King Richard did come to meet his adversary in a place that was compassed with towns whose termination was in *ton* (what number is adjacent may, by the map, be perceived), that there he should come to great distress; or else, upon the same occasion, did happen to lodge at a place beginning and ending with the same syllable of *An* (as this of *Anbian*), that there he should lose his life, to expiate that wicked murder of his late wife Anne, daughter and coheir of Richard Neville Earl of Salisbury and Warwick." This is essentially a local tradition. The prediction and the vision were in all likelihood rife in Sutton, and Shenton, and Sibson, and Coton, and Dadlington, and Stapleton, and Atherston, in the days of Shakspere's boyhood. Anbian, or Ambiam, a small wood, is in the center of the plain called Bosworth Field. Tradition has pointed out a hillock where Richard harangued his army; and also a little spring, called King Richard's Well. Dr. Parr, about forty years ago, found out a well "in dirty, mossy ground," in the midst of this plain; and then a Latin inscription was to be set up to enlighten the peasantry of the district, and to preserve the memory of the spot for all time. Two words about the well in Shakspere would have given it a better immortality.—Knight, *Pictorial Shakspere.*

POPULARITY OF THE PLAY

The tragedy of *Richard the Third* held possession of the stage long after the other plays of this class had been expelled from it by the improved taste and diminished patience of the public. It is certainly tragic enough to satisfy the most voracious appetite for horrors: murder follows murder with breathless rapidity; the jocose royal assassin, who in a former play had dismissed Henry the Sixth and the Prince of Wales to their account, begins this tragedy by the slaughter of his brother Clarence, and then goes on with the coolness of a butcher, killing one inconvenient friend or relative after another, till our memory becomes perplexed by the attempt to recall the names of his victims. An interest kept up by such means can hardly be thought artistic, but this interest is kept up from the opening of the play till its close, when the scoffing regal criminal makes his exit in a blaze of intrepidity. —St. John, *Essays on Shakespeare and his Works.*

RANK OF THE PLAY

Measured by the Shakespearean standard of excellence, *Richard III*, however popular and successful on the stage, can only rank as a second or third rate performance; and this, I make no doubt, is to be attributed to the fact that it was not of Shakespeare's original composition, but the work of the author or authors of *Henry VI* series of plays; his part in this as in those, being merely that of a reviser or re-writer.—Daniel, *Richard III in the Shakespeare Quarto Fac-Simile.*

HISTORICAL PLAYS

The dramatist was bound by fidelity to his main purpose, to subordinate the details of history; and according to the preponderance of the dramatic or the historic, we have a tragedy like Macbeth or a chronicle like Richard III. We are neither misled nor deceived therefore, when we find in these historical plays what would have no place in formal history. The very anachronisms of the poet are often most valuable in the interpretation of events described, just as a discord in music heralds the resolving chords which introduce new harmonies. "They are perfect," these plays, in their way, "because there is no care about centuries in them."—Warner, *English History in Shakespeare's Plays.*

Othello

Preface

By Israel Gollancz, M.A.

THE EARLY EDITIONS

The First Edition of *Othello* was a Quarto, published in 1622, with the following title-page:

"The | Tragædy of Othello, | The Moore of Venice. | *As it hath beene diuerse times acted at the* | Globe, and at the Black-Friers, by | *his Maiesties Seruants.* | *Written by* William Shakespeare. | [Vignette] | London, | Printed by N.O. for Thomas Walkley, and are to be sold at his | shop, at the Eagle and Child, in Brittans Bursse. | 1622."[1]

In 1623 appeared the First Folio, containing *Othello* among the "Tragedies" (pp. 310-339); the text, however, was not derived from the same source as the First Quarto; an independent MS. must have been obtained. In addition to many improved readings, the play as printed in the Folio contained over one hundred and fifty verses omitted in the earlier edition, while, on the other hand, ten or fifteen lines in the Quarto were not represented in

1. Prefixed to this First Quarto were the following lines:

"The Stationer to the Reader.

"*To set forth a booke without an Epistle, were like to the old English prouerbe,* A blew coat without a badge,? *the Author being dead, I thought good to take that piece of worke upon mee: To commend it, I will not, for that which is good, I hope euery man will commend, without intreaty: and I am the bolder, because the author's name is sufficient to vent his worke. Thus leauing euery one to the liberty of iudgement; I haue ventered to print this play, and leaue it to the generall censure. Yours,* Thomas Walkley."

the folio version. Thomas Walkley had not resigned his interest in the play; it is clear from the *Stationers' Register* that it remained his property until March 1, 1627 (*i.e.* 1628) when he assigned "Orthello *the More of Venice*" unto Richard Hawkins, who issued the Second Quarto in 1630. A Third Quarto appeared in 1655; and later Quartos in 1681, 1687, 1695.

The text of modern editions of the play is based on that of the First Folio, though it is not denied that we have in the First Quarto a genuine play-house copy; a notable difference, pointing to the Quarto text as the older, is its retention of oaths and asseverations, which are omitted or toned down in the Folio version.

DATE OF COMPOSITION

This *last* point has an important bearing on the date of the play, for it proves that *Othello* was written before the Act of Parliament was issued in 1606 against the abuse of the name of God in plays. External and internal evidence seem in favor of 1604, as the birth-year of the tragedy, and this date has been generally accepted since the publication of the *Variorum Shakespeare* of 1821, wherein Malone's views in favor of that year were set forth (Malone had died nine years before the work appeared). After putting forward various theories, he added: "We know it was acted in 1604, and I have therefore placed it in that year." For twenty years scholars sought in vain to discover upon what evidence he *knew* this important fact, until at last about the year 1840 Peter Cunningham announced his discovery of certain *Accounts of the Revels at Court*, containing the following item:

> *By the King's* 'Hallamas Day, being the first of Nov,
> *Matis Plaiers*. A play at the bankettinge House att
> Whitehall, called the Moor of Venis [1604].'[1]

We now know that this manuscript was a forgery, but strange to say there is every reason to believe that though "the book" itself is spurious, the information which it yields is genuine, and that Malone had some such entry in his possession when he wrote his emphatic statement (*vide* Grant White's account of the whole story, quoted in Furness' *Variorum* edition; *cp*. pp. 351-357).

1. *v. Shakespeare Society Publications*, 1842.

The older school of critics, and Malone himself at first, assigned the play to *circa* 1611 on the strength of the lines, III, iv, 46, 47:

> The hearts of old gave hands;
> But our new heraldry is hands, not hearts,

which seemed to be a reference to the arms of the order of Baronets, instituted by King James in 1611; Malone, however, in his later edition of the play aptly quoted a passage from the *Essays* of Sir Wm. Cornwallis, the younger, published in 1601, which may have suggested the thought to Shakespeare: "*They (our forefathers) had wont to give their hands and their hearts together, but we think it a finer grace to look asquint, our hand looking one way, and our heart another.*"

THE ORIGINAL OF OTHELLO

From the elegy on the death of Richard Burbage in the year 1618, it appears that the leading character of the play was assigned to this most famous actor:

> But let me not forget one chiefest part
> Wherein, beyond the rest, he mov'd the heart,
> The grievèd Moor, made jealous by a slave,
> Who sent his wife to fill a timeless grave,
> Then slew himself upon the bloody bed.
> All these and many more with him are dead.[1]

THE SOURCE OF THE PLOT

The story of *Il Moro di Venezia* was taken from the *Heccatommithi* of the Italian novelist Giraldi Cinthio; it is the seventh tale of the third decade, which deals with "The unfaithfulness of Husbands and Wives." No English translation of the novel existed in Shakespeare's time (at least we know of none), but a French translation appeared in the year 1584, and through this medium the work may have come to England. Cinthio's novel may have been of Oriental origin, and in its general character it somewhat resembles the tale of *The Three Apples* in *The Thousand and One Nights*; on the other hand it has

1. *v*. Ingleby's *Centurie of Prayse* (*New Shak. Soc.*), 2nd edition, p. 131, where the elegy is discussed, and a truer version printed.

been ingeniously maintained that "a certain Christophal Moro, a Luogotenente di Cipro, who returned from Cyprus in 1508, after having lost his wife, was the original of the Moor of Venice of Giraldi Cinthio." "Fronting the summit of the *Giants' Stair*," writes Mr. Rawdon Brown, the author of this theory, "where the Doges of Venice were crowned, there are still visible four shields spotted with mulberries (*strawberries* in the description of Desdemona's handkerchief), indicating that that part of the palace portal on which they are carved was terminated in the reign of Christopher Moro, whose insignia are three mulberries sable and three bends azure on a field argent; the word *Moro* signifying in Italian either mulberry-tree or blackamoor." Perhaps Shakespeare learned the true story of *his* Othello from some of the distinguished Venetians in England; "Cinthio's novel would never have sufficed him for his *Othello*"[1] (*vide* Furness, pp. 372-389). Knowing, however, Shakespeare's transforming power, we may well maintain that, without actual knowledge of Christopher Moro's history, he was capable of creating Othello from Cinthio's savage Moor, Iago from the cunning cowardly ensign of the original, the gentle lady Desdemona from "the virtuous lady of marvelous beauty, named Disdemona (*i.e.* 'the hapless one')," [2] who is beaten to death "with a stocking filled with sand," Cassio and Emilia from the vaguest possible outlines. The tale should be read side by side with the play by such as desire to study

1. The title of the novel summarizes its contents as follows:

   "A Moorish Captain takes to wife a Venetian Dame, and his Ancient accuses her of adultery to her husband: it is planned that the Ancient is to kill him whom he believes to be the adulterer; the Captain kills the woman, is accused by the Ancient, the Moor does not confess, but after the infliction of extreme torture, is banished; and the wicked Ancient, thinking to injure others, provided for himself a miserable death."
2. This is the only name given by Cinthio. Steevens first pointed out that "Othello" is found in Reynold's *God's Revenge against Adultery*, standing in one of his arguments as follows: "She marries Othello, an old German soldier." The name "Iago" also occurs in the book. It is also found in *The first and second fart of the History of the famous Euordanus, Prince of Denmark. With the strange adventures of Iago, Prince of Saxonie: and of both their several fortunes in Love. At London*, 1605.

the process whereby a not altogether artless tale of horror[1] has become the subtlest of tragedies—"perhaps the greatest work in the world."[2] "The most pathetic of human compositions."[3]

DURATION OF ACTION

The action seems to cover three days: Act I—one day; interval for voyage; Act II—one day; Acts III, IV, V—one day. In order to get over the difficulty of this time-division various theories have been advanced, notably that of Double Time, propounded by Halpin and Wilson; according to the latter, "Shakespeare counts off days and hours, as it were, by two clocks, on one of which the true Historic Time is recorded, and on the other the Dramatic Time, or a false show of time, whereby days, weeks, and months may be to the utmost contracted" (Furness, pp. 358-372).

According to Mr. Fleay, the scheme of time for the play is as follows:

Act I—one day. Interval for voyage. Act II—one day. Act III—one day (Sunday). Interval of a week, at least. Act IV, sc. i, ii, iii; Act V, sc. i, ii, iii—one day. Where Act IV begins with what is now Act III, sc. iv, and Act V with the present Act IV, sc. iii.

> Dreams, Books, are each a world: and books, we know,
> Are a substantial world, both pure and good;
> Round them with tendrils strong as flesh and blood,

---

1. Mrs. Jameson rightly calls attention to a striking incident of the original story: Desdemona does not accidentally drop the handkerchief: it is stolen from her by Iago's little child, an infant of three years old, whom he trains and bribes to the theft. The love of Desdemona for this child, her little playfellow—the pretty description of her, taking it in her arms and caressing it, while it profits by its situation to steal the handkerchief from her bosom, are well imagined and beautifully told, *etc.*
2. Macaulay.
3. Wordsworth: "The tragedy of *Othello*, Plato's records of the last scenes in the career of Socrates, and Izaak Walton's *Life of George Herbert* are the most pathetic of human compositions." (A valuable summary of criticisms, English and foreign, will be found in Furness' *Othello*, pp. 407-453.)

Our pastime and our happiness will grow.
There find I personal theme, a plenteous store,
Matter wherein right voluble I am,
To which I listen with a ready ear;
Two shall be named pre-eminently dear,—
The gentle Lady married to the Moor;
And heavenly Una, with her milk-white Lamb.

Introduction

By Henry Norman Hudson, A.M.

Il Moro di Venezia is the title of one of the novels in Giraldi Cinthio's *Hecatommithi*. The material for *The Tragedy of Othello, the Moor of Venice*, was partly derived from this source. Whether the story was accessible to Shakespeare in English, we have no certain knowledge. No translation of so early a date has been seen or heard of in modern times; and we have already in several cases found reason to think he knew enough of Italian to take the matter directly from the original. We proceed, as usual, to give such an abstract of the tale as may fully discover the nature and extent of the Poet's obligations:

There lived in Venice a valiant Moor who was held in high esteem for his military genius and services. Desdemona, a lady of great virtue and beauty, won by his noble qualities, fell in love with him. He also became equally enamored of her, and, notwithstanding the opposition of her friends, married her. They were altogether happy in each other until the Moor was chosen to the military command of Cyprus. Though much pleased with this honor, he was troubled to think that he must either part from his wife or else expose her to the dangers of the voyage. She, seeing him troubled and not knowing the cause, asked him one day how he could be so melancholy after being thus honored by the Senate; and, on being told the reason, begged him to dismiss such idle thoughts, as she was resolved to follow him wherever he should go, and, if there were any dangers in the way, to share them with him. So, the necessary preparations being made, he soon afterwards embarked with his wife, and sailed for Cyprus.

In his company he had an ensign, of a fine looking person, but exceedingly depraved in heart, a boaster and a coward, who by his craftiness and pretension had imposed on the Moor's simplicity, and gained his friendship. This rascal also took his wife along, a handsome and discreet woman, who, being an Italian, was much cherished by Desdemona. In the same company was also a lieutenant to whom the Moor was much attached, and often had him to dine with him and his wife; Desdemona showing him great attention and civility for her husband's sake.

The ensign, falling passionately in love with Desdemona, and not daring to avow it lest the Moor should kill him, sought by private means to make her aware of his passion. But when he saw that all his efforts came to nothing, and that she was too much wrapped up in her husband to think of him or any one else, he at last took it into his head that she was in love with the lieutenant, and determined to work the ruin of them both by accusing them to the Moor of adultery. But he saw that he would have to be very artful in his treachery, else the Moor would not believe him, so great was his affection for his wife, and his friendship for the lieutenant. He therefore watched for an opportunity of putting his design into act; and it was not long before he found one. For, the lieutenant having drawn his sword and wounded a soldier upon guard, the Moor cashiered him. Desdemona tried very hard to get him pardoned, and received again to favor. When the Moor told his ensign how earnest she was in the cause, the villain saw it was the proper time for opening his scheme: so, he suggested that she might be fond of the lieutenant's company; and, the Moor asking him why, he replied,—"Nay, I do not choose to meddle between man and wife; but watch her properly, and you will then understand me." The Moor could get no further explanation from him, and, being stung to the quick by his words, kept brooding upon them, and trying to make out their meaning; and when his wife, some time after, again begged him to forgive the lieutenant, and not to let one slight fault cancel a friendship of so many years, he at last grew angry, and wondered why she should trouble herself so much about the fellow, as he was no relation of hers. She replied with much sweetness, that her only motive in speaking was the pain she felt in seeing her husband deprived of so good a friend.

Upon this solicitation, he began to suspect that the ensign's words meant that she was in love with the lieutenant. So, being full of melancholy thoughts, he went to the ensign, and tried to make him speak more intelligibly; who, feigning great reluctance to say more, and making as though he yielded to his pressing entreaties, at last replied,—"You must know, then, that Desdemona is grieved for the lieutenant only because, when he comes to your house, she consoles herself with him for the disgust she now has at your blackness." At this, the Moor was more deeply stung than ever; but, wishing to be informed further, he put on a threatening look, and said,—"I know not what keeps me from cutting out that insolent tongue of yours, which has thus attacked the honor of my wife." The ensign replied that he expected no other reward for his friendship, but still protested that he had spoken the truth. "If," said he, "her feigned affection has blinded you to such a degree that you cannot see what is so very visible, that does not lessen the truth of my assertion. The lieutenant himself, being one of those who are not content unless some others are made privy to their secret enjoyments, told me so; and I would have given him his death at the time, but that I feared your displeasure: but, since you thus reward my friendship, I am sorry I did not hold my tongue." The Moor answered in great passion,—"If you do not make me see with my own eyes the truth of what you tell me, be assured that I will make you wish you had been born dumb."—"That would have been easy enough," said the ensign, "when the lieutenant came to your house; but now that you have driven him away, it will be hard to prove it. But I do not despair of causing you to see that which you will not believe on my word."

The Moor then went home with a barbed arrow in his side, impatient for the time when he was to see what would render him forever miserable. Meanwhile, the known purity of Desdemona made the ensign very uneasy lest he should not be able to convince the Moor of what he said. He therefore went to hatching new devices of malice. Now, Desdemona often went to his house, and spent part of the day with his wife. Having observed that she brought with her a handkerchief which the Moor had given her, and which, being delicately worked in the Moorish style, was much prized by them both, he devised to steal it. He had a little girl of three years old, who was much caressed by Desdemona. So, one day, when she was at his house, he put the child into her arms, and while she was pressing the little girl to her bosom, he stole away the handkerchief so dexterously that she did not perceive it. This put him in high spirits. And the lady, being occupied with other things, did not think of the handkerchief till some days after, when, not being able to find it, she began to fear lest the Moor should ask for it, as he often did. The ensign, watching his opportunity, went to the lieutenant, and left the handkerchief on his bolster. When the lieutenant found it, he could not imagine how it came there; but, knowing it to be Desdemona's, he resolved to carry it to her: so, waiting till the Moor was gone out, he went to the back door and knocked. The Moor, having that instant returned, went to the window, and asked who was there; whereupon the lieutenant, hearing his voice, ran away without answering. The Moor then went to the door, and, finding no one there, returned full of suspicion, and asked his wife if she knew who it was that had knocked. She answered with truth that she did not; but he, thinking it was the lieutenant, went to the ensign, told him what had happened, and engaged him to ascertain what he could on the subject.

The ensign, being much delighted at this incident, contrived one day to have an interview with the lieutenant in a place where the Moor could see them. In the course of their talk, which was on a different subject, he laughed much, and by his motions expressed great surprise. As soon as they had parted, the Moor went to the ensign, to learn what had passed between them; and he, after much urging, declared that the lieutenant withheld nothing from him, but rather boasted of his frequent wickedness with Desdemona, and how, the last time he was with her, she made him a present of the handkerchief her husband had given her. The Moor thanked him, and thought that if his wife no longer had the handkerchief, this would be a proof that the ensign had told him the truth. So, one day after dinner he asked her for it; and she, being much disconcerted at the question, and blushing deeply, all which was carefully observed by the Moor, ran to her wardrobe, as if to look for it; but, as she could not find it, and wondered what had become of it, he told her to look for it some other time; then left her, and began to reflect how he might put her and the lieutenant to death so as not to be held responsible for the murder.

The lieutenant had in his house a woman who, struck with the beauty of the handkerchief, determined to copy it before it should be returned. While she was at the work, sitting by a window where any one passing in the street might see her, the ensign pointed it out to the Moor, who was then fully persuaded of his wife's guilt. The ensign then engaged to kill both her and the lieutenant. So, one dark night, as the lieutenant was coming out of a house where he usually spent his evenings, the ensign stealthily gave him a cut in the leg with his sword, and brought him to the ground, and then rushed upon him to finish the work. But the lieutenant, who was very brave and skillful, having drawn his sword, raised himself for defense, and cried out murder as loud as he could. As the alarm presently drew some people to the spot, the ensign fled away, but quickly returned, pretended that he too was brought thither by the noise, and condoled with the lieutenant as much as if he had been his brother. The next morning, Desdemona, hearing what had happened, expressed much concern for the lieutenant, and this greatly strengthened the Moor's conviction of her guilt. He then arranged with the ensign for putting her to death in such a manner as to avoid suspicion. As the Moor's house was very old, and the ceiling broken in divers places, the plan agreed upon at the villain's suggestion was, that she should be beaten to death with a stocking full of sand, as this would leave no marks upon her; and that when this was done they should pull down the ceiling over her head, and then give out that she was killed by a beam falling upon her. To carry this purpose into effect, the Moor one night had the ensign hidden in a closet opening into his chamber. At the proper time, the ensign made a noise, and when Desdemona rose and went to see what it was, he rushed forth and killed her in the manner proposed. They then placed her on the bed, and when all was done according to the arrangement, the Moor gave an alarm that his house was falling. The neighbors running thither found the lady dead under the beams. The next day, she was buried, the whole island mourning for her.

The Moor, not long after, became distracted with grief and remorse. Unable to bear the sight of the ensign, he would have put him openly to death, but that he feared the justice of the Venetians; so he drove him from his company and degraded him, whereupon the villain went to studying how to be revenged on the Moor. To this end, he disclosed the whole matter to the lieutenant, who accused the Moor before the Senate, and called the ensign to witness the truth of his charges. The Moor was imprisoned, banished, and afterwards killed by his wife's relations. The ensign, returning to Venice, and continuing his old practices, was taken up, put to the torture, and racked so violently that he soon died.

Such are the materials out of which was constructed this greatest of domestic dramas. A comparison of Cinthio's tale with the tragedy built upon it will show the measure of the Poet's judgment better, perhaps, than could be done by an entirely original performance. For, wherever he departs from the story, it is for a great and manifest gain of truth and nature; so that he appears equally judicious in what he borrowed and in what he created, while his resources of invention seem boundless, save as they are self-restrained by the reason and logic of art. The tale has nothing anywise answering to the part of Roderigo, who in the drama is a vastly significant and effective occasion, since upon him the most profound and subtle traits of Iago are made to transpire, and that in such a way as to lift the characters of Othello and Desdemona into, a much higher region, and invest them with a far deeper and more pathetic interest and meaning. And even in the other parts, the Poet can scarce be said to have taken any thing more than a few incidents and the outline of the plot; the character, the passion, the pathos, the poetry, being entirely his own.

Until a recent date, *The Tragedy of Othello* was commonly supposed to have been among the last of Shakespeare's writing. Chalmers assigned it to 1614, Drake, to 1612; Malone at first set it down to 1611, afterwards to 1604. Mr. Collier has produced an extract from *The Egerton Papers*, showing that on August 6, 1602, the sum of ten pounds was paid "to Burbage's Players for *Othello*." At that time, Queen Elizabeth was at Harefield on a visit to Sir Thomas Egerton, then Lord Keeper of the Great Seal, afterwards Lord Ellesmere; and it appears that he had the tragedy performed at his residence for her delectation. The company that acted on this occasion were then known as the Lord Chamberlain's Servants, and in *The Egerton Papers* were spoken of as Burbage's Players, probably because Richard Burbage was the leading actor among them. And an elegy on the death of Burbage, lately discovered among Mr. Heber's manuscripts, ascertains him to have been the original performer of Othello's part. After mentioning various characters in which this actor had been distinguished, the writer proceeds thus:

> But let me not forget one chiefest part
> Wherein, beyond the rest, he mov'd the heart;
> The grieved Moor, made jealous by a slave,
> Who sent his wife to fill a timeless grave,
> Then slew himself upon the bloody bed.

When selected for performance at Harefield, *Othello* was doubtless in the first blush and freshness of its popularity, having probably had a run at the Globe in the spring of that year, and thus recommended itself to the audience of the Queen. Whether the play were then in its finished state, we have no means of ascertaining. Its workmanship certainly bespeaks the Poet's highest maturity of power and art; which has naturally suggested, that when first brought upon the stage it may have been as different from what it is now, as the original *Hamlet* was from the enlarged copy. Such is the reasonable conjecture of Mr. Verplanck,—a conjecture not a little approved by the fact of the Poet's having rewritten so many of his dramas after his mind had outgrown their original form. The style, however, of the play is throughout so even and sustained, so perfect is the coherence and congruity of part with part, and its whole course so free from redundancy and impertinence, that, unless some further external evidence should come to light, the question will have to rest in mere conjecture.

The drama was not printed during the author's life. On October 6, 1621, it was entered at the Stationers' by Thomas Walkley, "under the hands of Sir George Buck and of the Wardens." Soon after was issued a quarto pamphlet of forty-eight leaves, the title-page reading thus: "The Tragedy of Othello, the Moor of Venice. As it hath been divers times acted at the Globe and at the Blackfriars, by his Majesty's Servants. Written by William Shakespeare. London: Printed by N.O. for Thomas Walkley, and are to be sold at his shop, at the Eagle and Child, in Britain's Bourse. 1622." This edition was set forth with a short preface by the publisher, which will be found in the footnote on page vii.

In the folio of 1623, *Othello* stands the tenth in the division of Tragedies, has the acts and scenes regularly marked, and at the end a list of the persons, headed, "The Names of the Actors." Iago is here called "a villain," and Roderigo "a gull'd gentleman." In the folio, the play has a number of passages, some of them highly important, amounting in all to upwards of 160 lines, which are not in the preceding quarto. On the other hand, the folio omits a few lines that are found in the earlier issue.

The play was again set forth in quarto form in 1630, with a title-page reading substantially the same as that of 1622, save as regards the name and address of the publisher.

Neither one of these copies was merely a repetition of another: on the contrary, all three of them were printed from different and probably independent manuscripts.

The island of Cyprus became subject to the republic of Venice, and was first garrisoned with Venetian troops, in 1471. After this time, the only attempt ever made upon that island by the Turks, was under Selim the Second, in 1570. It was then invaded by a powerful force, and conquered in 1571; since which time it has continued a part of the Turkish empire. We learn from the play, that there was a junction of the Turkish fleet at Rhodes, in order for the invasion of Cyprus; that it first sailed towards Cyprus, then went to Rhodes, there met another squadron, and then resumed its course to Cyprus. These are historical facts, and took place when Mustapha, Selim's general, attacked Cyprus, in May, 1570; which is therefore the true period of the action.

In respect of general merit, *Othello* unquestionably stands in the same rank with the Poet's three other great tragedies, *Macbeth*, *Lear*, and *Hamlet*. As to the particular place it is entitled to hold among the four, the best judges, as we might expect, are not agreed. In the elements and impressions of moral terror, it is certainly inferior to *Macbeth*; in breadth and variety of characterization, to *Lear*; in compass and reach of thought to *Hamlet*: but it has one advantage over all the others, in that the passion, the action, the interest, all lie strictly within the sphere of domestic life; for which cause the play has a more close and intimate hold on the common sympathies of mankind. On the whole, perhaps it may be safely affirmed of these four tragedies, that the most competent readers will always like that best which they read last.

Dr. Johnson winds up his excellent remarks on this tragedy as follows: "Had the scene opened in Cyprus, and the preceding incidents been occasionally related, there had been little wanting to a drama of the most exact and scrupulous regularity." This means, no doubt, that the play would have been improved by such a change. The whole of Act I would thus have been spared, and we should have, instead, various narrations in the form of soliloquy, but addressed to the audience. Here, then, would be two improprieties,—the turning of the actor into an orator by putting him directly in communication with the audience, and the making him soliloquize matter inconsistent with the nature of the soliloquy.

But, to say nothing of the irregularity thus involved, all the better meaning of Act I would needs be lost in narration. For the very reason of the dramatic form is, that action conveys something which cannot be done up in propositions. So that, if narrative could here supply the place of the scenes in question, it does not appear why there should be any such drama at all. We will go further: This first Act is the very one which could least be spared, as being in effect fundamental to the others, and therefore necessary to the right understanding of them.

One great error of criticism has been, the looking for too much simplicity of purpose in works of art. We are told, for instance, that the end of the drama is, to represent actions; and that, to keep the work clear of redundances, the action must be one, with a beginning, a middle, and an end; as if all the details, whether of persons or events, were merely for the sake of the catastrophe. Thus it is presumed, that any one thing, to be properly understood, should be detached from all others. Such is not the method of nature: to accomplish one aim, she carries many aims along together. And so the proper merit of a work of art, which is its truth to nature, lies in the harmony of divers coördinate and concurrent purposes, making it, not like a flat abstraction, but like a round, plump fact. Unity of effect is indeed essential; but unity as distinguished from mere oneness of effect comes, in art as in nature, by complexity of purpose;—a complexity wherein each purpose is alternately the means and the end of the others.

Whether the object of the drama be more to represent action, or passion, or character, cannot be affirmed, because in the nature of things neither of these can be represented save in vital union with the others. If, however, either should have precedence, doubtless it is character, for-as-much as this is the common basis of the other two: but the complication and interaction of several characters is necessary to the development of any one; the persons serving as the playground of each other's transpirations, and reciprocally furnishing motives, impulses, and occasions. For every society, whether actual or dramatic, is a *concresence* of individuals: men do not grow and develop alone, but by and from each other; so that many have to grow up together in order for any one to grow; the best part even of their individual life coming to them from or through the social organization. And as men are made, so they must be studied; as no one can grow by himself, so none can be understood by himself: his character being partly derived, must also be partly interpreted, from the particular state of things in which he lives, the characters that act with him, and upon him.

It may be from oversight of these things, that the first Act in *Othello* has been thought superfluous. If the rise, progress, and result of the Moor's passion were the only aim of the work, that Act might indeed be dispensed with. But we must first know something of his character and the characters that act upon him, before we can rightly decide what and whence his passion is. This knowledge ought to be, and in fact is, given in the opening scenes of the play.

Again: We often speak of men as acting thus or thus, according as they are influenced from without. And in one sense this is true, yet not so, but that the man rather determines the motive, than the motive the man. For the same influences often move men in different directions, according to their several predispositions of character. What is with one a motive to virtue, is with another a motive to vice, and with a third no motive at all. On the other hand, where the outward motions are the same, the inward springs are often very different: so that we cannot rightly interpret a man's actions, without some forecast of his actuating principle; his actions being the index of his character, and his character the light whereby that index is to be read. The first business, then, of a drama is, to give some preconception of the characters which may render their actions intelligible, and which may itself in turn receive further illustration from the actions.

Now, there are few things in Shakespeare more remarkable than the judgment shown in his first scenes; and perhaps the very highest instance of this is in the opening of *Othello*. The play begins strictly at the beginning, and goes regularly forward, instead of beginning in the middle, as Johnson would have it, and then going both ways. The first Act gives the prolific germs from which the whole is evolved; it is indeed the seminary of the whole play, and unfolds the characters in their principles, as the other Acts do in their phenomena. The not attending duly to what is there disclosed has caused a good deal of false criticism on the play; as, for example, in the case of Iago, who, his earlier developments being thus left out of the account, or not properly weighed, has been supposed to act from revenge; and then, as no adequate motives for such a revenge are revealed, the character has been thought unnatural.

The main passions and proceedings of the drama all have their *primum mobile* in Iago; and the first Act amply discloses what he is made of and moved by. As if on purpose to prevent any mistake touching his springs of action, he is set forth in various aspects having no direct bearing on the main course of the play.

He comes before us exercising his faculties on the dupe Roderigo, and thereby spilling out the secret of his habitual motives and impulses. That his very frankness may serve to heighten our opinion of his sagacity, the subject he is practising upon is at once seen to be a person who, from strength of passion, weakness of understanding, and want of character, will be kept from sticking at his own professions of villainy. So that the freedom with which he here unmasks himself only lets us into his keen perceptions of his *whens* and *hows*.

We know from the first, that the bond of union between them is the purse. Roderigo thinks he is buying up Iago's talents and efforts. This is just what Iago means to have him think; and it is something doubtful which glories most, the one in having money to bribe talents, or the other in having wit to catch money. Still it is plain enough that Iago, with a pride of intellectual mastery far stronger than his love of lucre, cares less for the money than for the fun of wheedling and swindling others out of it.

But while Iago is selling pledges of assistance to his dupe, there is the stubborn fact of his being in the service of Othello; and Roderigo cannot understand how he is to serve two masters at once whose interests are so conflicting. In order, therefore, to engage his faith without forsaking the Moor, he has to persuade Roderigo that he follows the Moor but to serve his turn upon him. A hard task indeed; but, for that very cause, all the more grateful to him, since, from its peril and perplexity, it requires the great stress of cunning, and gives the wider scope for his ingenuity. The very anticipation of the thing oils his faculties into ecstacy; his heart seems in a paroxysm of delight while venting his passion for hypocrisy, as if this most Satanical attribute served him for a muse, and inspired him with an energy and eloquence not his own.

Still, to make his scheme work, he must allege some reasons for his purpose touching the Moor: for Roderigo, gull though he be, is not so gullible as to entrust his cause to a groundless treachery; he must know something of the strong provocations which have led Iago to cherish such designs. Iago understands this perfectly: he therefore pretends a secret grudge against Othello, which he is but holding in till he can find or make a fit occasion; and therewithal assigns such grounds and motives as he knows will secure faith in his pretense; whereupon the other gets too warm with the anticipated fruits of his treachery to suspect any similar designs on himself. Wonderful indeed are the arts whereby the rogue wins and keeps his ascendancy over the gull! During their conversation, we can almost see the former worming himself into the latter, like a corkscrew into a cork.

But Iago has a still harder task, to carry Roderigo along in a criminal quest of Desdemona; for his character is marked rather by want of principle than by bad principle, and the passion with which she has inspired him is incompatible with any purpose of dishonoring her. Until the proceeding before the Senate, he hopes her father will break off the match with Othello, so that she will again be open to an honorable solicitation; but, when he finds her married, and the marriage ratified by her father, he is for giving up in despair. But Iago again besets him, like an evil angel, and plies his witchcraft with augmented vigor. Himself an atheist of female virtue, he has no way to gain his point but by debauching Roderigo's mind with his own atheism. With an overweening pride of wealth Roderigo unites considerable respect for womanhood. Therefore Iago at once flatters his pride by urging the power of money, and inflames his passion by urging the frailty of woman: for the greatest preventive of dishonorable passion is faith in the virtue of its object. Throughout this undertaking, Iago's passionless soul revels amid lewd thoughts and images, like a spirit broke loose from the pit. With his nimble fancy, his facility and felicity of combination, fertile, fluent, and apposite in plausibilities, at one and the same time stimulating Roderigo's inclination to believe, and stifling his ability to refute, what is said, he literally overwhelms his power of resistance. By often iterating the words, "put money in your purse," he tries to make up in earnestness of assertion whatever may be wanting in the cogency of his reasoning, and, in proportion as Roderigo's mind lacks room for his arguments, to subdue him by mere violence of impression. Glorying alike in mastery of intellect and of will, he would so make Roderigo part of himself, like his hand or foot, as to be the immediate organ of his own volitions. Nothing can surpass the fiendish chuckle of self-satisfaction with which he turns from his conquest to sneer at the victim:

Thus do I ever make my fool my purse;
For I mine own gain'd knowledge should profane,
If I would time expend with such a snipe,
But for my sport and profit.

So much for Iago's proceedings with the gull. The sagacity with which he feels and forescents his way into Roderigo is only equaled by the skill with which, while clinching the nail of one conquest, he prepares the subject, by a sort of forereaching process, for a further conquest.

Roderigo, if not preoccupied with vices, is empty of virtues; so that Iago has but to play upon his vanity and passion, and ruin him through these. But Othello has no such avenues open: the villain can reach him only through his virtues; has no way to work his ruin but by turning his honor and integrity against him. And the same exquisite tact of character, which prompts his frankness to the former, counsels the utmost closeness to the latter. Knowing Othello's "perfect soul," he dare not make to him the least tender of dishonorable services, lest he should repel his confidence, and incur his resentment. Still he is quite moderate in his professions, taking shrewd care not to whiten the sepulcher so much as to provoke an investigation of its contents. He therefore rather modestly acknowledges his conscientious scruples than boasts of them; as though, being a soldier, he feared that such things might speak more for his virtue than for his manhood. And yet his reputation for exceeding honesty has something suspicious about it, for it looks as though he had studied to make that virtue somewhat of a speciality in his outward carriage; whereas true honesty, like charity, naturally shrinks from being matter of public fame, lest by notoriety it should get corrupted into vanity or pride.

Iago's method with the Moor is, to intermix confession and pretension in such a way that the one may be taken as proof of modesty, the other, of fidelity. When, for example, he affects to disqualify his own testimony, on the ground that "it is his nature's plague to spy into abuses," he of course designs a contrary impression; as, in actual life, men often acknowledge real vices, in order to be acquitted of them. That his accusation of others may stand the clearer of distrust, he prefaces it by accusing himself. Acting, too, as if he spared no pains to be right, yet still feared he was wrong, his very opinions carry the weight of facts, as having forced themselves upon him against his will. When, watching his occasion, he proceeds to set his scheme of mischief at work, his mind seems struggling with some terrible secret which he dare not let out, yet cannot keep in; which breaks from him in spite of himself, and even because of his fear to utter it. He thus manages to be heard and still seem overheard, that so he may not be held responsible for his words, any more than if he had spoken in his sleep. In those well-known lines,—"Good name, in man and woman, is the immediate jewel of their souls," etc.,—he but gives out that he is restrained only by tenderness to others from uttering what would blast them. And there is, withal, a dark, frightful significance in his manner, which puts the hearer in an agony of curiosity: the more he refuses to tell his thoughts, the more he sharpens the desire to know them: when questioned, he so states his reasons for not speaking, that in effect they compel the Moor to extort the secret from him. For his purpose is, not merely to deceive Othello, but to get his thanks for deceiving him.

It is worth remarking, that Iago has a peculiar classification, whereby all the movements of our nature fall under the two heads of sensual and rational. Now, the healthy mind is marked by openness to impressions from without; is apt to be overmastered by the inspiration of external objects; in which case the understanding is kept subordinate to the social, moral, and religious sentiments. But our ancient despises all this. Man, argues he, is made up altogether of intellect and appetite, so that whatever motions do not spring from the former must be referred to the latter. The yielding to inspirations from without argues an ignoble want of spiritual force; to be overmastered by external objects, infers a conquest of the flesh over the mind; all the religions of our nature, as love, honor, reverence, according to this liberal and learned spirit are but "a lust of the blood and a permission of the will," and therefore things to be looked down upon with contempt. Hence, when his mind walks amidst the better growings of humanity, he is "nothing, if not critical": so he pulls up every flower, however beautiful, to find a flaw in the root; and of course flaws the root in pulling it. For, indeed, he has, properly speaking, no susceptibilities; his mind is perfectly unimpressible, receives nothing, yields to nothing, but cuts its way through every thing like a flint.

It appears, then, that in Iago intellectuality itself is made a character; that is, the intellect has cast off all allegiance to the moral and religious sentiments, and become a law and an impulse to itself; so that the mere fact of his being able to do a thing is sufficient reason for doing it. For, in such cases, the mind comes to act, not for any outward ends or objects, but merely for the sake of acting; has a passion for feats of agility and strength; and may even go so far as to revel amid the dangers and difficulties of wicked undertakings. We thus have, not indeed a craving for carnal indulgences, but a cold, dry pruriency of intellect, or as Mr. Dana aptly styles it, "a lust of the brain," which naturally manifests itself in a fanaticism of mischief, a sort of hungering and thirsting after unrighteousness. Of course, therefore, Iago shows no addiction to sensualities: on the contrary, all his passions are concentrated in the head, all his desires eminently spiritual and Satanical; so that he scorns the lusts of the flesh, or, if indulging them at all, generally does it in a criminal way, and not so much for the indulgence as for the criminality involved. Such appears to be the motive principle of Satan, who, so far as we know, is neither a glutton, nor a wine-bibber, nor a debauchee, but an impersonation of pride and self-will; and therefore prefers such a line of action as will most exercise and demonstrate his power.

Edmund in *King Lear*, seeing his road clear but for moral restraints, politely bows them out of door, lest they should hinder the free working of his faculties. Iago differs from him, in that he chooses rather to invade than elude the laws of morality: when he sees Duty coming, he takes no pains to play round or get by her, but rather goes out of his way to meet her, as if on purpose to spit in her face and walk over her. That a thing ought not to be done, is thus with him a motive for doing it, because, the worse the deed, the more it shows his freedom and power. When he owns to himself that "the Moor is of a constant, loving, noble nature," it is not so much that he really feels these qualities in him, as that, granting him to have them, there is the greater merit in hating him. For anybody can hate a man for his faults; but to hate a man for his virtues, is something original; involves, so to speak, a declaration of moral independence. So, too, in the soliloquy where he speaks of loving Desdemona, he first disclaims any unlawful passion for her, and then adds, parenthetically, "though, peradventure, I stand accountant for as great a sin"; as much as to say, that whether guilty or not he did not care, and dared the responsibility at all events. So that, to adopt a distinction from Dr. Chalmers, he here seems not so much an atheist as an antitheist in morality. We remember that the late Mr. Booth, in pronouncing these words, cast his eyes upwards, as if looking Heaven in the face with a sort of defiant smile!

That Iago prefers lying to telling the truth, is implied in what we have said. Perhaps, indeed, such a preference is inseparable from his inordinate intellectuality. For it is a great mistake to suppose that a man's love of truth will needs be in proportion to his intellectuality: on the contrary, an excess of this may cause him to prefer lies, as yielding larger scope for activity and display of mind. For they who thrive by the truth naturally attribute their thrift to her power, not to their own; and success, coming to them as a gift, rather humbles than elates them. On the other hand, he who thrives by lying can reckon himself an overmatch for truth; he seems to owe none of his success to nature, but rather to have wrung it out in spite of her. Even so, Iago's characteristic satisfaction seems to stand in a practical reversing of moral distinctions; for example, in causing his falsehood to do the work of truth, or another's truth, the work of falsehood. For, to make virtue pass for virtue, and pitch for pitch, is no triumph at all; but to make the one pass for the other, is a triumph indeed! Iago glories in thus seeming to convict appearance of untruth; in compelling nature, as it were, to own her secret deceptions, and acknowledge him too much for her. Hence his adroit practice to appear as if serving Roderigo, while really using him. Hence his purpose, not merely to deceive the Moor, but to get his thanks for doing so. Therefore it is that he takes such a malicious pleasure in turning Desdemona's conduct wrong side out; for, the more angel she, the greater his triumph in making her seem a devil.

There is, indeed, no touching the bottom of Iago's art: sleepless, unrelenting, inexhaustible, with an energy that never flags, and an alertness that nothing can surprise, he outwits every obstacle and turns it into an ally; the harder the material before him, the more greedily does he seize it, the more adroitly work it, the more effectively make it tell; and absolutely persecutes the Moor with a redundancy of proof. When, for instance, Othello drops the words, "and yet how nature, erring from itself"; meaning simply that no woman is altogether exempt from frailty; Iago with inscrutable sleight-of-hand forthwith steals in upon him, under cover of this remark, a cluster of pregnant insinuations, as but so many inferences from his suggestion; and so manages to impart his own thoughts to the Moor by seeming to derive them from him. Othello is thus brought to distrust all his original perceptions, to renounce his own understanding, and accept Iago's instead. And such, in fact, is Iago's aim, the very earnest and pledge of his intellectual mastery. Nor is there any thing that he seems to take with more gust, than the pain he inflicts by making the Moor think himself a fool; that he has been the easy dupe of Desdemona's arts; and that he owes his deliverance to the keener insight and sagacity of his honest, faithful ancient.

But there is scarce any wickedness conceivable, into which such a lust and pride of intellect and will may not carry a man. Craving for action of the most exciting kind, there is a fascination for him in the very danger of crime. Walking the plain, safe, straight-forward path of truth and nature, does not excite and occupy him enough; he prefers to thread the dark, perilous intricacies of some hellish plot, or to balance himself, as it were, on a rope stretched over an abyss, where danger stimulates and success demonstrates his agility. Even if remorse overtake such a man, its effect is to urge him deeper into crime; as the desperate gamester naturally tries to bury his chagrin at past losses in the increased excitement of a larger stake.

Critics have puzzled themselves a good deal about Iago's motives. The truth is, "natures such as his spin motives out of their own bowels." What is said of one of Wordsworth's characters in *The Borderers*, holds equally true of our ancient:

> There needs no other motive
> Than that most strange incontinence in crime
> Which haunts this Oswald. Power is life to him
> And breath and being; where he cannot govern,
> He will destroy.

If it be objected to this view, that Iago states his motives to Roderigo; we answer, Iago is a liar, and is trying to dupe Roderigo; and knows he must allege some motives, to make the other trust him. Or, if it be objected that he states them in soliloquy, when there is no one present for him to deceive; again we answer, Yes there is; the very one he cares most to deceive, namely, himself. And indeed the terms of this statement clearly denote a foregone conclusion, the motives coming in only as an after-thought. The truth is, he cannot quite look his purpose in the face; it is a little too fiendish for his steady gaze; and he tries to hunt up or conjure up some motives, to keep the peace between it and his conscience. This is what Coleridge justly calls "the motive-hunting of a motionless malignity"; and well may he add, "how awful it is!"

Much has been said about Iago's acting from revenge. But he has no cause for revenge, unless to deserve his love be such a cause. For revenge supposes some injury received, real or fancied; and the sensibility whence it springs cannot but make some discrimination as to its objects. So that, if this were his motive, he would respect the innocent while crushing the guilty, there being, else, no revenge in the case. The impossibility, indeed, of accounting for his conduct on such grounds is the very reason why the character, judged on such grounds, has been pronounced unnatural. It is true, he tries to suspect, first Othello, and then Cassio, of having wronged him: he even finds or feigns a certain rumor to that effect; yet shows, by his manner of talking about it, that he does not himself believe it, or rather does not care whether it be true or not. And he elsewhere owns that the reasons he alleges are but pretenses after all. Even while using his divinity, he knows it is the "divinity of hell," else he would scorn to use it; and boasts of the intention to entrap his victims through their friendship for him, as if his obligations to them were his only provocations against them. For, to bad men, obligations often are provocations. That he ought to honor them, and *therefore* envies them, is the only wrong they have done him, or that he thinks they have done him; and he means to indemnify himself for their right to his honor, by ruining them through the very gifts and virtues which have caused his envy. Meanwhile, he amuses his reasoning powers by inventing a sort of *ex-post-facto* motives for his purpose; the same wicked busy-mindedness, that suggests the crime, prompting him to play with the possible reasons for it.

We have dwelt the longer on Iago, because without a just and thorough insight of him Othello cannot be rightly understood, as the source and quality of his action require to be judged from the influences that are made to work upon him. The Moor has for the most part been regarded as specially illustrating the workings of jealousy. Whether there be any thing, and, if so, how much, of this passion in him, may indeed be questions having two sides; but we may confidently affirm that he has no special predisposition to jealousy; and that whatsoever of it there may be in him does not grow in such a way, nor from such causes, that it can justly be held as the leading feature of his character, much less as his character itself; though such has been the view more commonly taken of him. On this point, there has been a strange ignoring of the inscrutable practices in which his passion originates. Instead of going behind the scene, and taking its grounds of judgment directly from the subject himself, criticism has trusted overmuch in what is said of him by other persons in the drama, to whom he must perforce seem jealous, because they know and can know nothing of the devilish cunning that has been at work with him. And the common opinion has no doubt been much furthered by the stage, Iago's villainy being represented as so open and barefaced, that the Moor must have been grossly stupid or grossly jealous not to see through him; whereas, in fact, so subtle is the villain's craft, so close and involved are his designs, that Othello deserves but the more respect and honor for being taken in by him.

Coleridge is very bold and clear in defense of the Moor. "Othello," says he, "does not kill Desdemona in jealousy, but in a conviction forced upon him by the almost superhuman art of Iago,—such a conviction as any man would and must have entertained, who had believed Iago's honesty as Othello did. We, the audience, know that Iago is a villain from the beginning; but, in considering the essence of the Shakespearean Othello, we must perseveringly place ourselves in his situation, and under his circumstances. Then we shall immediately feel the fundamental difference between the solemn agony of the noble Moor, and the wretched fishing jealousy of Leontes." Iago describes jealousy as "the monster that doth make the meat it feeds on." And Emilia speaks to the same sense, when Desdemona acquits her husband of jealousy on the ground that she has never given him cause: "But jealous souls will not be answer'd so; they are not ever jealous for the cause, but jealous, for they're jealous."

If jealousy be indeed such a thing as is here described, it seems clear enough that a passion thus self-generated and self-sustained ought not to be confounded with a state of mind superinduced, like Othello's, by forgery of external proofs,—a forgery wherein himself has no share but as the victim. And we may safely affirm that he has no aptitude for such a passion; it is against the whole grain of his mind and character. Iago evidently knows this; knows the Moor to be incapable of spontaneous distrust; that he must see, before he'll doubt; that when he doubts, he'll prove; and that when he has proved, he will retain his honor at all events, and retain his love, if it be compatible with honor. Accordingly, lest the Moor should suspect himself of jealousy, Iago pointedly warns him to beware of it; puts him on his guard against such self-delusions, that so his mind may be more open to the force of evidence, and lest from fear of being jealous he should entrench himself in the opposite extreme, and so be proof against conviction.

The struggle, then, in Othello is not between love and jealousy, but between love and honor; and Iago's machinations are exactly adapted to bring these two latter passions into collision. Indeed it is the Moor's very freedom from a jealous temper, that enables the villain to get the mastery of him. Such a character as his, so open, so generous, so confiding, is just the one to be taken in the strong toils of Iago's cunning; to have escaped them, would have argued him a partaker of the strategy under which he falls. It is both the law and the impulse of a high and delicate honor, to rely on another's word, unless we have proof to the contrary; to presume that things and persons are what they seem: and it is an impeachment of our own veracity to suspect falsehood in one who bears a character for truth. Such is precisely the Moor's condition in respect to Iago; a man whom he has long known, and never caught in a lie; whom he as often trusted, and never seen cause to regret it. So that, in our judgment of the Moor, we ought to proceed as if his wife were really guilty of what she is charged with; for, were she ever so guilty, he could scarce have stronger proof than he has; and that the evidence owes all its force to the plotting and lying of another, surely makes nothing against him.

Nevertheless, we are far from upholding that Othello does not at any stage of the proceedings show signs of jealousy. For the elements of this passion exist in the strongest and healthiest minds, and may be kindled into a transient sway over their motions, or at least so as to put them on the alert; and all we mean to affirm is, that jealousy is not Othello's characteristic, and does not form the actuating principle of his conduct. It is indeed certain that he doubts before he has proof; but then it is also certain that he does not act upon his doubt, till proof has been given him. As to the rest, it seems to us there can be no dispute about the thing, but only about the term; some understanding by *jealousy* one thing, some another. We presume that no one would have spoken of the Moor as acting from jealousy, in case his wife had really been guilty: his course would then have been regarded simply as the result of conviction upon evidence; which is to our mind nearly decisive of the question.

Accordingly, in the killing of Desdemona we have the proper marks of a judicial as distinguished from a revengeful act. The Moor goes about her death calmly and religiously, as a duty from which he would gladly escape by his own death, if he could; and we feel that his heart is wrung with inexpressible anguish, though his hand is firm. It is a part of his heroism, that as he prefers her to himself, so he prefers honor to her; and he manifestly contemplates her death as a sacrifice due to the institution which he fully believes, and has reason to believe, she has mocked and profaned. So that we cordially subscribe to the words of Ulrici respecting him: "Jealousy and revenge seize his mind but transiently; they spring up and pass away with the first burst of passion; being indeed but the momentary phases under which love and honor, the ruling principles of his soul, evince the deep wounds they are suffering."

The general custom of the stage has been, to represent Othello as a full-blooded Negro; and criticism has been a good deal exercised of late on the question whether Shakespeare really meant him for such. The only expression in the play that would fairly infer him to be a Negro, is Roderigo's "thick-lips." But Roderigo there speaks as a disappointed lover, seeking to revenge himself on the cause of his disappointment. We all know how common it is for coxcombs like him, when balked and mortified in rivalry with their betters, to fly off into extravagant terms of disparagement and reproach; their petulant vanity easing and soothing itself by calling them any thing they may wish them to be. It is true, the Moor is several times spoken of as black; but this term was often used, as it still is, of a tawny skin in comparison with one that is fair. So in *Antony and Cleopatra* the heroine speaks of herself as being "with Phœbus' amorous pinches *black*"; and in *The Two Gentlemen of Verona* Thurio, when told that Silvia says his face is a fair one, replies,—"Nay, then the wanton lies: my face is *black*." But, indeed, the calling a dark-complexioned white person black is as common as almost any form of speech in the language.

It would seem, from Othello's being so often called "the Moor," that there ought to be no question about what the Poet meant him to be. For the difference between Moors and Negroes was probably as well understood in his time as it is now; and there is no more evidence in this play that he thought them the same, than there is in *The Merchant of Venice*, where the Prince of Morocco comes as a suitor to Portia, and in a stage-direction of the old quarto is called "a *tawny* Moor." Othello was a Mauritanian prince, for Iago in Act IV, sc. ii, speaks of his purposed retirement to Mauritania as his home. Consistently with this, the same speaker in another place uses terms implying him to be a native of Barbary, Mauritania being the old name of one of the Barbary States. Iago, to be sure, is an unscrupulous liar; but then he has more cunning than to lie when telling the truth will stand with his purpose, as it evidently will here. So that there needs no scruple about endorsing the argument of Mr. White, in his *Shakespeare's Scholar*. "Shakespeare," says he, "nowhere calls Othello an Ethiopian, and also does not apply the term to Aaron in the horrible *Titus Andronicus*; but he continually speaks of both as Moors; and as he has used the first word elsewhere, and certainly had use for it as a reproach in the mouth of Iago, it seems that he must have been fully aware of the distinction in grade between the two races. Indeed I never could see the least reason for supposing that Shakespeare intended Othello to be represented as a Negro. With the Negroes, the Venetians, had nothing to do, that we know of, and could not have in the natural course of things; whereas, with their over-the-way neighbors, the Moors, they were continually brought in contact. These were a warlike, civilized, and enterprising race, which could furnish an Othello."

That the question may, if possible, be thoroughly shut up and done with, we will add the remarks of Coleridge on the aforesaid custom of the stage: "Even if we supposed this an uninterrupted tradition of the theater, and that Shakespeare himself, from want of scenes, and the experience that nothing could be made too marked for the senses of his audience, had practically sanctioned it,—would this prove aught concerning his own intention as a poet for all ages? Can we imagine him so utterly ignorant as to make a barbarous Negro plead royal birth,—at a time, too, when Negroes were not known except as slaves? As for Iago's language to Brabantio, it implies merely that Othello was a Moor, that is, black. Though I think the rivalry of Roderigo sufficient to account for his willful confusion of Moor and Negro; yet, even if compelled to give this up, I should think it only adapted for the acting of the day, and should complain of an enormity built on a single word, in direct contradiction to Iago's 'Barbary horse.' Besides, if we could in good earnest believe Shakespeare ignorant of the distinction, still why should we adopt one disagreeable possibility, instead of a ten times greater and more pleasing probability? It is a common error to mistake the epithets applied by the *dramatis personæ* to each other, as truly descriptive of what the audience ought to see or know. No doubt, Desdemona 'saw Othello's visage in his mind'; yet, as we are constituted, and most surely as an English audience was disposed in the beginning of the seventeenth century, it would be something monstrous to conceive this beautiful Venetian girl falling in love with a veritable Negro. It would argue a disproportionateness, a want of balance in Desdemona, which Shakespeare does not appear to have in the least contemplated."

The character of Othello, direct and single in itself, is worked out with great breadth and clearness. And here again the first Act is peculiarly fruitful of significant points; furnishing, in respect of him as of Iago, the seminal ideas of which the subsequent details are the natural issues and offshoots. In the opening scene we have Iago telling various lies about the Moor; yet his lying is so managed as, while affecting its immediate purpose on the gull, to be at the same time more or less suggestive of the truth: he caricatures Othello, but is too artful a caricaturist to let the peculiar features of the subject be lost in an excess of misrepresentation; that is, there is truth enough in what he says, to make it pass with one who wishes it true, and whose mind is too weak to prevent such a wish from growing into belief.

Othello's mind is strongly charged with the natural enthusiasm of high principle and earnest feeling, and this gives a certain elevated and imaginative turn to his manner of thought and speech. In the deportment of such a man there is apt to be something upon which a cold and crafty malice can easily stick the imputation of being haughty and grandiloquent, or of "loving his own pride and purposes." Especially, when urged with unseasonable or impertinent solicitations, his answers are apt to be in such a style, that they can hardly pass through an Iagoish mind, without catching the air of strutting and bombastic evasion. For a man like Othello will not stoop to be the advocate or apologist of himself: it is enough that he stands justified to his own sense of right; and if others dislike his course, this does not shake him, as he did not take it with a view to please them: he acts from his own mind; and to explain his conduct, save where he is responsible, looks like soliciting an endorsement from others, as though the consciousness of rectitude were not enough to sustain him. Such a man, if his fortune and his other parts be at all in proportion, commonly succeeds; for by his strength of character he naturally creates a sphere which himself alone can fill, and so makes himself necessary. On the other hand, a subtle and malignant rogue, like Iago, while fearing to be known as the enemy of such a man, envies his success, and from this envy affects contempt of his qualities. For the proper triumph of a bad man over his envied superiors is, to scoff at the very gifts which gnaw him.

The intimations, then, derived from Iago lead us to regard the Moor, before we meet with him, as one who deliberates calmly, and therefore decides firmly. His refusing to explain his conduct where he is not responsible, is a pledge that he will not shrink from any responsibility where he truly owes it. In his first reply when urged by Iago to elude Brabantio's pursuit, our expectations are made good. We see that, as he acts, from honor and principle, so he will cheerfully abide the consequences. Full of equanimity and firmness, he is content to let the reasons of his course appear in the issues thereof; whereas Iago delights in stating his reasons, as giving scope for mental activity and display.

From his characteristic intrepidity and calmness, the Moor, as we learn in the sequel, has come to be esteemed, by those who know him best, as one whom "passion cannot shake." For the passions are in him both tempered and strengthened by the energy of higher principles; and, if kept under reason, the stronger they are, the more they exalt reason. This feature of Othello is well seen at his meeting with Brabantio and attendants, when the parties are on the point of fighting, and he quiets them by exclaiming, "Keep up your bright swords, for the dew will rust them;" where the belligerent spirit is as much charmed down by his playful logic, as overawed by his sternness of command. So, too, when Brabantio calls out, "Down with him, thief!" and he replies, "Good signior, you shall more command with years than with your weapons."

Such is our sturdy warrior's habitual carriage: no upstart exigency disconcerts him; no obloquy exasperates him to violence or recrimination: peril, perplexity, provocation rather augment than impair his self-possession; and the more deeply he is stirred, the more calmly and steadily he acts. This calmness of intensity is most finely displayed in his address to the Senate, where the words, though they fall on the ear as softly as an evening breeze, seem charged with life from every part of his being. All is grace and modesty and gentleness, yet what strength and dignity! the union of perfect repose and impassioned energy. Perhaps the finest point of contrast between Othello and Iago lies in the method of their several minds. Iago is morbidly introversive and self-explicative; his mind is ever busy spinning out its own contents; and he takes no pleasure either in viewing or in showing things, till he has baptized them in his own spirit, and then seems chuckling inwardly as he holds them up reeking with the slime he has dipped them in. In Othello, on the contrary, every thing is direct, healthy, objective; and he reproduces in transparent diction the truth as revealed to him from without; his mind being like a clear, even mirror which, invisible itself, renders back in its exact shape and color whatsoever stands before it.

We know of nothing in Shakespeare that has this quality more conspicuous than the Moor's account "how he did thrive in this fair lady's love, and she in his." The dark man eloquent literally speaks in pictures. We see the silent blushing maiden moving about her household tasks, ever and anon turning her eye upon the earnest warrior; leaving the door open as she goes out of the room, that she may catch the tones of his voice; hastening back to her father's side, as though draw to the spot by some new impulse of filial attachment; afraid to look the speaker in the face, yet unable to keep out of his presence, and drinking in with ear and heart every word of his marvelous tale: the Moor, meanwhile, waxing more eloquent when this modest listener was by, partly because he saw she was interested, and partly because he wished to interest her still more. Yet we believe all he says, for the virtual presence of the things he describes enables us, as it were, to test his fidelity of representation.

In his simplicity, however, he lets out a truth of which he seems not to have been aware. At Brabantio's fireside he has been unwittingly making love by his manner, before he was even conscious of loving; and thought he was but listening for a disclosure of the lady's feelings, while he was really soliciting a response to his own: for this is a matter wherein heart often calls and answers to heart, without giving the head any notice of its proceedings. His quick perception of the interest he had awakened is a confession of the interest he felt, the state of his mind coming out in his anxiety to know that of hers. And how natural it was that he should thus honestly think he was but returning her passion, while it was his own passion that caused him to see or suspect she had any to be returned! And so she seems to have understood the matter; whereupon, appreciating the modesty that kept him silent, she gave him a hint of encouragement to speak. In his feelings, moreover, respect keeps pace with affection; and he involuntarily seeks some tacit assurance of a return of his passion as a sort of permission to cherish and confess it. It is this feeling that originates the delicate, reverential courtesy, the ardent, yet distant, and therefore beautiful regards, with which a truly honorable mind instinctively attires itself towards its best object;—a feeling that throws a majestic grace around the most unpromising figure, and endows the plainest features with something more eloquent than beauty.

The often-alleged unfitness of Othello's match has been mainly disposed of by what we have already said respecting his origin. The rest of it, if there be any, may be safely left to the facts of his being honored by the Venetian Senate and of his being a cherished guest at Brabantio's fireside. At all events, we cannot help thinking that the noble Moor and his sweet lady have the very sort of resemblance which people thus united ought to have; and their likeness seems all the better for being joined with so much of unlikeness. It is the chaste, beautiful wedlock of meekness and magnanimity, where the inward correspondence stands the more approved for the outward diversity; and reminds us of what we are too apt to forget, that the stout, valiant soul is the chosen home of reverence and tenderness. Our heroic warrior's dark, rough exterior is found to enclose a heart strong as a giant's, yet soft and sweet as infancy. Such a marriage of bravery and gentleness proclaims that beauty is an overmatch for strength; and that true delicacy is among the highest forms of power.

Equally beautiful is the fact, that Desdemona has the heart to recognize the proper complement of herself beneath such an uninviting appearance. Perhaps none but so pure and gentle a being could have discerned the real gentleness of Othello through so many obscurations. To her fine sense, that tale of wild adventures and mischances, which often did beguile her of her tears,—a tale wherein another might have seen but the marks of a rude, coarse, animal strength,—disclosed the history of a most meek, brave, manly soul. Nobly blind to whatsoever is repulsive in his manhood's vesture of accidents, her thoughts are filled with "his honors and his valiant parts"; his ungracious aspect is lost to her in his graces of character; and the shrine, that were else so unattractive to look upon, is made beautiful by the life with which her chaste eye sees it irradiated.

In herself, Desdemona is not more interesting than several of the Poet's women; but perhaps none of the others is in a condition so proper for developing the innermost springs of pathos. In her character and sufferings there is a nameless something that haunts the reader's mind, and hangs like a spell of compassionate sorrow upon the beatings of his heart: his thoughts revert to her and linger about her, as under a mysterious fascination of pity which they cannot shake off, and which is only kept from being painful by the sacred charm of beauty and eloquence that blends with the feeling while kindling it. It is remarkable, that the sympathies are not so deeply moved in the scene of her death, as in that where by the blows of her husband's hand and tongue she is made to feel that she has lost him. Too innocent to suspect that she is suspected, she cannot for a long time understand nor imagine the motive of his harshness; and her errings in quest of excuses and apologies for him are deeply pathetic, inasmuch as they manifestly spring from her incapability of an impure thought. And the sense that the heart of his confidence is gone from her, and for what cause it is gone, comes upon her like a dead stifling weight of agony and woe, which benumbs her to all other pains. She does not show any thing that can be properly called pangs of suffering; the effect is too deep for that; the blow falling so heavy that it stuns her sensibilities into a sort of lethargy.

Desdemona's character may almost be said to consist in the union of purity and impressibility. All her organs of sense and motion seem perfectly ensouled, and her visible form instinct in every part with the spirit and intelligence of moral life.

We understood
Her by her sight; her pure and eloquent blood
Spoke in her cheeks, and so distinctly wrought,
That one might almost say her body thought.

Hence her father describes her as a "maiden never bold; of spirit so still and quiet, that her motion blush'd at itself." Which gives the idea of a being whose whole frame is so receptive of influences and impressions from without, who lives so entranced amid a world of beauty and delight, that her soul keeps ever looking and listening; and if at any time she chance upon a stray thought or vision of herself, she shrinks back surprised and abashed, as though she had caught herself in the presence of a stranger whom modesty kept her from looking in the face. It is through this most delicate impressibility that she sometimes gets frightened out of her real character; as in her equivocation about the handkerchief, and her childlike pleading for life in the last scene; where her perfect candor and resignation are overmastered by sudden impressions of terror.

But, with all her openness to influences from without, she is still susceptive only of the good. No element of impurity can insinuate itself. Her nature seems wrought about with some subtle texture of moral sympathies and antipathies, which selects as by instinct whatsoever is pure, without taking any thought or touch of the evil mixed with it. Even Iago's moral oil-of-vitriol cannot eat a passage into her mind: from his envenomed wit she extracts the element of harmless mirth, without receiving or suspecting the venom with which it is charged. Thus the world's contagions pass before her, yet dare not touch nor come near her, because she has nothing to sympathize with them or own their acquaintance. And so her life is like a quiet stream,

In whose calm depth the beautiful and pure
Alone are mirror'd; which, though shapes of ill
Do hover round its surface, glides in light,
And takes no shadow from them.

Desdemona's heroism, we fear, is not of the kind to take very well with such an age of individual ensconcement as the present. Though of a "high and plenteous wit and invention," this quality never makes any special report of itself: like Cordelia, all the parts of her being speak in such harmony that the intellectual tones may not be distinctly heard. Besides, her mind and character were formed under that old-fashioned way of thinking which, regarding man and wife as socially one, legislated *round* them, not *between* them; so that the wife naturally sought protection *in* her husband, instead of resorting to legal methods for protection *against* him. Affection does indeed fill her with courage and energy of purpose: she is heroic to link her life with the man she loves; heroic to do and suffer with him and for him after she is his; but, poor gentle soul! she knows no heroism that can prompt her, in respect of him, to cast aside the awful prerogative of defenselessness: that she has lost him, is what hurts her; and this is a hurt that cannot be salved with anger or resentment: so that her only strength is to be meek, uncomplaining, submissive in the worst that his hand may execute. Swayed by that power whose "favorite seat is feeble woman's breast," she is of course "a child to chiding," and sinks beneath unkindness, instead of having the spirit to outface it.

They err greatly, who think to school Desdemona in the doctrine of woman's rights. When her husband has been shaken from his confidence in her truth and loyalty, what can she care for her rights as a woman? To be under the necessity of asserting them, is to have lost and more than lost them. A constrained abstinence from evil deeds and unkind words bears no price with her; and to be sheltered from the wind and storm, is worse than nothing, unless she have a living fountain of light and warmth in the being that shelters her. But, indeed, the beauty of the woman is so hid in the affection and obedience of the wife, that it seems almost a profanation to praise it. As brave to suffer wrong as she is fearful to do it, there is a holiness in her mute resignation which ought, perhaps, to be kept, where the Poet has left it, veiled from all save those whom a severe discipline of humanity may have qualified for duly respecting it. At all events, whoever would get at her secret, let him study her as a pupil, not as a critic; and until his inmost heart speaks her approval, let him rest assured that he is not competent to judge her. But if he have the gift to see that her whole course, from the first intimation of the gentle, submissive daughter, to the last groan of the ever-loving, ever-obedient, broken-hearted wife, is replete with the beauty and grace and holiness of womanhood, then let him weep, weep, for her; so may he depart "a sadder and a wiser man." As for her unresisting submissiveness, let no man dare to defend it! Assuredly, we shall do her a great wrong, if we suppose for a moment that she would not rather die by her husband's hand, than owe her life to any protection against him. What, indeed, were life, what could it be to her, since suspicion has fallen on her innocency? That her husband could not, would not, *dare* not wrong her, even because she had trusted in him, and because in her sacred defenselessness she could not resist nor resent the wrong,—this is the only protection from which she would not pray to be delivered.

Coleridge has justly remarked upon the art shown in Iago, that the character, with all its inscrutable depravity, neither revolts nor seduces the mind: the interest of his part amounts almost to fascination, yet there is not the slightest moral taint or infection about it. Hardly less wonderful is the Poet's skill in carrying the Moor through such a course of undeserved infliction, without any loosening from him of our sympathy or respect. Deep and intense as is the feeling that goes along with Desdemona, Othello fairly divides it with her: nay, more; the virtues and sufferings of each are so managed as to heighten the interest of the other. The impression still waits upon him, that he does "nought in hate, but all in honor." Nor is the mischief made to work through any vice or weakness perceived or left in him, but rather through such qualities as lift him higher in our regard. Under the conviction that she, in whom he had built his faith and garnered up his heart,—that she, in whom he looked to find how much more blessed it is to give than to receive, has desecrated all his gifts, and turned his very religion into sacrilege;—under this conviction, all the poetry, the grace, the consecration, every thing that can beautify or gladden existence is gone; his whole being, with its freight of hopes, memories, affections, is reduced to a total wreck; a last farewell to whatsoever has made life attractive, the conditions, motives, prospects of noble achievement, is all there is left him: in brief, he feels literally unmade, robbed not only of the laurels he has won, but of the spirit that manned him to the winning of them; so that he can neither live nobly nor nobly die, but is doomed to a sort of living death, an object of scorn and loathing unto himself. In this state of mind, no wonder his thoughts reel and totter, and cling convulsively to his honor, which is the only thing that now remains to him, until in his efforts to rescue this he loses all, and has no refuge but in self-destruction. He approaches the awful task in the bitterness as well as the calmness of despair. In sacrificing his love to save his honor, he really performs the most heroic self-sacrifice; for the taking of Desdemona's life is to him something worse than to lose his own. Nor could he ever have loved her so much, had he not loved honor more. Her love for him, too, is based upon the very principle that now prompts and nerves him to the sacrifice. And as at last our pity for her rises into awe, so our awe of him melts into pity; the catastrophe thus blending their several virtues and sufferings into one most profound, solemn, sweetly-mournful impression. "Othello," says Coleridge, "had no life but in Desdemona:—the belief that she, his angel, had fallen from the heaven of her native innocence, wrought a civil war in his heart. She is his counterpart; and, like him, is almost sanctified in our eyes by her absolute unsuspiciousness, and holy entireness of love. As the curtain drops, which do we pity the most?"

Comments

By Shakespearean Scholars

OTHELLO

In Othello, Shakespeare means us to recognize the man of action, whose life has been spent in deeds of military prowess and adventure, but who has had little experience either of the ways of society or of the intrigues of weaker men. Moreover, he is a man apart. A renegade from his own faith and an outcast from his own people, he is, indeed, the valued servant of the Venetian state, but is not regarded as on an equality with its citizens, and that though, as being of kingly descent, he regards himself as being at least the equal of its republican citizens. A homeless man, who had never experienced the soothing influences of domesticity. In short, a man strong in action but weak in intellectuality, of natural nobility of character, knowing no guile in himself and incapable of seeing it in others; but withal sensitive on the subject of his birth, and inclined to regard himself as an inheritor of the curse of outcast Ishmael.—Ransome, *Short Studies of Shakespeare's Plots.*

Othello has a strong and healthy mind and a vivid imagination, but they deal entirely with first impressions, with obvious facts. If he trusts a man, he trusts him without the faintest shadow of reserve. Iago's suggestion that Desdemona is false comes upon him like a thunderbolt. He *knows* this man to be honest, his every word the absolute truth. He is stunned, and his mind accepts specious reasonings passively and without examination. Yet his love is so intense that he struggles against his own nature, and for a time *compels* himself to think, though not upon the great question whether she is false. He cannot bring his intellect to attack Iago's conclusions, and only argues the minor point: *Why* is she false? But even this effort is too much for him. It is, I have said, against nature; and nature, after the struggle has been carried on unceasingly for hours, revenges herself—he falls into a fit. That this is the legitimate climax of overpowering emotion on an intensely real and single character is plain. This obstruction and chaos of the faculties is the absolute opposite of the brilliant life into which Hamlet's intellect leaps on its contact with tremendous realities.—Rose, *Sudden Emotion: Its Effect upon Different Characters as Shown by Shakespere.*

What a fortunate mistake that the Moor, under which name a baptized Saracen of the northern coast of Africa was unquestionably meant in the novel, has been made by Shakespeare, in every respect, a negro! We recognize in Othello the wild nature of that glowing zone which generates the most raging beasts of prey and the most deadly poisons, tamed only in appearance by the desire of fame, by foreign laws of honor, and by nobler and milder manners. His jealousy is not the jealousy of the heart, which is incompatible with the tenderest feeling and adoration of the beloved object; it is of that sensual kind from which, in burning climes, has sprung the disgraceful ill-treatment of women and many other unnatural usages. A drop of this poison flows in his veins, and sets his whole blood in the most disorderly fermentation. The Moor seems noble, frank, confiding, grateful for the love shown him; and he *is* all this, and, moreover, a hero that spurns at danger, a worthy leader of an army, a faithful servant of the state; but the mere physical force of passion puts to flight in one moment all his acquired and accustomed virtues, and gives the upper hand to the savage in him over the moral man. The tyranny of the blood over the will betrays itself even in the expression of his desire of revenge against Cassio. In his repentance when he views the evidence of the deed, a genuine tenderness for his murdered wife, and the painful feeling of his annihilated honor, at last burst forth; and he every now and then assails himself with the rage a despot shows in punishing a runaway slave. He suffers as a double man;

at once in the higher and lower sphere into which his being was divided.—Schlegel, *Lectures on Dramatic Art and Literature.*

DESDEMONA

The suffering of Desdemona is, unless I mistake, the most nearly intolerable spectacle that Shakespeare offers us. For one thing, it is *mere* suffering; and, *ceteris paribus*, that is much worse to witness than suffering that issues in action. Desdemona is helplessly passive. She can do nothing whatever. She cannot retaliate even in speech; no, not even in silent feeling. And the chief reason of her helplessness only makes the sight of her suffering more exquisitely painful. She is helpless because her nature is infinitely sweet and her love absolute. I would not challenge Mr. Swinburne's statement that we *pity* Othello even more than Desdemona; but we watch Desdemona with more unmitigated distress. We are never wholly uninfluenced by the feeling that Othello is a man contending with another man; but Desdemona's suffering is like that of the most loving of dumb creatures tortured without cause by the being he adores.—Bradley, *Shakespearean Tragedy.*

Nothing in poetry has ever been written more pathetic than the scene preceding Desdemona's death; I confess I almost always turn away my eyes from the poor girl with her infinitely touching song of "Willow, willow, willow," and I would fain ask the Poet whether his tragic arrow, which always hits the mark, does not here pierce almost too deeply. I would not call the last word with which she dies a lie, or even a "noble" lie; this qualification has been wretchedly misused. The lie with which Desdemona dies is divine truth, too good to come within the compass of an earthly moral code.—Horn, *Shakespeare's Schauspiele erläutert.*

THE MURDER OF DESDEMONA

When Othello thus bows his own lofty nature before the groveling but most acute worldly intellect of Iago, his habitual view of "all qualities" had been clouded by the breath of the slanderer. His confidence in purity and innocence had been destroyed. The sensual judgment of "human dealings" had taken the place of the spiritual. The enthusiastic love and veneration of his wife had been painted to him as the result of gross passion:

"Not to affect many proposed matches," &c.

His belief in the general prevalence of virtuous motives and actions had been degraded to a reliance on the libertine's creed that all are impure:

——"there's millions now alive," &c.

When the innocent and the high-minded submit themselves to the tutelage of the man of the world, as he is called, the process of mental change is precisely that produced in the mind of Othello. The poetry of life is gone. On them, never more

The freshness of the heart can fall like dew.

They abandon themselves to the betrayer, and they prostrate themselves before the energy of his "gain'd knowledge." They feel that in their own original powers of judgment they have no support against the dogmatism, and it may be the ridicule, of experience. This is the course with the young when they fall into the power of the tempter. But was not Othello in all essentials *young*? Was he not of an enthusiastic temperament, confiding, loving,—most sensitive to opinion,—jealous of his honor,—truly wise, had he trusted to his own pure impulses?—But he was most weak, in adopting an evil opinion against his own faith, and conviction, and proof in his reliance upon the honesty and judgment of a man whom he really doubted and had never proved. Yet this is the course by which the highest and noblest intellects are too often subjected to the dominion of the subtle understanding and the unbridled will. It is an unequal contest between the principles that are struggling for the master in the individual man, when the attributes of the serpent and the dove are separated, and become conflicting. The wisdom which belonged to Othello's enthusiastic temperament was his confidence in the truth and purity of the being with whom his life was bound up, and his general reliance upon the better part of human nature, in his judgment of his friend. When the confidence was destroyed by the craft of his deadly enemy, his sustaining power was also destroyed;—the balance of his sensitive temperament was lost;—his enthusiasm became wild passion;—his new belief in the dominion of grossness over the apparently pure and good, shaped itself into gross outrage; his honor lent itself to schemes of cruelty and revenge. But even amidst the whirlwind of this passion, we every now and then hear something which sounds as the softest echo of love and gentleness. Perhaps in the whole compass of the Shaksperean pathos there is nothing deeper than "But yet the pity of it, Iago! O, Iago, the pity of it, Iago." It is the contemplated murder of Desdemona which thus tears his heart. But his "disordered power, engendered within itself to its own destruction," hurries on the catastrophe. We would ask, with Coleridge, "As the curtain drops, which do we pity the most?"—Knight, *Pictorial Shakspeare.*

Finally, let me repeat that Othello does not kill Desdemona in jealousy, but in a conviction forced upon him by the almost superhuman art of Iago,—such a conviction as any man would and must have entertained who had believed Iago's honesty as Othello did. We, the audience, know that Iago is a villain from the beginning; but in considering the essence of the Shaksperian Othello, we must perseveringly place ourselves in his situation, and under his circumstances. Then we shall immediately feel the fundamental difference between the solemn agony of the noble Moor, and the wretched fishing jealousies of Leontes, and the morbid suspiciousness of Leonatus, who is, in other respects, a fine character. Othello had no life but in Desdemona:—the belief that she, his angel, had fallen from the heaven of her native innocence, wrought a civil war in his heart. She is his counterpart; and, like him, is almost sanctified in our eyes by her absolute unsuspiciousness, and holy entireness of love. As the curtain drops, which do we pity the most?—Coleridge, *Lectures on Shakspere.*

IAGO

The Moor has in his service as "ancient" a young Venetian, Iago, of tried military capacity, cheerful temperament and bluff honesty of bearing. No one, to outward seeming, could be less of a villain, and yet this plausibly respectable exterior covers a fiend in human shape. Iago is the arch-criminal of Shaksperean drama—"more fell than anguish, hunger and the sea." Richard III is in many features his prototype, but the hunchback king is incited to his unnatural deeds by the consciousness of his physical deformity. Moreover, though he has taken "Machiavel" as his master, he is after all an "Italianate" Englishman, not an Italian, and though he crushes conscience, as he believes, out of existence, it asserts its power at the last. But in Iago conscience is completely wanting. He is, as Coleridge has said, "all will in intellect." He is the incarnation of absolute egotism, an egotism that without passion or even apparent purpose is at chronic feud with the moral order of the world. His mind is simply a non-conductor of spiritual elements in life. "Virtue" is to him a "fig," love "a lust of the blood, and a permission of the will;" reputation, "an idle and most false imposition," whose loss is a trifle compared with a bodily wound. Hamlet in the agony of disillusion had compared the world to an unweeded garden, occupied solely by things rank and gross in nature. This is Iago's habitual view, and to him it causes no particle of pain. Evil is his native element, and the increase of evil an end in itself. It is, therefore, unprofitable to discuss in detail the grounds of his hatred towards Othello or his other victims. His is at bottom, to use Coleridge's phrase, a "motiveless malignity," and he can scarcely be in earnest with the pretexts which he urges for his misdeeds, and which vary from day to day. Othello's advancement, over his head, of Cassio, a Florentine who knows nothing of war but "the bookish theoric," might seem a genuine grievance, yet it is noticeable that after the first few lines of the play Iago scarcely alludes to this, and makes more of what are evidently imaginary offenses by Othello and Cassio against his honor as a husband. In one passage he hints vaguely that he loves Desdemona, and it is significant that this is the only trace left of the ensign's motive for revenge in Cinthio's novel. That Shakspere departed so widely from his original proves that he meant Iago to be actuated by nothing but sheer *diablerie.*—Boas, *Shakspere and his Predecessors.*

Some allege that Iago is too villainous to be a natural character, but those allegers are simpleton judges of human nature: Fletcher of Saltoun has said that there is many a brave soldier who never wore a sword; in like manner, there is many an Iago in the world who never committed murder. Iago's "*learned spirit*" and exquisite intellect, happily ending in his own destruction, were as requisite for the moral of the piece as for the sustaining of Othello's high character; for we should have despised the Moor if he had been deceived by a less consummate villain than "honest Iago." The latter is a true character, and the philosophical truth of this tragedy makes it terrible to peruse, in spite of its beautiful poetry. Why has Aristotle said that tragedy purifies the passions? for our last wish and hope in reading *Othello* is that the villain Iago may be well tortured.—Campbell, *Remarks on the Life and Writings of Shakespeare*.

But Iago! Aye! there's the rub. Well may poor Othello look down to his feet, and not seeing them different from those of others, feel convinced that it is a fable which attributes a cloven hoof to the devil. Nor is it wonderful that the parting instruction of Lodovico to Cassio [*sic*] should be to enforce the most cunning cruelty of torture on the hellish villain, or that all the party should vie with each other in heaping upon him words of contumely and execration. His determination to keep silence when questioned, was at least judicious; for with his utmost ingenuity he could hardly find anything to say for himself. Is there nothing, then, to be said for him by anybody else?

No more than this. He is the sole exemplar of studied personal revenge in the plays. The philosophical mind of Hamlet ponders too deeply, and sees both sides of the question too clearly, to be able to carry any plan of vengeance into execution. Romeo's revenge on Tybalt for the death of Mercutio is a sudden gust of ungovernable rage. The vengeance in the Historical Plays are those of war or statecraft. In Shylock, the passion is hardly personal against his intended victim. A swaggering Christian is at the mercy of a despised and insulted Jew. The hatred is national and sectarian. Had Bassanio or Gratiano, or any other of their creed, been in his power, he would have been equally relentless. He is only retorting the wrongs and insults of his tribe in demanding full satisfaction, and imitating the hated Christians in their own practices. It is, on the whole, a passion remarkably seldom exhibited in Shakespeare in any form. Iago, as I have said, is its only example as directed against an individual. Iago had been affronted in the tenderest point. He felt that he had strong claims on the office of lieutenant to Othello. The greatest exertion was made to procure it for him, and yet he was refused.

What is still worse, the grounds of the refusal are military; Othello assigns to the civilians reasons for passing over Iago, drawn from his own trade, of which they, of course, could not pretend to be adequate judges. And worst of all, when this practised military man is for military reasons set aside, who is appointed? Some man of greater renown and skill in arms? *That* might be borne; but it is no such thing.—Maginn, *Shakespeare Papers*.

EMILIA

A few words on the character of Emilia: when we change meter to rhythm, we vary the stress on our syllables; but a stronger accent in one part of our line implies a weaker accent in another part; it may even happen that to produce our fullest music we allow the whole accentual stress of the line to fall on one syllable; this, as we saw in our review of "Julius Cæsar," is Shakespeare's method in dealing with his characters; one is heightened if another is lowered; and it may turn out that the method gives us a sense of unfairness; I have some such feeling when I approach the character of Emilia; I refer especially to the conversation between Emilia and her mistress (IV, iii, 60-106). Emilia had summed up her views of the subject by a line—"The ills we do, their ills instruct us so"; which Desdemona rightly condemns—and with the line all the foregoing remarks of Emilia. It is well to gaze upon one entire and perfect chrysolite, but ill for the foil thereof, when the foil is another woman—the woman, moreover, who would right the wrong though she lost twenty lives—who did lose her life through her devotion, and whose last words were of faithful love—"O, lay me by my mistress' side.—Luce, *Handbook to Shakespeare's Works*.

From the moment when Emilia learns Othello's deed from his own lips, the poet disburdens us in a wonderful manner of all the tormenting feelings which the course of the catastrophe had awakened in us. Emilia is a woman of coarser texture, good-natured like her sex, but with more spite than others of her sex, light-minded in things which appear to her light, serious and energetic when great demands meet her; in words she is careless of her reputation and virtue, which she would not be in action. At her husband's wish she has heedlessly taken away

Desdemona's handkerchief, as she fancied for some indifferent object. Thoughtless and light, she had cared neither for return nor for explanation, even when she learned that this handkerchief, the importance of which she knows, had caused the quarrel between Othello and Desdemona; in womanly fashion she observes less attentively all that is going on around her, and thus, in similar but worse unwariness than Desdemona, she becomes the real instrument of the unhappy fate of her mistress. Yet when she knows that Othello has killed his wife, she unburdens our repressed feelings by her words, testifying to Desdemona's innocence by loud accusations of the Moor. When she hears Iago named as the calumniator of her fidelity, she testifies to the purity of her mistress by unsparing invectives against the wickedness of her husband, and seeks to enlighten the slowly apprehending Moor, whilst she continues to draw out the feelings of our soul and to give them full expression from her own full heart. At last, when she entirely perceives Iago's guilt in the matter of the handkerchief, and therefore her own participation in it, her devoted fidelity to her mistress and her increasing feeling rise to sublimity; her testimony against her husband, in the face of threatening death, now becomes a counterpart to Othello's severe exercise of justice, and her death and dying song upon Desdemona's chastity is an expiatory repentance at her grave, which is scarcely surpassed by the Moor's grand and calm retaliation upon himself. The unravelment and expiation in this last scene are wont to reawaken repose and satisfaction even in the most deeply agitated reader.—Gervinus, *Shakespeare Commentaries*.

RODERIGO

Roderigo is a florid specimen of one of Shakespeare's simpleton lovers. He has placed his whole fortune at the disposal of Iago, to use for the purpose of winning favor for him with Desdemona, not having the courage and ability to woo for himself; or rather, having an instinctive knowledge of his own incompetence, with so profound and devout a respect for the talent of his adviser, as to leave the whole management of the diplomacy in his hands. Although Roderigo is a compound of vacillation and weakness, even to imbecility; although he suddenly forms resolutions, and as suddenly quenches them at the rallying contempt and jeering of Iago; and even, although being entangled in the wily villain's net, he is gradually led on to act unconsonantly with his real nature; yet withal, Roderigo has so much of redemption in him, that we commiserate his weakness, and wish him a better fate; for he is not wholly destitute of natural kindness: he really is in love with Desdemona, and was so before her marriage. Iago has had his purse, "as though the strings were his own," to woo her for him; and yet we find, with all Roderigo's subserviency to the superior intellect, that the very first words of the play announce his misgiving that his insidious friend has played him false, since he knew of the projected elopement of Desdemona with Othello, and did not apprise him of it. With this first falsehood palpable to him, he again yields to the counsel of Iago, who schools him into impatience with the promise that he shall yet obtain his prize.—Clarke, *Shakespeare-Characters*.

THE SOURCE OF THE PATHOS

The source of the pathos throughout—of that pathos which at once softens and deepens the tragic effect—lies in the character of Desdemona. No woman differently constituted could have excited the same, intense and painful compassion, without losing something of that exalted charm, which invests her from beginning to end, which we are apt to impute to the interest of the situation, and to the poetical coloring, but which lies, in fact, in the very essence of the character. Desdemona, with all her timid flexibility and soft acquiescence, is not weak; for the negative alone is weak; and the mere presence of goodness and affection implies in itself a species of power; power without consciousness, power without effort, power with repose—that soul of grace!—Jameson, *Shakespeare's Heroines*.

INTERMARRIAGE OF THE RACES

Great efforts are often made to show that Othello as conceived by Shakespeare was not a Negro; and true it is that such an addition as "thick lips," given contemptuously, does not prove it. Othello, however, himself, says that he is black; and I have been convinced that Shakespeare had in his mind the proper negro complexion and physiognomy too, and that he even assigned some mental characteristics of the negro type. To these I think belong an over-affection for high sounding words, for the sake of the sound, an affectation of stateliness that verges upon stiffness, and value for conspicuous position with somewhat excessive feeling for parade—for the pride and pomp of circumstance, the report of the artillery and the waving of the ensign. There are other coincidences besides these, and I cannot divest myself of the sense that Othello embodies the ennobled characteristics of the colored division of the human family; and in his position relatively to the proudest aristocracy of Europe, his story exemplifies the difficulty the world has yet to solve between the white and the black. The feuds and antipathies of race can be fully conciliated at no other altar than the nuptial bed; and the marriage of Desdemona, and its consequences, typify the obstacles to this conclusion. Some critics moralize the fate of Desdemona as punishment for undutiful and ill-assorted marriage, yet the punishment falls quite as severely on the severity of Brabantio—on his cruelty, we may say, for he is the first—and out of unnatural pique, to belie his own daughter's chastity—

> Look to her, Moor—have a quick eye to see;

and if we must needs make out a scrupulous law of retribution, we shall come at last to an incongruity, and that can in no sense be pious. The revolt of Desdemona was a revolt against custom and tradition, but it was in favor of the affections of the heart; and if the result was pitiable, it may have been not because custom and tradition were right, but because they were strong, and because there was the greater reason for abating their strength by proving it assailable; the justest war does not demand the fewest victims; and the heroes who are left on the field were no whit less right, but only less fortunate, than their comrades who survive to carry home the laurels. For the matter in hand, however, it is most certain that the most important advance that has yet been made towards establishing even common cordiality between the races has been due as in the case of Desdemona and the redeemed slave, Othello, if not to the love at least to the compassionate sympathy of woman.—Lloyd, *Critical Essays*.

THE FAULT OF THE PLAY

The fault of the play lies in the fact that Othello has no moral right to conviction. Yet he has more right than Claudio (in *Much Ado*), far more than Posthumus, and *a fortiori* more than the hardly sane Leontes. A little closer questioning of Emilia, however, would have brought out the truth; and this fact concerns Iago's conduct as well as Othello's.—Seccombe and Allen, *The Age of Shakespeare*.

BEAUTIES OF THE PLAY

The beauties of this play impress themselves so strongly upon the attention of the reader, that they can draw no aid from critical illustration. The fiery openness of Othello, magnanimous, artless, and credulous, boundless in his confidence, ardent in his affection, inflexible in his resolution, and obdurate in his revenge; the cool malignity of Iago, silent in his resentment, subtle in his design, and studious at once of his interest and his vengeance; the soft simplicity of Desdemona, confident of merit, and conscious of innocence, her artless perseverance in her suit, and her slowness to suspect that she can be suspected, are such proofs of Shakespeare's skill in human nature as, I suppose, it is in vain to seek in any modern writer. The gradual progress which Iago makes in the Moor's conviction, and the circumstances which he employs to enflame him, are so artfully natural, that, though it will perhaps not be said of him [Othello] as he says of himself, that he is "a man not easily jealous," yet we cannot but pity him, when at last we find him "perplexed in the extreme."—Johnson.

THE FASCINATION OF THE PLAY

The noblest earthly object of the contemplation of man is man himself. The universe, and all its fair and glorious forms, are indeed included in the wide empire of imagination; but she has placed her home and her sanctuary amidst the inexhaustible varieties and the impenetrable mysteries of the mind. *Othello* is, perhaps, the greatest work in the world. From what does it derive its power? From the clouds? From the ocean? From the mountains? Or from love strong as death, and jealousy cruel as the grave?—Macaulay, *Essay on Dante*.

PUNISHMENT

In every character of every play of Shakespeare's the punishment is in proportion to the wrong-doing. How mild is the punishment of Desdemona, of Cordelia for a slight wrong; how fearful that of Macbeth,—every moment from the commission of his crime to his death, he suffers more than all the suffering of these two women. His deliberate crime belongs to the cold passions; as the deed is done with forethought and in cold blood, so it is avenged by the long-continued tortures of conscience.—Ludwig, *Shakespeare-Studien*.

King Lear

Preface

By Israel Gollancz, M.A.

THE EARLY EDITIONS

Two quarto editions of *King Lear* appeared in the year 1608, with the following title-pages—(i) "M. William Shak-speare: | HIS | True Chronicle Historie of the life and | death of King Lear and his three Daughters. | *With the unfortunate life of* Edgar, *fonne* | and heire to the Earle of Gloster, and his | sullen and assumed humor of | Tom of Bedlam: | *As io was played before the Kings Maieftie at Whitehall vpon* | *S.* Stephans *night in Chriftmas Hollidayes.* | By his Maiesties Seruants playing vsually at the Gloabe | on the Bancke-fide. [Device.] London, | Printed for *Nathaniel Butter*, and are to be sold at his fhop in *Pauls* | Church-yard at the figne of the Pide Bull neere | St. Auftins Gate, 1608."

(ii) The title of the second quarto is almost identical with that of (i), but the device is different, and there is no allusion to the shop "at the signe of the Pide Bull."

It is now generally accepted that the "Pide Bull" quarto is the first edition of the play, but the question of priority depends on the minutest of bibliographical criteria, and the Cambridge editors were for a long time misled in their chronological order of the quartos; the problem is complicated by the fact that no two of the extant six copies of the first quarto are exactly alike;[1] they differ in having one, two, three, or four, uncorrected sheets.

1. Capell's copy; the Duke of Devonshire's; the British Museum's two copies; the Bodleian two copies.

The Second Quarto was evidently printed from a copy of the First Quarto, having three uncorrected sheets. A reprint of this edition, with many additional errors, appeared in 1655.

The Folio Edition of the play was derived from an independent manuscript, and the text, from a typographical point of view, is much better than that of the earlier editions; but it is noteworthy that some two hundred and twenty lines found in the quartos are not found in the folio, while about fifty lines in the folio are wanting in the quartos.[1]

Much has been written on the discrepancies between the two versions; among modern investigations perhaps the most important are those (i) Delius and (ii) Koppel; according to (i), "in the quartos we have the play as it was originally performed before King James, and before the audience of the Globe, but sadly marred by misprints, printers' sophistications, and omissions, perhaps due to an imperfect and illegible MS. In the Folio we have a later MS., belonging to the Theater, and more nearly identical with what Shakespeare wrote. The omissions of the Quartos are the blunders of the printers; the omissions of the Folios are the abridgments of the actors;" according to (ii), "it was Shakespeare's own hand that cut out many of the passages both in the Quarto text and the Folio text.... The *original* form was, essentially, that of the Quarto, then followed a *longer* form, *with the additions in the Folio*, as substantially *our modern editions have again restored them*; then the shortest form, as it is preserved for us in the Folio."[2]

1. To the latter class belong I. ii. 124-131; I. iv. 347-358; III. i. 22-29; III. ii. 80-96; to the former, I. iii. 17-23; I. iv. 155-171, 256-259; II. ii. 150-153; III. vi. 19-60, 110-123; III. vii. 99-108; IV. i. 60-67; IV. ii. 31-50, 53-59, 62-69; IV. iii.; IV. vii. 88-95; V. i. 23-28; V. iii. 54-59, 207-224. *Vide* Prætorius' facsimiles of Q. 1 and Q. 2; Vietor's Parallel Text of Q. 1 and F. 1 (Marburg, 1886), Furness' Variorum, *etc*.
2. Delius' *Essay* appeared originally in the German Shakespeare Society Year-Book, X.; and was subsequently translated into English (*New Shak. Soc. Trans*. 1875-76).

   Dr. Koppel's investigations are to be found in his *Text-Kritische Studien über Richard III. u. King Lear* (Dresden, 1877). A *resume* of the various theories is given in Furness' edition, pp. 359-373.

It seems probable that the quarto represents a badly printed revised version of the original form of the play, specially prepared by the poet for performance at Court, whereas the folio is the actors' abridged version. It seems hardly possible to determine the question more definitely.

TATE'S VERSION

For more than a century and a half, from the year 1680 until the restoration of Shakespeare's tragedy at Covent Garden in 1838, Tate's perversion of *Lear* held the stage,[1] delighting audiences with "the Circumstances of Lear's Restoration, and the virtuous Edgar's Alliance with the amiable Cordelia." It was to this acting-edition that Lamb referred in his famous criticism, "Tate has put his hook into the nostrils of this leviathan for Garrick and his followers," etc. Garrick, Kemble, Kean, and other great actors were quite content with this travesty, but "the Lear of Shakespeare cannot be acted."

DATE OF COMPOSITION

The play of *King Lear* may safely be assigned to the year 1605: (i) According to an entry in the Stationers' Register, dated November 26, 1607, it was "played before the King's Majesty at Whitehall upon S. Stephens' night at Christmas last," *i.e.*, on December 26, 1606; (ii) the names of Edgar's devils, and many of the allusions in Act III, sc. iv, were evidently derived from Harsnett's *Declaration of egregrious Popish Impostures*, which was first published in 1603; (iii) the substitution of "*British man*" for "*Englishman*" in the famous nursery-rhyme (Act III, sc. iv, 192) seems to point to a time subsequent to the Union of England and Scotland under James I; the poet Daniel in a congratulatory address to the King (printed in 1603) wrote thus:

O thou mightie state,
Now thou art all *Great Britain*, and no more,
No *Scot*, no *English* now, nor no debate;[2]

1. *Vide Furness*, pp. 467-478.
2. It is noteworthy that in Act IV. scene vi. 260 the Folio reads "*English*," where the Quartos have "*British*."

(iv) the allusions to the "late eclipses" (Act I, sc. ii, 117, 158, 164) have been most plausibly referred to the great eclipse of the sun, which took place in October, 1605, and this supposition is borne out by the fact that John Harvey's *Discoursive Probleme Concerning Prophesies*, printed in 1588, actually contains a striking prediction thereof (hence the point of Edmund's comment, "*I am thinking of a prediction I read this other day,*" *etc.*); perhaps, too, there is a reference to the Gunpowder Plot in Gloucester's words, "*machinations*, hollowness, treachery, and all ruinous disorders follow us disquietly to our graves."

THE SOURCES OF THE PLOT

The story of "Leir, the son of Balderd, ruler over the Britaynes, in the year of the world 3105, at what time Joas reigned as yet in Juda," was among the best-known stories of British history. Its origin must be sought for in the dim world of Celtic legend, or in the more remote realm of simple nature-myths,[1] but its place in literature dates from Geoffrey of Monmouth's Latin history of the Britons, *Historia Britonum*, composed about 1130, based in all probability on an earlier work connected with the famous name of Nennius, though Geoffrey alleges his chief authority was "an ancient British book." To the *Historia Britonum* we owe the stories of Leir, Gorboduc, Locrine; there, too, we find rich treasures of Arthurian romance. Welsh, French, and English histories of Britain were derived, directly or indirectly, from this Latin history. The first to tell these tales in English verse was Layamon, son of Leovenath, priest of the Arley Regis, in Worcestershire, on the right bank of the Severn, who flourished at the beginning of the thirteenth century, and whose English *Brut* was based on Wace's French *Geste des Bretons*—a versified translation of Geoffrey's history. At the end of the century the story figures again in Robert of Gloucester's *Metrical Chronicle*; in the fourteenth century Robert of Brunne, in the fifteenth John Hardyng, re-told in verse these ancient British stories. In the sixteenth century we have Warner's *Albion's England*—the

1. According to some Celtic folk-lorists, "Lir" = Neptune; the two cruel daughters = the rough Winds; Cordelia = the gentle Zephyn I know no better commentary on the tempestuous character of the play; Shakespeare has unconsciously divined the germ of the myth.

popular metrical history of the period; we have also the prose chronicles of Fabyan, Rastell, Grafton, and over and above all, Holinshed's famous *Historie of England*;[1] the story of *Leir* is to be found in all these books. Three versions of the tale at the end of the sixteenth century show that the poetical possibilities of the subject were recognized before Shakespeare set thereon the stamp of his genius:[2]—(i) in the *Mirour for Magistrates* "Queene Cordila" tells her life's "tragedy," how "in dispaire" she slew herself "the year before Christ, 800"; (ii) Spenser, in Canto X of the Second Book of the *Faery Queene*, summarizes, in half a dozen stanzas, the story of "Cordelia"—this form of the name, used as a variant of "Cordeill" for metrical purposes, occurring here for the first time; the last stanza may be quoted to illustrate the closing of the story in the pre-Shakespearean versions:

So to his crown she him restor'd again
In which he died, made ripe for death by eld,
And after will'd it should to her remain:
Who peacefully the same long time did weld,
And all men's hearts in due obedience held;
Till that her sister's children woxen strong
Through proud ambition, against her rebell'd,
And overcommen kept in prison long,
Till weary of that wretched life herself she hong;

(iii) of special interest, however, is the pre-Shakespearean drama, which was entered in the books of the Stationers' Company as early as 1594 under the title of *The moste famous Chronicle historye of* Leire, *Kinge of England, and his Three Daughters*, but evidently not printed till the year 1605, when perhaps its publication was due to the popularity of the newer Chronicle History on the same subject; "The | True Chronicle Hi | story of King Leir | and his three | daughters, Gonorill, Ragan, and Cordella. | As it hath bene divers and sundry | times lately acted. | London | printed | by Simon Stafford for John | Wright, and are

1. In Camden's *Remains* the "Lear" story is told of the West-Saxon King Ina; in the *Gesta Romanorum* Theodosius takes the place of King Lear.
2. The ballad of *King Leir, and his Three Daughters* (*vide* Percy's *Reliques*) is, in all probability, later than Shakespeare's play.

to bee sold at his shop at | Christes Church dore, next Newgate- | Market, 1605."[1]

It is noteworthy that the play was entered in the Registers on May 8 as "the *tragicall* historie of Kinge Leir," though the play is anything but a "tragedy"—its ending is a happy one. It looks, indeed, as though the original intention of the publishers was to palm off their "*Leir*" as identical with the great tragedy of the day.

But however worthless it may seem when placed in juxtaposition with "the most perfect specimen of the dramatic art existing in the world,"[2] yet this less ambitious and humble production is not wholly worthless, if only for "a certain childlike sweetness" in the portraiture of "faire Cordella,"

> Myrrour of vertue, Phœnix of our age!
> Too kind a daughter for an unkind father!

It may be pronounced a very favorable specimen of the popular "*comedies*" of the period to which it belonged (*circa* 1592), with its conventional classicism, its characteristic attempts at humor, its rhyming couplets; like so many of its class, it has caught something of the tenderness of the Greenish drama, and something—rather less—of the aspiration of the Marlowan.[3]

---

1. *Vide* "Six Old Plays on which Shakespeare founded his *Measure for Measure*", etc.; Hazlitt's *Shakespeare's Library*, etc.; an abstract of the play is given by Furness, pp. 393-401.
2. Shelley, *Defence of Poetry,* Essays, &c., 1840, p. 20.
3. Here are a few lines—perhaps "the salt of the old play"—by way of specimen: [the Gallian king is wooing Cordella disguised as a Palmer],
"*King*. Your birth's too high for any but a king.
Cordella. My mind is low enough to love a palmer,
Rather than any king upon the earth.
King. O, but you never can endure their life
Which is so straight and full of penury.
Cordella. O yes, I can, and happy if I might:
I'll hold thy palmer's stag within my hand,
And think it is the sceptre of a queen.
Sometime I'll set thy bonnet on my head
And think I wear a rich imperial crown.
Sometime I'll help thee in thy holy prayers,
And think I am with thee in Paradise.
Thus I'll mock fortune, as she mocketh me,

"With all its defects," says Dr. Ward, "the play seems only to await the touch of a powerful hand to be converted into a tragedy of supreme effectiveness; and while Shakespeare's genius nowhere exerted itself with more transcendent force and marvelous versatility, it nowhere found more promising materials ready to its command."[1]

Yet Shakespeare's debt to the old play was of the slightest, and some have held that he may not even have read it, but in all probability he derived therefrom at least a valuable hint for the character of Kent, whose prototype Perillus is by no means unskillfully drawn; perhaps, too, the original of the steward Oswald is to be found in the courtier Scaliger; again it is noteworthy that messengers with incriminating letters play an important part in the earlier as in the later drama; and possibly the first rumblings of the wild storm-scene of *Lear* may be heard in the mimic thunder which in "*Leir*" strikes terror in the heart of the assassin hired to murder king and comrade—"the parlosest old men that ere he heard."

There is in the *Chronicle History* no hint of the under-plot of *Lear*, the almost parallel story of Gloster and Edmund, whereby Shakespeare subtly emphasizes the leading *motif* of the play; the vague original thereof is to be found in Sir Philip Sidney's *Arcadia* (Book II, pp. 138-158, ed. 1598), ("*the pitifull state and story of the Paphlagonian vnkinde king, and his kind sonne, first related by the son, then by the blind father*").

DURATION OF ACTION

The time of the play, according to Mr. Daniel (*vide Transactions of New Shakespeare Soc.*, 1877-1879), covers ten days, distributed as follows:

Day 1. Act. I, sc. i.

Day 2. Act I, sc. ii. *An interval of something less than a fortnight.*

Day 3. Act I, sc. iii, iv.

And never will my lovely choice repent:
For having thee, I shall have all content."

1. *History of English Dramatic Literature*, Vol. I., p. 126.

Day 4. Act II, sc. i, ii.

Day 5. Act II, sc. iii, iv; Act III, sc. i-vi.

Day 6. Act III, sc. vii; Act IV, sc. i.

Day 7. Act IV, sc. ii. Perhaps an *interval* of a day or two.

Day 8. Act IV, sc. iii.

Day 9. Act IV, sc. iv, v, vi.

Day 10. Act IV, sc. vii; Act V, sc. i-iii.

"The longest period, including intervals, that can be allowed for this play is one month; though perhaps little more than three weeks is sufficient."

Introduction

By Henry Norman Hudson, A.M.

The earliest notice that has reached us of *The Tragedy of King Lear* is an entry at the Stationers' by Nathaniel Butter and John Busby, dated November 26, 1607: "A book called Mr. William Shakespeare's History of King Lear, as it was played before the King's Majesty at Whitehall, upon St. Stephen's night at Christmas last, by his Majesty's Servants playing usually at the Globe on the Bank-side." This ascertains the play to have been acted on December 26, 1606. Three editions of the tragedy were also published in 1608, one of which, a quarto pamphlet of forty-one leaves, has a title-page reading as follows: "Mr. William Shakespeare: His True Chronicle History of the life and death of King Lear and his three Daughters. With the unfortunate life of Edgar, son and heir to the Earl of Gloster, and his sullen and assumed humor of Tom of Bedlam. As it was played before the King's Majesty at Whitehall upon St. Stephen's night in Christmas Holidays, by his Majesty's Servants playing usually at the Globe on the Bank-side. London: Printed for Nathaniel Butter, and are to be sold at his shop in Paul's Church-yard, at the sign of the Pied Bull, near St. Austin's Gate. 1608."

The title-pages of the other two quarto impressions vary from this only in omitting the publisher's address. As regards the text, the differences of the three quartos, though sometimes important, are seldom more than verbal. Mr. Collier, who seems to have examined them with great care, informs us that those without the publisher's address are more accurate than the other; and he thinks that the one with the address was issued first. All three of them, however, are printed in a very slovenly manner, and furnish divers specimens of most edifying typographical disorder.

As a noteworthy circumstance, we must mention that in the title-pages of the quartos the author's name is made very conspicuous, being placed at the top, and set forth in larger type than any thing else in the page. And the name, "Mr. William Shakespeare," is given with like prominence again at the head of the page on which the play begins. This was probably meant to distinguish the drama from another on the same subject, and to make the purchaser sure that he was getting the genuine work of Shakespeare: it also argues that the publisher found his interest, and perhaps his pride, in having that name prominent on the wares. Mr. Collier mentions it as a peculiarity not found in any other production that he recollects of that period.

There can be little doubt, if any, that the quarto issues of *King Lear* were unauthorized. The extreme badness of the printing would naturally infer that the publisher had not access to any competent proofreader. Moreover, none of the other authentic quartos was published by Butter. It is pretty certain, also, as we have before had occasion to observe, that at that time and for several years previous great care was used by the company to keep the Poet's dramas out of print. How Butter got possession of the copy is beyond our means of knowing, and it were vain to conjecture. The fact of three issues in one year shows that the play was highly popular; and this would of course increase the interest both of the publisher to get a copy, and of the company to keep it from him.

After 1608, there was no edition of King Lear, that we know of, till the folio of 1623, where it makes the ninth in the division of Tragedies, is printed with a fair degree of clearness and accuracy, and has the acts and scenes regularly marked throughout. The folio was evidently made up from manuscript, and not from any of the earlier issues; as it has a few passages that are not in the quartos. On the other hand, the play as there given is considerably abridged, and the omissions are such as to infer that they were made with a view to shorten the time of performance. As showing how much we are indebted to the quartos for the play as it now stands, we may mention that the whole of the third scene in Act IV is wanting in the folio; which scene, though not directly helping forward the action of the play, is one of the finest for reading in the whole compass of the Poet's dramas. Several other passages, of great excellence in themselves, and some of considerable length, are also wanting in the folio. The quartos have, in all, upwards of 220 lines that are not in the later edition; while, on the other hand, the folio has about 50 lines that are wanting in the quartos.

We have seen that *King Lear* was performed at Court on December 26, 1606. Doubtless it had become favorably known on the public stage before it was called for at Whitehall. On the other side, divers names and allusions used in setting forth the assumed madness of Edgar were taken from Harsnet's *Declaration of Popish Impostures*, which was published in 1603. Thus much is all the information we have as to the time when the play was written. So that the Poet must have been not far from his fortieth year when this stupendous production came from his hand.

We have already spoken of another drama on the subject of King Lear. This was entered at the Stationers' as early as May 14, 1594, and again on May 8, 1605, and published the latter year by Simon Stafford and John Wright, with the following title: "The True Chronicle History of King Leir and his three Daughters, Gonorill, Ragan, and Cordelia. As it hath been divers and sundry times lately acted." Malone and some others think the publication of this play was owing to the successful course which Shakespeare's drama was at that time running on the stage. It seems nowise improbable that such may have been the case. Whether there was any earlier edition of the old play, is unknown: it is quite likely, at all events, that Shakespeare was acquainted with it; though the resemblances are such as need infer no knowledge of it but what might have been gained by seeing it on the stage. Probably he took from that source some hints for the part of Kent. Perhaps it should be remarked that his most judicious departures from the history, such as the madness of Lear and the death of Lear and Cordelia at the close, were entirely original with him; the older play adhering, in these points, to the story as told by the chroniclers.

Campbell the poet has worked out a very pleasant comparison of the two dramas, which we probably cannot do better than subjoin. "The elder tragedy," says he, "is simple and touching. There is one entire scene in it,—the meeting of Cordelia with her father, in a lonely forest,—which, with Shakespeare's *Lear* in my memory and heart, I could scarcely read with dry eyes. The *Lear* antecedent to our Poet's *Lear* is a pleasing tragedy; yet the former, though it precedes the latter, is not its prototype, and its mild merits only show us the wide expanse of difference between respectable talent and commanding inspiration. The two Lears have nothing in common but their aged weakness, their general goodness of heart, their royal rank, and their misfortunes. The ante-Shakespearean Lear is a patient, simple old man; who bears his sorrows very meekly, till Cordelia arrives with her husband the King of France, and his victorious army, and restores her father to the throne of Britain. Shakespeare's Lear presents the most awful picture that was ever conceived of the weakness of senility, contrasted with the strength of despair. In the old play, Lear has a friend Perillus, who moves our interest, though not so deeply as Kent. But, independently of Shakespeare's having created a new Lear, he has sublimated the old tragedy into a new one, by an entire originality in the spiritual portraiture of its personages."

The story of King Lear and his three daughters is one of those old legends with which mediæval romance peopled "the dark backward and abysm of time," where fact and fancy appear all of the same color and texture. Milton, discoursing of ante-historical Britain, finely compares the gradual emerging of authentic history from the shadows of fable and legend, to the course of one who, "having set out on his way by night, and traveled through a region of smooth or idle dreams, arrives on the confines, where daylight and truth meet him with a clear dawn, representing to his view, though at a far distance, true colors and shapes." In Shakespeare's day, the legendary tale which forms the main plot of this drama was largely interwoven with the popular literature of Europe. It is met with in various forms and under various names, as in that old repository of popular fiction, the *Gesta Romanorum*, in the *Romance of Perceforest*, in *The Mirror for*

Magistrates, in Spenser's *Faerie Queene*, in Camden's *Remains*, and in Warner's *Albion's England.* The oldest extant version of the tale in connection with British history is in Geoffrey of Monmouth, a Welch monk of the twelfth century, who translated it from the ancient British tongue into Latin. From thence it was abridged by the Poet's favorite old chronicler, Holinshed. This abridgment is copied at length in the editions of Knight and Verplanck: for variety's sake, we subjoin the legend mostly in the words of Milton, as given in his *History of England.*

Lear, the son of Bladud, became ruler over the Britons in the year of the world 3105, at which time Joas reigned in Judea. Lear was a prince of noble demeanor, governed laudably, and had three daughters, but no son. At last, failing through age, he determines to bestow his daughters in marriage, and to divide his kingdom among them. But first, to try which of them loved him best, he resolves to ask them solemnly in order; and which should profess largest, her to believe. Gonorill the eldest, apprehending too well her father's weakness, makes answer, invoking Heaven, "That she loved him above her soul." "Therefore," quoth the old man, "since thou so honorest my declining age, to thee and the husband whom thou shalt choose I give the third part of my realm." So fair a speeding for a few words soon uttered was to Regan, the second, ample instruction what to say. She, on the same demand, spares no protesting; and the gods must witness, "That she loved him above all creatures": so she receives an equal reward with her sister. But Cordella the youngest, though hitherto best loved, and now having before her eyes the rich hire of a little easy soothing, and the loss likely to betide plain dealing, yet moves not from the solid purpose of a sincere and virtuous answer. "Father," saith she, "my love towards you is as my duty bids: what should a father seek, what can a child promise more?" When the old man, sorry to hear this, and wishing her to recall those words, persisted asking; with a loyal sadness at her father's infirmity, but something harsh, and rather glancing at her sisters than speaking her own mind, she made answer, "Look, how much you have, so much is your value, and so much I love you." "Then hear thou," quoth Lear, now all in passion, "what thy ingratitude hath gained thee: because thou hast not reverenced thy aged father equal to thy sisters, part of my kingdom, or what else is mine, reckon to have none." And, without delay, he gives his other daughters in marriage, Goronill to Maglanus, Duke of Albania, Regan to Henninus, Duke of Cornwall; with them in present half his kingdom; the rest to follow at his death.

Meanwhile, fame was not sparing to divulge the wisdom and other graces of Cordelia, insomuch that Aganippus, a great king in Gaul, seeks her to wife; and, nothing altered at the loss of her dowry, receives her gladly in such manner as she was sent him. After this, King Lear, more and more drooping with years, became an easy prey to his daughters and their husbands; who now, by daily encroachment, had seized the whole kingdom into their hands; and the old king is put to sojourn with his eldest daughter, attended only by threescore knights. But they, in a short while grudged at as too numerous and disorderly for continual guests, are reduced to thirty. Not brooking that affront, the old king betakes him to his second daughter; but there also, discord soon arising between the servants of differing masters in one family, five only are suffered to attend him. Then back he returns to the other, hoping that she could not but have more pity on his gray hairs; but she now refuses to admit him, unless he be content with one only of his followers. At last the remembrance of Cordelia comes to his thoughts; and now, acknowledging how true her words had been, he takes his journey into France.

Now might be seen a difference between the silent affection of some children and the talkative obsequiousness of others, while the hope of inheritance overacts them, and on the tongue's end enlarges their duty. Cordelia, out of mere love, at the message only of her father in distress pours forth true filial tears. And, not enduring that her own or any other eye should see him in such forlorn condition as his messenger declared, she appoints one of her servants first to convey him privately to some good sea-town, there to array him, bathe him, cherish him, and furnish him with such attendance and state as beseemed his dignity; that then, as from his first landing, he might send word of his arrival to her husband. Which done, Cordelia, with her husband and all the barony of his realm, who then first had news of his passing the sea, go out to meet him; and, after all honorable and joyful entertainment, Aganippus surrenders him, during his abode there, the power of his whole kingdom; permitting his wife to go with an army, and set her father upon his throne. Wherein her piety so prospered, that she vanquished her impious sisters and their husbands; and Lear again three years obtained the crown. To whom, dying, Cordelia, with all regal solemnities, gave burial; and then, as right heir succeeding, ruled the land five years in peace; until her two sisters' sons, not bearing that a kingdom should be governed by a woman, make war against her, depose her, and imprison her; of which impatient, and now long unexercised to suffer, she there, as is related, killed herself.

In *The Mirror for Magistrates*, the same incidents are narrated in full, under the title, "How Queen Cordila in despair slew herself, the year before Christ 800," The Queen is here represented as telling the story of her own life, in a poem of forty-nine stanzas, each stanza consisting of seven lines. The poem was written by John Higgins, and originally set forth with a dedication dated December 7, 1586. The workmanship has considerable merit; but there is no sign that Shakespeare made any particular use of it, though he was most likely well acquainted with it. *The Mirror for Magistrates* is a collection of poems and legends, begun in Mary's reign by Sackville, Earl of Dorset, and continued from time to time by different hands. It was a work of very great popularity, and went through various editions before 1610. There were little need of saying so much about the thing here, but that it shows how widely the story was known when Shakespeare invested it with such tragic glory. We have but to add, that the main circumstances of the tale are briefly told by Spenser, in *The Faerie Queene*, Book ii, Canto 10, stanzas 27-32, which made its appearance in 1590. It was from Spenser that Shakespeare borrowed the softening of *Cordella or Cordila* into *Cordelia.*

The subordinate plot of Gloster and his sons was probably taken from an episodical chapter in Sidney's *Arcadia*, entitled "The pitiful State and Story of the Paphlagonian unkind King, and his kind Son; first related by the son, then by the blind father." Here Pyrocles, the hero of Arcadia, and his companion,

Musidorus, are represented as traveling together in Galatia, when, being overtaken by a furious tempest, they were driven to take shelter in a hollow rock. Staying there till the violence of the storm was passed, they overheard two men holding a strange disputation, which made them step out, yet so as to see, without being seen. There they saw an aged man, and a young, both poorly arrayed, extremely weather-beaten; the old man blind, the young man leading him; yet through those miseries in both appeared a kind of nobleness not suitable to that affliction. But the first words they heard were these of the old man: "Well, Leonatus, since I cannot persuade thee to lead me to that which should end my grief and thy trouble, let me now intreat thee to leave me. Fear not; my misery cannot be greater than it is, and nothing doth become me but misery: fear not the danger of my blind steps; I cannot fall worse than I am." He answered,—"Dear father, do not take away from me the only remnant of my happiness: while I have power to do you service, I am not wholly miserable."

These speeches, and some others to like purpose, moved the princes to go out unto them, and ask the younger what they were. "Sirs," answered he, "I see well you are strangers, that you know not our misery, so well here known. Indeed, our state is such, that, though nothing is so needful to us as pity, yet nothing is more dangerous unto us than to make ourselves so known as may stir pity. This old man whom I lead was lately rightful prince of this country of Paphlagonia; by the hardhearted ungratefulness of a son of his, deprived not only of his kingdom, but of his sight, the riches which nature grants to the poorest creatures. Whereby, and by other unnatural dealings, he hath been driven to such grief, that even now he would have had me lead him to the top of this rock, thence to cast himself headlong to death; and so would have made me, who received life from him, to be the worker of his destruction. But, noble gentlemen, if either of you have a father, and feel what dutiful affection is engrafted in a son's heart, let me intreat you to convey this afflicted prince to some place of rest and security."

Before they could answer him, his father began to speak: "Ah, my son! how evil an historian are you, to leave out the chief knot of all the discourse, my wickedness. And if thou doest it to spare my ears, assure thyself thou dost mistake me. I take witness of that sun which you see, that nothing is so welcome to my thoughts as the publishing of my shame. Therefore, know you, gentlemen, that what my son hath said is true. But this is also true: that, having had in lawful marriage this son, and so enjoyed men's expectations of him, till he was grown to justify their expectations, I was carried by a bastard son of mine, first to mislike, then to hate, lastly to do my best to destroy this son. If I should tell you what ways he used to bring me to it, I should trouble you with as much hypocrisy, fraud, malice, ambition, and envy, as in any living person could be harbored: but, methinks, the accusing his trains might in some manner excuse my fault, which I loathe to do. The conclusion is, that I gave, order to some servants of mine, whom I thought as apt for such charities as myself, to lead him out into a forest, and there to kill him.

"But those thieves spared his life, letting him go to learn to live poorly; which he did, giving himself to be a private soldier in a country hereby. But, as he was ready to be advanced for some noble service, he heard news of me; who, drunk in my affection to that unlawful son, suffered myself so to be governed by him, that, ere I was aware, I had left myself nothing but the name of a king. Soon growing weary of this, he threw me out of my seat, and put out my eyes; and then let me go, full of wretchedness, fuller of disgrace, and fullest of guiltiness. And as he came to the crown by unjust means, as unjustly he keeps it, by force of strange soldiers in citadels, the nests of tyranny; disarming all his countrymen, that no man durst show so much charity as to lend a hand to guide my dark steps; till this son of mine, forgetting my wrongs, not recking danger, and neglecting the way he was in of doing himself good, came hither to do this kind office, to my unspeakable grief: for well I know, he that now reigneth will not let slip any advantage to make him away, whose just title may one day shake the seat of a never-secure tyranny. And for this cause I craved of him to lead me to the top of this rock, meaning, I must confess, to free him from so serpentine a companion as I am; but he, finding what I purposed, only therein, since he was born, showed himself disobedient to me. And now, gentlemen, you have the true story, which, I pray you, publish to the world, that my mischievous proceedings may be the glory of his filial piety, the only reward now left for so great a merit."

The story then goes on to relate how Plexirtus, the wicked son, presently came with a troop of horse to kill his brother; whereupon Pyrocles and Musidorus, joining with Leonatus, beat back the assailants, killing several of them. Other allies soon coming in on both sides, there follows a war between the two parties, which ends in the overthrow of Plexirtus, and the crowning of Leonatus by his blind father; in which very act the old man expires.

The reader now has before him, we believe, a sufficient view of all the known sources which furnished any hints or materials for this great tragedy; unless we should add, that there is an old ballad on the subject, entitled "A lamentable Song of the Death of King Lear and his three Daughters," and reprinted in Percy's *Reliques of Ancient Poetry*. The ballad, however, was probably of a later date than the play, and partly founded upon it.

There has been a good deal of impertinent criticism spent upon the circumstance, that in the details and costume of this play the Poet did not hold himself to the date of the legend which he adopted as the main plot. That date, as we have seen, was some 800 years before Christ; yet the play abounds in manners, sentiments, and allusions of a much later time. Malone is scandalized, that while the old chroniclers have dated Lear's reign from the year of the world 3105, yet Edgar speaks of Nero, who was not born till 800 or 900 years after. The painstaking Mr. Douce, also, is in dire distress at the Poet's blunders in substituting the manners of England under the Tudors for those of the ancient Britons. Now, to make these points, or such as these, any ground of impeachment, is to mistake totally the nature and design of the work. For the play is not, nor was it meant to be, in any proper sense of the term a history: it is a tragedy altogether, and nothing else; and as such it is as free of local and chronological conditions and circumscriptions, as human nature itself. Whatsoever of historical or legendary matter there is in it, neither forms nor guides the structure or movement of the piece; but is used in strict and entire subservience to the general ends of tragic representation. Of course, therefore, it does not fall within the lines of any jurisdiction for settling dates: it is amenable to no laws but the laws of art, any more than if it were entirely of the Poet's own creation: its true whereabout is in the reader's mind; and the only proper question is, whether it keeps to the laws of this whereabout; in which reference it will probably stand the severest inquisitions that criticism has strength to prosecute.

On this point, Mr. Verplanck has given us, under the head of Costume, one of the choicest pieces of criticism that we have met with; part of which we subjoin. After referring to the various uses which the story was made to serve, "in poem, ballad, and many ruder ways," he goes on as follows:

"Thus Lear and his 'three daughters fair' belong to the domain of old romance and popular tradition. They have nothing to do with the state of manners or arts in England, in any particular year of the world. They belong to that unreal but 'most potently believed' history, whose heroes were the household names of Europe,—St. George and his brother champions, King Arthur and Charlemagne, Don Bellianis, Roland, and his brother Paladins, and many others, for part of whom time has done, among those 'who speak the tongue that Shakespeare spake,' what the burning of Don Quixote's library was meant to do for the knight.

"Now, who, that is at all familiar with this long train of imaginary history, does not know that it had its own customs and costume, as well defined as the heathen mythology or Roman history? All the personages wore the arms and habiliments and obeyed the ceremonial mediæval chivalry, very probably because these several tales were put into legendary or poetic form in those days; but whatever was the reason, it was in that garb alone that they formed the popular literature of Europe in Shakespeare's time. It was a costume well fitted for poetical purposes, familiar in its details to the popular understanding, yet so far beyond the habitual associations of readers, as to have some tinge of antiquity, while it was eminently brilliant and picturesque.

"To have deviated from this conventional costume of fiction, half-believed as history, for the sake of stripping off old Lear's civilized 'lendings,' and bringing him to the unsophisticated state of a painted Pictish king, would have shocked the sense of probability in an audience of Elizabeth's reign, as perhaps it would even now. The positive objective truth of his history would appear far less probable than the received truth of poetry and romance, of the nursery and the stage. Accordingly, Shakespeare painted Lear and his times in the attire in which they were most familiar to the imagination of his audience; just as Racine did in respect to the half-fabulous personages of Grecian antiquity when he reproduced them on the French stage; and, of the two, probably the English bard was the nearest to historical truth.

"Such is our theory, in support of which we throw down our critical glove, daring any champion to meet us on some wider field than our present limits can afford. The advantages of this theory are so obvious and manifold, that it certainly deserves to be true, if not so in fact. To the reader it clears away all anxiety about petty criticisms or anachronisms, and 'such small deer,' while it presents the drama to his imagination in the most picturesque and poetical attire of which it is susceptible. The artist, too, may luxuriate at pleasure in his decorations, whether for the stage or the canvass, selecting all that he judges most appropriate to the feeling of his scene, from the treasures of the arts of the middle ages, and the pomp and splendor of chivalry, without having before his eyes the dread of some critical antiquary to reprimand him for encasing his knights in plate-armor, or erecting Lear's throne in a hall of Norman architecture, a thousand years or more before either Norman arch or plate-armor had been heard of in England."

This we regard as an ample vindication of the play not only from the criticisms cited, but from whatsoever others of the like sort have been or can be urged. It throws the whole subject, we think, on just the right ground; leaving to the drama all the freedom and variety that belong to the Gothic architecture, where the only absolute law is, that the parts shall all meet in one concent, and stand in mutual intelligence; and the more the structure is diversified in form, aspect, purpose, and expression, the grander and more elevating is the harmony resulting from the combination. It is clearly in the scope and spirit of this great principle of Gothic art, that *King Lear* was conceived and worked out. Herein, to be sure, it is like other of the Poet's dramas; only, it seems to us, more so than any of the rest. There is almost no end to the riches here drawn together: on attempting to reckon over the parts and particulars severally, one is amazed to find what varied wealth of poetry, character, passion, pathos, and high philosophy, is accumulated in the work. Yet there is a place for every thing, and every thing is in its place, at once fitting it and filling it: there is nothing but what makes good its right to be where and as it is; nothing but what seems perfectly in keeping and at home with all the rest: so that the accumulation is not more vast and varied in form and matter, than it is united and harmonious in itself. We have spoken of a primary and a secondary plot in the drama; and we may add, that either of these has scope enough for a great tragedy by itself: yet, be it observed, the two plots are so woven together in organic reciprocity and interdependence, as to be hardly distinguishable, and not at all separable; we can scarce think of them apart or perceive when one goes out, and the other comes in.

Accordingly, of all Shakespeare's dramas, this, on the whole, is the one which, whether we regard the qualities of the work or the difficulties of the subject, best illustrates to our mind the measure of his genius; his masterpiece in that style or order of composition which he, we will it say created, but certainly carried so much higher than any one else, as to make it his peculiar province. The play, indeed, stands as our ideal of what the spirit and principle of Gothic art are capable of in the form of dramatic representation; in a word, the highest specimen of what has been aptly called the Gothic drama, that literature has to show. Shelley, in his *Defence of Poetry*, has a passage, referring to the Fool of this play, which ought not to be omitted here. "The modern practice," says he, "of blending comedy with tragedy, though liable to great abuse, is undoubtedly an extension of the dramatic circle; but the comedy should be, as in *King Lear*, universal, ideal, and sublime. It is, perhaps, the intervention of this, which determines the balance in favor of *King Lear* against the *Œdipus Tyrannus* or the *Agamemnon*; unless the intense power of the choral poetry should be considered as restoring the equilibrium. *King Lear*, if it can sustain that comparison, may be judged the most perfect specimen of the dramatic art existing in the world."

The style and versification of *King Lear* do not differ from those of other plays written at or about the same period; save that here they seem attracted, as by imperceptible currents of sympathy, into a freedom and variety of movement answerable to the structure of the piece. There seems, in this case, no possible tone of mind or feeling, but that the Poet has a congenial form of imagery to body it forth, and a congenial pitch of rhythm and harmony to give it voice. Certainly, in none of his plays do we more feel the presence and power of that wonderful diction, not to say language, which he gradually wrought out and built up for himself, as the fitting and necessary organ of his thought. English literature has nothing else like it; and whatsoever else it has, seems tame, stiff, and mechanical, in the comparison. Nor is there any of the Poet's dramas wherein we have, in larger measure, the sentiments of the individual, as they are kindled by special circumstances and exigencies, forthwith expanding into general truth, and so lifting the whole into the clear daylight of a wise and thoughtful humanity. It is by this process that the Poet so plays upon the passions, as, through them, to instruct the reason; while at the same time the passion so fills the mind, that the instruction steals in unobserved, and therefore yields no food for conceit.

Touching the improbability, often censured, of certain incidents in this tragedy, it seems needful that somewhat be said. Improbable enough, we grant, some of the incidents are. But these nowise touch the substantial truth of the drama: the Poet but uses them as the occasion for what he has to develop of the inner life of nature and man. Besides, he did not invent them. They stood dressed in many attractive shapes before him, inviting his hand. And his use of them is amply justified in that they were matters of common and familiar tradition, and as such already domesticated in the popular mind and faith of the time.

As to the *alleged* improbabilities of character, this is another and a much graver question. The play, it must be confessed, sets forth an extreme diversity of moral complexion, but especially a boldness and lustihood of crime, such as cannot but seem unnatural, if tried by the rule, or even by the exceptions, of what we are used to see of nature. Measuring, indeed, the capabilities of man by the standard of our own observations, we shall find all the higher representations of art, and even many well-attested things of history, too much for belief. But this is not the way to deal with such things; our business is, to be taught by them as they are, and not to crush them down to the measures of what we already know. And so we should bear in mind, that the scene of this play is laid in a period of time when the innate peculiarities of men were much less subjected, than in our day, to the stamp of a common impression. For the influences under which we live cannot but generate more uniformity of character; thus making us apt to regard as monstrous that rankness of growth, those great crimes and great virtues, which are recorded of earlier times, and which furnish the material of deep tragedy. For the process of civilization, if it do not kill out the aptitudes for heroic crime, at least involves a constant discipline of prudence, that keeps them in a more decorous reserve. But suppose the pressure of conventional motives and restraints to be wanting, and it will not then appear so very incredible that there should be just such spontaneous outcomings of wicked impulse, just such redundant transpirations of original sin, as are here displayed. Accordingly, while we are amid the Poet's scenes, and subject to his power, he seems to enlarge our knowledge of nature, not to contradict it; but when we fall back and go to comparing his shows with our experiences, he seems rather to have beguiled us with illusions, than edified us with truth. All which, we suspect, is more our fault than his. And that criticism is best, which is born rather of what he makes us, than of what we are without him.

In speaking of the several characters of the play, we scarce know where to begin. Much has been written upon them, and the best critics seem to have been so raised and kindled by the theme as to surpass themselves. The persons of the drama are variously divisible into groups, according as we regard their domestic or their moral affinities. We prefer to consider them as grouped upon the latter principle. And as the main action of the piece is shaped by the prevailing energy of evil, we will begin with those from whom that energy springs.

There is no accounting for the conduct of Goneril and Regan but by supposing them possessed with a very instinct and original impulse of malignity. The main points of their action, as we have seen, were taken from the old story. Character, in the proper sense of the term, they have none in the legend; and the Poet but invested them with characters suitable to the part they were believed to have acted.

Whatever of soul these beings possess, is all in the head: they have no heart to guide or inspire their understanding; and but enough of understanding to seize occasions and frame excuses for their heartlessness. Without affection, they are also without shame; there being barely so much of human blood in their veins, as may serve to quicken the brain, without sending a blush to the cheek. Their hypocrisy acts as the instructive cunning of selfishness; with a sort of hell-inspired tact they feel their way to a fit occasion, but drop the mask as soon as their ends are reached. There is a smooth, glib rhetoric in their professions of love, unwarmed with the least grace of real feeling, and a certain wiry virulence and intrepidity of thought in their after-speaking, that is almost terrific. No touch of nature finds a response in their bosoms; no atmosphere of comfort can abide their presence: we feel that they have somewhat within that turns the milk of humanity into venom, which all the wounds they can inflict are but opportunities for casting.

The subordinate plot of the drama serves the purpose of relieving the improbability of their conduct towards their father. Some, indeed, have censured this plot as an embarrassment to the main one; forgetting, perhaps, that to raise and sustain the feelings at any great height, there must be some breadth of basis. A degree of evil, which, if seen altogether alone, would strike us as superhuman, makes a very different impression, when it has the support of proper sympathies and associations. This effect is in a good measure secured by Edmund's independent concurrence with Goneril and Regan in wickedness. It looks as if some malignant planet had set the elements of evil astir in several hearts at the same time; so that "unnaturalness between the child and the parent" were become, sure enough, the order of the day.

Besides, the agreement of the sister-fiends in filial ingratitude might seem, of itself, to argue some sisterly attachment between them. So that, to bring out their character truly, it had to be shown, that the same principle which united them against their father would, on the turning of occasion, divide them against each other. Hence the necessity of bringing them forward in relations adapted to set them at strife. In Edmund, accordingly, they find a character wicked enough, and energetic enough in his wickedness, to interest their feelings; and because they are both alike interested in him, therefore they will cut their way to him through each other's life. Be it observed, too, that their passion for Edmund grows out of his treachery to his father; as though from such similarity of action they inferred a congeniality of mind. For even to have hated each other from love of any one but a villain, and because of his villainy, had seemed a degree of virtue.

Having said so much, perhaps we need not add, that the action of Goneril and Regan seems to us the most incredible thing in the play. Nor are we quite able to shake off the feeling, that before the heart could get so thoroughly ossified the head must cease to operate. On the whole, we find it not easy to think of Goneril and Regan otherwise than as instruments of the plot; not so much ungrateful persons as personifications of ingratitude. And it is considerable that they both appear of nearly the same mind and metal; are so much alike in character, that we can scarce distinguish them as individuals.

For the union of wit and wickedness, Edmund stands next to Richard and Iago. His strong and nimble intellect, his manifest courage, his energy of character, and his noble, manly person and presence, prepare us on our first acquaintance to expect from him not only great undertakings, but great success in them. But while his personal advantages naturally generate pride, his disgraces of fortune are such as, from pride, to generate guilt. The circumstances of our first meeting with him, the matter and manner of Gloster's conversation about him and to him, sufficiently explain his conduct; while the subsequent outleakings of his mind in soliloquy let us into his secret springs of action. With a mixture of guilt, shame, and waggery, his father, before his face, and in the presence of one whose respect he craves, makes him and his birth the subject of gross and wanton discourse;

confesses himself ashamed yet compelled to acknowledge him; avows the design of keeping him from home, as if to avoid the shame of his presence; and makes comparisons between him and "another son some year elder than this," such as could hardly fail at once to wound his pride, to stimulate his ambition, and awaken his enmity. Thus the kindly influences of human relationship and household ties are turned to their contraries. He feels himself the victim of a disgrace for which he is not to blame; which he can never hope to outgrow; which no degree of personal worth can ever efface; and from which he sees no escape but in pomp and circumstance of worldly power.

Nor is this all. Whatever aptitudes he may have to filial piety are thwarted by his father's open impiety towards his mother. Nay, even his duty to her seems to cancel his obligations of love to him; the religious awe with which we naturally contemplate the mystery of our coming hither, and the mysterious union of those who brought us hither, is kept out of mind by his father's levity respecting his birth and her who bore him. Thus the very beginnings of religion are stifled in him by the impossibility of revering his parents: there is no sanctity about the origin and agents of his being, to inspire him with awe: as they have no religion towards each other, so he can have none towards them. He can only despise them for being his parents; and the consciousness, that he is himself a living monument of their shame, tends but to pervert and poison the felicities of his nature.

Moreover, by his residence and education abroad, he is cut off from the fatherly counsels and kindnesses which might else cause him to forget the disgraces entailed upon him. His shame of birth, however, nowise represses his pride of blood: on the contrary, it furnishes the conditions wherein such pride, though the natural auxiliary of many virtues, is most apt to fester into crime. For while his shame begets scorn of family ties, his pride passes into greediness of family possessions: the passion for hereditary honors is unrestrained by domestic attachments; no love of Edgar's person comes in to keep down a lust for his distinctions; and he is led to envy as a rival the brother whom he would else respect as a superior.

Always thinking, too, of his dishonor, he is ever on the lookout for signs that others are thinking of it; and the jealousy thus engendered construes every show of respect into an effort of courtesy;—a thing which inflames his ambition while chafing his pride. The corroding suspicion, that others are perhaps secretly scorning his noble descent while outwardly acknowledging it, leads him to find or fancy in them a disposition to indemnify themselves for his personal superiority out of his social debasement. The stings of reproach, being personally unmerited, are resented as wrongs; and with the plea of injustice he can easily reconcile his mind to the most wicked schemes. Aware of Edgar's virtues, still he has no relentings, but shrugs his shoulders, and laughs off all compunctions with an "I must," as if justice to himself were a sufficient excuse for his criminal purposes.

With "the plague of custom" and "the curiosity of nations" Edmund has no compact: he did not consent to them, and therefore is not bound by them. He came into the world in spite of them; and may he not thrive in the world by outwitting them? Perhaps he owes his gifts to a breach of them: may he not, then, use his gifts to circumvent them? Since his dimensions are so well compact, his mind so generous, and his shape so true, he prefers nature as she has made him to nature as she has placed him; and freely employs the wit she has given, to compass the wealth she has withheld. Thus our philosopher appeals from convention to nature and, as usually happens in such cases, takes only so much of nature as will serve his turn. For convention is itself a part of nature; it being just as natural that men should grow up together in communities, as that they should grow up severally as individuals. But the same principle which prompts the appeal orders the tribunal. Nor does nature in such cases ever contradict, or debate, or try conclusions with men; but nods assent to their propositions, and lets them have their own way, as knowing that "the very devils cannot plaguc them better."

Nevertheless, there is not in Edmund, as in Iago, any spontaneous or purposeless wickedness. Nay, he does not so much commit crimes, as devise accidents, and then commit his cause to them; not so much makes war on morality, as bows and smiles and shifts her off out of the way, that his wit may have free course. He deceives others without scruple indeed, but then he does not consider them bound to trust him; and tries to avail himself of their credulity or criminality without becoming responsible for it. True, he is a pretty bold experimenter, but that is because he has nothing to lose if he fails, and much to gain if he succeeds. Nor does he attempt to disguise from himself, or gloss over, or anywise palliate his designs; but boldly confronts and stares them in the face, as though assured of sufficient external grounds to justify or excuse them.

Edmund's strength and acuteness of intellect, unsubjected as they are to the moral and religious sentiments, of course exempt him from the superstitions that prevail about him. He has an eye to discern the error of such things, but no sense for the greater truth they involve. For such superstitions are but the natural suggestions of the religious instincts unenlightened by revelation. So that he who would not be superstitious without revelation, would probably be irreligious with it; and that there is more of truth in superstition than in irreligion, is implied in the very fact of religious instincts. It is merely the atheism of the heart that makes Edmund so discerning of error in what he does not like; in which case the subtleties of the understanding lead to the rankest unwisdom.

As a portraiture of individual character Lear himself holds, to our mind, much the same pre-eminence over all others, which we accord to the tragedy as a dramatic composition. Less complex and varied, perhaps, than Hamlet, the character is, however, much more remote from the common feelings and experiences of human life. Few of us arrive at the age, fewer have the capacity, and fewer still are ever in a condition to feel what Lear feels, do what he does, and suffer what he suffers. The delineation impresses us, beyond any other, with the truth of what some one has said of Shakespeare,—that if he had been the author of the human heart, it seems hardly possible he should have better understood what was in it, and how it was made.

From our first interview with Lear, it becomes manifest that, with his body tottering beneath the weight of years and cares of state, his mind is sliding into that second childhood which is content to play with the shadows of things past, as the first is, with the shadows of things that are to be. The opening of the play informs us that the division of the kingdom has been already resolved upon, the terms of the division arranged, and the several portions allotted. The trial of professions, therefore, is clearly but a trick of the king's, designed, perhaps, to surprise his children into expressions which filial modesty would else forbid. Not that Lear distrusts his daughters; but he has a morbid hungering after the outward tokens of affection; is not satisfied to know the heart beats for him, but craves to feel and count over its beatings. And he naturally looks for the strongest professions where he feels the deepest attachment. And the same doting fondness that suggested the device makes him angry at its defeat; while its success with the first two heightens his irritation at its failure with the third. Balked of his hope, and that too where he is at once the most confident and the most desirous of success, he naturally enough flies off in a transport of rage. Still it is not so much a doubt of Cordelia's love, as a dotage of his trick, that frets and chafes him; for the device is evidently a *pet* with him.

And there appears something of obstinacy and sullenness in Cordelia's answer, as if she would resent the old man's credulity to her sisters' lies by refusing to tell him the truth. But the fact is, she cannot, if she wills, talk much about what she is, and what she intends. For there is a virgin delicacy in genuine and deep feeling, that causes it to keep in the background of the life; to be heard rather in its effects than in direct and open declarations; and the more it is ashamed to be seen, the more it *blushes* into sight. Such is the beautiful instinct of true feeling to embody itself sweetly and silently in deeds, lest, from showing itself in words, it should turn to matter of vanity or pride. It is not strange, therefore, that Cordelia should make it her part to "love and be silent." And perhaps it is as little strange that Lear, impetuous by nature, irritable through age, and self-willed from habit, on the tiptoe of anticipation, and in the full tide of successful experiment, should be surprised by her answer into a tempest of passion. Of course his anger at the failure is proportioned to his confidence of success; and in the disorder of his thoughts he forgets the thousand little acts that have insensibly wrought in him to love her most, and to expect most love from her. In all which the old king, enamored of his trick, and vexed at its defeat, is like a peevish fretful child who, if prevented from kissing his nurse, falls to striking her.

Men sometimes take a secret pleasure in the mere exercise of the will without or against reason, as if they could make that right or true which is not so in itself. For such a course has to their feelings the effect of ascertaining and augmenting their power. The very shame, too, of doing wrong sometimes hurries men into a barring of themselves off from retreat. Such appears to be the case with Lear in his treatment of Cordelia. In the first place, he *will* do the thing, because he knows it to be wrong, and then the uneasy sense of a wrong done prompts him to bind the act with an oath; that is, because he ought not to have driven the nail, therefore he *clinches* it. It is clear from what follows, especially from his shrinking soreness of mind as shown when the Fool's grief at the loss of Cordelia is spoken of, that he cannot suppress the feeling that he has done her wrong.

But the great thing in the delineation of Lear, is the effect and progress of his passion in redeveloping his faculties. For the character seems designed in part to illustrate the power of passion to reawaken and raise the faculties from the tomb wherein age hath inurned them. In Lear, accordingly, we have, as it were, a handful of tumult embosomed in a sea, gradually overspreading, and pervading, and fearfully convulsing the entire mass. Coming before us at first full of paternal love and of faith in filial piety, his noble mind, freed from the cares of state and settled into repose, seems about to run through the vale of age so deep and smooth and still as to leave us unadmonished of its flowing. The possibility of filial desertion appears never to have entered his thoughts; for so absolute is his trust, that he can scarce admit the evidence of sight against his cherished expectations. Bereft, as he thinks, of one, he clings the closer to the rest, assuring himself that they will spare no pains to make up the loss. Cast off and struck on the heart by another, he flies with still greater confidence to the third. Though proofs that she, too, has fallen off are multiplied upon him, still he cannot give her up, cannot be provoked to curse her; he *will* not see, will not own to himself the fact of her revolt.

When, however, the truth is forced home, and he can no longer evade or shuffle off the conclusion, the effect is indeed awful. So long as his heart had something to lay hold of, and cling to, and rest upon, his mind was the abode of order and peace. But now that his feelings are rendered objectless, torn from their accustomed holdings, and thrown back upon themselves, there springs up a wild chaos of the brain, a whirling tumult and anarchy of the thoughts, which, until imagination has time to work, chokes his utterance. The crushing of his aged spirit brings to light its hidden depths and buried riches. Thus his terrible energy of thought and speech, as soon as imagination rallies to his aid, proceeds naturally from the struggle of his feelings,—a struggle that seems to wrench his whole being into dislocation, convulsing and upturning his soul from the bottom.

In the transition of his mind from its first stillness and repose to its subsequent tempest and storm; in the hurried revulsions and alternations of feeling,—the fast-rooted faith in filial virtue, the keen sensibility to filial ingratitude, the mighty hunger of the heart, thrice repelled, yet ever strengthened by repulse; and in the turning up of sentiments and faculties deeply imbedded beneath the incrustations of time and place;—in all this we have a retrospect of the aged sufferer's whole life; the abridged history of a mind that has passed through many successive stages, each putting off the form, yet retaining and perfecting the grace of those that preceded.

As to the representation here given of madness, we would not willingly trust ourselves to undertake to describe it. Nor need we. The elder Kean's revelations of art (for such they may well be called) were before our day. But they were witnessed by a countryman of ours, who has put on record good evidence that his eye and tongue were equal to the greatest things that even that great artist could do. We refer to Mr. Richard H. Dana's noble paper on Kean's acting,—a paper that may be regarded as settling the question whether criticism be capable of rising into an art. We subjoin that portion of it which relates to the point in hand:

"It has been said that Lear is a study for one who would make himself acquainted with the workings of an insane mind. And it is hardly less true, that the acting of Kean was an embodying of these workings. His eye, when his senses are fast forsaking him, giving an inquiring look at what he saw, as if all before him was undergoing a strange and bewildering change which confused his brain; the wandering, lost motions of his hands, which seemed feeling for something familiar to them, on which they might take hold and be assured of a safe reality; the under monotone of his voice, as if he was questioning his own being, and what surrounded him; the continuous, but slight, oscillating motion of the body;—all these expressed, with fearful truth, the bewildered state of a mind fast unsettling, and making vain and weak efforts to find its way back to its wonted reason. There was a childish, feeble gladness in the eye, and a half-piteous smile about the mouth, at times, which one could scarce look upon without tears. As the derangement increased upon him, his eye lost its notice of objects about him, wandering over things as if he saw them not, and fastening upon the creatures of his crazed brain. The helpless and delighted fondness with which he clings to Edgar, as an insane brother, is another instance of the justness of Kean's conceptions. Nor does he lose the air of insanity, even in the fine moralizing parts, and where he inveighs against the corruption of the world. There is a madness even in his reason."

Mrs. Jameson aptly says of Cordelia, that "every thing in her lies beyond our view, and affects us in such a manner that we rather feel than perceive it." And it is very remarkable that, though but little seen or heard, yet the whole play seems full of her. All that she utters is, forty-three lines in Act I, twenty-four in the fourth and thirty-seven in the seventh scene of Act IV, and five in Act V. Yet we had read the play occasionally for several years, before we could fully realize but she was among the principal speakers; and even now, on taking up the play, we can scarce persuade ourselves but that the time of reading is to be spent chiefly with her.

It is in this remoteness, we take it, this gift of presence without appearance, that the secret of her power mainly consists. Her character has no foreground; nothing outstanding, or that touches us in a definable way: she is all perspective, self-withdrawn; so that she comes to us rather by inspiration than by vision. Even when before us, we rather feel than see her: so much "more is meant than meets the eye," that what is shown is in a manner lost sight of in what is suggested. Thus she affects us through deeper and finer susceptibilities than consciousness can grasp; as if she at once used, and developed in us, higher organs of communication than sense; or as if her presence acted in some mysterious way on our very life, so that when it works in us most we perceive it least.

Thus what was stated before respecting her affection is true of her character generally. For she has the same deep, quiet reserve of thought as of feeling, so that her mind becomes conspicuous by its retiringness, and wins the attention by shrinking from it. Though she nowhere says any thing indicating much intelligence, yet she always strikes us somehow as very intelligent, and even the more so, that her intelligence does not appear. And indeed what she knows is so bound up with her affections, that she cannot draw it off into expression by itself; it is held in perfect solution, as it were, with all the other elements of her nature, and nowhere falls down in a sediment, so as to be producible in a separate state. She has a deeper and truer knowledge of her sisters, than any one else about them; but she knows them rather by heart than by head; and so can *feel* and *act*, but not *articulate*, a prophecy of what they will do. Ask her, indeed, what she thinks on any subject, and she will answer, that she thinks,—nay, she cannot *tell*, she can only *show* you what she thinks: for her thinking involuntarily shapes itself into life, not into speech; and she uses the proper language of her mind, when, bending over her "child-chang'd father," she invokes restoration to "hang its medicine on her lips," or, kneeling beside him, intreats him to "hold his hands in benediction o'er her."

All which shows a peculiar fitness in Cordelia for the part she was designed to act; which was, to exemplify the workings of filial piety, as Lear exemplifies those of paternal love. To embody this sentiment, the whole character, in all its movements and aspects, is made essentially religious. For filial piety is religion acting under the sacredest relation of human life. And religion, we know or ought to know, is a life, and not a language; and life is the simultaneous and concurrent action of *all* the elements of our being. Which is illustrated to perfection in Cordelia; who, be it observed, never thinks of her piety at all, because her piety prompts her to think only of her father. And so she can reveal her good thoughts only by veiling them in good deeds, as the spirit is veiled and revealed in the body; nay, has to be so veiled, in order to be revealed; for, if the veil be torn off, the spirit is no longer there.

Therefore it is, that Cordelia affects us so deeply and constantly without our being able to perceive how or why. Hence, also, the impression of reserve that runs through her character; for where the whole moves equally and at once, the parts are not distinctly seen, and so seem held in reserve. And she affects those about her in the same insensible way as she affects us; that is, she keeps their thoughts and feelings busy, by keeping what she thinks and feels hidden beneath what she does: an influence goes forth from her by stealth, and stealthily creeps into them;—an influence which does not appear, and yet is irresistible, and is therefore irresistible because it does not appear; and which becomes an undercurrent in their minds, circulates in their blood, as it were, and enriches their life with a beauty which seems their own, and yet is not their own: so that she steals upon us through them, and we think of her the more, because they, without suspecting it, remind us of her.

Accordingly, her father loves her most, yet knows not why; has no assignable reasons for his feeling, and therefore cannot reason it down. Having cast her off from his bounty, but not out of his heart, he grows full of unrest, as if there were some secret power about her which he cannot be without, though he did not dream of its existence while she was with him. And "since her going into France the Fool has much pined away"; as though her presence were necessary to his health; so that he sickens upon the loss of her, yet he suspects not wherefore, and knows but that she was by and his spirits were nimble, she is gone and his spirits are drooping.

Such is the influence of a right-minded and right-mannered woman on those about her: she does not know it, they do not know it; her influence is all the better and stronger, that neither of them knows it: she begins to lose it when she goes about to use it and make them sensible of it: with noiseless step it glides into them unnoticed and unsuspected, but disturbs and repels them as soon as it seeks to make itself heard. For, indeed, her power lies not in what she values herself upon, and voluntarily brings forward, and makes use of, but in something far deeper and diviner than all this, which she knows not of and cannot help.

Finally, we know of nothing with which to compare Cordelia, nothing to illustrate her character by. An impersonation of the holiness of womanhood, herself alone is her own parallel; and all the objects that lend beauty when used to illustrate other things, seem dumb or ineloquent of meaning beside her. Superior, perhaps, to all the rest of Shakespeare's women in beauty of character, she is nevertheless inferior to none of them as a living and breathing reality. We see her only in the relation of daughter, and hardly *see* her even there; yet we know what she is or would be in every relation of life, just as well as if we had seen her in them all. "Formed for all sympathies, moved by all tenderness, prompt for all duty, prepared for all suffering," we seem almost to hear her sighs, and see her tears, and feel her breath, as she hangs like a ministering spirit over her reviving father: the vision sinks sweetly and silently into the heart, and in its reality to our feelings, abides with us more as a remembrance than an imagination, instructing and inspiring us as that of a friend whom we had known and loved in our youth.

It is an interesting feature of this representation, that Lear's faith in filial piety is justified by the event, though not his judgment as to the persons in whom it was to be found. Wiser in heart than in understanding, he mistook the object, but was right in the feeling. In his pride of sovereignty, he thought to command the affection of his children, and to purchase the dues of gratitude by his bounty to them; but he is at last indebted to the unbought grace of nature for that comfort which he would fain owe to himself; what he seeks, and even more than he seeks, comes as the free return of a love which thrives in spite of him, and which no harshness or injustice of his could extinguish. Thus the confirmation of his faith grows by the ruin of his pride. Such is the frequent lesson of human life. For the fall has hardly more defaced the beauty of human character, than it has marred our perception of what remains; and not the least punishment of our own vices is, that they take from us the power to discern the virtue of others.

There is a strange assemblage of qualities in the Fool, and a strange effect arising from their union and position, which we are not a little at loss to describe. It seems hardly possible that Lear's character should be properly developed without him: indeed he serves as a common gauge and exponent of all the characters about him,—the mirror in which their finest and deepest lineaments are reflected. Though a privileged person, with the largest opportunity of seeing and the largest liberty of speaking, he every where turns his privileges into charities, making the immunities of the clown subservient to the noblest sympathies of the man. He is therefore by no means a mere harlequinian appendage of the scene, but moves in vital intercourse with the character and passion of the drama. He makes his folly the vehicle of truths which the king will bear in no other shape, while his affectionate tenderness sanctifies all his nonsense. His being heralded to us by the announcement of his pining away at the banishment of Cordelia, sends a consecration before him: that his life feeds on her presence, hallows every thing about him. Lear manifestly loves him, partly for his own sake, and partly for hers; for we feel a delicate, scarce-discernible play of sympathy between them on Cordelia's account; the more so, perhaps, that neither of them makes any clear allusion to her; their very reserve concerning her indicating that their hearts are too full to speak.

We know not, therefore, how to describe the Fool otherwise than as the soul of pathos in a sort of comic masquerade; one in whom fun and frolic are sublimed and idealized into tragic beauty; with the garments of mourning showing through and softened by the law of playfulness. His "laboring to outjest Lear's heart-struck injuries" shows that his wits are set a-dancing by grief; that his jests bubble up from the depths of a heart struggling with pity and sorrow, as foam enwreaths the face of deeply-troubled waters. So have we seen the lip quiver and the cheek dimple into a smile, to relieve the eye of a burden it was reeling under, yet ashamed to let fall. There is all along a shrinking, velvet-footed delicacy of step in the Fool's antics, as if awed by the holiness of the ground; and he seems bringing diversion to the thoughts, that he may the better steal a sense of woe into the heart. It is hard to tell whether the inspired antics, that sparkle from the surface of his mind, be in more impressive contrast with the dark tragic scenes into which they are thrown like rockets into a midnight tempest, or with the undercurrent of deep tragic thoughtfulness out of which they falteringly issue and play.

If the best grace and happiness of life consist in a forgetting of self and a living for others, Kent and Edgar are those of Shakespeare's men whom one should most wish to resemble. Strikingly similar in virtues and situation, these two persons are, notwithstanding, widely different in character. Brothers in magnanimity and in misfortune; equally invincible in fidelity, the one to his King, the other to his father; both driven to disguise themselves, and in their disguise both serving where they stand condemned;—Kent, too generous to control himself, is always quick, fiery, and impetuous; Edgar, controlling himself even because of his generosity, is always calm, collected, and deliberate. Yet it is difficult which of them to prefer. For, if Edgar be the more judicious and prudent, Kent is the more unselfish, of the two: the former disguising himself for his own safety, and then turning his disguise into an opportunity of service; the latter disguising himself merely *in order* to serve, and then periling his life in the same course whereby the other seeks to preserve it. Nor is Edgar so lost to himself and absorbed in others but that he can and does survive them; whereas Kent's life is so bound up with others, that their death plucks him after. Nevertheless it is hard saying whether one would rather be the subject or the author of Edgar's tale,—"Whilst I was big in clamor," etc.

In Kent and Oswald we have one of those effective contrasts with which the Poet often deepens the harmony of his greater efforts. As the former is the soul of goodness clothed in the assembled nobilities of manhood; so the latter is the very extract and embodiment of meanness; two men, than whom "no contraries hold more antipathy." To call the steward wicked, were a misuse of the term: he is absolutely beneath serious censure; one of those convenient packhorses whereon guilt often rides to its ends. Except the task of smoothing the way for the passions of a wicked mistress, there were no employment base enough for him. None but a reptile like him could ever have got hatched into notice in such an atmosphere as Goneril's society; were he any thing else, there could not be sympathy enough between them to admit the relation of superior and subaltern.

The surpassing power of this drama is most felt in the third and fourth acts, especially those parts where Lear appears. The fierce warring of the elements around the old King, as if mad with enmity against him, while he seeks shelter in their strife from the tempest in his mind, his preternatural illumination of mind when tottering on the verge of insanity; his gradual settling into that unnatural calmness which is far more appalling than any agitation, because it marks the pause between order gone and anarchy about to begin; the scattering out of the mind's jewels in the mad revel of his unbound and disheveled faculties, until he finally sinks, broken-hearted and broken-witted, into the sleep of utter prostration;—all this, joined to the incessant groanings and howlings of the storm; the wild, inspired babblings of the Fool; the desperate fidelity of Kent, outstripping the malice of the elements with his ministries of love; the bedlamitish jargon of Edgar, whose feigned madness, striking in with Lear's real madness, takes away just enough of its horror, and borrows just enough of its dignity, to keep either from becoming insupportable;—the whole at last dying away into the soft, sweet, solemn discourse of Cordelia, as though the storm had faltered into music at her coming; and winding up with the revival of Lear, his faculties touched into order and peace by the voice of filial sympathy;—in all this we have a masterpiece of art, of which every reader's feelings must confess the power, though perhaps no analysis can fathom the secret.

It would hardly do to leave the subject without referring to the improvement which this mighty drama has suffered at the hands of one Nahum Tate, for the purpose, as would seem, of dwarfing and dementing it down to the capacity of some theatrical showman. Nor need we deem it so very strange that the Tatified *Lear* should have gotten and kept possession of the stage, considering how many there are in our day, who prefer some modern berhyming of the Psalms to the Psalms as God and David wrote them. A part of Tate's work lay in rectifying the catastrophe, so as to make Lear and Cordelia come off triumphant, thus rewarding their virtue with worldly success. The cutting out of the precious Fool, and the turning of Cordelia into a lovesick hypocrite, who feigns indifference to her father in order to cheat and enrage him, that so he may abandon her to a forbidden match with Edgar, completes this execrable piece of profanation. Tate improve *Lear!* Set a tailor at work, rather, to improve Niagara!

For the rest that we would say on this point and some others, we will substitute Lamb's immortal criticism on the tragedy with reference to the capacities of the stage. "The Lear of Shakespeare," says he, "cannot be acted. The contemptible machinery, by which they mimic the storm he goes out in, is not more inadequate to represent the horrors of the real elements, than any actor can be to represent Lear: they might more easily propose to personate the Satan of Milton on a stage, or one of Michael Angelo's terrible figures. The greatness of Lear is not in corporal dimension, but in intellectual: the explosions of his passion are terrible as a volcano; they are storms turning up and disclosing to the bottom that sea, his mind, with all its vast riches. It is his mind which is laid bare. This case of flesh and blood seems too insignificant to be thought on; even as he himself neglects it. On the stage we see nothing but corporal infirmities and weaknesses, the impotence of rage: while we read it, we see not Lear, but we are Lear,—we are in his mind;.we are sustained by a grandeur which baffles the malice of his daughters and storms: in the aberrations of his reason, we discover a mighty irregular power of reasoning, immethodized from the ordinary purposes of life, but exerting its powers, as the wind blows where it listeth, at will upon the corruptions and abuses of mankind. What have looks or tones to do with that sublime identification of his age with that of the *heavens themselves*, when, in his reproaches to them for conniving at the injustice of his children, he reminds them that 'they themselves are old'? What gestures shall we appropriate to this? What has the voice or the eye to do with such things? But the play is beyond all art, as the tamperings with it show: it is too hard and stony; it must have love-scenes, and a happy ending. It is not enough that Cordelia is a daughter, she must shine as a lover too. Tate has put his hook in the nostrils of this Leviathan, for Garrick and his followers, the showmen of the scene, to draw the mighty beast about more easily. A happy ending!—as if the living martyrdom that Lear had gone through, the flaying of his feelings alive, did not make a fair dismissal from the stage of life the only decorous thing for him. If he is to live and be happy after, if he could sustain this world's burden after, why all this pudder and preparation,—why torment us with all this unnecessary sympathy? As if the childish pleasure of getting his gilt robes and scepter again could tempt him to act over again his misused station,—as if, at his years and with his experience, any thing was left but to die."

Comments

By Shakespearean Scholars

LEAR

But this drama is primarily the drama of Lear. Lear disturbs the harmony of the ethical institutions of both State and Family. Long years of absolute power have developed the tyrant dominated by selfishness; weary of care, he would shirk the responsibilities of government, but retain the pleasures of its outward show; he forsakes reason and suffers the penalty of reason forsaking him; the State is nothing to him; he would throw government aside like a cast-off garment; his daughter Cordelia cannot play false like her treacherous sisters, and he thrusts her aside as easily as an impatient child tosses away the toy which cannot obey his bidding. If she goes with some bitterness in her heart, her inherent love of truth develops into the truth of love, and she returns only to be sacrificed.

Since Lear's sin is so great that Nemesis will only be satisfied with his tragic end, his deed returns upon his own head. Nemesis follows Regan and Goneril, and they suffer the penalty of their own wicked deeds; if we see in Cordelia's violent death only "dramatic pathos," this by no means infringes upon the general law of retribution, but simply shows that while evil deeds bring their own punishment, all misfortune is not necessarily the result of wrongdoing.—Ferris-Gettemy, *Outline Studies in Shakespearean Drama*.

Of all Shakspere's plays *Macbeth* is the most rapid, *Hamlet* the slowest, in movement. *Lear* combines length with rapidity,—

like the hurricane and the whirlpool, absorbing while it advances. It begins as a stormy day in summer, with brightness; but that brightness is lurid, and anticipates the tempest.

It was not without forethought, nor is it without its due significance, that the division of Lear's kingdom is in the first six lines of the play stated as a thing already determined in all its particulars, previously to the trial of professions, as the relative rewards of which the daughters were to be made to consider their several portions. The strange, yet by no means unnatural, mixture of selfishness, sensibility, and habit of feeling derived from, and fostered by, the particular rank and usages of the individual;—the intense desire of being intensely beloved,—selfish, and yet characteristic of the selfishness of a loving and kindly nature alone;—the self-supportless leaning for all pleasure on another's breast;—the cravings after sympathy with a prodigal disinterestedness, frustrated by its own ostentation, and the mode and nature of its claims;—the anxiety, the distrust, the jealousy, which more or less accompany all selfish affections, and are amongst the surest contradistinctions of mere fondness from true love, and which originate Lear's eager wish to enjoy his daughter's violent professions, whilst the inveterate habits of sovereignty convert the wish into claim and positive right, and an incompliance with it into crime and treason;—these facts, these passions, these moral verities, on which the whole tragedy is founded, are all prepared for, and will to the retrospect be found implied, in these first four or five lines of the play. They let us know that the trial is but a trick; and that the grossness of the old king's rage is in part the natural result of a silly trick suddenly and most unexpectedly baffled and disappointed.—Coleridge, *Lectures on Shakspere*.

The thoughtless confidence of Lear in his children has something in it far more touching than the self-beggary of Timon; though both one and the other have prototypes enough in real life, and as we give the old king more of our pity, so a more intense abhorrence accompanies his daughters and the evil characters of that drama than we spare for the miserable sycophants of the Athenian.... There seems to have been a period of Shakespeare's life when his heart was ill at ease, and ill-content with the world as his own conscience; the memory of hours misspent, the pang of affection misplaced or unrequited, the experience of man's worser nature which intercourse with unworthy associates, by choice or circumstance, peculiarly teaches;—these, as they sank down into the depths of his great mind, seem not only to have inspired into it the conception of Lear and Timon, but that of one primary character, the censurer of mankind.—Hallam, *Introduction to the Literature of Europe*.

CORDELIA

There is in the beauty of Cordelia's character an effect too sacred for words, and almost too deep for tears; within her heart is a fathomless well of purest affection, but its waters sleep in silence and obscurity,—never failing in their depth and never overflowing in their fullness. Every thing in her seems to lie beyond our view, and affects us in a manner which we feel rather than perceive. The character appears to have no surface, no salient points upon which the fancy can readily seize: there is little external development of intellect, less of passion, and still less of imagination. It is completely made out in the course of a few scenes, and we are surprised to find that in those few scenes there is matter for a life of reflection, and materials enough for twenty heroines. If *Lear* be the grandest of Shakespeare's tragedies, Cordelia in herself, as a human being, governed by the purest and holiest impulses and motives, the most refined from all dross of selfishness and passion, approaches near to perfection; and in her adaptation, as a dramatic personage, to a determinate plan of action, may be pronounced altogether perfect. The character, to speak of it critically as a poetical conception, is not, however, to be comprehended at once, or easily; and in the same manner Cordelia, as a woman, is one whom we must have loved before we could have known her, and known her long before we could have known her truly.—Jameson, *Shakespeare's Heroines*.

"Of the heavenly beauty of soul of Cordelia, pronounced in so few words, I will venture to speak." This was the impression which Shakspere's Cordelia produced upon Schlegel. In the whole range of the Shakspearean drama there is nothing more extraordinary than the effect upon the mind of the character of

Cordelia. Mrs. Jameson has truly said, "Everything in her seems to lie beyond our view, and affects us in a manner which we feel rather than perceive." In the first act she has only forty-three lines assigned to her: she does not appear again till the fourth act, in the fourth scene of which she has twenty-four lines, and, in the seventh, thirty-seven. In the fifth act she has five lines. Yet during the whole progress of the play we can never forget her; and, after its melancholy close, she lingers about our recollections as if we had seen some being more beautiful and purer than a thing of earth, who had communicated with us by a higher medium than that of words. And yet she is no mere abstraction;—she is nothing more nor less than a personification of the holiness of womanhood. She is a creature formed for all sympathies, moved by all tenderness, prompt for all duty, prepared for all suffering; but she cannot talk of what she is, and what she purposes. The King of France describes the apparent reserve of her character as

> A tardiness in nature,
> Which often leaves the history unspoke
> That it intends to do.

She herself says,—

> If for I want that glib and oily art,
> To speak, and purpose not; since what I well intend,
> I'll do 't before I speak.

—Knight, *Pictorial Shakspere*

REGAN AND GONERIL

At the first moment the two sisters display no characteristic difference; "as like as a crab is to a crab," says the fool; on a closer inspection it is surprising what a wide and clearly defined contrast there is between the two. The elder, Goneril, with the "wolfish visage" and the dark "frontlet" of ill-humor, is a masculine woman, full of independent purposes and projects, whilst Regan appears more feminine, rather instigated by Goneril, more passive, and more dependent. Goneril's boundless "unbordered" nature, which renders her a true child of that fearful age, shows itself in bloody undertakings, originating in her own brain; whilst Regan's evil nature appears rather in her urging on the atrocities of others, as when Kent is set in the stocks and Gloster's eyes are torn out. The worst of the two is married to a noble gentleman (Albany), whom she reviles as "a moral fool," whose mildness and repose seem to her "milky gentleness," and whose quiet power and resolute manliness she only later finds reason to discover. The better sister has the worst husband in Cornwall, a man whose wrathful disposition allows of no impediment and bears no remonstrance. Goneril at first appears to govern her husband, who recognizes her depth of foresight, and, until he penetrates her character, avoids discords with her; she pursues her aims independently, scarcely listening to him, and scarcely deigning to answer him; Regan, on the contrary, is obsequious and dependent towards the gloomy, laconic, and powerful Cornwall, who is immovable and resolute in his determination. At the first occasion (Act I, sc. i) Goneril appears as the instigator and Regan as her echo. She it is who afterwards begins to put restraints upon the king; she first treats him disrespectfully, halves and dismisses his attendants, whilst Regan avoids her father with some remains of awe. But she fears her sister still more than her father; she rather suffers her father's messenger to be mistreated than Goneril's servant. Her sister knows her weakness; she does not consider it sufficient to write to her; she goes to her and follows her in order to be sure of her co-operation in her measures. Regan cannot hurl forth vehement and hasty words like Goneril; she has not the same fierce eyes, her glance (though Lear in his madness indeed calls it a squint) is more full of comfort, her nature is softer and more cordial, and Lear, it seems, hardly trusts himself to penetrate her character closely; when, in his delusion, he sits in judgment upon her, he desires to have her heart anatomized. She utters inoffensively harsher things to her father than Goneril does, and yet her father hesitates to pronounce his curse upon her as upon her sister—a curse even twice repeated against Goneril. The latter receives it with marble coldness, but Regan shudders, and fears to draw upon herself the like malediction. It is not until Goneril in her presence has entirely laid open her own unblushing cruelty and barbarity towards their old father, that Regan grows bolder also, and drives away the king's train of knights; she will have no one but himself. When Goneril afterwards insists that the old man shall taste the consequences of his obstinacy and folly, and forbids Gloster, in spite of the raging storm, to harbor him, she chimes in with her usual dependent weakness. After the brood of serpents have got rid of the old father, there begins a domestic feud between the families. Goneril digs deeper mines, to which the mistreatment of Lear has been only the prelude. She wishes to seize on the whole kingdom, she betroths herself to Edmund during her husband's life; she rejoices in Cornwall's death, poisons Regan, joins with Edmund in ordering Cordelia's execution, and finally attempts the life of her husband, whom she now fears, because he had discovered with horror her misdeeds. Here, again, Regan appears throughout less blamable and vile; she makes no engagement with Edmund till after Cornwall's death; she unsuspectingly confides letters for Edmund to Goneril's treacherous servant; she falls a victim to her sister's poison, being herself clear from all attempts of the kind; in every respect she is more contracted in her nature than her sister, whose "woman's will is of undistinguish'd space."—Gervinus, *Shakespeare Commentaries*.

It would be an interesting subject for a prize essay which of the two is the worse, Regan or Goneril. I confess, I am unable to answer the question satisfactorily. I believe Shakespeare meant to leave it a question. It may be said that Goneril, as she was the first to ill-treat her father, was the worse; but it may be justly replied, that Regan was still worse, inasmuch as the sight of the tortured old man, so far from moving her, only causes her to torture him anew, so that nothing is left but madness, which, as we have already intimated, can be regarded as only a relief. On the whole, the fool was in the right when he said that both were of a height, and that one tasted as much like the other as a crab does to a crab.—Franz Horee, *Shakspeare's Schauspiele erläutert*.

EDGAR

As all proceeds so rapidly, and Edgar, one hardly understands how, is driven by lies from his father's house, it is, as represented on the stage, scarcely intelligible. That Edgar comes on the stage as a crazy beggar is no more clearly explained, yet the reasons of it may be imagined; but that, in this disguise of a madman, he utters, without any necessity, so much useless talk, becomes extremely wearisome, while the much-admired scene in the hut, through its length, and the inexhaustible stream of crazy speeches, is, according to our feeling, equally fatiguing. It might even be conjectured that Shakespeare intended to give us here a sort of dramatic extravaganza, showing us specimens of three different kinds of fools all together, one really crazy, one pretending to be crazy, and one a Fool by profession—these he sets upon the scene side by side, and lets all three figure away in the finest style.—Rumelin, *Shakespeare-Studien.*

THE STEWARD

In the character of the steward to Queen Goneril, Shakespeare has given an impersonation of blind feudal attachment. He is the reverse of Kent. He, from the mere servility of slavish obedience, would perpetrate any enormity of vice or of good service with the implicit punctuality and passiveness of a machine. It is no question with him whether an act be just or unjust, merciful or cruel. Kent speaks of him to this effect when he indignantly describes him as one of those who "turn their halcyon beaks with every gale and vary of their masters; knowing naught, like dogs, but following." He is, in short, a serf, and carries out the will of his mistress, as an axe obeys the hand of an executioner. The spirit of active and passive fidelity was never more aptly contrasted than in the two characters of Kent and Oswald the steward. The whole world would not stand between Kent and his zeal to serve his friend; and he has given proof that the whole world would not bring him to commit an unjust act, or to approve of it. The steward goes to his death in the service of his mistress, and with his dying breath entreats Edgar, who has killed him, to deliver the treasonable letter, upon his person, from Goneril to Edmund. He is accurately the character that Edgar gives him: "A serviceable villain, as dexterous to the vices of his mistress as badness would desire."—Clarke, *Shakespeare-Characters.*

THE FOOL

Shakespeare has many fools in his plays; but the fool in *King Lear* is different from all the rest. Shakespeare designs him to be one of those poor half-witted kindly creatures who, having once received an idea into their brain, are incapable of parting with it, but whose mental activity consists solely in harping upon the same string, sometimes with a weird ingenuity, sometimes humorously, sometimes bitterly, but calculated by continual repetition to create an impression upon those who are thrown in their company. He thus acts as a sort of conscience, and that appears to be the chief function of the fool in *King Lear*. Up to the point of the arrival of Kent, the folly of his action in parting with his crown does not seem to have occurred to Lear at all. "A very honest-hearted fellow, and as poor as the king," says Kent. "If thou be as poor for a subject as he is for a king, thou art poor enough." It is from the speeches of Kent and the fool that the gross folly of his conduct is gradually made apparent to Lear; and it is part of Lear's punishment that whereas in the first scene he is able to banish conscience in the shape of Kent, in the latter part of the play he is forced to hug remorse, in the shape of the fool, as his only companion.—Ransome, *Short Studies in Shakespeare's Plots*.

Genuine humor breaks forth only out of a loving heart, and through his unbounded love for his master the Fool has purchased the right to tell him the bitter truth, and hold up the mirror before the wrong that he has done. As the Fool represents truth in the guise of humor, he cannot be brought forward until the rupture with the moral law has taken place; the disguised truth waits; the king has not for two days seen the Fool. In his grief for Cordelia's banishment, the Fool has almost forgotten his part, and this affords us a pledge that, under the veil of humor, the deepest earnestness is concealed. Only in slight allusions does he touch the fault of the King, for roughly to waken up the injury done were the office not of love but of scorn.

Hence the Fool makes the folly of the King the target of his humor; the harmless words he throws out conceal a deep and penetrating significance. When, immediately after Goneril's first rude speech to her father, the Fool breaks out with the apparently random words, "Out went the candle, and we were left darkling"—the words of an old song—the point is, that the light of the moral world has now ceased to shine, and the darkness incessantly increases. (Compare the words addressed to Kent by the Fool, Act II, sc. iv. with the words: "We'll set thee to school to an ant," etc.) As, however, the old king draws ever nearer to the brink of the abyss, the arrows of the Fool, aimed at the folly of the king, grow fewer, he catches oftener at some harmless, jesting remark, to cheer the suffering of his master, and to lighten the burden of his own grief. The whole depth and power of his sorrow he crowds into a little song, for he has become thus rich in songs since the king, as he says, has made his daughters his mothers. In a similar way he expresses his impregnable devotion to the king in those deeply significant verses in which he promises not to desert the king in the storm, and the particular theme of which is that the wise are fools before God, but the fools in the eye of the world are justified by a higher power. The Fool has his place in the tragedy only so long as the king is able to perceive the truth veiled by the Fool's humor. There is no longer room or need for him after the king has become crazed. This crisis is the end of the Fool. He vanishes, "goes to bed at mid-day," when his beloved master is hopelessly lost.—Heuse, *Vorträdge über ausgewählte dramatishe Dichtungen Shakespeare's, Schiller's, und Goethe's.*

We have yet a few words to say of a chief person of the piece, which, because this person stands by himself, a single specimen of the kind, we have kept for the last; we mean the Fool. His appearance in this tragedy is very significant, as the tragic effect is heightened in the greatest degree by his humor and the sharpness of his wit. No one but the Fool dared venture to turn Lear's attention to his great folly (the resignation of his power in his life-time). It is of the greatest importance that this unwise proceeding of the king should be directly pointed at, as with the finger of another, and it is made ever plainer to him how foolishly, and, in relation to Cordelia, how unjustly he has acted. But the shrewd Fool knew how to clothe his mockeries so skillfully, and to produce them so opportunely, that, although they are none the less cutting, their design is not so prominent, and the king takes them because they come from the Fool, who is bound to speak truth, and to whom Lear is attached, even as the fool, with the most devoted love, is attached to Lear. But it is not only his wit, never running dry, although indeed alloyed to many a platitude, nor his invariable good humor and his clear understanding by which the Fool commands our sympathy; but, in an almost still higher degree, it is the lovableness of his character that interests us. He has pined away—as we learn before he appears—after the youngest of the princesses has gone to France, and has sorrowed the more for what the knight who relates his condition cannot mention to the king, namely, the unhappy circumstances under which the departure of Cordelia has taken place. And how faithfully does he cling to the king in that fearful night, and, by forcing himself to appear merrier than he possibly could be in that condition, try in every way to calm the wild excitement of his master, and lure him from his heartrending, maddening pain at the shameful ingratitude of his degenerate daughters. But the more the Fool is saddened at the sight of Lear's failing mind, the fewer are his words, until at last the Poet, and with perfect truth, lets him disappear from the scene, as his later appearance would be without significance, and have a disturbing effect. But that we do not learn what becomes of him certainly seems strange, but it is not hard to explain it. It remained for Lear to inquire for him, or, in one way or another, to make mention of him, but Lear is subsequently so engrossed with his own fortunes and Cordelia's, and so, as it were, buried in them, that he could not turn his thoughts to anything which was remote from these fortunes. It is highly probable that the Fool's heart was broken by trouble and grief at Lear's cruel fate.—Schick, *Shakespeare's King Lear.*

THE MOVEMENT OF THE PLAY

The general action of the play has essentially two movements, which pass into each other by the finest and most intricate network There is in it a double guilt and a double retribution. The first movement (embracing mainly three acts) exhibits the complete disintegration of the family. It portrays the first guilt and the first retribution—the wrong of the parents and its punishment. Lear banishes his daughter; his daughters in turn drive him out of doors. Gloster expels from home and disinherits his true and faithful son in favor of the illegitimate and faithless son, and is then himself falsely accused and betrayed by the latter. Cordelia, too, falls into guilt in her attempt to avenge the wrongs of her father. Thus the disruption is complete—the parents expelled, the false triumphant, the faithful in disguise and banishment. Such is the first movement—the wrong done by parents to their children, and its punishment. The second movement will unfold the second retribution, springing from the second guilt—the wrong done by the children to their parents, and its punishment. It must be observed, however, that the deeds of the children which are portrayed in the first movement of the drama constitute their guilt. In the one hand they are instruments of retribution, but on the other hand their conduct is a violation of ethical principles as deep as that of their parents. They are the avengers of guilt, but in this very act become themselves guilty, and must receive punishment. The general result, therefore, of the second movement will be the completed retribution. Lear and his three guilty daughters—for we have to include Cordelia under this category—as well as Gloster and his guilty son, perish. The faithful of both families come together, in their banishment, in order to protect their parents; thereby, however, Cordelia assails the established State. The consequence of her deed is death. The faithless of both families also come together; though they triumph in the external conflict, there necessarily arises a struggle among themselves—for how can the faithless be faithful to one another? The jealousy of the two sisters leads to a conspiracy, and to their final destruction. Edmund, faithless to both, falls at last by the hand of his brother, whom he has deeply wronged.—Snider, *System of Shakespeare's Dramas*.

THE BEST OF SHAKESPEAR'S PLAYS

It is the best of all Shakspear's plays, for it is the one in which he was the most in earnest. He was here fairly caught in the web of his own imagination. The passion which he has taken as his subject is that which strikes its root deepest into the human heart; of which the bond is the hardest to be unloosed; and the canceling and tearing to pieces of which gives the greatest revulsion to the frame. This depth of nature, this force of passion, this tug and war of the elements of our being, this firm faith in filial piety, and the giddy anarchy and whirling tumult of the thoughts at finding this prop failing it, the contrast between the fixed, immovable basis of natural affection, and the rapid, irregular starts of imagination, suddenly wrenched from all its accustomed holds and resting-places in the soul, this is what Shakespear has given, and what nobody else but he could give. So we believe.—The mind of Lear, staggering between the weight of attachment and the hurried movements of passion, is like a tall ship driven about by the winds, buffeted by the furious waves, but that still rides above the storm, having its anchor fixed in the bottom of the sea; or it is like the sharp rock circled by the eddying whirlpool that foams and beats against it, or like the solid promontory pushed from its basis by the force of an earthquake.—Hazlitt, *Characters of Shakespear's Plays.*

THE CHARM OF THE PLAY

What Lear has in common with Othello is the soul of the Poet, dark, melancholy, deeply wounded, well-nigh shattered by the world; only here, in Lear, still more than in Othello, has he concentrated in his work, painted in burning colors, all the bitterness which the depravity of human nature must generate in a sensitive heart. The Poet had daughters; that he had, perhaps, similar experiences may be supposed; divested of the historical costume, the features of Lear look out upon us with the naturalness of ordinary life, so that we seem to see an unhappy citizen of the year 1600 wrestling with madness rather than an old English king, much as Lear insists upon his regal dignity. Here is the charm which the poem has for the great public: Lear suffers from the domestic cross which is never wholly absent in any single family. It needs but a small quantity of hypochondria to magnify a situation of small occasions into such giant proportions. In this view, the poem may be styled the poetry or the tragedy of the choleric temperament, as Hamlet is of the melancholic, and Romeo of the sanguine nature. In Lear all is precipitous, in wild haste, thundering on, and this is the case even in the subordinate parts.—Rapp, *Shakspere's Schauspiele, Einleitung.*

How is it, now, that this defective drama so overpowers us that we are either unconscious of its blemishes or regard them as almost irrelevant? As soon as we turn to this question we recognize, not merely that *King Lear* possesses purely dramatic qualities which far outweigh its defects, but that its greatness consists partly in imaginative effects of a wider kind. And, looking for the sources of these effects, we find among them some of those very things which appeared to us dramatically faulty or injurious. Thus, to take at once two of the simplest examples of this, that very vagueness in the sense of locality which we have just considered, and again that excess in the bulk of the material and the number of figures, events and movements, while they interfere with the clearness of vision, have at the same time a positive value for imagination. They give the feeling of vastness, the feeling not of a scene or particular place, but of a world; or, to speak more accurately, of a particular place which is also a world. This world is dim to us, partly from its immensity, and partly because it is filled with gloom; and in the gloom shapes approach and recede, whose half-seen faces and motions touch us with dread, horror, or the most painful pity,—sympathies and antipathies which we seem to be feeling not only for them but for the whole race. This world, we are told, is called Britain; but we should no more look for it in an atlas than for the place, called Caucasus, where Prometheus was chained by Strength and Force and comforted by the daughters of Ocean, or the place where Farinata stands erect in his glowing tomb, "Come avesse lo Inferno in gran dispitto."—Bradley, *Shakespearean Tragedy*.

THE LESSON OF THE PLAY

Briefly, I take this to be the lesson of *King Lear*—

There's nothing we can call our own but love.

Some learn this lesson for themselves; to some it must be taught; and the teaching may be stern or bitter; it was to King Lear. But, the lesson once learned, the whole man is changed; and though the very gates of death are opened through the learning, that makes no difference; death is then the consummation of life; *for love implies sacrifice throughout life unto death, and the ideal death of love in tragedy only makes the sacrifice apparent*. Or we may put it thus: If Lear had lived, he would henceforth have lived for love; as it was, he died for love; ultimately there is no difference;

death after this is a mere accident; it will come when it will come. And the same is true of Cordelia, although she had learned the lesson, and death to her was always "the consummation of life."—Luce, *Handbook to Shakespeare's Works.*

What are we to make of it all? Was Gloucester right when he spoke of humanity as the quarry of malignant, irresponsible deities?

As flies to wanton boys, are we to the gods;
They kill us for their sport.

Is the dead march with which the play closes not only the dirge over the bodies of those that are no more, but over the futility of human ideals, over fruitless loyalties, and martyrdoms in vain? Is it all one to be a Cordelia or a Goneril, since in death they are not divided? Is that Shakspere's "message" to the world, and was the eighteenth century right after all when it rejected such a cheerless conclusion, and showed us Cordelia victorious and happily wedded to Edgar?

No! this most representative of Shaksperean tragedies is not born of the pessimism that despairs of all things human, nor of the facile optimism that thinks everything is for the best in the best of all possible worlds. It is, as Kreyssig has called it, "the tragedy of the categorical imperative." It boldly recognizes that in the sphere of outward circumstances virtue is not always triumphant nor vice cast down. Amidst the clash of the iron forces of the universe, love and purity are often crushed.

Streams will not curb their pride
The just man not to entomb,
Nor lightnings go aside
To give his virtues room;
Nor is that wind less rough which blows a good man's barge.

But there is an inner sanctuary inviolable by these shocks from without. In the kingdom of the spirit nothing matters except "the good will," and there Cordelia's ardor of love is justified of itself. It exists, and in its existence lies its triumph. But, even on the sternest interpretation of Shaksperean ethics, such glorious self-abandonment wins a benediction from above:

Upon such sacrifices, my Cordelia,
The gods themselves throw incense.

And may we not even venture to interpret Lear's own words as a prophetic salutation, and to think of her as "a soul in bliss," one of "the just spirits that wear victorious palms"?—Boas, *Shakspere and his Predecessors*.

Macbeth

Preface

By Israel Gollancz, M.A.

THE FIRST EDITION

Macbeth was first printed in the First Folio, where it occupies pp. 131 to 151, and is placed between *Julius Cæsar* and *Hamlet*. It is mentioned among the plays registered in the books of the Stationers' Company by the publishers of the Folio as "not formerly entered to other men." The text is perhaps one of the worst printed of all the plays, and textual criticism has been busy emending and explaining away the many difficulties of the play. Even the editors of the Second Folio were struck by the many hopeless corruptions, and attempted to provide a better text. The first printers certainly had before them a very faulty transcript, and critics have attempted to explain the discrepancies by assuming that Shakespeare's original version had been tampered with by another hand.

"Macbeth" and Middleton's "Witch"

Some striking resemblances in the incantation scenes of *Macbeth* and Middleton's *Witch* have led to a somewhat generally accepted belief that Thomas Middleton was answerable for the alleged un-Shakespearean portions of *Macbeth*. This view has received confirmation from the fact that the stage-directions of *Macbeth* contain allusions to two songs which are found in Middleton's *Witch* (viz. "*Come away, come away*," III, v; "*Black spirits and white,*" IV, i). Moreover, these very songs are found in

D'Avenant's re-cast of *Macbeth* (1674).[1] It is, however, possible that Middleton took Shakespeare's songs and expanded them, and that D'Avenant had before him a copy containing additions transferred from Middleton's cognate scenes. This view is held by the most competent of Middleton's editors, Mr. A.H. Bullen, who puts forward strong reasons for assigning the *Witch* to a later date than *Macbeth*, and rightly resents the proposals on the part of able scholars to hand over to Middleton some of the finest passages of the play.[2] Charles Lamb had already noted the essential differences between Shakespeare's and Middleton's Witches. "Their names and some of the properties, which Middleton has given to his hags, excites smiles. The Weird Sisters are serious things. Their presence cannot co-exist with mirth. But in a lesser degree, the Witches of Middleton are fine creatures. Their power, too, is in some measure over the mind. They raise jars, jealousies, strifes, *like a thick scurf o'er life*" (*Specimens of English Dramatic Poets*).

THE PORTER'S SPEECH

Among the passages in *Macbeth*, that have been doubted are the soliloquy of the Porter, and the short dialogue that follows between the Porter and Macduff. Even Coleridge objected to "the low soliloquy of the Porter"; he believed them to have been written for the mob by some other hand, perhaps with Shakespeare's consent, though he was willing to make an exception in the case of the Shakespearean words, "*I'll devil-porter it no further: I had thought to let in some of all professions, that go the primose way*

1. The first of these songs is found in the edition of 1673, which contains also two other songs not found in the Folio version.
2. The following are among the chief passages supposed to resemble Middleton's style, and rejected as Shakespeare's by the Clarendon Press editors: Act I. Sc. ii. iii. 1-37; Act II. Sc. i. 61, iii. (Porter's part); Act III. Sc. v.; Act IV. Sc. i. 39-47, 125-132; iii. 140-159; Act V. (?) ii., v. 47-50; viii. 32-33, 35-75.
   The second scene of the First Act is certainly somewhat disappointing, and it is also inconsistent (*cp*. ll. 52, 53, with Sc. iii., ll. 72, 73, and 112, etc.), but probably the scene represents the compression of a much longer account. The introduction of the superfluous Hecate is perhaps the strongest argument for rejecting certain witch-scenes, viz.: Act III. Sc. v.; Act IV. Sc. i. 39-47, 125-132.

to the everlasting bonfire." But the Porter's Speech is as essential a part of the design of the play as is the Knocking at the Gate, the effect of which was so subtly analyzed by De Quincey in his well-known essay on the subject. "The effect was that it reflected back upon the murderer a peculiar awfulness and a depth of solemnity...when the deed is done, when the work of darkness is perfect, then the world of darkness passes away like a pageantry in the clouds; the knocking at the gate is heard; and it makes known audibly that the reaction: has commenced; the human has made its reflex upon the fiendish; the pulses of life are beginning to beat again; and the reëstablishment of the goings-on of the world in which we live first makes us profoundly sensible of the awful parenthesis that had suspended them."

The introduction of the Porter, a character derived from the Porter of Hell in the old Mysteries, is as dramatically relevant, as are the grotesque words he utters; and both the character and the speech are thoroughly Shakespearean in conception (*cp. The Porter in Macbeth, New Shak. Soc.*, 1874, by Prof. Hales).

DATE OF COMPOSITION

The undoubted allusion to the union of England and Scotland under James I (Act IV, Sc. i, 120), gives us one limit for the date of *Macbeth*, viz., March, 1603, while a notice in the MS. diary of Dr. Simon Forman, a notorious quack and astrologer, gives 1610 as the other limit; for in that year he saw the play performed at the Globe.[1] Between these two dates, in the year 1607, "*The Puritan, or, the Widow of Watling Street*," was published, containing a distinct reference to Banquo's Ghost—"*Instead of a jester we'll have a ghost in a white sheet sit at the upper end of the table.*"[2]

1. The Diary is among the Ashmolean MSS. (208) in the Bodleian Library; its title is a *Book of Plaies and Notes thereof for common Pollicie.* Halliwell-Phillipps privately reprinted the valuable and interesting booklet. The account of the play as given by Forman is not very accurate.
2. Similarly, in Beaumont and Fletcher's *Knight of the Burning Pestle*, produced in 1611:

   When thou art at the table with thy friends,
   Merry in heart and fill'd with swelling wine,
   I'll come in midst of all thy pride and mirth,
   Invisible to all men but thyself.

It is remarkable that when James visited Oxford in 1605 he was "addressed on entering the city by three students of St. John's College, who alternately accosted his Majesty, reciting some Latin verses, founded on the prediction of the weird sisters relative to Banquo and Macbeth." The popularity of the subject is further attested by the insertion of the *Historie of Macbeth* in the 1606 edition of *Albion's England*. The former incident may have suggested the subject to Shakespeare; the latter fact may have been due to the popularity of Shakespeare's play. At all events authorities are almost unanimous in assigning *Macbeth* to 1605-1606; and this view is borne out by minor points of internal evidence.[1] As far as metrical characteristics are concerned the comparatively large number of light-endings, twenty-one in all (contrasted with eight in *Hamlet*, and ten in *Julius Cæsar*) places *Macbeth* near the plays of the Fourth Period.[2] With an early play of this period, viz. *Antony and Cleopatra*, it has strong ethical affinities.

THE SOURCES OF THE PLOT

Shakespeare derived his materials for *Macbeth* from Holinshed's *Chronicle of England and Scotland*, first published in 1577, and subsequently in 1587; the latter was in all probability the edition used by the poet. Holinshed's authority was Hector Boece, whose *Scotorum Historæ* was first printed in 1526; Boece drew from the work of the Scotch historian Fordun, who lived in the fourteenth century. Shakespeare's indebtedness to Holinshed for the plot of the present play is not limited to the chapters dealing with Macbeth; certain details of the murder of Duncan belong to the murder of King Duffe, the great grandfather of Lady Macbeth. Shakespeare's most noteworthy departure from his original is to be found in his characterization of Banquo.

---

1. *E.g.* II. iii. 5, "*expectation of plenty*" probably refers to the abundance of corn in the autumn of 1606; the reference to the "*Equivocator*" seems to allude to Garnet and other Jesuits who were tried in the spring of 1606.
2. Macbeth numbers but two weak-endings, while *Hamlet* and *Julius Cæsar* have none. *Antony and Cleopatra* has not less than seventy-one light-endings and twenty-eight weak-endings. It would seem that Shakespeare, in this latter play, broke away from his earlier style as with a mighty bound.

The Macbeth of legend has been whitened by recent historians; and the Macbeth of history, according to Freeman, seems to have been quite a worthy monarh; (*cp.* Freeman's *Norman Conquest*, Skene's *Celtic Scotland*, etc.).

Shakespeare, in all probability, took some hints from Scot's *Discoverie of Witchcraft* (1584) for his witch-lore. It should also be noted that King James, a profound beliver in witchcraft, published in 1599 his *Demonologie*, maintaining his belief against Scot's skepticism. In 1604 a statute was passed to suppress witches.

There may have been other sources for the plot; possibly an older play existed on the subject of Macbeth; in Kempe's *Nine Days' Wonder* (1600) occur the following words: "I met a proper upright youth, only for a little stooping in the shoulders, all heart to the heel, a penny poet, whose first making was the miserable story of Mac-doel, or Mac-dobeth, or Mac-somewhat," etc. Furthermore, a ballad (? a stage-play) on Macdobeth was registered in the year 1596.

DURATION OF ACTION

The Time of the play, as analyzed by Mr. P.A. Daniel (*New Shakespeare Soc.* 1877-79) is nine days represented on the stage, and intervals:

Day 1. Act I, sc. i to iii.

Day 2. Act I, sc. iv to vii.

Day 3. Act II, sc. i to iv. *An interval*, say a couple of weeks.

Day 4. Act III, sc. i to v. [Act III, sc. vi, an impossible time.]

Day 5. Act IV, sc. i.

Day 6. Act IV, sc. ii. *An interval*, Ross's journey to England.

Day 7. Act IV, sc. iii, Act V, sc. 1. *An interval.* Malcolm's return to Scoland.

Day 8. Act V, sc. ii and iii.

Day 9. Act V, sc. iv to viii.

Introduction

By Henry Norman Hudson, A.M.

In the folio of 1623 *The Tragedy of Macbeth*, as it is there called, makes the seventh in the list of Tragedies. In modern editions generally, the Chiswick among others, it stands as first in the division of Histories—an order clearly and entirely wrong. Macbeth has indeed something of an historical basis, and so have *Hamlet* and *Lear*; but in all three the historical matter is so merged in the form and transfigured with the spirit of tragedy, as to put it well nigh out of thought to class them as histories; since this is subjecting them to wrong tests, implies the right to censure them for not being what they were never meant to be. In them historical truth was nowise the Poet's aim; they are to be viewed simply as works of Art: so that the proper question concerning them is, whether and how far they have that truth to nature, that organic proportion and self-consistency which the laws of Art require.

The tragedy was never printed that we know of till in the folio, and was registered in the Stationers' books by Blount and Jaggard, November 8, 1623, as one of the plays "not formerly entered to other men." The original text is remarkably clear and complete, the acts and scenes being regularly marked throughout.

Malone and Chalmers agreed upon the year 1606 as the time when *Macbeth* was probably written; their chief ground for this opinion being what the Porter says in Act II, sc. iii: "Here's a farmer that hang'd himself on the expectation of plenty"; and again,—"Here's an equivocator, that could swear in both scales against either scale: who committed treason enough for God's sake, yet could not equivocate to Heaven." As 1606 was indeed a year of plenty, Malone thought the former passage referred to that fact; and that the latter "had a direct reference to the doctrine of equivocation avowed and maintained by Henry Garnet, superior of the order of Jesuits in England, at his trial for the Gunpowder Treason, March 28, 1606." These arguments, we confess, neither seem strong enough to uphold the conclusion, nor so weak, on the other hand, as to warrant the scorn which Mr. Knight has vented upon them. And, however inadequate the basis, the conclusion appears to be about right; at least no better one has been offered.

That *Macbeth* was probably written after the union of the three kingdoms, has been justly inferred from what the hero says in his last interview with the Weird Sisters, Act IV, sc. i: "And some I see, that twofold balls and treble scepters carry." James I came to the throne of England in March, 1603; but the English and Scottish crowns were not *formally* united, at least the union was not proclaimed, till October, 1604. That they *were to be united*, was doubtless well understood some time before it actually took place: so that the passage in question does not afford a *certain* guide to the date of the composition. The most we can affirm is, that the writing was probably after 1604, and *certainly* before 1610; the ground of which certainty is from Dr. Simon Forman's *Book of Plays, and Notes thereof, for common Policy*; a manuscript discovered by Mr. Collier in the Ashmolean Museum. Forman gives a minute and particular account of the plot and leading incidents of Macbeth, as he saw it played at the Globe Theater, April 20, 1610. The notice is too long for our space.

The play in hand yields cause, in the accuracy of local description and allusion, for thinking the Poet had been in Scotland. And these internal likelihoods are not a little strengthened by external arguments. It hath been fully ascertained that companies of English players did visit Scotland several times during Shakespeare's connection with the stage. The earliest visit of this kind that we hear of was in 1589, when Ashby, the English minister at the Scottish court, wrote to Burleigh how "my Lord Both-well sheweth great kindness to our nation, using *Her Majesty's Players* and Canoniers with all courtesy." And a like visit was again made in 1599, as we learn from Archbishop Spottiswood, who writing the history of that year has the following: "In the end of the year happened some new jars betwixt the King and the ministers of Edinburgh; because of a company of English comedians whom the King had licensed to play within the burgh. The ministers, being offended with the liberty given them, did exclaim in their sermons against stage-players, their unruliness and immodest behavior; and in their sessions made an act, prohibiting people to resort unto their plays, under pain of church censures. The King, taking this to be a discharge of his license, called the sessions before the council, and ordained them to annul their act, and not to restrain the people from going to these comedies: which they promised, and accordingly performed; whereof publication was made the day after, and all that pleased permitted to repair unto the same, to the great offense of the ministers."

This account is confirmed by the public records of Scotland, which show that the English players were liberally rewarded by the King, no less a sum than 828*l*. 5*s*. 4*d*. being distributed to them between October, 1599, and December, 1601. And it appears from the registers of the Town Council of Aberdeen, that the same players were received by the public authorities of that place, under the sanction of a special letter from the King, styling them "our servants." There, also, they had a gratuity of 32 marks, and the freedom of the city was conferred upon "Laurence Fletcher, Comedian to His Majesty," who, no doubt, was the leader of the company. That this was the same company to which Shakespeare belonged, or a part of it, is highly probable from the patent which was made out by the King's order, May 7, 1603, authorizing Laurence Fletcher, William Shakespeare, Richard Burbage, and others, to perform plays in any part of the kingdoms. In this instrument the players are termed "our servants,"—the same title whereby the King had recommended them to the authorities of Aberdeen. All which, to be sure, is no positive proof that Shakespeare was of the number who went to Scotland; yet we do not well see how it can fail to impress any one as making strongly that way, there being no positive proof to the contrary. And the probability thence arising, together with the internal likelihoods of Macbeth, may very well warrant a belief of the thing in question.

At the date of Shakespeare's tragedy the story of Macbeth, as handed down by tradition, had been told by Holinshed, whose *Chronicles* first appeared in 1577, and by George Buchanan, the learned preceptor of James I, who has been termed the Scotch Livy, and whose *History of Scotland* came forth in 1582. In the main features of the story, so far as it is adopted by the Poet, both these writers agree, save that Buchanan represents Macbeth to have merely dreamed of meeting with the Weird Sisters, and of being hailed by them successively as Thane of Angus, of Murray, and as King. We shall see hereafter that Holinshed was Shakespeare's usual authority in matters of British history. And in the present case the Poet shows no traces of obligation to Buchanan, unless, which is barely possible, he may have taken a hint from the historian, where, speaking of Macbeth's reign, he says,—"Multa hic fabulose quidam nostrorum affingunt; sed quia *theatris* aut Milesiis fabulis sunt aptiora quam historiæ, ea omitto." A passage which, as showing the author's care for the truth of what he wrote, perhaps should render us wary of trusting too much in later writers, who would have us believe that, a war of factions breaking out, Duncan was killed in battle, and Macbeth took the crown by just and lawful title. It is considerable that both Hume and Lingard acquiesce in the old account which represents Macbeth to have murdered Duncan and usurped the throne. The following outline of the story as told by Holinshed may suffice to show both whence and how much the Poet borrowed.

Malcolm, king of Scotland, had two daughters, Beatrice and Doada, severally married to Abbanath Crinen and to Sinel, thanes of the Isles and of Glamis, by whom they had each a son, named Duncan and Macbeth. The former succeeded his grandfather in the kingdom; and, being of a soft and gentle nature, his reign was at first very quiet and peaceable, but afterwards, by reason of his slackness, greatly harassed with troubles and seditions, wherein his cousin, who was of a valiant and warlike spirit, did great service to the state. His first exploit was in company with Banquo, thane of Lochquaber, against Macdowald, who had headed a rebellion, and drawn together a great power of natives and foreigners. The rebels being soon broken and routed, Macdowald sought refuge in a castle with his family, and when he saw he could no longer hold the place, he first slew his wife and children, then himself; whereupon Macbeth entered, and, finding his body among the rest, had his head cut off, set upon a pole, and sent to the king. Macbeth was very severe, not to say cruel, towards the conquered; and when some of them murmured thereat he would have let loose his revenge upon them, but that he was partly appeased by their gifts, and partly dissuaded by his friends. By the time this trouble was well over, Sweno, king of Norway, arrived with an army in Fife, and began to slaughter the people without distinction of age or sex. Which caused Duncan to bestir himself in good earnest: he went forth with all the forces he could rally, himself, Macbeth, and Banquo leading them, and met the invaders at Culros, where after a fierce fight the Scots were beaten. Then Sweno, thinking he could now have the people for his own without killing them, gave order that none should be hurt but such as were found in an attitude of resistance. Macbeth went forthwith to gathering a new power, and Duncan, having fled into the castle of Bertha, and being there hotly besieged by Sweno, opened a communication with him to gain time, and meanwhile sent a secret message to Macbeth to wait at a certain place till he should hear further. When all things were ready, Duncan, having by this time settled the terms of surrender, offered to send forth a good supply of food and refreshment to the besiegers; which offer they gladly accepted, being much straitened for the means of living: whereupon the Scots mixed the juice of mekilwort berries in the bread and ale, and thereby got their enemies into so sleepy a state that they could make no defense; in which condition Macbeth fell upon them, and cut them to pieces, only Sweno himself and ten others escaping to the ships. While the people were giving thanks for this victory word came that a fleet of Danes had landed at King-corn, sent thither by Canute, Sweno's brother. Macbeth and Banquo, being sent against the new invaders, slew part of them, and chased the rest back to their ships. Thereupon a peace was knit up between the Scots and Danes, the latter giving a great sum of gold for the privilege of burying their dead in Colmes Inch.

Not long after, Macbeth and Banquo being on their way to Fores where the king then lay, as they were passing through the fields without other company, three women in strange and wild apparel suddenly met them; and while they were rapt with wonder at the sight, the first woman said,—All hail, Macbeth, thane of Glamis; the second,—Hail, Macbeth, thane of Cawdor; the third,—All hail, Macbeth, that hereafter shalt be king of Scotland. Then said Banquo,—What manner of women are you, that to my fellow here, besides high offices, ye assign the kingdom, but promise nothing at all to me? Yes, said the first, we promise greater things to thee; for he shall reign indeed, but with an unlucky end, and shall have no issue to succeed him; whereas thou indeed shalt not reign, but from thee shall spring a long line of kings. Then the women immediately vanished. At first Macbeth and Banquo thought this was but a fantastical illusion, insomuch that Banquo would call Macbeth king in jest, and Macbeth in like sort would call him father of many kings. But afterwards the women were believed to be the Weird Sisters; because, the thane of Cawdor being condemned for treason, his lands and titles were given to Macbeth. Whereupon Banquo said to him jestingly,—Now, Macbeth, thou hast what two of the Sisters promised; there remaineth only what the other said should come to pass. And Macbeth began even then to devise how he might come to the throne, but thought he must wait for time to work his way, as in the former preferment. But when, shortly after, the king made his oldest son Prince of Cumberland, thereby in effect appointing him successor, Macbeth was sorely troubled thereat, as it seemed to cut off his hope; and, thinking the purpose was to defeat his title to the crown, he studied how to usurp it by force. For the law of Scotland then was, that if at the death of a king the lineal heir were not of sufficient age for the government, the next in blood should take it in his stead. Encouraged by the words of the Weird Sisters, and urged on by his wife, who was "burning with unquenchable desire to bear the name of queen," Macbeth at length whispered his design to some trusty friends, of whom Banquo was chief, and, having a promise of their aid, slew the king at Inverness: then, by the help of his confederates, he got himself proclaimed king, and forthwith went to Scone where, by common consent, he was invested after the usual manner. Duncan's body was first buried at Elgin, but afterwards removed to Colmekill, and laid in a sepulcher with his predecessors.

Macbeth now set himself about the administration of the state, as though he would fain make up for his want of title by his fitness for the office; using great liberality towards the nobles, enforcing justice on all offenders, and correcting the abuses that had grown up in Duncan's feeble reign; insomuch that he was accounted the sure defense and buckler of innocent people: he made many wholesome laws, and, in short, so good was his government, that had he attained it by lawful means, and continued as just and upright as he began, he might well have been numbered among the best princes that ever were. But it turned out that all this was done but to gain popular favor. For the pricking of conscience made him fear lest another should serve him as he had served Duncan; and the promise of the Weird Sisters to Banquo would not out of his mind. So he had a great supper, and invited Banquo and his son Fleance, having hired certain murderers to kill them as they were going home, that himself might seem clear of the crime, should it ever be laid to his charge. It chanced, however, through the darkness, that Fleance escaped, and, being afterwards warned of what was in plot against him, he fled into Wales. Thenceforth nothing went well with Macbeth. For men began to fear for their lives, so that they scarce dared come in his presence; and as many feared him, so he stood in fear of many, and therefore by one pretense or another made away with such as were most able to work him any danger. And he had double profit by this course, in that both those whom he feared were got rid of, and his coffers were enriched with their goods, thus enabling him to keep a guard of armed men about his person: for which causes he at length found such sweetness in putting the nobles to death, that his thirst of blood might nowise be satisfied. For better security against the growing dangers, he resolved to build a strong castle on the top of a very high hill called Dunsinane, and to make the thanes of each shire come and help on the building in turn. When the turn fell to Macduff, thane of Fife, he sent his men well furnished, telling them to be very diligent in the work, but himself stayed away; which when Macbeth knew, he said,—I perceive this man will never obey me till he be ridden with a snaffle: nor could he afterwards bear to look upon Macduff, either because he thought him too powerful for a subject, or because he had been warned to beware of him by certain wizards in whom he trusted; and indeed he would have put him to death, had not the same counselors assured him that he should never be slain by any man born of a woman, nor be vanquished till the wood of Birnam came to the castle of Dunsinane. Trusting in this prophecy, he now became still more cruel from security than he had been from fear. At last Macduff, to avoid peril of life, purposed with himself to flee into England; which purpose Macbeth soon got wind of, for in every nobleman's house he had one sly fellow or another in fee, to let him know all that was going on: so he hastened with a power into Fife, to besiege Macduff's castle; which being freely opened to him, when he found Macduff was already gone, he caused his wife and children to be slain, confiscated his goods, and proclaimed him a traitor.

After the murder of Duncan his two sons, named Malcolm and Donaldbain, had taken refuge, the one in England, where he was well received by Edward the Confessor, and the other in Ireland, where he also was kindly treated by the king of that land. The mother of these two princes was sister to Siward, Earl of Northumberland. Macduff, therefore, went straight to Malcolm as the only hope of poor Scotland, and earnestly besought him to undertake the deliverance of his suffering country, assuring him that the hearts and hands of the people would be with him, if he would but go and claim the crown. But the prince feigned to excuse himself, because of his having certain incurable vices which made him totally unfit to be king. For, said he, so great is my lust that I should seek to deflower all the young maids and matrons; which intemperance would be worse than Macbeth's cruelty. Macduff answered that this was indeed a very great fault, and had ruined many kings: nevertheless, said he, there are women enough in Scotland: make thyself king, and I will procure you satisfaction herein so secretly that no man shall know of it. Malcolm then said, I am also the most avaricious being on earth, insomuch that, having the power, I should make pretenses for slaying most of the nobles, that I might enjoy their estates. The other replied,—This is a far worse fault than the former, for avarice is the root of all evil: notwithstanding, follow my counsel; there are riches enough in Scotland to satisfy thy greediness. Then said the prince again, I am furthermore given to lying and all kinds of deceit, and nothing delights me more than to betray all such as put any trust in my words. Thereupon Macduff gave over the suit, saying. This is the worst of all, and here I leave thee. O miserable Scotchmen, ye have one cursed tyrant now reigning over you without any right; and this other that hath the right is nothing fit to reign; for by his own confession he is not only full of lust and avarice, but so false withal that no trust is to be put in aught he says. Adieu, Scotland, for now I account myself a banished man forever. Then, he being about to depart, the prince said, Be of good cheer, Macduff, for I have none of those vices, and have only jested with thee, to prove thy mind; for Macbeth hath often sought by such means to get me into his hands: but the slower I have seemed to entertain thy request the more diligent I shall be to accomplish it. Hereupon, after embracing and swearing mutual fidelity, they fell to consulting how they might bring their wishes to good effect. Macduff soon repaired to the borders of Scotland, and sent letters thence to the nobles, urging them to assist the prince with all their powers, to recover the crown out of the usurper's hands.

Now the prince, being much beloved of good King Edward, procured that his uncle Siward might go with ten thousand men to aid him in the enterprise. Meanwhile the Scottish nobles, apprised of what was on foot, drew into two factions, some siding with Malcolm, others with Macbeth. When Macbeth saw how the prince was strengthening with allies, he retreated to Dunsinane, meaning to abide there in a fortified camp; and, being advised to withdraw into the Isles and there wait for better times, he still refused, trusting in the prophecies of the Weird Sisters. Malcolm, following close upon his retreat, came at night to Birnam wood, where, his men having taken food and rest, he gave order for them to get each a bough as big as he could carry, and march therewith, so as to hide their strength from the enemy. The next day Macbeth, seeing their approach, at first marveled what it meant, then, calling to mind the prophecy, thought it was like to be fulfilled: nevertheless, he resolved to fight, and drew up his men in order of battle; but when those of the other side cast away their boughs, and he saw how many they were, he betook himself to flight. Macduff was hot in pursuit, and overhauled him at Lanfanan, where at last Macbeth sprung from his horse, saying, Thou traitor, why dost thou thus follow me in vain, who am not to be slain by any man that was born of a woman? Macduff answered,—It is true, Macbeth; and now shall thy cruelty end; for I am even he that the wizards told thee of, who was never born of my mother, but ripped out of her womb: therewithal he stepped forth and slew him, then cut off his head, and set it upon a pole, and brought it to Malcolm.—The murder of Duncan took place in 1039, and Macbeth was killed in 1054; so that the events of the play, viewed historically, stretch over a period of more than fifteen years.

From another part of the same history Shakespeare took several circumstances of the assassination. It is where Holinshed relates how King Duff, being the guest of Donwald and his wife at their castle in Fores, was there murdered. We will condense so much of the narrative as bears upon the matter in hand.

The king having retired for the rest of the night, his two chamberlains, as soon as they saw him well abed, came forth again, and fell to banqueting with Donwald and his wife, who had prepared many choice dishes and drinks for their rear-supper; wherewith they so gorged themselves, that their heads no sooner got to the pillow than they were so fast asleep that the chamber might have been removed without-waking them. Then Donwald, goaded on by his wife, though in heart he greatly abhorred the act, called four of his servants, whom he had already framed to the purpose with large gifts, and instructed them how to proceed; and they, entering the king's chamber a little before cock's crow, without any bustle cut his throat as he lay asleep, and immediately carried the body forth into the fields. In the morning, a noise being made that the king was slain, Donwald ran thither with the watch, as though he knew nothing of it, and finding cakes of blood in the bed and on the floor, forthwith slew the chamberlains as guilty of the murder.

Thomas Middleton has a play called *The Witch*, wherein are delineated with considerable skill the vulgar hags of old superstition, whose delight was to "raise jars, jealousies, strifes, and heart-burning disagreements, like a thick scurf o'er life." Much question has been had whether this or *Macbeth* were written first, with the view on one side, as would seem, to make out for Middleton the honor of contributing somewhat towards the Poet's Weird Sisters. Malone has perhaps done all the case admits of, to show that *The Witch* was not written before 1613; but in truth there is hardly enough to ground an opinion upon one way or the other. And the question may be safely dismissed as altogether vain; for the two plays have nothing in common, but what may well enough have been derived from Scot's *Discoverie of Witchcraft*, or from the floating witchcraft lore of the time, some relics of which have drifted down in the popular belief to a period within our remembrance.

The old witches of superstition were foul, ugly, mischievous beings, generally actuated by vulgar envy or hate; not so much wicked as mean, and therefore apt to excite disgust, but not to inspire terror or awe; who could inflict injury, but not guilt; could work men's physical ruin, but not win them to work their own spiritual ruin. The Weird Sisters of Shakespeare, as hath been often remarked, are essentially different, and are beholden to them for little if any thing more than the drapery of the representation. Resembling old women, save that they have long beards, they bubble up in human shape, but own no human relations; are without age, or sex, or kin; without birth or death: passionless and motiveless. A combination of the terrible and the grotesque, unlike the Furies of Eschylus they are petrific, not to the senses, but to the thoughts. At first, indeed, on merely looking *at* them, we can scarce help laughing, so uncouth and grotesque is their appearance: but afterwards, on looking *into* them, we find them terrible beyond description; and the more we look, the more terrible do they become; the blood almost curdling in our veins, as, dancing and singing their infernal glees over embryo murders, they unfold to our thoughts the cold, passionless, inexhaustible malignity and deformity of their nature. Towards Macbeth they have nothing of personal hatred or revenge: their malice is of a higher strain, and savors as little of any such human ranklings as the thunderstorms and elemental perturbations amidst which they come and go. But with all their essential wickedness there is nothing gross, or vulgar, or sensual about them. They are the very purity of sin incarnate; the vestal virgins, so to speak, of hell; in whom every thing seems reversed; whose ascent is downwards; whose proper eucharist is a sacrament of evil; and the law of whose being is violation of law!

The later critics, Coleridge, especially, dwell much on what they conceive to be the most distinctive and essential feature of Shakespeare's art, affirming it to be the organic involution of the universal in the particular; that his characters are classes individualized; that his men and women are those of his own age and nation indeed, yet not in such sort but that they are equally the men and women of all ages and nations; for which cause they can never become obsolete, or cease to be natural and true. Herein the Weird Sisters are thoroughly Shakespearean, there being nothing in his whole circle of character, wherein this method of art is more profoundly exemplified. Probably no form of superstition ever prevailed to any great extent, but that it had a ground and principle of truth. The old system of witchcraft was no doubt an embodiment of some natural law, a local and temporary outgrowth from something as general and permanent as human nature itself. Our moral being must breathe, and because it must have breath, therefore, in defect of other provision, it puts forth some such arrangement of breathing organs, as a tree puts forth leaves. The point of art, then, in this case was to raise and transfigure the literal into the symbolical; to take the body, so brittle and perishable in itself, and endow it with immortality; which of course could be done only by filling and animating it with the efficacy of imperishable truth. Accordingly the Poet took enough of current and traditionary matter to enlist old credulity in behalf of agents suited to his peculiar purpose; representing to the age its own thoughts, and at the same time informing the representation with a deep moral significance suited to all ages alike. In *The Witch,* we have but the literal form of a transient superstition: in *Macbeth* that form is made the transparent vehicle of a truth coeval and coextensive with the workings of human guilt. In their literal character the Weird Sisters answer to something that was, and is not; in their symbolical character they answer to something that was, and is, and will abide; for they represent the mysterious action and reaction between the evil mind and external nature.

For the external world serves in some sort as a looking-glass, wherein man beholds the image of his fallen nature; and he still regards that image as his friend or his foe, and so parleys with it or turns from it, according as his will is more disposed to evil or to good. For the evil suggestions, which seem to us written in the face or speaking from the mouth of external objects and occasions, are in reality but projections from our own evil hearts: these are instances wherein "we do receive but what we give": the things we look upon seem inviting us to crime, whereas in truth our wishes construe their innocent meanings into wicked invitations. In the spirit and virtue of which principle the Weird Sisters symbolize the inward moral history of each and every man, and therefore may be expected to live in the faith of reason so long as the present moral order of things shall last. So that they may be aptly enough described as poetical or mythical impersonations of evil influences; as bodying forth in living form the fearful echo which the natural world gives back to the evil that speaks out from the human heart. And the secret of their power over Macbeth lies mainly in that they present to him his embryo wishes and half-formed thoughts: at one time they harp his fear aright, at another time his hope; and that, too, even before such hope and fear have distinctly reported themselves in his consciousness; and by thus harping them, strengthen them into resolution and develop them into act. As men often know they would something, yet know not clearly what, until they hear it spoken by another; and sometimes even dream of being told things which their minds have been tugging at, but could not put into words.

All which may serve to suggest the real nature and scope of the effect which the Weird Sisters have on the action of the play; that their office is not so properly to deprave as to develop the characters whereon they act; not to create the evil heart, but to untie the evil hands. They put nothing into Macbeth's mind, but only draw out what was already there, breathing fructification upon his indwelling germs of sin, and thus acting as mediators, so to speak, between the secret upspringing purpose and the final accomplishment of crime. It is quite worthy of remark how Buchanan represents their appearance and prophecies to have been the coinage of his dreams; as if his mind were so swollen with ambitious thoughts, that they must needs haunt his pillow and people his sleep; and afterwards, when a part of the dream came to pass without his help, this put him upon working out for himself the fulfillment of the remainder. And in this view of the matter it is not easy to see but that a dream would every way satisfy the moral demands of the case, though it would by no means answer the purposes of the drama.

And the Poet evidently supposes from the first that Macbeth already had the will, and that what he wanted further was an earnest and assurance of success. And it is the ordering of things so as to meet this want, and the tracing of the mental processes and the subtle workings of evil consequent thereon, that renders this drama such a paragon of philosophy organized into art. The Weird Sisters rightly strike the keynote and lead off the terrible chorus; because they embody and realize to us, and even to the hero himself, that secret preparation of evil within him, out of which the whole action proceeds. In their fantastical and unearthly aspect, awakening mingled emotions of terror and mirth; in their mysterious reserve and oracular brevity of speech, so fitted at once to sharpen curiosity and awe down skepticism; in the circumstances of their prophetic greeting,—a blasted heath, as a spot sacred to infernal orgies,—the influences of the place thus falling in with the preternatural style and matter of their disclosures;—in all this we may discern a peculiar aptness to generate even in strong minds a belief in their predictions. And such belief, for aught appears, takes hold on Banquo equally as on Macbeth; yet the only effect thereof in the former is to test and approve his virtue. He sees and hears them with simple wonder; has no other interest in them than that of a natural and innocent curiosity; questions them merely with a view to learn what they are, not to draw out further promises; remains calm, collected, and perfectly planless, his thoughts being wholly taken up with what is before him; and because he sees nothing of himself in them, and has no germs of wickedness for them to work upon, therefore he "neither begs nor fears their favors nor their hate." Macbeth, on the other hand, kindles and starts at their words, his heart leaps forth to catch what they say, and he is eager and impatient to have them speak further; they seem to mean more than meets the ear, and he craves to hear that meaning expressed in full: all which is because they show him his own mind, and set astir the wicked desires his breast is teeming with: his mind all at once becomes strangely introversive, self-occupied, and absent from what is before him, "that he seems rapt withal"; and afterwards, as soon as his ear is saluted with a partial fulfillment of their promise, he forthwith gets lost in thought, and shudders and goes into an ecstasy of terror at the horrid suggestions awakened within him, and his shuddering at them is even because of his yielding to them.

It is observable that Macbeth himself never thinks of making the Weird Sisters anywise responsible for his acts or intentions. The workings of his mind all along manifestly infer that he feels himself just as free to do right, and therefore just as guilty in doing wrong, as if no supernatural soliciting had come near him. He therefore never offers to soothe his conscience or satisfy his reason on the score of his being drawn or urged on by any fatal charm or fascination of hell; it being no less clear to him than to us, that whatsoever of such mighty magic there may be in the prophetic greeting is all owing to his own moral predisposition. For, in truth, the promise of the throne by the Weird Sisters, how firmly soever believed in, is no more an instigation to murder for it, than a promise of wealth in like sort would be to steal. To a truly just and virtuous man such a promise, in so far as he had faith therein, would preclude the motives to theft; his argument would be, that inasmuch as he was fated to be rich he had nothing to do but wait for the riches to come. If, however, he were already a thief at heart, and kept from stealing only by fear of the consequences, he would be apt to construe the promise of wealth into a promise of impunity in theft. Which appears to strike something near the difference between Banquo and Macbeth; for, in effect, with Banquo the prophetic words preclude, but with Macbeth themselves become, the motives to crime. So much for the origin of the murderous purpose, and the agency of the Weird Sisters in bringing it to a head.

Henceforth Macbeth's doubts and difficulties, his shrinkings and misgivings, spring from the peculiar structure and movement of his intellect, as sympathetically inflamed and wrought upon by the poison of meditated guilt. His whole state of man suffers an insurrection; conscience forthwith sets his understanding and imagination into morbid, irregular, convulsive action, insomuch that the former disappears in the tempestuous agitations of thought which itself stirs up: his will is buffeted and staggered with prudential reasonings and fantastical terrors, both of which are self-generated out of his disordered and unnatural state of mind. Here begins his long and fatal course of self-delusion. He misderives his scruples, misplaces his apprehensions, mistranslates the whispers and writhings of conscience into the suggestions of prudence, the forecastings of reason, the threatenings of danger. His strong and excitable imagination, set on fire of conscience, fascinates and spell-binds the other faculties, and so gives an objective force and effect to its internal workings. Under this guilt-begotten hallucination, "present fears are less than horrible imaginings." Thus, instead of acting directly in the form of remorse, conscience comes to act circuitously through imaginary terrors, which again react on the conscience, as fire is kept burning by the current of air which itself generates. Hence his apparent freedom from compunctious visitings even when he is really most subject to them. It is probably from oversight of this that some have set him down as a timid, cautious, remorseless villain, withheld from crime only by a shrinking, selfish apprehensiveness. He does indeed seem strangely dead to the guilt and morbidly alive to the dangers of his enterprise; free from remorses of conscience, and filled with imaginary fears: but whence his uncontrollable irritability of imagination? how comes it that his mind so swarms with horrible imaginings, but that his imagination itself is set on fire of hell? So that he seems remorseless, because in his mind the agonies of remorse project and translate themselves into the specters of a conscience-stricken imagination.

His conscience thus acting, as it were, in disguise and masquerade, the natural effect at first is, to make him wavering and irresolute: the harrowings of guilty fear have a certain prospective and preventive operation, causing him to recoil, he scarce knows why, from the work he has in hand. So that he would never be able to go through, but for the coming in of a partner and helpmeet in the wicked purpose. But afterwards, the first crime having passed from prospect into retrospect, the self-same working of conscience has the effect of goading and hurrying him on from crime to crime. He still mistakes his inward pangs for outward perils: guilt peoples his whereabout with fantastical terrors, which in seeking to beat down he only multiplies. Amidst his efforts to dissimulate he loses his self-control, and spills the awful secret he is trying to hide; and in giving others cause to suspect him, he makes himself cause to suspect them. Thus his cowardice of conscience urges him on to fresh murders, and every murder but adds to that cowardice; the very blood which he spills to quiet his fears sprouting up in "gorgons and chimeras dire" to awaken new fears and call for more victims.

The critics of a certain school have in characteristic fashion found fault with the huddling together and confusion of metaphors, which Macbeth pours forth when his mind is preternaturally heated and wrought up. Doubtless they would have him talk always according to the rules of grammar and rhetoric. Shakespeare was content to let him talk according to his state of mind and the laws of his character. Nor, in this view, could any thing better serve the Poet's purpose, than this preternatural rush and redundancy of imagination, hurrying on from thought to thought, and running and massing a multitude of half-formed images together. And such a cast of mind in the hero was necessary to the health of the drama: otherwise such a manifold tragedy had been in danger of turning out an accumulation of horrors. As it is, the impression is at once softened and deepened, after a style of art which Shakespeare alone could evoke and manage: the terrible is made to tread, sometimes to tremble, on the outmost edge, yet never passes into the horrible; what were else too frightful to be born being thus kept within the limits of pleasurable emotion. Macbeth's imagination so overwrought and self-accelerating, this it is that glorifies the drama with such an interfusion of tragic terror and lyrical sweetness, and pours over the whole that baptism of terrible beauty which forms its distinctive excellence.

In the structure and working of her mind and moral frame Lady Macbeth is the opposite of her husband, and for that reason all the better fitted to piece out and make up his deficiency. Of a firm, sharp, wiry, matter-of-fact intellect, doubly charged with energy of will she has little in common with him save a red-hot ambition; for which cause, while the prophetic disclosures have the same effect on her will as on his, and she forthwith jumps into the same purpose, the effect on her mind is just the reverse; she being subject to no such involuntary and uncontrollable tumults of thought: without his irritability of understanding and imagination, she therefore has no such prudential misgivings or terrible illusions to make her shake, and falter, and recoil. So that what terrifies him, transports her; what stimulates his reflective powers, stifles hers.

Almost any other dramatist would have brought the Weird Sisters to act immediately upon Lady Macbeth, and through her upon her husband, as thinking her more open to superstitious allurements and charms. Shakespeare seems to have understood that aptness of mind for them to work upon would have unfitted her for working upon her husband in aid of them. Enough of such influence has already been brought to bear: what is wanted further is quite another sort of influence; such a sort as could only be wielded by a mind not much accessible to the former. There was strong dramatic reason, therefore, why nothing should move or impress her, when awake, but facts; why she should not be of a constitution and method of mind, that the evil which has struck its roots so deep within should come back to her in the elements and aspects of nature, either to mature the guilty purpose, or to obstruct the guilty act. It is quite remarkable that she never once recurs to the Weird Sisters, or lays any stress on their salutations: they seem to have no weight with her but for the impression they have made on Macbeth; that which impression may grow to the desired effect she refrains from using it or meddling with it, and seeks only to fortify it with such other impressions as lie in her power to make. Does not all this look as though she were skeptical touching the contents of his letter, and durst not attempt to influence him with arguments that had no influence with herself, lest her want of sincerity therein should still further unknit his purpose? And what could better set forth her incomparable shrewdness and tact, than that, instead of overstraining this one motive, and thereby weakening it, she should thus let it alone, and endeavor to strengthen it by mixing others with it? Moreover, it does not elude her penetration, that his fears still more than his hopes are wrought up by the preternatural soliciting: for the Weird Sisters represent in most appalling sort the wickedness of the purpose which they suggest; and the thought of them scares up a throng of horrid images, and puts him under a fascination of terror: the instant he reverts to them his imagination springs into action,—an organ whereof while ambition works the bellows, conscience still governs the stops and keys. So that her surest course is to draw his thoughts off to the natural motives and solicitings of the opportunity that has made itself to his hands: otherwise there is danger that the opportunity will unmake him; for, so long as his mind is taken up with those stimulants of imagination, outward facilities for his purpose augment his inward recoilings from the act.

Coleridge justly remarks upon her consummate art in first urging in favor of the deed those very circumstances which to her husband's conscience plead most movingly against it. That the King has unreservedly cast himself upon their loyalty and hospitality, this she puts forth as the strongest argument for murdering him. An awful stroke of character indeed! and therefore awful, because natural. By thus anticipating his greatest drawbacks, and urging them as the chief incentives, she forecloses all debate, and leaves him nothing to say; which is just what she wants; for she knows well enough that the thing is a horrible crime, and will not stand the tests of reason a moment; and therefore that the more he talks the less apt he will be for the work. And throughout this dreadful wrestling-match she surveys the whole ground and darts upon the strongest points with all the quickness and sureness of instinct: her powers of foresight and self-control seem to grow as the horrors thicken; the exigency being to her a sort of practical inspiration. The finishing touch in this part of the picture is when, her husband's resolution being all in a totter, she boldly cuts the very sinews of retreat by casting the thing into a personal controversy and making it a theme of domestic war, so that he has no way but either to fall in with her leading or else to take her life. To gain the crown she literally hazards all, putting it out of the question for them to live together, unless he do the deed, and thus embattling all the virtues and affections of the husband against the conscience of the man. He accordingly goes about the deed, and goes through it, with an assumed ferocity caught from her.

Nor is it to be supposed that this ferocity is native to her own breast: in her case, too, surely it is assumed; for though in her intense overheat of expectant passion it be temporarily fused and absorbed into her character, it is disengaged and thrown off as soon as that heat passes away. Those will readily take our meaning, who have ever seen how, from the excitement of successful effort, men will sometimes pass for a while into and become identified with a character which they undertake to play. And so Lady Macbeth, for a special purpose, begins with acting a part which is really foreign to her, but which, notwithstanding, such is her iron fixedness of will, she braves out to issues so overwhelming as to make her husband and many others believe it is her own. In herself, indeed, she is a great bad woman whom we fear and pity; yet neither so great nor so bad, we are apt to think, as she is generally represented. She has closely studied her husband, and penetrated far into the heart of his mystery; yet she knows him rather as he is to her than as he is in himself: hence in describing his character she interprets her own, and shows more of the warm-hearted wife than of the cool-headed philosopher. Mr. Verplanck, with great felicity, distinguishes her as "a woman of high intellect, bold spirit, and lofty desires, who is mastered by a fiery thirst for power, and that for her husband as well as herself."

Two very different characters, however, may easily be made out for her, according as we lay the chief stress on what she says, or what she does. For surely none can fail to remark, that the promise of a fiend conveyed in her earlier speeches is by no means made good in her subsequent acts. That Shakespeare well understood the principle whereon Sophocles sprinkled the songs of nightingales amid the grove of the Furies, could not be better shown than in that, when Lady Macbeth looks upon the face of her sleeping Sovereign, at whose heart her steel is aimed, and sees the murderous thought passing, as it were, into a fact before her, a gush of womanly feeling or of native tenderness suddenly stays her uplifted arm. And, again, when she hears from Macbeth how he has done two or more murders to screen the first, she sinks down at the tale, thus showing that the woman she had so fearfully disclaimed has already returned to torment and waste her into the grave. So that the sequel proves her to have been better than she was herself aware; for at first her thoughts were so centered and nailed to the object she was in quest of, that she had no place for introversion, and did not suspect what fires of hell she was planting in her bosom. In truth, she had undertaken too much: in her efforts to screw her own and her husband's courage to the sticking-place there was exerted a force of will which answered the end indeed, but at the same time cracked the sinews of nature; though that force of will still enables her to hide the dreadful work that is doing within. She has quite as much if not more of conscience than Macbeth; but its workings are retrospective, proceed upon deeds, not thoughts; and she is not so made, she has no such sensitive redundancy of imagination, that conscience should be in her senses, causing the howlings of the storm to syllable the awful notes of remorse. And as her conscience is without an organ to project and body forth its revenges, so she may indeed possess them in secret, but she can never repress them: subject to no fantastical terrors nor moral illusions, she therefore never loses her self-control: the unmitigable corrodings of her rooted sorrow may destroy, but cannot betray her, unless when her energy of will is bound up in sleep. And for the same cause she is free alike from the terrible apprehensions which make her husband flinch from the first crime, and from the maddening and merciless suspicions of guilty fear that lash and spur him on to other crimes. But the truth of her inward state comes out with an awful mingling of pathos and terror, in the scene where her conscience, sleepless amid the sleep of nature, nay, most restless even when all other cares are at rest, drives her forth, open-eyed, yet sightless, to sigh and groan over spots on her hands, that are visible to none but herself, nor even to herself, but when she is blind to every thing else. And what an awful mystery, too, hangs about her death! We know not, the Poet himself seems not to know, whether the gnawings of the undying worm drive her to suicidal violence, or themselves cut asunder the cords of her life: all we know is, that the death of her body springs somehow from the inextinguishable life and the immedicable wound of her soul. What a history of her woman's heart is written in her thus sinking, sinking away whither imagination shrinks from following, under the violence of an invisible yet unmistakable disease, which still sharpens its inflictions and at the same time quickens her sensibility!

This guilty couple are patterns of conjugal virtue. A tender, delicate, respectful affection sweetens and dignifies their intercourse; the effect of which is rather heightened than otherwise by their ambition, because they seem to thirst for each other's honor as much as for their own. And this sentiment of mutual respect even grow by their crimes, since their inborn greatness is developed through them, not buried beneath them. And when they find that the crown, which they have waded through so much blood to grasp, does but scald their brows and stuff their pillow with thorns, this begets a still deeper and finer play of sympathies between them. Thenceforth, (and how touching its effect!) a soft subdued undertone of inward sympathetic woe and anguish mingles audibly in the wildrushing of the moral tempest that hangs round their footsteps. Need we add how free they are from any thing little or mean, vulgar or gross? the very intensity of their wicked passion seeming to have assoiled their minds of all such earthly and ignoble incumbrances. And so manifest withal is their innate fitness to reign, that their ambition almost passes as the instinct of faculty for its proper sphere.

Dr. Johnson observes with rare infelicity that this play "has no nice discriminations of character." How far from just is this remark, we trust hath already been made clear enough. In this respect the hero and heroine are equaled only by the Poet's other masterpieces,—by Shylock, Hamlet, Lear, and Iago; while the Weird Sisters, so seemingly akin (though whether as mothers, or sisters, or daughters, we cannot tell) to the thunder-storms that keep them company, occupy the summit of his preternatural creations. Nevertheless it must be owned that the grandeur of the dramatic combination oversways our impression of the individual characters, and, unless we make a special effort that way, prevents a due notice of their merits; that the delicate limning of the agents is apt to be lost sight of in the magnitude, the manifold unity, and thought-like rapidity of the action.

The style of this drama is pitched in the same high tragic key as the action: throughout we have an explosion, as of purpose into act, so also of thought into speech, both literally kindling with their own swiftness. No sooner thought than said, no sooner said than done, is everywhere the order of the day. And therewithal, thoughts and images come crowding and jostling each other in so quick succession that none can gain full utterance a second till leaping upon the tongue before the first is fairly off. Thus the Poet seems to have endeavored his utmost how much of meaning could be conveyed in how little of expression; with the least touching of the ear to send vibrations through all the chambers of the mind. Hence the large manifold suggestiveness that lurks in the words; they seem instinct with something which the speakers cannot stay to unfold. And between the invitations to linger and the continual drawings onward, the reader's mind is kindled into an almost preternatural illumination and activity. Doubtless this prolonged stretch and tension of thought would at length grow wearisome, and cause an inward flagging and faintness but that the play, moreover, is throughout a fierce conflict of antagonist elements and opposite extreme, which are so managed as to brace up the interest on every side; so that the effect of the whole is to refresh, not exhaust the powers, the mind being sustained in its long and lofty flight by the wings that grow forth of their own accord from it superadded life. In general, the lyrical, instead of being interspersed here and there in the from of musical lulls and pauses, is thoroughly interfused with the dramatic; while the ethical sense underlies them both, and is occasionally forced up through them by their own pressure. May we not say, in short, that the entire drama is, as it were, a tempest set to music?

Many writers have spoken strongly against the Porter-scene; Coleridge denounces it as unquestionably none of Shakespeare's work. Which mikes us almost afraid to trust our own judgment concerning it; yet we cannot but feel it to be in the true spirit of the Poet's method. This strain of droll broad humor, oozing out, so to speak amid such a congregation of terrors, has always in our case deepened their effect, the strange but momentary diversion causing them to return with the greater force. Of the murder scene, the banquet scene, and the sleep-walking scene, with their dagger of the mind, and Banquo of the mind, and blood-spots of the mind, it were vain to speak. Yet over these sublimely-terrific passages there hovers a magic light of poetry, at once disclosing the horrors, and annealing them into matter of delight.—Hallam sets Macbeth down as being, in the language of Drake, "the greatest effort of our author's genius, the most sublime and impressive drama which the world has ever beheld";—a judgment from which most readers will probably be less inclined to dissent, the older they grow.

Comments

By Shakespearean Scholars

MACBETH

To the Christian moralist Macbeth's guilt is so dark that its degree cannot be estimated, as there are no shades in black. But to the mental physiologist, to whom nerve rather than conscience, the function of the brain rather than the power of the will, is an object of study, it is impossible to omit from calculation the influences of the supernatural event, which is not only the starting-point of the action, but the remote causes of the mental phenomena.—Bucknill, *The Mad Folk of Shakespeare.*

Macbeth wants no disguise of his natural disposition, for it is not bad; he does not affect more piety than he has: on the contrary, a part of his distress arises from a real sense of religion: which makes him regret that he could not join the chamberlains in prayer for God's blessing, and bewail that he has "given his eternal jewel to the common enemy of man." He continually reproaches himself for his deeds; no use can harden him; confidence cannot silence, and even despair cannot stifle, the cries of his conscience. By the first murder he put "rancor in the vessel of his peace"; and of the last he owns to Macduff, "My soul is too charged with blood of thine already."—Whately, *Remarks on Some Characters of Shakespere.*

LADY MACBETH

We may be sure that there were few "more thoroughbred or fairer fingers" in the land of Scotland than those of its queen, whose bearing in public towards Duncan, Banquo and the nobles, is marked by elegance and majesty; and, in private, by affectionate anxiety for her sanguinary lord. He duly appreciated her feelings, but it is a pity that such a woman should have been united to such a man. If she had been less strong of purpose, less worthy of confidence, he would not have disclosed to her his ambitious designs; less resolute and prompt of thought and action, she would not have been called upon to share his guilt; less sensitive or more hardened, she would not have suffered it to prey forever like a vulture upon her heart. She affords, as I consider it, only another instance of what women will be brought to, by a love which listens to no considerations, which disregards all else beside, when the interests, the wishes, the happiness, the honor, or even the passions, caprices, and failings of the beloved object are concerned: and if the world, in a compassionate mood, will gently scan the softer errors of sister-woman, may we not claim a kindly construing for the motives which plunged into the Aceldama of the blood-washed tragedy the sorely-urged and broken-hearted Lady Macbeth?—Maginn, *Shakespeare Papers.*

Lady Macbeth is not thoroughly hateful, for she is not a virago, not an adulteress, not impelled by revenge. On the contrary, she expresses no feeling of personal malignity towards any human being in the whole course of her part. Shakespeare could have easily displayed her crimes in a more commonplace and accountable light, by assigning some feudal grudge as a mixed motive of her cruelty to Duncan; but he makes her a murderess in cold blood, and from the sole motive of ambition, well knowing that if he had broken up the inhuman serenity of her remorselessness by the ruffling of anger, he would have vulgarized the features of the splendid Titaness.

By this entire absence of petty vice and personal virulence, and by concentrating all the springs of her conduct into the one determined feeling of ambition, the mighty poet has given her character a statue-like simplicity, which, though cold, is spirit-stirring, from the wonder it excites, and which is imposing, although its respectability consists, as far as thc heart is concerned, in merely negative decencies. How many villains walk the earth in credit to their graves, from the mere fulfillment of these negative decencies! Had Lady Macbeth been able to smother her husband's babblings, she might have been one of them.—Campbell, *Life of Mrs. Siddons.*

As she is commonly represented, Lady Macbeth is *nothing* more than the maximum of ambition, a person, who, in order to obtain a crown, avails herself of every means, even the most horrible. Such, indeed, is she, and much more. It may be said that she would set half the earth on fire to reach the throne of the other half. But,—and here lies the depth of her peculiar character,—not for herself alone; but for him, her *beloved* husband. She is a tigress who could rend all who oppose her; but her mate, who, in comparison with her, is gentle, and disposed somewhat to melancholy, him she embraces with genuine love. In relation to him her affection is great and powerful, and bound up with all the roots and veins of her life, and consequently it passes into *weakness*. The connection of this fearful pair is not without a certain touching passionateness, and it is through this that the Lady first *lives* before us, as otherwise she would be almost without distinctive features, and would appear only as the *idea* of the most monstrous criminality. Ambition without Love is cold, French-tragic, and incapable of awakening deep interest. Here Love is the more moving as it reigns in the conjugal relation; and truly, to the atrocious crimes perpetrated by this pair, there was need of such a counterpoise, in order that they may appear as *human beings* suffering wreck, and not as perfect devils.—Horn, *Shakespeare Erläutert.*

This is certain, that Shakespeare in the part of Lady Macbeth, as in all his parts, actually relied upon the young actor to whom the part might be assigned to carry out and complete the representation; and therefore at the present day it becomes the special duty of the actress in this part not in tone, look, or gesture to aggravate the abhorrence which might thus be excited, but to alleviate it, so that to intelligent spectators will be presented not the picture of a Northern Fury, nor of a monster, still less of a heroine or martyr to conjugal love, but that of a woman capable of the greatest elevation, but seized mysteriously by the magic of Passion, only to fall the more terribly, and thus, in spite of our horror at her crime, wringing from us our deepest sympathy. —Von Friesen, *Jahrbuch der deutschen Shakespeare-Gesellschaft.*

THE GHOST

It is the skepticism as to the objective reality of Banquo's Ghost which has originated the question as to whether he should be made visible to the spectators in the theater, since, as the skeptics observe, he is invisible to all the assembled guests, and does not speak at all. But for this skepticism, it would never have been doubted that the Ghost should be made visible to the theater, although he is invisible to Macbeth's company, and although no words are assigned to him. This doubt existing, illustrates to us how stage-management itself is affected by the philosophy which may prevail upon certain subjects. Upon the Spiritualist view, Banquo's Ghost, and the Witches themselves, are all in the same category, all belonging to the spiritual world, and seen by the spiritual eye; and the mere fact that the Ghost does not speak, is felt to have no bearing at all upon the question of his presentation as an objective reality.

The Spiritualist, when contending for the absolute objectivity of Banquo's Ghost, may possibly be asked whether he also claims a *like* reality for "the air-drawn dagger." To this he would reply, that, to the best of his belief, a *like* reality was *not* to be affirmed of that dagger, which he conceives to have been a representation, in the spiritual world, of a dagger, not, however, being on that account less real (if by unreality we are to understand that it was, in some incomprehensible way, generated in the material brain), but only differing from what we should term a real *bonâ fide* dagger, as a painting of a dagger differs from a real one.—Roffe, *An Essay upon the Ghost Belief of Shakespeare.*

THE WEIRD SISTERS

The Weird Sisters who preside over the play as the ministers of evil are partly "metaphysical," as Coleridge, following Lady Macbeth's phrase of "metaphysical aid," justly called them. It has been said that Shakespeare meant them to be no more than the witches of his day as they were commonly conceived. This is quite incredible when we think of that high poetic genius in him which could not have left them unspiritualized by imagination, and which must have felt that these personages, if conceived only as the vulgar witches, would be below the dignity of his tragedy. It is also said that all that was not vulgar in them was in the soul of Macbeth, and not in them. That is a credible theory, but it is not borne out by the text; and it seems to assert that Shakespeare did not believe in, or at least did not as a poet conceive of, spiritual creatures, other than ghosts, who dwelt in a world outside of humanity, and yet could touch it at intervals when certain conditions were fulfilled. These spiritual creatures, as he conceived them, had chiefly to do with nature; were either embodiments of its elemental forces, or their masters. Such were Oberon and Ariel, but they had most to do with the beneficent forces of nature. Here the Weird Sisters command its evil forces. Whether Shakespeare believed in this half-spiritual world of beings, dwelling and acting in a supposed zone between us and the loftier spiritual world, and having powers over the natural world—I cannot tell, but at least he conceived this realm; and if he believed in it, there were hundreds of persons at his time who were with him in that belief, as there are numbers now who share in it, in spite of science. I do not think, then, that the spiritual part of his conception of the witches was intended by him to exist solely in the mind of Macbeth. On the contrary, I hold that it is incredible Shakespeare should have taken up witches into his tragedy and left them as James I and the rest of the world commonly conceived them. His imagination was far too intense, his representing power much too exacting, to allow him to leave them unidealized. It is true he kept their vulgar elements for the sake of the common folk who did not think; but for those who did, Shakespeare unvulgarized the witches. They materialize themselves only for their purpose of temptation; their normal existence is impalpable, invisible, unearthly.—Brooke, *Lectures on Shakespeare*.

Shakespeare's picture of the witches is truly magical: in the short scenes where they enter, he has created for them a peculiar language, which, although composed of the usual elements, still seems to be a collection of formulæ of incantation. The sound of the words, the accumulation of rhymes, and the rhythmus of the verse, form, as it were, the hollow music of a dreary dance of witches. These repulsive things, from which the imagination shrinks back, are here a symbol of the hostile powers which operate in nature, and the mental horror outweighs the repugnance of our senses. The witches discourse with one another like women of the very lowest class, for this was the class to which witches were supposed to belong; when, however, they address Macbeth, their tone assumes more elevation; their predictions, which they either themselves pronounce, or allow their apparitions to deliver, have all the obscure brevity, the majestic solemnity, by which oracles have in all times contrived to inspire mortals with reverential awe. We here see that the witches are merely instruments; they are governed by an invisible spirit, or the ordering of such great and dreadful events would be above their sphere.—Schlegel, *Lectures on Shakespeare.*

THE INCANTATION SCENES

It has been objected to the incantation scenes in Macbeth, that the subjects and language in them are revolting. They are so; nothing, however, can be more irrational than to take exception against them on that score. The witches are an impersonation of those qualities which are antagonist to all that is gentle, and lovely, and peaceful, and good. They are loathsome abstractions of the "evil principle," and are the precursors, as well as providers of all the stormy passions that shake this poor citadel of man. They represent the repulsive as well as the cruel propensities of our nature; every one, therefore, who is a slave to his lower passions, is spell-bound by the "weird sisters"; and this, I have little doubt, was the moral that Shakespeare intended to read to his brother mortals: for, we should bear in mind that Macbeth was, by nature, an honorable and even generous man; but as he was unable to withstand the impulse of an unworthy ambition, and could not resist the sneers of his uncompromising partner, he rushed into that bottomless hell of torment—a guilty and an upbraiding conscience.—Clarke, *Shakespeare-Characters.*

THE INFLUENCE OF THE UNSEEN WORLD

Every device of Shakespeare has been designed to accentuate the overweening influence of the unseen world. So long as Macbeth is striving to bring about the fulfillment of the prophecy, he is a bungler; but at every turn the unseen agency brings fortune to his aid. So soon, however, as he bends his efforts to defeat the intentions of the supernatural world, fortune deserts him. Everything goes wrong. Fleance escapes. Suspicion seizes his nobles. Macduff flies, and Macbeth's insensate revenge has the effect of bringing to a head the smouldering anger of the nobility. Finally, the unseen universe interferes directly in the scene, and by its deceitful oracles lulls him into a state of false security. Were it not for the prophecy about Birnam wood, Macbeth would have met s foes in the field, and not cooped himself up in his castle of Dunsinane, where, as he says himself, "he is tied as a bear to the stake." Had it not been for his belief in his charmed existence he would never have risked his life in single combat with all and sundry of the besieging host. He the *protégé* of destiny had attempted to defy his patron; and to the last farthing he was called upon to pay the price of his temerity.—Ransome, *Short Studies in Shakespeare's Plots.*

THE KEYNOTE

The keynote of this, the most picturesque, the most lurid and fiercely rapid of all tragedies, is struck in the first scene by a miracle of imagination, and maintained to the end in spite of inequalities. A storm of fear blows through the short five acts. Macbeth's imagination appals him; he struggles entangled in a hellish net. His wife screws her courage to a point at which it will not stick, and the cord snaps under the tension.—Seccombe and Allen, *The Age of Shakespeare.*

DARKNESS IN THIS TRAGEDY

Darkness, we may even say blackness, broods over this tragedy. It is remarkable that almost all the scenes which at once recur to memory take place either at night or in some dark spot. The vision of the dagger, the murder of Duncan, the murder of Banquo, the sleep-walking of Lady Macbeth, all come in night-scenes. The Witches dance in the thick air of a storm, or, "black and midnight hags," receive Macbeth in a cavern. The blackness of night is to the hero a thing of fear, even of horror; and that which he feels becomes the spirit of the play. The faint glimmerings of the western sky at twilight are here menacing: it is the hour when the traveler hastens to reach safety in his inn, and when Banquo rides homeward to meet his assassins; the hour when "light thickens," when "night's black agents to their prey do rouse," when the wolf begins to howl, and the owl to scream, and withered murder steals forth to his work. Macbeth bids the stars hide their fires that his "black," desires may be concealed; Lady Macbeth calls on thick night to come, palled in the dunnest smoke of hell. The moon is down and no stars shine when Banquo, dreading the dreams of the coming night, goes unwillingly to bed, and leaves Macbeth to wait for the summons of the little bell. When the next day should dawn, its light is "strangled," and "darkness does the face of earth entomb." In the whole drama the sun seems to shine only twice: first, in the beautiful but ironical passage where Duncan sees the swallows flitting round the castle of death; and, afterwards, when at the close the avenging army gathers to rid the earth of its shame. Of the many slighter touches which deepen this effect I notice only one. The failure of nature in Lady Macbeth is marked by her fear of darkness; "she has light by her continually." And in the one phrase of fear that escapes her lips even in sleep, it is of the darkness of the place of torment that she speaks.—Bradley, *Shakespearean Tragedy*.

POPULARITY OF "MACBETH"

One might have expected that *Macbeth* would prove the most popular of Shakespeare's tragedies, both with the actors and with audiences. Such has, however, not been the case. Except on rare occasions, *Macbeth*, despite its apparent supremacy as an "acting play," has less attraction than *Lear*, *Othello*, and, above all, *Hamlet*. Nor is the reason far to seek. Of the two elements which Aristotle's definition requires in tragedy, it has but one. It works by terror alone, and does not touch the springs of pity. It has no bursts and swells of pathos, no outpours of tenderness, no sweet dews of hapless love. Lacking these, it lacks charm. The characters on whom the interest is concentrated are not the innocent sufferers, but the guilty workers of woe, and, if not outcasts from our sympathy in the woe they thereby bring upon themselves, they are far from making any demands upon our affection. *Macbeth* stands alone among Shakespeare's great productions as a picture of crime and retribution unrelieved by any softer features. Like some awful Alpine peak, girdled with glaciers and abysses, with no glimpses of flower-bespangled vales and pastures.—Kirke, *Atlantic Monthly*, April, 1895.